Hidden Histories

Discovering the Heritage of Wales

HIDDEN HISTORIES

DISCOVERING THE HERITAGE OF WALES

Edited by Peter Wakelin and Ralph A. Griffiths

COMISIWN BRENHINOL HENEBION CYMRU

ROYAL COMMISSION ON THE ANCIENT AND HISTORICAL MONUMENTS OF WALES

ISBN 978-1-871184-35-8
(A Welsh-language edition is also available, ISBN 978-1-871184-36-5)

British Library Cataloguing in Publication Data. A catalogue record for this book is available from the British Library.

Editorial advisory panel: David Browne, Dr Toby Driver, Professor Ralph A. Griffiths, Stephen Hughes,
Penny Icke, Brian Malaws, Richard Suggett, Dr Peter Wakelin
Copy editing: David Browne, Patricia Moore
Design: John Johnston
Digitisation: Fleur James
Indexing: John Noble

Comisiwn Brenhinol Henebion Cymru
Royal Commission on the Ancient and Historical Monuments of Wales
Crown Building, Plas Crug, Aberystwyth, Ceredigion, SY23 1NJ, United Kingdom
Telephone: 01970 621200   *e-mail:* nmrwales@rcahmw.gov.uk   www.rcahmw.gov.uk

All text and images are Crown Copyright, Royal Commission on the Ancient and Historical Monuments of Wales
unless otherwise stated on page 317.

Contents

Foreword

Huw Edwards

The story of Wales is endlessly rich and varied. This book tells that story using one of our greatest national treasures – the vast collection of images gathered by the Royal Commission on the Ancient and Historical Monuments of Wales.

The Royal Commission was established in 1908, and we celebrate its centenary with pride and gratitude. The other great Welsh institutions of the Edwardian era, the National Library and the National Museum, were created in 1907. Together, these three great collections represent the heritage of Wales.

The Royal Commission is like a big detective agency: its experts promote a deeper understanding of Wales. They reveal subjects, places, buildings and personalities whose significance has been hidden from us for far too long. That is why BBC Wales decided it would make an ideal subject for a television documentary series, and why I was pleased to be involved with it and to take the cameras to one of my favourite Welsh buildings, Capel Als in Llanelli (which I have written about overleaf).

The BBC series, Hidden Histories, followed the work of the Commission for over a year as its experts offered new interpretations of the heritage of Wales. Those interpretations ranged from the mysteries of Iron Age hillforts and Roman complexes, to medieval houses, to sites of the Industrial Revolution and to monuments of the Victorian age. The filming followed the Commission's photographer working at night to try to recapture eroded inscriptions on the Pillar

of Eliseg, its aerial archaeologist discovering a lost medieval church through cropmarks, one of its surveyors decoding the construction methods used to build Pontcysyllte aqueduct, and its tree-ring dating experts interpreting the origins of Newton House at Llandeilo.

The scale of the task is astonishing. The Commission holds the most extensive photographic archive in Wales, with over 1.5 million photographs, as well as 100,000 plans and drawings, 40,000 maps and some 3 million pages of text. People all over the world can obtain information through the Commission's websites on some 80,000 sites, ranging from burial mounds to blast furnaces. They can identify what records the Commission holds and view digital images.

A century after its birth, the Commission is still hard at work. In many senses, its task can never be finished. The historic environment is interpreted in new ways: chapels are now as worthy of study as castles; off-shore archaeology is as important as upland sites. New tools have transformed the potential to discover sites and reveal evidence about them. There is an archive of permanent value to be maintained and developed. Public expectation for learning about the historic environment is at an all-time high.

The Royal Commission is emphatically about the future of Wales, as well as its past. I am delighted to be associated with the Commission's invaluable work, and I hope you enjoy this celebration of what is being achieved.

Huw Edwards is one of Britain's foremost broadcast journalists. He spent fourteen years as the BBC's Chief Political Correspondent and presents its flagship Ten O'Clock News. He has written and presented documentaries about politics, classical music, history and the Welsh language and is writing a book about Welsh chapels.

001 A Great Welsh Chapel: Capel Als, Llanelli

Created by working men and women: the superb carpentry, plasterwork and organ at Capel Als.
DS2008_186_001 NPRN 6419

Above: A detail of woodcarving in the interior.
DS2008_186_015 NPRN 6419

Top right: The façade of Capel Als in Marble Halls Road, Llanelli, with its Sunday school to the left.
DS2008_186_001 NPRN 6419

W elsh chapels have not always been considered worthy of meaningful study. This is changing rapidly. As chapels disappear, a mighty chunk of Welsh culture and heritage disappears with them. The Royal Commission takes its responsibility in this regard very seriously. On a recent visit to Llanelli's oldest nonconformist chapel, Capel Als, I met some of the Commission's investigators as we filmed a sequence for the BBC series, Hidden Histories.

Why Capel Als? It was not my boyhood chapel, so I can be relatively impartial. Capel Als represents two of the principal forces of nonconformist worship in my part of Wales. It was a markedly working-class church whose membership was entirely Welsh-speaking. In addition, its ministers were political as well as religious figures. One of those ministers can be classed as one of the giants of his time. David Rees, a Carmarthenshire man, came to Llanelli in 1829 and led Capel Als for 40 years. He is remembered as a great religious leader, but his roles as a social reformer, political campaigner and daring propagandist deserve just as much attention. His leadership placed Capel Als right in the mainstream of the radical politics of his age. He fought against Anglican domination, and demanded religious freedom for nonconformists. He campaigned for better conditions for workers. He was instrumental in creating Llanelli's first savings bank, and the town's first lending library. He believed strongly in the church's duty to help the poor and underlined the social responsibility that came with wealth. He was extremely unpopular in some quarters, and the English press abused and attacked him many times – the ultimate badge of honour.

In my view, David Rees is the greatest figure in the history of Llanelli. No individual has done more to improve the quality of life in the town. Under his

leadership, Capel Als grew into one of the strongest chapels in Wales. The chapel we see today is not the building left by David Rees. The structure is broadly similar, but it was greatly expanded and improved in 1894-5, during the ministry of Dr Thomas Johns.

Capel Als had already installed Llanelli's first chapel pipe-organ in 1880, built by Bishop of London. When Mr Bishop came to Llanelli to collect his money, he was astonished to be given a bag with 300 gold coins in it. Many years later, he described his very nervous journey back to London by train, never letting the bag out of his grasp. The chapel has a superb musical tradition, and for many years the chapel choir and orchestra held week-long music festivals attended by thousands of people from every part of south and west Wales. The Bishop organ was reinstalled after the rebuilding of the chapel supervised by Owen Morris Roberts, the renowned chapel architect based in Porthmadog. The resulting building was a slightly odd mix: a clumpy, boxy exterior which does not prepare the first-time visitor for the utterly glorious interior. The quality of the carpentry, the plaster-work (especially the wonderful ceiling), the tiling and the stained glass (unusual for a chapel) combine to take the breath away. I have visited many times, but each visit is a delight.

There are several outstanding chapels in Llanelli, including Zion, Tabernacl and Capel Newydd [see essay 071]. But the combination of grandeur and social significance places Capel Als at the top of the list every time. It stands as a reminder to Llanelli's future generations of what was once achieved by the ordinary working men and women of their town.

Many of our best chapels are at risk. The Royal Commission has recorded almost 7,000 across Wales in conjunction with Capel, the Chapels Heritage Society. Their work has been vital in making sure that we know more about the chapels, and understand their place in our national heritage.

Huw Edwards

Right: An example of the unusually rich stained glass for a nonconformist chapel.
DS2008_186_018 NPRN 6419

Introduction: Hidden Histories

Peter Wakelin

The landscapes of Wales have been moulded by millennia of human activity: by people who have farmed, provided shelter for their families, hunted, worshipped, fought, dug away the earth in mines and quarries, organised, played, travelled, traded. Each generation has lived in ways that differed subtly – sometimes significantly – from those of the generation before. All have left their marks, still there to be detected in the fabric of our surroundings.

This book tells the story of Wales through one hundred picture essays that explore landscapes, buildings, sites, monuments and maritime remains. The images are drawn overwhelmingly from the rich archive of the Royal Commission on the Ancient and Historical Monuments of Wales, whose work since 1908 has helped to lay the foundations for knowledge of the country's heritage. Each picture essay expands upon an image made or collected by the Royal Commission as curator of the national record of Wales's heritage. Among the images are early photographic prints, original architects' drawings, maps, aerial views, imaginative reconstructions, digital models and evocative photographs of hillforts and castles, cottages and mansions, collieries and farms.

The book celebrates the Royal Commission's first century. Its contributors include current or former staff, Commissioners and partners who have contributed in recent years to the development of knowledge about our built heritage. The essays are grouped chronologically from prehistory to the present and are introduced by a concise overview of each era, with cross-references to essays in square brackets [001 to 100]. An indication of where sites are located is given by their familiar historic counties, a map of which is provided with the index. Further reading is suggested at the end of the book and every site or building pictured can be found on the Commission's online database, Coflein, by using the National Primary Record Number (NPRN) below each caption. Coflein can also be searched for other sites, buildings, landscapes and maritime remains: it holds 80,000 records and the number increases every year.

Some of Wales's most famous monuments are explored in this book, including the great town walls of Conwy [picture essay 041], graceful Pontcysyllte aqueduct [058], and Clough Williams-Ellis's delightful fantasy, Portmeirion [090]. However, most of the picture essays highlight treasures that are not so well known. Many emphasise the everyday life of past generations, for example the struggles of hunter-gatherers to survive in harsh environments [006], how farmers protected their crops and animals in the Iron Age [020], and how people took their leisure in the Middle Ages [044]. Some reveal unexpected stories, for example about the Neolithic people who built a timber enclosure three times the size of the enormous Avebury henge in Wiltshire [013] or the farmers in Glamorgan who built elaborate houses for their pigs [055].

Opposite: The mechanism in the clock tower of Golden Grove, Llandeilo, a country house of 1826-32.

DI2005_1145 NPRN 17391

Below: The history of Cardiff Castle has been unpicked by research and survey. The large earthen motte was built by William the Conqueror in 1081, while the keep was added in 1140 and the gate tower in around 1300.

DI2005_0667 NPRN 33

Above: The traditional buildings of Wales have been increasingly well cared for in recent decades, partly thanks to the Royal Commission's work to raise awareness of their importance: the sixteenth- to eighteenth-century Llowes Court, at Glasbury in Radnorshire.

DI2005_0783 NPRN 81340

Right: New archaeological sites are discovered every year through the Royal Commission's aerial reconnaissance. The parchmark in this field shows the site of a medieval church at Llwydfaen in the Conwy valley discovered in July 2006.

AP_2006_4256 NPRN 404665

In 1908 there was a sense in which the whole of Welsh history could be said to be in the 'dark ages'. Far less was understood about our past than has been learned a hundred years later. Knowledge has been transformed by independent researchers, university lecturers, museum curators and the staff of bodies such as the Welsh Archaeological Trusts, the Ancient Monuments Inspectorate and the Royal Commission. The longevity and range of the Commission's contribution as a heritage detective agency (as Huw Edwards calls it in his Foreword) has been particularly remarkable.

Many picture essays in this book describe how investigators have worked, as well as what they have discovered. More often than not they have pieced histories together from scattered fragments. An understanding of the Roman occupation, for example, has been assembled patiently and slowly from stray finds and methodical deductions, revealing the network of Roman roads [023] and the pattern of military fortifications [022]. A cumulative knowledge-bank derived from skilfully recording thousands of private homes enabled the patterns of indigenous architectural development to be identified in *Houses of the Welsh Countryside* [004]. Techniques of investigation have developed continuously. In 1908 an aeroplane had yet to fly through Welsh skies; in 1925 the Commission published aerial photographs for the first time; since the 1980s systematic aerial reconnaissance has identified thousands of lost archaeological remains from ephemeral evidence in crops and grassland

[010, 035]; now remote sensing techniques are fast developing.

Monuments of international importance are now better understood as a result of detailed study by the Royal Commission and its partners, for example Paviland Cave on the Gower cliffs [006], St David's Cathedral [039] and Cardiff Castle [073]. Occasionally, individual lives may be elucidated: we know at least the name of Rustica, an early medieval teenage girl [026]; we can begin to understand the motives of an extraordinary priest, Dr John Davies of Mallwyd [050]; and we can see the home and the workplace of the novelist Kate Roberts [088, 094]. There are still many unanswered questions, as the recent *Introducing a Research Framework for the Archaeology of Wales* (2008) has shown, but an enormous amount has been achieved.

A hundred years ago few researchers were interested in prehistory as a subject and important types of monument had yet to be recognised, such as the Neolithic ceremonial complexes detectable from crop marks [010] or the widespread, enigmatic

piles of charred and broken stones known as burnt mounds. Today, evidence of the complexity of prehistoric settlements is still emerging [016, 019] and many mysteries persist: for example, while there is a persuasive case that Neolithic people carried the Stonehenge bluestones all the way from Pembrokeshire [011], it is possible that they were brought by glacial action. The study of early medieval archaeology had barely begun a century ago. Since then light has been shed on this fascinating era, when Wales started to emerge as a distinct cultural entity. The painstaking decoding of inscribed stones in particular has been a revelation [033]. For the Middle Ages, whereas attention once focused largely on Anglo-Norman castles and monasteries – the works of the occupiers rather than the defenders – more recently the castle-building of the Welsh princes has been explored [037]. The global value of the industrial heritage has been properly appreciated only in the last few decades, for example by uncovering the genius of indigenous artisan engineers, the vitality of early railway

Above: In 1899 investigations such as S. Baring Gould's fieldwork at Foel Trigarn in Pembrokeshire, where Iron Age ramparts encircle Bronze Age burials, had only just begun to examine successive phases of prehistoric construction.

DI2007_1582 NPRN 94948

13

builders [057], and how communities adapted to the Industrial Revolution [061].

The landscape has not stopped developing. Two chapters of this book review the archaeology and buildings of the past century, a period of enormous change and profound disturbance brought by two world wars [081, 085]. In 1908 some major chapels were yet to be built, and the practice of the leading Arts and Crafts architect Herbert L. North had been open for only a few years [079]. During the twentieth century the Royal Commission's recording programmes had to keep pace with the decline of rural cottages [088], the closure of the coal industry [083] and contemporary projects of historical significance [096].

One outcome of all this investigation has been that thousands of monuments and buildings have been protected on the advice of the Commission since its first inventory was published in 1911, among them many now appreciated as jewels of the nation [002]. The Commission continues to make recommendations to the Welsh Assembly Government, especially through the Uplands Archaeology Initiative and aerial survey, and it is helping to assess historic battlefields [100]. Seminal studies like *Houses of the Welsh Countryside* and *Copperopolis*, the Commission's web services,

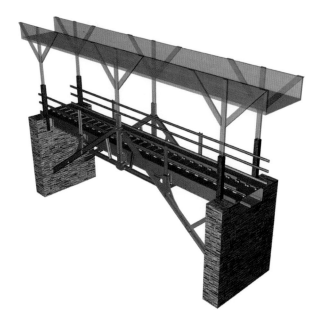

Right: Pont-y-cafnau, Merthyr Tydfil, designed around 1793 by the innovative local engineer, Watkin George. Horse-drawn trams crossed the deck, and water to power Cyfarthfa ironworks was carried by both an iron trough underneath and a timber launder above. It is believed to be the first iron aqueduct or railway bridge ever built.

PYCA04 NPRN 34860

Above and right: Bethania Welsh Baptist chapel in Maesteg, Glamorgan, is one of the triumphs of Beaux Arts style, designed by William Beddoe Rees in every detail from façade to door handles in 1908, the year the Royal Commission was established.

DS2006_118_022 NPRN 13780

outreach activities and exhibitions have informed the management of sites and stimulated the commitment of owners and communities, which can be just as potent as statutory protection in achieving conservation benefits. Attitudes have changed considerably: for example, industrial sites were under constant threat of reclamation when the Commission began studying them forty years ago, and vernacular buildings regularly suffered from unsympathetic alteration.

Historic buildings and archaeological sites are fragile resources liable to decay, neglect or clearance, and understanding their significance is essential to their management with scarce resources. The Commission's records have provided vital information to repair fire-damaged or derelict buildings [043], and they preserve knowledge about hundreds that have been lost entirely, such as Brynmawr's Dunlop Semtex factory [086] and Pen Llystyn Roman fort [003]. Older records are also valuable in reflecting what has been lost – the postcard views loaned to the National Monuments Record for copying by Thomas Lloyd evoke demolished houses and much-altered streetscapes [074]. Planners, teachers, custodians and private individuals want authoritative information and evaluations uninfluenced by vested interests or political imperatives. Whereas decision-makers need impartial sources, developers on the one hand and pressure groups on the other provide information reflecting their own purposes. Even heritage attractions encounter tensions between offering historical understanding and a good day out. All of

us are tempted to judge past conditions by the standards of the present if their context is not clear – for example, to view hillforts as desperate, primitive defences rather than swaggering expressions of power and wealth [018], or to sensationalise industrial work as more inhumane than the alternatives that drove people to it.

Why uncover hidden histories, except to satisfy our curiosity? People appreciate the past as a tool for understanding the present, a reminder of diversity, a force for the community, and a creative inspiration. Understanding history is a mark of a mature society, and nothing confronts us with it more directly than the concrete evidence all around. It is often said that history is like personal memory, without which one cannot know one's own identity and it is impossible to learn. A phrase in Welsh emphasises how this relates to communities: *cof cenedl*, or 'people's memory'. In all sorts of practical ways the past sheds light on the issues of the here and now – for

example making the possibilities of climate change more real by revealing sea-level changes since the Mesolithic or how people had to adapt late in the Bronze Age to declining food supplies. Any present hardships are put in perspective by the conflicts of the early middle ages [034], the devastation of the First World War [082] or the hard labour of women like Mrs Matthews who barrowed ore at a Swansea copperworks [056]. Narratives from history amplify our personal experiences and broaden our horizons, and this has sustained the growth of family history and its broadening from genealogy to inquiring how and where ancestors lived and worked.

This book addresses hidden histories, in the plural, to celebrate the sense of place and the diversity born of differences between north and south, border and heartland, timber and stone, upland and coastal, rich and poor, male and female. Patterns of regional building traditions are among the foundations of local distinctiveness; the marks left by

Above: Photographs in the National Monuments Record provide a moving record of life in cottages and houses at a time of rapid social change. The kitchen at Plas Penmynydd, Anglesey, was photographed in around 1930.

CD2003_626_036 NPRN 15829

Right: Allt-yr-yn synagogue in Newport, reputed to be the smallest in Britain, with one of its senior members, Mr Harry Poloway BEM, MBE, CStJ, photographed in 2007.

DS2007_188_003 NPRN 406440

the peoples who have flowed through Wales help us to recognise our national complexity – this land has been a home to Neanderthals, Beaker people, Celts, Romans, Vikings, Anglo-Saxons, Normans, Jews, Flemings, families pulled to the south Wales valleys at their zenith from Ireland, England, Italy and Spain, and twentieth-century immigrants and refugees from Germany, Somalia, Pakistan, Iraq. Appropriately, the Royal Commission's recording reaches beyond churches and chapels to Sikh gurdwaras, synagogues, mosques, Buddhist shrines and Hindu temples.

If western economies depend in the twenty-first century on creativity and innovation, the built heritage is invaluable as a source of inspiration. Deprived post-industrial communities are reminded of the energy and entrepreneurship that once made them thrive, architects are influenced by traditional building styles [092], lessons about sustainability are learned from cottage-building crafts that make the most of locally-available materials [066], and the sites investigated by the Royal Commission during its centenary year have inspired a beautifully filmed

BBC television series. Recently, *Planet* magazine commissioned leading poets to take creative inspiration from the Royal Commission's rich image bank in a series entitled 'Ancient Monuments: Present Words'. Gillian Clarke, the National Poet of Wales, chose an aerial photograph of Castell y Bere, perched atop a narrow rock in Merioneth, and wrote a poem that meditates on much that knowing about history brings to mind – image and poem are reproduced below with her kind permission.

There is no doubt that heritage can play a central role in forging stronger communities by fostering identity and pride. People have been enriched by knowing more about their past, whether in old-established towns like Denbigh [048], inner-city areas or dispersed upland communities [062]. Intricate mapping of the surviving industrial landscape at Blaenavon helped to win the area international recognition as a World Heritage Site and to change how it was perceived by both visitors and local people.

There is much to be proud of in our hidden histories and in how knowledge about them has been transformed in the last one hundred years. Even those most familiar with Wales need to remind themselves from time to time what treasures can be found here and what depths of history they represent. This book aims to help them do just that.

Below: The hilltop ruins of Castell y Bere, Merioneth, built in the early thirteenth century by Llywelyn the Great during his campaign to create a single state that would encompass much of Wales.
GTJ00182 NPRN 93719

Castell y Bere
(Llywelyn ab Iorwerth 1173-1240)

Not hard to imagine them,
slipshod and slow on the slope to the summit,
hauling a castle up to the sky
in rain and wind, summer and winter,
stone by stone and timber by timber,
for his masons, carpenters, stone-carvers,
his craftsmen in leather and glass.
In sixty years it was over, surrendered.
Now, seven centuries on,
rain and wind, summer and winter
have scoured it of terror and blood.
All gone to grass. What remains
are Llywelyn's dream and his name,
and the vertebrae of a sheep –
a broken rosary dropped from the sky –
and two kites circling.

Gillian Clarke

One Hundred Years of Investigation

David Browne and Ralph A. Griffiths[1]

On 10 August 1908 a Royal Commission was authorised and appointed by King Edward VII to 'make an inventory of the Ancient and Historical Monuments and Constructions connected with or illustrative of the contemporary culture, civilisation and conditions of life of the people in Wales and Monmouthshire from the earliest times, and to specify those which seem most worthy of preservation'. This last injunction was the most urgent purpose of the Commission in the eyes of the legislators, but the inventory was its essential preliminary. The protection of significant sites under the Ancient Monuments Act of Queen Victoria's reign had been severely hampered by a basic lack of knowledge of the country's stock of monuments. So it was felt that an independent and official body was needed to prepare a reliable inventory from which examples could be selected and recommended for statutory protection. At the time some may have thought that the new Royal Commission would do its work in short order and that, like most Royal Commissions, it could then be disbanded. But as the years passed, it was gradually appreciated that the historic environment constantly changes and that each generation develops its own interest in it and increasingly sophisticated means of understanding it. And so the Royal Commission still exists after 100 years, and recording and assessing our sites and monuments remain at its heart today.

This need was not peculiar to Wales, and in 1908 identical Royal Commissions were established for Scotland and England too. What is striking, however, is that the Commission for Wales coincided with a national cultural renaissance which had recently seen the creation of the University of Wales (1893) and the National Library and National Museum of Wales (both in 1907), all of which would be closely connected with the new Royal Commission.

The early commissioners were distinguished men (there was no woman) who were notable figures in Welsh cultural life, each with a distinctive contribution to make to the task ahead. They represented that voluntarist tradition in British public service which still lingers in cultural quarters. Their involvement in such long-established scholarly institutions as the Cambrian Archaeological Association and the Honourable Society of Cymmrodorion proved invaluable to the Royal Commission from the beginning.

It might be thought a disadvantage that for the first four decades of its existence it was based, like other Royal Commissions, in London, but this meant easy access to the British Museum, the Public Record Office and the Cymmrodorion Society, which also had its headquarters in the capital.

The Royal Commission's first chairman was Sir John Rhys (died 1915), philologist and professor of Celtic at Oxford. He oversaw the publication of the first four inventory volumes [002], which appeared in quick succession: for Montgomeryshire (1911), Flintshire (1912), Radnorshire (1913) and Denbighshire (1914). The second chairman (until his death in 1934) was Evan Vincent Evans, whose background was quite different. By profession an accountant and journalist, he was a friend of Welsh politicians and a stalwart of eisteddfodau and the Cymmrodorion – he greatly encouraged scholars without claiming to be one himself.

The early commissioners, too, represented varied backgrounds. Edward Anwyl (died 1914) was another philologist, professor of Welsh and Comparative Philology at the University College of Wales, Aberystwyth. G. Hartwell Jones (died 1944) was an Anglican clergyman living in Surrey but also chairman of the Cymmrodorion Society. Robert Hughes was a former lord mayor of Cardiff, which had recently been created a city. Henry Owen, a lawyer, was a notable Pembrokeshire historian and another leading light of the Cymmrodorion. J. A. (later Sir Joseph) Bradney, who was the pre-eminent historian of Monmouthshire, was appointed a commissioner during the Great War, when he was also a lieutenant-colonel in the militia. The last of these early commissioners to be appointed (in 1920) was John Morris-Jones, poet and professor of Welsh in the University College of North Wales, Bangor.

None of these men could claim to be a practising archaeologist by any later definition of the term; rather they represented an antiquarian tradition focussed on the 'Celtic' past. Two other commissioners were in a different mould, however. W. E. Llewellyn Morgan, who was on the army retired list, had spent several decades penning field descriptions of monuments; those which he made for the Royal Commission, drawing on his earlier notes, were sufficiently respected to be included in the Pembrokeshire inventory (1925).

Opposite: The first commissioners and staff, probably taken at Llanfihangel Abercywyn, Carmarthenshire (from left to right): Evan Vincent Evans, unknown clergyman, George Eyre Evans (investigator), Sir Edward Anwyl, Edward Owen (Secretary), Sir John Rhys (Chairman), Griffith Hartwell Jones. DI2007_0097 NPRN 54624

[1] With contributions by Hilary Malaws, David Percival and Peter White.

Wash drawing of St Asaph Cathedral by Mervyn Pritchard, 1912.

DI2008_0381 NPRN 140540

Finally, R. C. Bosanquet (died 1925) was professor of Classical Archaeology at the University of Liverpool: the high quality of the Roman entries in the first inventories may be attributed to him. Together, these commissioners were knowledgeable of every part of Wales and influential in scholarly and public circles at a time when the professions of archaeology and history were still in the early stages of their development.

The day-to-day work of the new Commission required specialist staff, and its first secretary was Edward Owen, a man after the commissioners' own hearts. Between 1908 and 1928 he did much to establish the Commission on sound and respected foundations. A reputable historian of Anglesey origins, he was trained as a lawyer and had served, like many a British civil servant, in the India Office, where he supervised the military store accounts and prepared statistical statements for India. As overall editor of the inventories, he was at pains to extend his knowledge beyond his own expertise in medieval and later manuscripts. His scholarship was widely admired by the Cymmrodorion and the Carmarthenshire Antiquarian Society among others. He was also closely involved with the University of Liverpool, where he became reader in Welsh Medieval Antiquities (1921) during his time as the Commission's secretary.

Owen's staff was a varied, not to say eccentric, group of talented individuals whose writings are often admired today. His assistant in 1908, Edward Thomas, was a fine writer and observer of the landscape but he found the Commission's work uncongenial (he regarded himself 'a fish out of water') and resigned to concentrate on literature. Thomas proved to be one of Britain's finest war poets, but in 1917 he was killed in action at Arras. Three other of the early staff made greater contributions to the Commission. George Eyre Evans's life (1857-1939) spanned the formative years of modern archaeology. As a prolific antiquary with many publications to his name before he joined the Commission, he was most closely associated with Carmarthenshire, particularly the county museum and the antiquarian society. Alfred Neobard Palmer (1847-1915) was appointed in 1910 as a 'temporary assistant inspector of Ancient Monuments' for six months, at 15s. a day with a guinea for subsistence and travelling. Palmer suffered ill health, and his appointment was an act of kindness by Edward Owen, who had earlier secured him a government pension in recognition of his historical researches. A chemist by profession, Palmer turned himself into a meticulous local historian, particularly of Wrexham, where the local studies library is named after him. He brought a scientist's rigour to his use of documentary evidence, but he was an inexperienced fieldworker and had difficulty reading maps – entries in the inventories based on his fieldwork can be unreliable.

It was, perhaps, Mervyn Pritchard, an architect employed by HM Office of Works and Public Buildings, who had the most lasting contribution to make. His services were loaned to the Commission to make plans and drawings for the inventories and he seems to have been responsible for much of the photography. The wash drawing of St Asaph Cathedral that is the frontispiece of the Flintshire volume is by Pritchard, and his plans and pen-and-ink drawings can be seen in the inventories for Denbighshire (1914), Carmarthenshire (1917) and Merioneth (1921). The Pembrokeshire inventory displays his talents most effectively: his drawings were traced in the studio from a series of photographs taken in July 1922 and though lacking the technical detail to facilitate close analysis, they transmit the nature and qualities of their subjects admirably.

Following the publication of the first inventories (of Montgomeryshire and Flintshire in 1911-12), the Commission's work was praised in Parliament for its quality and value for money; but the Great War naturally slowed things down. Edward Owen, now unpaid, managed to keep the work going and the Carmarthenshire volume was published at the height of the war in 1917. At the same time (and although he was in his sixties), Owen was anxious to contribute to the war effort through a position in the newly-formed statistics department of the War Office, but he was turned down. For a brief period after the war Owen ran the Commission from his home in Wrexham, until new offices could be found in London. During his visits to the capital he took to sleeping in the office to carry out the work expected of him – which earned a mild rebuke from the Chief Commissioner of Works.

The future of the Royal Commission was in some doubt during the years of austerity, when the Office of Works considered a purge of Royal Commissions. This prompted the chairman, Vincent Evans, to urge Owen to publish the Merioneth volume as soon as possible, and when it appeared in 1921 Evans shrewdly sent a copy to the Prime Minister, David Lloyd George, who responded by congratulating the commissioners for 'doing a real public service'. The Commission's continuance was not questioned again for nearly seventy years. Nevertheless, financial cut-backs delayed the appearance of the Pembrokeshire inventory, and the Commission itself did not meet formally for two and a half years.

The fundamental nature of the inventories was bound to lead the Commission into other areas concerned with the historic sites and monuments it was recording, and this has characterised the Commission throughout its life. As early as 1916 Owen was allowed to make representations to the town clerk of Chepstow about the proposed destruction of a stretch of medieval town wall, and in 1926 the Commission was represented on the committees running the excavations at the Roman fort at Kanovium (Caerhun). Owen himself was in constant demand to give talks to national and local societies, and a steady stream of requests for information came in – for example on the Roman fort at Tomen-y-mur, Whitland Abbey, stone circles, place names and, especially, genealogy.

During the mid-1920s developments in professional archaeology exerted growing pressure for change in the approaches, methodology and structure of the Royal Commission. While the Commission had fulfilled its role of identifying monuments worthy of preservation, the volume on Pembrokeshire (1925) attracted criticism for its dearth of original fieldwork and its failure to keep up with advances in architectural recording and interpretation.

Edward Owen was prepared to defend the Commission's approach to its work, which had the merit of publishing lists of sites and monuments swiftly in the county inventories. But Owen also saw the need to keep abreast of scholarly advances, even though the financial climate of the post-war years made it difficult to find suitably qualified staff when they would be expected to work for practically nothing. A thorough review of the Commission's operations resulted in major revision of his original guidelines. The Commission had been fortunate in recruiting Cyril Fox, the new director of the National Museum of Wales, as a commissioner; supported by R. C. Bosanquet, he was largely responsible for the changes that were now made. What survived of Owen's guidelines were the county arrangement of inventories and the broad classification scheme he had devised. There was a shift in focus from the use of documents and antiquarian reports to fieldwork, and an insistence on a full record of each site, building or object, with original plans and descriptions made by the Commission itself. Categories or types of structures and objects were henceforward to be identified routinely, noting any significant variations of detail, and reference to the methods used by the English and Scottish Commissions in describing and mapping monuments would be more frequent.

Cyril Fox, 1882-1967, Royal Commissioner and Director of the National Museum of Wales, 1926-48; knighted in 1935.

Courtesy Mrs Migallon

The opportunity was not taken to extend the remit of the Commission's investigators to buildings dated after 1714, but this year was an advance on the earlier guidelines. Special attention would now be drawn to domestic structures of all sorts, including 'humbler dwellings'. Another novelty was consultation with 'official referees' whose specialist advice would supplement the expertise of the small number of commissioners, especially in new and developing fields of knowledge. This enabled the Commission to recruit advisers of the calibre of J. E. Lloyd (the distinguished medieval historian) and Mortimer Wheeler (the go-ahead archaeologist who became keeper of the London Museum after resigning as director of the National Museum of Wales in 1926).

In the remaining two years of his secretaryship Owen put in order the work already done on Anglesey. It was left to his successor, Wilfred J. Hemp, to oversee the full implementation of the new guidelines. As an experienced inspector of Welsh monuments in the Office of Works and a plain-speaking advocate of archaeology and archaeologists, in many ways Hemp was ideal for the task. On the other hand, he found the administrative burdens in a period of economic depression tiresome and his insistent attempts to squeeze resources from the 'singularly ill-informed' Treasury seem to have been less effective than the efforts of Vincent Evans, who was familiar with the corridors of Whitehall.

The annual budget of the Commission was raised from £1,250 to £1,700 at the time of Hemp's appointment, but the story of the next decade is essentially one of constant struggle by both chairman and secretary to secure expert investigative staff and refine the quality of reporting, building on the principles of 1926. Leonard Monroe, a trained architect, was appointed as the secretary's assistant, and Hemp decided to employ Stuart Piggott, a young archaeologist with a distinguished career ahead of him, instead of a typist (but on a typist's salary of £3 a week). Convinced that each specialist member of 'a skeleton staff of three should be a first rate man', Hemp nevertheless estimated that it would take forty years to complete the county inventories to the standard now adopted.

The test of the Commission's revised strategy and Hemp's stewardship was the Anglesey inventory, on which work had been proceeding since the mid-1920s. In November 1929 Hemp estimated that 'it should be completed in about four years, if the services of a typist can be obtained'. In Hemp's mind it also depended on strengthening the complement of staff,

particularly in field archaeology; but, as the government grappled with economic crises over the next few years, there was little sympathy shown at the Treasury. A desperate Leonard Monroe repeatedly threatened to resign, and in 1933 Stuart Piggott did so. Even Hemp was moved to tell the commissioners that henceforward they could only count on receiving the 'statutory allowance' of his time.

In the event, the Anglesey book was published in 1937. Its approach and structure set the pattern for the inventory volumes that would follow over the next half-century. One of its most striking features was its emphasis on the comparative study of sites and buildings and on the use of examples to establish types of structures so as to provide a deeper understanding of past societies. Site descriptions were arranged by parishes, maps and plans were generously provided, the spelling of Welsh place names followed principles recommended by J. E. Lloyd rather than the antiquated practices of the Ordnance Survey, and a helpful glossary of terms was included. The book was praised because it 'not only set a fresh standard for work in Wales, but also dealt more comprehensively with the archaeology and history of the district concerned than did the publications of the fellow Commissions for England and Scotland'. Sadly, Vincent Evans, the long-serving chairman who had presided over the transformation of the Commission's work, died in November 1934, before the Anglesey inventory was published. He was succeeded by the Earl of Plymouth.

The next item on the agenda was the Caernarfonshire inventory. There was much to be said for applying the knowledge gained in Anglesey to the county immediately across the Menai Strait, and sporadic collection of materials on Caernarfonshire had taken place already. But the Second World War caused major disruption to the Commission's plans for this volume. During the war Hemp ran the evacuated Commission from his home in Criccieth. This enabled him to devote happy days to research and writing on a county that was the Commission's priority. His long-standing interest in history, genealogy and heraldry was applied to the wealth of medieval stone carvings and inscriptions, and his experience as an inspector for the Office of Works enabled him to report in 1941 on clearances at Conwy Castle so that additions could be made to its newly-surveyed plan. Soon after the war ended, Hemp retired and Leonard Monroe moved elsewhere. In terms of experienced staff, and therefore continuance of its work, the Commission stood at a crossroads.

During the war another strand of investigation and recording began that was later to be bound into the Royal Commission. This was the creation in 1940 of the National Buildings Record for England, Scotland and Wales because of concern that buildings might be destroyed by enemy action without any record ever having been made of them. With limited resources, it set about the formidable task of rapidly compiling a national architectural archive, and in a very short space of time it amassed an impressive collection of photographs and drawings, including the Courtauld Institute's already established Conway Library. Leonard Monroe was seconded to the National Buildings Record from the Royal Commission to cover south Wales. Photographers around the country were also engaged to photograph buildings in areas judged to be at greatest risk: most prolific of those working in Wales was George Bernard Mason, who produced photographs of exceptional quality. After the war the National Buildings Record photographers took to recording buildings ahead of the new threat posed by demolition, as owners of many fine houses could no longer

afford to maintain them.

In 1946 the Royal Commission was clear about its programme of future work: to complete the Caernarfonshire inventory along modern lines. But more immediate decisions were needed about where the Commission should be based and who was to lead its small staff. A. H. A. Hogg (died 1989) was appointed the secretary in 1949. Hogg was by profession a civil engineer, but he had strong interests and field experience in archaeology going back to his teenage years. He came to the Royal Commission from a lectureship in engineering at Cambridge University. Hogg was par excellence a field worker, who imbued two generations of investigators with the principles and practices of rigorous recording, using chain, tape and theodolite. Probably at his urging, it was decided to base the Commission in Aberystwyth rather than return to London. Aberystwyth had the advantages of a central location in Wales and scholarly facilities close by in the National Library of Wales. The Commission has remained in Aberystwyth ever since.

By 1949 the rest of the Commission's staff was

Conwy Castle and Stephenson's railway bridge in a photograph from the National Buildings Record.

CD 2003_624_001 NPRN 121

One of the photographs from the survey by G. B. Mason of Faenol Fawr, Bodelwyddan, for the National Buildings Record in 1954.

DI2008_0368 NPRN 35813

mostly young and inexperienced, with the singular exception of C. N. Johns, who had wide knowledge as a crusader castle archaeologist in the Palestine Department of Antiquities in the 1930s and '40s, and immediately after the war had been seconded from the Royal Commission to be the British controller of antiquities and excavations in Libya. His was a name to conjure with in Middle Eastern archaeology for long after, and he applied his field experience to good effect in north Wales. During the years of recovery and growing prosperity in the '50s and early '60s, the staff grew in number and became more specialised in both field survey and site and building recording, eventually with a specialist photographer and professional illustrator, all of whose services ensured that the three Caernarfonshire volumes published between 1956 and 1964 maintained and enhanced the standards achieved in the Anglesey book twenty years earlier.

Petrol rationing at first had delayed the fieldwork, which was made more difficult, too, by mountainous terrain and bad weather. An important modification of the principles was made to extend the cut-off date for recording vernacular architecture from 1714 to 1750, with some examination of buildings constructed between then and 1850. These changes in the evolution of the Commission's interpretation of 'historic monuments' reflected the passage of time and the life of buildings, as well as ideas about what should be recorded and preserved. In the more industrialised counties of Wales this would shortly raise very large issues for the Commission's future programme. Like the earlier stress on 'humbler dwellings' in the Anglesey inventory (of which a new edition appeared in 1960), the modifications doubtless owed much to Cyril Fox, still one of the commissioners, and to the publication of his and Lord Raglan's three volumes on Monmouthshire houses in 1951-4.

The Caernarfonshire books broke new ground in their recording of hundreds of huts and field systems, site descriptions like that of Caernarfon Castle (in Volume II), and the space given to local vernacular architecture and the small churches of the Caernarfonshire countryside. Volume II recorded the discoveries of the Roman marching camp at Penygwryd and Roman fort at Pen Llystyn. Volume III included the first complete survey ever made of Bardsey, the Isle of Saints. The whole enterprise was informed by a multiplicity of skilful plans and maps, as well as by hundreds of photographs.

In 1963 responsibility for the National Buildings Record was transferred to the three Royal Commissions and it was amalgamated with the records gathered during the course of their own work over the previous half-century. The Commissions were explicitly empowered to continue this established architectural work. In Wales Peter Smith was assigned as the emergency recorder with special responsibility for domestic architecture. By this stage the Commission had also amassed a considerable archive of measured drawings, surveys and photographs through its own inventory programme. These records documented archaeological sites and buildings of all periods, and the amalgamation created a substantial national archive which was renamed the National Monuments Record of Wales to reflect its unique scope and importance. Its primary functions were 'to provide an index of all monuments, so that inquirers can be directed at once to the best information concerning any structure; and to fill the gaps in that information'. These ambitious and important aims resulted in a classified card index, innovatory in its day, for every known site and structure in Wales. Managed by C. H. Houlder, it laid the foundation of the Commission's structured archive, database and enquiry service as they are today.

When the Commission came to survey the county of Glamorgan, it faced a much larger and more complex body of architecture than that in previous inventories. A greater proportion of investigators' time was needed for architectural survey than for traditional earthwork archaeology, and it was realised that it would be possible to progress the work more efficiently if the system of recording by parishes were abandoned in favour of recording by a combination of period and monument type. Volume I, published in 1976, therefore focussed exclusively on prehistoric and early medieval Glamorgan and represented a major departure. This and the plans for further thematic volumes in the Glamorgan inventory were essentially the work of A. H. A. Hogg and his team. Although Hogg himself had retired as secretary in 1973, he continued to lend his services to the Commission until his late seventies.

In the meantime several other important

developments had broadened the Royal Commission's responsibilities. In 1969 it took the initiative to list all known field monuments in Wales as a source of information for local authorities. Commissioners were sensitive to the inevitably slow progress of the authoritative, detailed inventory programme, and it seemed helpful to complement it with a rapid survey of those monuments that were increasingly at risk from development: they were defined as 'all types of ancient structures which are no longer capable of active use', a definition that allowed the inclusion of certain industrial monuments but excluded churches and mansions. A further advantage of this new project was that priority could be given to two counties that so far had no inventories. Yet only two of these new lists were issued: the first for Cardiganshire in 1970 and the second in 1973 for the 'Early Monuments' of Monmouthshire.

A second experiment capitalised on the Commission's growing archive of excavated and recorded sites. In 1971 it published what it saw as 'the first of a series of reports by which... the National Monuments Record of Wales hopes to provide accounts of the major field monuments for which no adequate descriptions exist'. This was a detailed survey of the hut settlement on Gateholm Island, Pembrokeshire [027]. The commissioners turned for another development to one of the senior investigators, Peter Smith, who had been studying over a number of years the historical and stylistic evolution of house types in Wales. The resulting book, *Houses of the Welsh Countryside*, which was brought out at the end of 1975 to coincide with 'Architectural Heritage Year', decisively demonstrated that the inventories could take yet another form, as national studies of a topic [004]. Smith's book, a contribution of European importance to the history of domestic architecture, was published to great acclaim, and an expanded edition appeared in 1988.

Excavation was a prominent activity of the Royal Commission during Hogg's period as secretary, reflecting his own interests and the dearth of other organisations to carry them out. For example, between 1957 and 1960 staff were diverted to the rescue excavation of the Roman fort at Pen Llystyn, Caernarfonshire [003], and in 1962 Hogg directed rescue excavations associated with a hydro-electric scheme on the site of Bronze Age cairns at Aber Camddwr, Cardiganshire. For several seasons in the 1960s, L. A. S. Butler conducted excavations in medieval Conwy, including in the vicarage garden where a medieval building had possibly been destroyed during Owain Glyn Dŵr's revolt. Other excavations at this time were part of the inventory programme for Glamorgan, such as at Harding's Down in Gower, where a rampart section was cut and an entrance and two hut platforms were revealed in an Iron Age hillfort. The Commission made many significant archaeological discoveries, not the least being the identification of six new Roman marching camps between 1954 and 1972.

Of great significance for the future were the trials which the Commission made in the early 1970s of the use of vertical aerial photography to speed up the survey of nationally important sites: of the Pembrokeshire hillforts Gaer Fawr and Carn Ingli in 1973, and in 1974 of Carn Goch, a hillfort in Carmarthenshire. The methodology was also adopted for the medieval site of Cefnllys Castle in Radnorshire.

The Commission's staff was active in the wider archaeological world in the post-war period, when there were relatively few qualified field archaeologists in Wales. Hogg was particularly noted for his contribution to hillfort studies and for several years he had a fruitful partnership with the castle historian, D. J. C. King, to compile lists of early castles and masonry castles in Wales and the Marches. He and several colleagues collaborated to publish the reports of pre-Second World War excavations at the hillfort of Pen Dinas, Aberystwyth. It was a deserved tribute that Hogg should be presented in 1981 with a volume in his honour that included essays on hillforts in both Britain and continental Europe.

In all these ways, some traditional and others novel, the Commission transformed the meaning of its original remit. While the concept of the inventory remained at its core, the Commission's role in recording and interpreting the historic landscape had much expanded.

In the late twentieth century the obligation to convey this knowledge to the public became progressively more urgent; at the same time, the reorganisation of archaeology in Wales presented a number of challenges which led to yet another reorientation. These came to a head in the 1980s and enabled the Commission to develop a distinctive focus to its activities.

The fourth secretary of the Royal Commission, Peter Smith (from 1973 to 1991), had joined the organisation in 1949 after a brief period as a trainee architect during which he became disillusioned with the prevailing modernist trend in architecture. At the outset his principal aim was to continue with the

Glamorgan inventory, and five massive volumes were published between 1976 and 2000 which were highly praised – though even as the millennium ended the plan had not been fully realised [005]. At the same time progress was made on the sites and monuments of Brecknock and a revision of the Radnorshire book of 1913 was begun to bring it up to modern scholarly standards. However, these continuations of the county inventory programme began to seem anachronistic as government policy laid heavier stress on speed of publication, economy and accessibility to a wider public. Yet other avenues were profitably explored. Perhaps with the needs of Glamorgan in mind, and certainly in the light of the decay of Wales's heavy industries, the chairman of the Commission, W. F. Grimes, encouraged greater interest in industrial remains – though he himself was a notable prehistorian. Particular attention was given to the early communications systems of the Swansea valley: a prelude to much more extensive studies of Wales's canals and the remains of the Swansea region's industries.

In the post-war decades the Royal Commission had consistently supported the county history movement in Wales, and in due time practically all the volumes that appeared – and continue to appear – in the series of histories of the counties of Glamorgan, Cardigan, Pembroke, Merioneth and Monmouth have drawn on the Commission's archive for striking illustrations and, in some cases, on its staff and commissioners for chapters.

On the other hand, the Royal Commission's role in excavation was bound to change from the 1970s onwards. Both rescue and research excavation were time-consuming and expensive, and they deflected work from the writing of the inventories. The strains became ever clearer as a result of the profound economic and social changes of contemporary Britain. These brought heightened public awareness of threats to the historic environment, for example from the increasing pace of destruction of buildings like country houses and churches (the so-called 'lost houses' and 'lost churches' of Wales) and from industrial decline and redevelopment of the landscape. The creation of the four Welsh Archaeological Trusts as excavating units removed the need for the Commission to be as centrally involved in such activity as it once had been, particularly now that urgent 'rescue' archaeology was the order of the day. The need to survey and record the rapidly changing historic landscape was equally urgent and the Commission was able to concentrate on this part of its mission.

Excavations at Cefn y Fan, Caernarfonshire. In the centre of the front row is A. H. A. Hogg, Secretary of the Royal Commission 1949-73; at the left end of the front row, C. H. Houlder. In the rear middle left is W. E. Griffiths and to his left Peter Smith, secretary 1973-91.

DI2008_0182 NPRN 26248

Following the formation of English Heritage to cover historic environment functions in England, it was decided to take a fresh look at the Royal Commissions. Management consultants were engaged by the government to examine 'value for money'. As far as Wales was concerned, in 1988 their report stated that 'Our strong impression of RCAHMW is that the best has become the enemy of the good. It is inward-looking, rather with the aura of an old-fashioned university department, it has not recognised the need for good management practices and the Commission has not fully recognised the value of integrating non-inventory activities into its priorities… If RCAHMW is to represent good value for money, there needs to be major re-orientation of effort.' This blunt report was accepted by the government.

The debate about the usefulness of 'static' county inventories in a changing world where developers, planners and owners needed direct access to current, reliable information about the historic environment had gone on for decades. The 1960s had seen the first shift away from inventory compilation with the establishment of the National Monuments Records in Wales, Scotland and England – making concrete the concept of the dynamic record. A decade later the Ancient Monuments Inspectorate supported the creation of a network of sites and monuments records (SMRs) capable of responding to current enquiries at a regional level.

In fact, an alternative to the static record of the inventories had been in being before the Commission's inception – the Ordnance Survey's (OS) record of archaeological sites for map depiction – and this would in due course be brought into the Royal Commissions. The Ordnance Survey's archaeology officer, C. W. Phillips, argued that, 'This continuous aspect of the work is of great importance and compares favourably with that of some other institutions which are unable to continue their work in it effectively once they have completed the inventory of a county, excellent though that inventory normally is'. He warned ruefully that, the Royal Commissions' completion of their inventories 'cannot be expected before much of the matter of their inquiry has been either damaged or destroyed'. Antiquities had been shown on OS maps from the late eighteenth century (at least two of the iconic features of these maps were introduced first in Wales: Gothic script for antiquities in 1812 and Egyptian typeface for Roman remains in 1816). Until the end of the Great War the identification and interpretation of antiquities had taken place in consultation with local experts and antiquaries, but in 1920 the Survey had appointed its first archaeological officer, O. G. S. Crawford, who built up a small but expert group, including W. F. Grimes, who later became chairman of the Welsh Commission. Throughout the 1950s and '60s the OS archaeology branch amassed a considerable body of material on antiquities, which went far beyond what was required for mapping. The sites index included a short description and interpretation of each site, with bibliographical references and field observations. These were usually accompanied by a measured plan, normally at the appropriate basic mapping scale but sometimes supplemented with enlarged surveys and cross-sections to aid interpretation and help in draughting the published map.

In 1983 the Survey's archaeological division was transferred to the three Royal Commissions along with its invaluable sites index and responsibility for surveying, interpreting and maintaining a record of archaeological sites depicted on OS maps. In Wales since then the Royal Commission itself has continued to provide mapping information to the Ordnance Survey for basic scales and for derived mapping such as the popular 1/50,000 scale Landranger series. The supply of this information is an invaluable product of the Royal Commission's archaeological survey projects, ensuring that every user of Ordnance Survey maps can appreciate the historic sites depicted.

The consultants in 1988 estimated that only 11 per cent of the Commission's resources were allocated to Wales's National Monuments Record. They accordingly recommended an adjustment of the balance with the Commission's publications programme: increased priority should be given to the National Monuments Record 'as the destination of… survey data' for Wales, and computer-based technologies should be developed for 'the storage, retrieval and dissemination of data'. Along with improved management structures and an emphasis on staff training to ensure the future capacity of the Commission, here was a clear remit for the new

chairman, Professor J. B. Smith, and the new secretary, Peter White, who came from English Heritage with extensive experience of administrative and financial management; both were appointed in 1991. In the following year a revised Royal Warrant confirmed the changed priorities of the Royal Commission.

The staffing needs for the multi-functional body that was now in prospect to serve a comparatively small country had still not been addressed – nor, indeed, had they ever been since 1908. However, in 1991 the crucial information technology post was created, and Terry James showed infinite patience and resourcefulness in recasting the Commission's data and introducing his colleagues to electronic recording. The use of the same software as that for the regional sites and monuments records helped the Commission to lead a partnership that resulted in data exchange through the Extended National Database (END) – a major advance in the development of a record for the whole of Wales.

No less significant were the expansion of the aerial survey programme of the 1980s and the introduction of the extraordinarily fruitful survey to cover all of the extensive Welsh uplands. Both of these initiatives continue to make distinctive contributions to Welsh archaeology by locating thousands of hitherto unsuspected sites. Greater managerial skills were needed to operate the Commission's increasingly complex infrastructure and the Plas Crug building at Aberystwyth, into which the Commission moved in 1990.

At the same time the undoubted professionalism and scholarship of the Commission's staff were harnessed to maximum effect. This was well demonstrated by the large Welsh Chapels project, which was carried forward in partnership with the National Library of Wales and the voluntary organisation, Capel. In time, all such projects came to be allocated to one of three branches, covering the main functions of survey and investigation, information management and public services, with close working between the staff of each.

The Commission's publications continued to prove a strength and extended far beyond the county inventories. Books were produced on topical subjects and particular sites or buildings. Studies of the collieries of Wales, Brecon Cathedral, Newport Castle (Pembrokeshire) and *Guns across the Severn* (the fortifications in the Severn channel) spring to mind. Gradually, from the 1990s onwards, there also developed a portfolio of outreach activity to complement management of the archive, supported by an education officer and organised from a

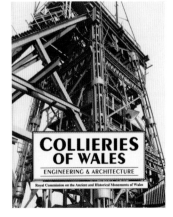

Collieries of Wales,
published 1994.

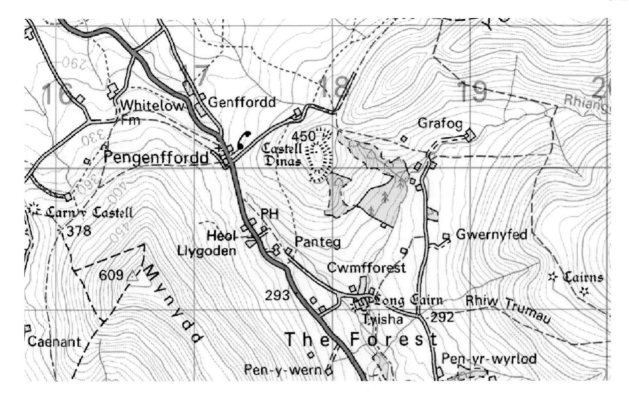

The Royal Commission is responsible for supplying the Ordnance Survey with surveys of ancient and historical sites to be represented on its different scales of mapping. This Landranger map extract from the Black Mountains in Powys shows five antiquities, including the complex fortification of Castell Dinas.

NPRN 92015
Crown copyright.
OS licence number 100017916

refurbished library that welcomes the public.

The Royal Commission's archive was a hidden strength which gave the organisation a renewed *raison d'être*. Years of under-capitalisation of the National Monuments Record had meant that it had no effective, modern finding aids. Computerisation of the records data now began to unlock its riches, including the collection of images, the largest of its kind in Wales and half as big again as that of the National Library. The National Monuments Record had become a nationwide resource of a nature different to that of the regional sites and monuments records. It expanded rapidly with significant donations from many public and private sources supplementing the detailed survey and photographic records of the Commission itself. Transfers from many other public organisations, including Cadw on behalf of the Welsh Assembly Government, take place from time to time. Important collections have been accepted from the private and commercial sectors, one of the most notable being the acquisition in 2008 of the Aerofilms collection of historic oblique air photographs. Today, the photographs in the National Monuments Record are Wales's largest national collection, with about 1.5 million images. A foretaste of the future was the Commission's participation in the Gathering the Jewels project, which provided an opportunity to make available online many notable images from the National Monuments Record and began a digitisation

programme which remains one of the Commission's priorities in its service to the public.

Providing public access to its collections is a paramount objective of the SWISH partnership (Shared Web Information Services for Heritage) to develop online public services. This collaboration with the Scottish Royal Commission, based in Edinburgh, was the first such project between the two devolved administrations that had recently come into being. SWISH supports Coflein, the Commission's free internet service, which at present carries details of some 80,000 sites as well as the National Monuments Record archive catalogue, and gives direct access to an ever expanding number of images and other digital records – a resource that would have far exceeded the expectations of the consultants in 1988. In 2006 SWISH began developing the Historic Wales Portal, which offers access to the historic environment records of a wide range of bodies, including the National Museum, Cadw, and the four Welsh Archaeological Trusts.

The SWISH partnership enabled access to the National Monuments Record using map searching online. In allocating additional funding to this imaginative project, the new Welsh Assembly Government demonstrated its confidence in the abilities and purposes of the Royal Commission and the role it plays in safeguarding and managing the nation's heritage.

002 The Early Inventories

ROYAL COMMISSION ON ANCIENT MONUMENTS IN WALES AND MONMOUTHSHIRE.

COUNTY OF MONTGOMERY.

MONUMENTS SPECIFIED BY THE COMMISSION AS ESPECIALLY WORTHY OF PRESERVATION.

No. in Inventory.	Parish.	Monument.	Remarks.
12	Bausley	Castle Camp	Forms (with Cefn Castell, parish of Middletown) part of the Breiddin scheme of defence.
33	Bettws Cedewen	'Cefn Ucheldre' Camp	Mound-and-bailey.
92	Castle Caereinion	Pen y foel Camp	
100	Castlewright	Caer din	
101	,,	Bishop's Moat	Mound-and-bailey.
143	Cletterwood	Buttington Church	Font formed of capital of pier from Strata Marcella Abbey.
149	Criggion	Breiddin	
174	Forden	Y Gaer	Roman.
214	Guilsfield	Gaer Fawr	
241	Hirnant	Carnedd Illog	
287	Kerry	Camp	
293	,,	The Double Dyche	
295	,,	Parish Church	
302	Leighton	Caer Digoll	
308/10	Llanbrynmair	Cairn and Circles	
311	,,	Tafolwern	Owain Cyfeiliog's mound-castle.
312	,,	Parish Church	Arcade of rude oak beams.
334	Llandinam	Cefn Carnedd	
364	Llandrinio	Parish Church	Norman arch and font.
387	Llandyssil	Cefn Bryntalch	Mound-and-bailey.
398	Llanerfyl	Parish Church	Inscribed Stone in churchyard.
419	Llanfair Caereinion	Y Gaer	Small Roman station.
420	,, ,,	Parish Church	14th-century effigy.
447	Llanfechain	Domen Gastell	Mound-and-bailey.
448	,,	Parish Church	Early English details.
463	Llanfihangel yng Ngwynfa	Beddau Cewri	Unexplored mounds of peculiar construction.

An extract from the first recommendations made by the Royal Commission of monuments worthy of preservation, from the Montgomeryshire inventory, published in 1911.

The first commissioners decided to compile their inventory of Wales's historic sites and monuments on a county basis. Material for the seven counties of Montgomery, Flint, Radnor, Denbigh, Carmarthen, Merioneth and Pembroke was accumulated quite rapidly up to 1915, when the Great War interrupted operations. Further fieldwork was then carried out for Pembrokeshire until 1923.

Edward Owen's guidelines for these seven inventories emphasised the use of known documentary sources rather than original fieldwork. Questionnaires were issued to local worthies, members of the Cambrian Archaeological Association were consulted, and witnesses were examined in public. The quality of the information gathered was naturally variable, and alternative views on (for example) Carmarthenshire 'cooking hearths' emerged. However, the list of 'Monuments specified by the Commissioners as especially worthy of preservation' was in all cases a firm outcome of permanent value.

A scheme was devised to place the monuments in classes, as far as possible in accordance with the scheme of the Congress of Archaeological Societies, and there were discussions with the Royal Commission for England on how best to classify certain sites. In a post-industrial age, the 'divisions' used seem distinctly old-fashioned: prehistoric sites (I), earthworks including hillforts (II), domestic buildings including castles (III), ecclesiastical buildings (IV), other sites like holy wells (V), sites prompted by place-name or other associations (VI), and, bringing up the rear, finds (VII). It was anticipated that every monument would be inspected in the field by an investigator, while the commissioners would confine their periodic inspections to typical monuments in each class. The work of compiling the inventories, coordinated by Owen, was the responsibility of the Commission's inspecting officers. Several commissioners, including Sir John Rhys and R. C. Bosanquet, also contributed.

In each book sites are reported by civil parish following the Census Reports of England and Wales of 1901, in alphabetical order. At the outset of the enterprise it was felt that generalised conclusions about the counties' histories were not advisable, 'without enlightenment from the use of the spade and the level, implements which this Commission has no power to requisition'. It was a sound, if cautious, instinct, since the earlier inventories have in truth been overtaken by later research. Although the books are now collectors' items, their detailed content has often been superseded, sometimes by the Royal Commission itself.

Right: A plan of Castell Pen-y-coed Iron Age defended enclosure, drawn by Mervyn Pritchard for the Carmarthenshire inventory, 1917.

DI2008_0385 NPRN 304193

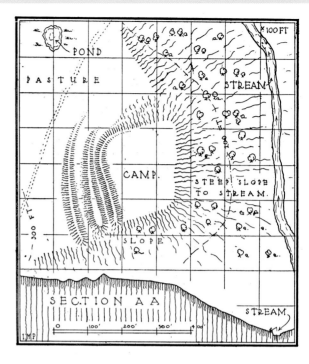

Above: An early photograph by the Commission: St Clears Castle in the Carmarthenshire inventory, 1917.

DI2008_0383 NPRN 105023

One of the most valuable parts of these early inventories remains the list of field names taken from such sources as tithe awards, for the light they might throw on 'lost' sites and monuments, as (for example) the hillfort of Croes Arthur in Carmarthenshire. Sometimes, the descriptions draw on excavation reports on which commissioners and field inspectors commented; the significance of antiquarian writings by Sion Dafydd Rhys, Edward Lhuyd and Thomas Pennant is noted in the entry on Caer Drewyn, Merioneth. By contrast, the site descriptions are poorly illustrated and some of the plans included were decades old. The small number of photographs in each inventory was often more decorative than analytical, though they provide a valuable record of sites. And the fact that Craig Rhiwarth in Montgomeryshire, a walled hillfort with over sixty huts then visible, hardly rated a mention was disappointing, to put it mildly. However, a substantial survey appears to have been made at Caer Digoll (Beacon Ring) within the framework of the published Ordnance Survey plan, and for the Carmarthenshire inventory a series of attractive, original plans of hillforts was prepared by Mervyn Pritchard.

David Browne

003 The Pen Llystyn Excavations

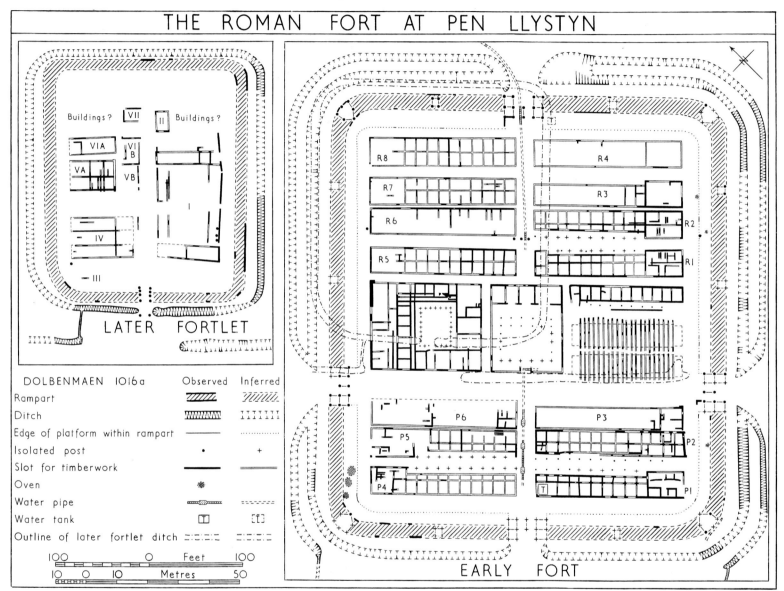

The Royal Commission's plan of the Roman fort at Pen Llystyn following the excavation.
DI2008_0103 NPRN 301056

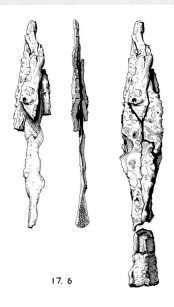

17. 6

Above: Record drawing of spearheads from the excavation.

DI2008_0104 NPRN 301056

Right: Ovens excavated adjacent to the quarry workings.

DI2008_0113 NPRN 301056

Below: Decorated samian pottery from Pen Llystyn.

DI2008_0110 NPRN 301056

One of the Royal Commission's most notable excavations was at the Roman site of Pen Llystyn. In 1957 the Commission's secretary, A. H. A. Hogg, wrote to an inspector of ancient monuments to announce the discovery of the Roman fort at a gravel pit at Bryncir, north of Cricieth.

A ditch had already been identified at the gravel pit, but it had yielded no artefacts. However, on a recent visit Hogg had been shown a piece of stamped samian pottery of Flavian date. This inspired him to organise the cutting of a few trenches, which made it clear that the site was that of a Roman fort with good preservation of the remains of timber buildings. Agreement was reached with the owner and the quarry company for Hogg's team to work within the quarry fence so long as gravel-digging was not delayed. The Commission kept a watching brief on soil-stripping operations, supplemented by controlled trenching, often in appalling weather, and built up a record of the fort. By November 1959 it was clear that a full rescue excavation was needed. The dig by volunteers and Royal Commission staff began in 1960 and lasted several seasons, directed by Hogg under the auspices of the Ministry of Works. The results were published by the Royal Archaeological Institute in 1969.

Observations and excavations together revealed the history of the site. Before the Roman fort, it had been occupied or used sporadically from the Early Bronze Age. Hollows, pits and small ditches represented phases of settlement of the Late Bronze Age or Iron Age, abandoned by the time the Roman army took possession of the hill.

This quite large auxiliary fort was built about AD 80, presumably to guard the approaches to and from the Llŷn peninsula; it was a good example of a Flavian-period layout. Within its ramparts it measured

117.3 metres by 132 metres, an enclosed area of 1.55 hectares. The defences were well adapted to the contours of the hill. The rampart was of gravel and boulders faced with turf; in front were two ditches. There were four double-passage gateways, each with a framework of fourteen large posts. Incorporated in the rampart were angle towers and intermediate turrets. In the *praetentura*, the area in front of the headquarters building, were four barracks and two stores or workshops. Across the centre of the fort were the commandant's house, the headquarters building, two granaries and, probably, the hospital. Behind the principal buildings, the *retentura* seems to have been subdivided by gates: two barrack blocks in one sector, and five barrack blocks and another building in the other. This evidence was taken to indicate that two units of infantry, 500 strong, were brigaded together. Cooking ovens and a water-supply through wooden pipes were also discovered.

The fort was occupied for less than twenty years, although evidence was found of short-lived later uses. It appears that the buildings were set on fire immediately after evacuation – almost certainly the act of the Roman army itself to leave nothing behind for the native population.

David Browne

004 Houses of the Welsh Countryside

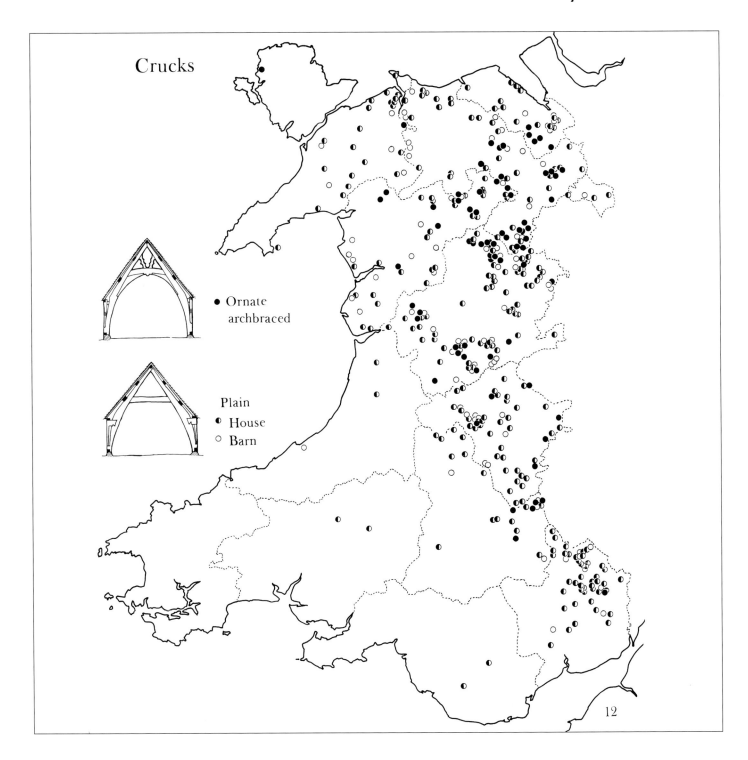

The numerous distribution maps in Houses of the Welsh Countryside *revealed the geographical patterns of vernacular architecture: map 12 showed the distribution of cruck construction across Wales.*

DI2008_0387
Crown copyright: RCAHMW. OS licence number 100017916

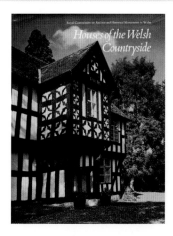

The cover of the first edition, showing the Old Vicarage, Berriew, 1975.

The two-phase house at Dduallt near Maentwrog, with the earlier, fifteenth- or sixteenth-century house to the right.

DI2006_1594 NPRN 28336

For much of the nineteenth and early twentieth centuries the study of farmhouses and cottages was pursued by antiquarians more or less independently of professional archaeologists and historians. In 1975 two path-breaking books on vernacular architecture were published: *English Vernacular Architecture* by Eric Mercer and *Houses of the Welsh Countryside* by Peter Smith, secretary of the Royal Commission. Both were departures from the Commission's style of inventories, and both were exhilarating combinations of empirical research and mature reflection. The books were very different in their attempts to make sense of an enormous amount of information. Mercer adopted an evolutionary approach, broadly arguing that domestic architecture passed through various stages of development irrespective of location; Smith's approach was diffusionist, tracing the spread of architectural innovation across the face of Wales.

The arrangement of *HWC* (as Smith's book is affectionately known) was novel. The sub-title, 'a study in historical geography', drew attention to the book's heart – a series of fifty maps that plotted the geographical distribution of distinctive architectural features of Welsh houses. The consolidated list of sites alone, arranged by county like the inventories,

extended to an astonishing thirty-six double-columned pages: it is an invaluable reference point. Smith's map-based approach was influenced by *The Personality of Britain* (1932) by Sir Cyril Fox, one of the earlier commissioners. Fox claimed that the whole of Wales belonged archaeologically to the 'highland zone' of Britain, yet Smith showed that the 'architectural personality' of Wales was complex, with differing regional distributions of features.

Peter Smith concluded from maps of date inscriptions that architectural innovation generally spread from east to west and he employed an amusing railway metaphor to make the point. Numerous maps plotted the medieval Welsh tradition of high-quality carpentry: the distribution of full roof-crucks showed at a glance the extraordinary numbers of surviving medieval houses in Wales and their uneven distribution. He also showed that medieval houses had a uniform plan and that they were succeeded by a diversity of regional house-types. The timing of the transition from open hall to storeyed house, and the reasons for the diversity of planning of post-medieval houses, are matters of intense interest today. Smith illustrated the different house-types with numerous plans and evocative cutaway drawings – models for future work in this field.

HWC was – and is – a voyage of discovery. It was possible to write it because of the rapid accumulation of survey information, catalogued in the reinvigorated National Monuments Record. It now seems astonishing that key sites like Ty-mawr, Castle Caereinion, and numerous other significant buildings were identified and put in context for the first time by Peter Smith and the Commission. These were by and large houses without a documented history: Smith showed that buildings were historical documents in their own right and that their study is integral to the study of history more generally. *HWC* enriched and broadened appreciation of the historic and vernacular architecture of Wales, leading to the conservation of many houses that would otherwise have disappeared.

HWC took its apt epigraph from O. M. Edwards's *Cartrefi Cymru*: 'Tybed fy mod wedi codi awydd ar rywun, yn y dalennau sydd yn y llyfr hwn, i fyned ar bererindod i rai o gartrefi Cymru....' (I wonder if I have, through the pages of this book, inspired anyone to venture on a pilgrimage to some of the houses of Wales).

Richard Suggett

005 The Glamorgan Inventories

A reconstruction drawing by Dylan Roberts of Coity Castle for the Glamorgan inventories.
DI2008_0373 NPRN 94504

It was sixty years before the Commission turned its attention to the highly industrialised parts of south Wales. Its survey team achieved work of considerable international importance in architectural history in compiling the Glamorgan inventory. The book about the county's *Greater Houses* (1981) was described enthusiastically as 'wonderful' and affording 'endless pleasure and instruction'. It attracted particular praise for its extensive use of line drawings, which had become one of the Commission's specialisms. It is recognised as a standard work of reference for the study of the early modern gentry and their houses – and not simply of Glamorgan.

In 1982 a second volume appeared, this time on *Medieval Non-defensive Secular Monuments*, which was scarcely less enthusiastically praised: C. J. Spurgeon's sections on moated sites and pillow mounds, and his historical introduction, were especially admired. At the time that this book was published the pressure to bring to an end the publication of large and expensive inventory volumes – even of this outstanding quality – was growing. Nevertheless, the volume on Glamorgan's *Farmhouses* was published in 1988 and was described by an eminent reviewer as 'the most impressive single volume to be published on vernacular architecture to date'. It concentrated on using illustrations rather than extensive texts to describe in detail the various architectural components of a class of building that had long deserved description.

Right: A cutaway drawing of the sixteenth-century mansion, Sker House.

GTJ00026 NPRN 19972

A Glamorgan farmhouse at Llandow.

DI2007_0397 NPRN 20008

The first of two spectacular volumes on the castles of Glamorgan – on *The Early Castles* of the conquest period up to 1217 – was published in 1991, by a team led by C. J. Spurgeon. The second volume, on *The Later Castles*, from 1217 to the end of the twentieth century and including the great masonry fortress of Caerphilly, by the same team, was published in 2000. These two authoritative volumes stand at the pinnacle of publication in castle studies internationally. They were essentially conceived during Peter Smith's time as the Commission's secretary, though he had retired in 1990.

Along similar lines, in 1987 the Commission had published the second part of what was intended to be the first volume of the Brecknock (or Breconshire) inventory. Compiled by David Browne, it described the hillforts and Roman remains of the county and was displayed at the Frankfurt Book Fair that year as an exemplar of the high-quality books then being published by Her Majesty's Stationery Office. The companion volume of 1997, edited by Stephen Briggs, described the later prehistoric monuments and unenclosed settlements of Brecknock down to AD 1000.

David Browne

The Prehistory of Wales

Toby Driver

The term 'prehistory' describes the time before written sources. The earliest surviving documentary descriptions of Wales date from some two thousand years ago, set down by Roman authors and shedding light on the culture of the Iron Age, albeit in its final phase. Both archaeological and written sources are available to interpret the material remains of cultures since then, each counterbalancing the biases of the other. In prehistory, however, we are reliant solely upon archaeological approaches.

The past century has seen archaeology progress from an antiquarian pursuit to a science, becoming a discipline informed by theoretical debate and the complementary ideas of anthropology, ethno-archaeology, geography and the environmental sciences. Archaeologists studying Wales, the staff of the Royal Commission among them, have achieved a great deal in discovering, surveying and interpreting field monuments, many of which had not been recognised before. In the Commission's earliest inventories prehistoric remains were documented as poorly understood curiosities of the rural landscape, frequently regarded as inferior to monumental castles or grand buildings. However, the profile of prehistoric archaeology has grown continuously since the Second World War: there has been development in scientific methods for surveying, dating and environmental analysis, and a growing appreciation of the chronology and significance of monuments and landscapes from different prehistoric periods. Royal Commission studies of Caernarfonshire, Glamorgan and Breconshire documented prehistoric burial places, forts, fields and farms, and augmented traditional field survey with excavations. These have stood the test of time, often providing the only record of tracts of prehistoric Wales. Thematic projects, uplands surveys and aerial reconnaissance have further broadened the Commission's recording of prehistory.

This essay summarises the prehistory of Wales, though the span of the prehistoric era is vast. Wales's earliest human remains are those of early Neanderthals, excavated at Pontnewydd cave, Denbighshire, and dating to about 225,000 years ago. Prehistorians have long been dissatisfied with the standard compart-mentalising of prehistoric epochs based on their prevailing tool technology – Stone Age (divided into Palaeolithic, Mesolithic and Neolithic), Bronze Age and Iron Age – though this division provides a useful chart with which to navigate the diversity of prehistory. Ways of life of the Mesolithic hunter or the Bronze Age farmer did not change overnight. Communities in every age doubtless achieved small technological advances and experienced imperceptible shifts in everyday practices, rituals and beliefs as the centuries passed. Very occasionally a visitor or migrant from distant parts may have arrived with radically different tools or knowledge, but generally change came gradually and cumulatively. Over thousands of years, usually mobile bands of hunters and gatherers gradually developed more complex social organisation, tool manufacture and artistic expression. Only with the arrival of knowledge of farming and cereal cultivation in north-western Europe at the start of the Neolithic is there evidence of permanent, settled communities, longer-term food storage, and the investment of effort to create communal monuments of wood and stone.

The environment that prehistoric people inhabited was also changing constantly, if imperceptibly to any single generation. During the timespan of the Palaeolithic and Mesolithic, continents and seas

Opposite page: The standing stone at Battle, Breconshire, stands nearly 4 metres high at the south end of a long stony cairn. It may once have been the focus for Bronze Age ritual and burial.
DI2007_0203 NPRN 301141

Below: Maesyfelin chambered long cairn at St Lythans in the Vale of Glamorgan is typical of the iconic prehistoric stone monuments of Wales.
DI2006_1024 NPRN 227289

The limestone cliffs of south-western Gower, viewed from the south. Paviland Cave is the narrow dark hole in the prominent whitish-yellow ridge, centre-right. Situated many miles inland during the Upper Palaeolithic, the cave mouth is now washed by winter storms.

AP_2006_2101 NPRN 300251

were reshaped by successive glaciations and the climate changed substantially. The start of the Neolithic saw sea levels around the British coast gradually stabilising several millennia after the most recent ice age, establishing new coastlines that are familiar today. In recent years archaeologists and oceanographers have recognised the research value of submerged former land surfaces, and advances in underwater prospection have allowed mapping of the Welsh land mass before the Neolithic, when land now covered by shallow seas would have been wooded plains. Changes in the prevailing regimes of temperature and precipitation were constant, and they continue today. Archaeologists have long relied on environmental data to provide a context for the study of particular sites and periods, and their findings are increasingly informing perceptions of the present environment and the susceptibility of our way of life to climate change.

Human settlement in Wales can be traced to the Palaeolithic. Discoveries of tools, animal bones and, occasionally, burials in caves tell us something about these early people, but human remains from the remotest periods are exceedingly rare. Only the durable remnants of jaws and teeth survive from the early Neanderthals of Pontnewydd cave, dating from the Lower Palaeolithic (around 225,000 years ago). The people of the Old Stone Age were not all cave-dwellers, but after successive glaciations of Wales (the most recent between about 21,000 and 14,000 years ago), caves are among the few places where tangible remains are preserved. Inhabited caves have been confirmed in the north and mid-Wales limestone regions and associated with open settlements in the south Wales limestone belt beyond the maximum limits of the glacial ice.

Finds of tools and hominin remains are more widespread from the Middle Palaeolithic (about 50,000 years ago) and the Upper Palaeolithic (about 30,000 years ago). At Coygan Cave, whose site is now a coastal promontory in Carmarthenshire but was once several miles inland, evidence for occupation by 'classic' Neanderthals was found. Bones of mammoth, woolly rhinoceros and hyena illustrate how distant this environment was from our own. Triangular handaxes show the mastery of stone tool technology. As well as describing Upper Palaeolithic sites and finds in the Royal Commission's inventories for Glamorgan (1976) and Breconshire (1997), the Commission assisted in surveying Paviland Cave, an Early Upper Palaeolithic site on the spectacular limestone coast of southern Gower. The cave is famous for the burial about 29,000 years ago of a young man (misnamed 'the Red Lady') with offerings of pierced shells, ivory rods or wands and two ivory bracelets [006]. Despite rich examples of cave art recorded in Europe, most famously at Lascaux in the Dordogne, Upper Palaeolithic cave art in Britain was recognised for the first time only in 2003, at Creswell Crags in Derbyshire. Portable art objects such as carved bones are more common, but the only such finds in Wales so far are those found in nineteenth-century excavations at Kendrick's Cave on the Great Orme, Llandudno: a decorated horse jawbone with zigzag incised lines is particularly fine and has been dated to around 10,000 years BC.

Following the retreat of the last glacial ice, nomadic bands of Mesolithic hunter-gatherers recolonised the warming land between about 8,000 and 5,000 BC. Sea levels were low and Britain was joined to the continent by a land bridge until about 8,500 years ago. A thick forest of pine and oak extended many miles into Cardigan and Carmarthen bays: ancient tree stumps are regularly exposed in eroding peat along coasts and estuaries. Mesolithic people left no visible monuments but traces of their hunting camps are found in coastal areas and sometimes in inland and mountainous regions. One such settlement and tool-making site was excavated at Waun Fignen Felen, on the eastern edge of the Black Mountain in Breconshire [007]. Environmental sampling and radiocarbon dating confirmed that there were episodes of forest clearance about 8,000 years ago, and surface collection and excavation recovered numerous microliths, left from the process of flint-knapping, and a perforated shale disc. One of the most famous Mesolithic sites to have been excavated is The Nab Head, on the west Pembrokeshire coast, where Mesolithic hunters made small flints and larger axes. Over 500 perforated shale beads were found here, as was a carved shale object that may represent a Venus figurine or a phallus, thought to be the only such carving from a Mesolithic context in Britain.

The gradual introduction of cereal farming from Europe in around 4,500 BC changed the subsistence

base and helped to produce more complex societies during the Neolithic (about 4,500 BC to 2,500 BC). Cultivation of crops required some people to abandon a mobile lifestyle and establish permanent farming settlements where they could prepare the soil, tend the crop during the growing season and then harvest and store the grain and by-products. Hunters of the Mesolithic must have had some sense of territory with regard to the land over which they roamed, but the new permanence of farming consolidated ideas of territorial possession and ancestral links to those who had farmed the land before. Slack times in the farming year and the ability to store the surplus from the harvest may have released time from food production for people in settled locations to expand craft activities: for example, to make fired clay pots and develop polished axes of fine-grained volcanic stone that were used for forest clearance and even ploughing. These changes also permitted communal enterprises such as the construction of chambered tombs, the most visible remains of the Neolithic in Wales [009].

Neolithic burial monuments took many forms, but they were generally mounds of earth or stone with a chamber or mortuary house inside or at one end. These monuments date from the Early Neolithic (roughly 4,500 BC to 3,500 BC) and are the oldest surviving standing structures in Europe. In Wales portal-dolmens are the best-known form, mostly sited along the south-west and north-west coasts. Their slim stone uprights supporting huge capstones

Carneddau Hengwm south cairn, Merioneth, looking along the stone-walled entrance of this basic passage grave, which was inserted into a pre-existing stone cairn by Neolithic builders, demonstrating a shift to new burial traditions.

DS2006_085_006 NPRN 302786

An aerial view of the site of the Graig Lwyd Neolithic axe factory (lower hill to right) on the north Caernarfonshire coast.

AP_2007_5246 NPRN 407068.

A possible causewayed enclosure at Flemingston, near St Athan in the Vale of Glamorgan. Discovered in 2006, the enclosure appears as two close-set, concentric ditches on a promontory, with a third ditch beyond.

AP_2006_3144 NPRN 404651

have long captured the imagination, though these structural elements have only been exposed through erosion of the mounds that covered them when built. Excavations have shown that some were surrounded by circular mounds of stone before being absorbed in larger, more complex cairns, often with further chambers constructed. Passage graves were more elaborate burial monuments, and in central and south-east Wales long cairns of 'Cotswold-Severn' type were built, with long rectangular mounds and one or more chambers. Such burial chambers were not quiet repositories for bones and offerings; excavations suggest that bones were regularly removed, replaced and tidied, possibly being taken away periodically for ancestral rites in villages or at other sacred locations.

Although chambered tombs have long attracted attention, many more features of the Neolithic ritual landscape have been identified. Aerial photography has revealed monuments generally hidden from view by ploughing and clearance, including cursus monuments and, from Late the Neolithic, circular henges – timber circles and massive palisaded enclosures that would have dominated the land [010]. In the lowlands of the Walton Basin in mid-Wales the largest Neolithic enclosure in Britain, at Hindwell, is matched by a concentration of other Neolithic monuments, including a cursus and a palisaded enclosure [013].

Ritual and burial sites are the predominant known monuments from the Neolithic and Bronze Ages, and houses and domestic enclosures are rarely discovered. One confirmed occupation site is the small defended outcrop at Clegyr Boia, Pembrokeshire. Traces of timber-built Neolithic houses have been discovered through excavations at Llandegai, beneath the chambered long cairn at Gwernvale, and elsewhere. Royal Commission aerial reconnaissance has been instrumental in discovering enigmatic causewayed enclosures, dating from the Neolithic and with characteristic multiple gaps in their perimeter banks and ditches. These have been interpreted as meeting places that drew together disparate communities, perhaps for markets, ceremonies and rituals, though they may have had more complex roles. Aerial photography from the mid-1990s has added five possible causewayed enclosures in the Vale of Glamorgan, Pembrokeshire and lowland Radnorshire to the single excavated example on Anglesey [008]. Eighty or so similar enclosures are so far known in the whole of the British Isles.

The farming communities of the Neolithic were not isolated. They produced polished axes and varied tools from outcrops and glacial erratics of fine-grained, igneous stone. Special qualities were required: the rock had to be easy to flake into a rough axe shape using a hammer-stone and bone or antler tools, but also tremendously strong and free from faults when used in heavy tasks such as tree-felling [012]. Axes were roughed-out at source. They were then traded to surrounding communities to be polished into finished, smooth axes. Networks of exchange could extend hundreds of miles. Recent research at Carn Meini in the Preseli Hills, Pembrokeshire, has confirmed the exploitation of the crags there over many centuries, including the production of bluestone pillars used in the construction of Stonehenge [011].

During the Late Neolithic (about 3,500 to 2,500 BC) chambered tombs were deliberately blocked or fell into disrepair, indicating new ritual and burial practices. The first of a series of new types of pottery emerged: Peterborough Ware, a decorated type quite different from plainer Neolithic bowls, and then Grooved Ware, consisting of flat-bottomed vessels adorned with striking grooves and surface patterns, appearing around 2,700 BC.

An ever greater variety of changes marked the beginning of the Early Bronze Age (roughly 2,500 to 1,400 BC). New types of burial and ritual monuments were constructed: cairns (circular mounds of stone) and barrows (circular mounds of earth) covered single or multiple cremation burials or whole-body inhumations. Stone and timber circles continued to be built in open, level areas and

may have been used for festivals, trading or religious ceremonies [014]. Standing stones, the most enigmatic of prehistoric monuments, were erected during the Early Bronze Age. While some may have been boundary markers or way markers, others identified burials or formed parts of ritual complexes of timber settings and buildings. New styles of pottery originating in European traditions were introduced to Britain.

The most momentous change visible in the Bronze Age was a knowledge of metal-working. Research and excavation have identified several Bronze Age mining sites, for example at Copa Hill in Cardiganshire, at Parys Mountain on Anglesey, and on the Great Orme at Llandudno, where prehistoric underground galleries are open to the public. The miners exploited veins of copper ore, fire-setting to fracture the rock

A cemetery of six striking Bronze Age cairns on the summit of Pen Pumlumon Arwystli, on the border between Cardiganshire and Montgomeryshire.
DI2006_0757 NPRN 289789

Cefn Sychbant ring cairn, occupying a high moorland saddle to the north-west of Merthyr Tydfil, was recorded for the first volume of the Royal Commission's Breconshire inventory.
DI2006_0770 NPRN 84666

Severn valley hillforts: the Breiddin hillfort (on the left-hand, distant hill), seen from beyond the wooded Gaer Fawr hillfort, Guilsfield. The woods are stripped away in the digital image on page 74.

AP_2007_4037 NPRN 141162 and 306997

and working with hammer-stones and antler picks. Artefact analysis is needed to understand the trading role of these mining sites in tool and weapon production. The Beaker culture (roughly 2,700 to 1,700 BC), straddling the end of the Neolithic and the beginning of the Bronze Age, represented a cultural revolution, during which new ideas were introduced by people coming from overseas regarding burial practice, metal-working, wealth and power. The pots or beakers from which the culture takes its name were highly decorated, delicate vessels that probably took many days to make, often bearing thousands of impressions on their surface in complex patterns. They were very different from the bulky, functional vessels that preceded them, and

were probably brought by migrants. The Beaker culture appears not to have been associated with any new monuments or radical changes in the economy, so the people who arrived with new beliefs may have been assimilated into British culture.

In the Middle and Late Bronze Age (around 1,400 to 700 BC), when the familiar stone circles, cairns and barrows ceased to be built, few visible monuments took their place. This was a time of growing population and more intensive land-use, in which farms were established with territories and boundaries. The clearance of Wales's rich tree-cover probably began before Neolithic times, but it accelerated through the Bronze Age as the population grew. The act of burning and clearing left fragile woodland soils

exposed to the elements, increasing soil moisture and starting the growth of blanket peat. Towards the end of the Late Bronze Age and at the beginning of the Iron Age it appears that the climate deteriorated markedly, becoming cooler and wetter. This is thought to have produced famine and unrest, with many upland communities apparently leaving their homelands and moving to the lowland peripheries, such as the borderlands and parts of coastal Pembrokeshire. However, there are problems in interpreting the evidence. The picture of settlement persisting in the lowlands may reflect geographical biases in the pattern of archaeological investigation. Future excavation at transitional sites in the mid-Wales hills may tell us more about how some later prehistoric communities survived the climatic deterioration.

Finds of swords, shields, axe heads and daggers, frequently in hoards, suggest greater aggression and conflict (conceivably spurred by population pressure and a desire to defend 'homelands'), but also greater wealth. The central borderlands prospered in the Late Bronze Age. By the ninth century BC a sizeable hillfort had been constructed on the Breiddin hill, dominating the surrounding lowlands [015]. The nearby Gaer Fawr hillfort could have equally early origins though it is more typically Iron Age in form, but it has yet to be excavated [016]. The Late Bronze Age Guilsfield hoard, found near these two sites, shows the prosperity of the area before the Iron Age: it included 120 pieces of locally-made metalwork such as sword blades, scabbard-covers and spearheads. In other parts of Wales hilltop settlements were built with strong ramparts and gateways that were the forerunners of the explosion in hillfort construction in the age that was to follow.

Bronze Age barrows showing as cropmarks despite being largely ploughed away, close to the coast at St Donat's, Vale of Glamorgan. Discoveries of lowland Bronze Age burials through aerial photography and excavation have overturned long-held assumptions that such burials were chiefly located on high ground.
AP_2006_3109 NPRN 404662

45

006 Paviland Cave and the Ice Age Hunters

Paviland Cave or Goat's Hole at low tide. The elongated fissure of the cave is at centre-left.
The cliffs would have looked out over fertile lowland plains.
DI2008_0218 NPRN 300251

Above: One of three bone spatulae from Goat's Hole believed to have both functional and symbolic significance.

Courtesy AC-NMW

Right: Survey plan of the interior of Goat's Hole, 1997.

DI2008_0409 NPRN 300251

Below: Stone tools from Paviland.

Courtesy AC-NMW

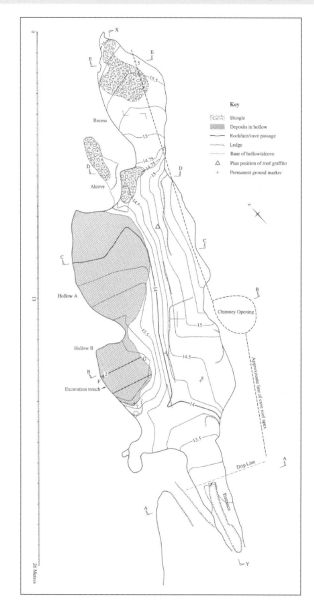

Caves have been a focus of human activity since the remotest periods of prehistory. Paviland Cave or Goat's Hole on the coast of Gower is the most significant archaeological site in Britain of the earlier Upper Palaeolithic period. It was the location of the first systematic excavation of a human skeleton and of the first recovery of a human fossil: the misnamed 'Red Lady'. Discovered in 1823, the fossilised skeleton was at first thought to be of recent date and female. However, it is now known to have been a ceremonially buried young adult male, a representative of the early humans who entered Europe around 40,000 years ago, during the last ice age.

The limestone fissure is easily accessible only at low tide. It has a history of exploration spanning almost two hundred years, beginning when archaeology was still an antiquarian pursuit and when the ancient origins of mankind were unsuspected. Material gathered from the cave has included many thousands of flints, animal bones, shells and worked ivory. In the 1990s concerns over marine erosion combined with a growing awareness of the site's importance led to a comprehensive review of the cave, its geological context, the artefacts and their dating, and the remaining deposits. A vital part of the research project, which engaged specialist partners from across the world, was a definitive survey of the cave: this was completed by the Royal Commission in 1997. Although all archaeological layers had been totally removed, scientific re-evaluation yielded important results.

The cave is now on the coast, but at the time of the Red Lady burial, when sea levels were about 80 metres lower than today, it was some 100 kilometres inland. It was sited in a cliff above a plain of varied topography, with wide views toward the Exmoor hills. The animal bones recovered are numerous and varied: an environment of rich, arid grassland supported mammoths, woolly rhinos, giant deer, bison, reindeer and horses. Game may have been driven to its death over the cliffs by Palaeolithic hunters. Predators included hyenas, wolves and bears, which competed with humans to occupy the cave; whether or not it was used regularly as a domestic site by humans is unclear.

The Red Lady burial has been radiocarbon-dated to about 29,000 years ago, during a mild climatic phase before the glacial maximum. It was placed alongside the cave wall, associated with a mammoth skull, stained with red ochre and accompanied by worked bone and ivory, perforated teeth and fragments of perforated shells, all likewise stained red. The DNA sequence from the skeleton shows the pedigree of modern Europeans, while the slightly warm-adapted body proportions, when viewed within the broader available sample of contemporary remains, point to their African ancestry. Artefact evidence also revealed the presence, more than 30,000 years ago, of indigenous Neanderthals, a human species eventually replaced by the newcomers.

The cave may have remained a sacred place, but in the millennia following the burial it lay in a remote region that was eventually abandoned as the climatic downturn intensified. Nevertheless, the growing ice sheet stopped short of this point, preserving the cave for future generations to investigate.

David Leighton

007   After the Ice Age

Waun Fignen Felen, a peat bog west of Craig-y-nos in the upper Swansea Valley, is a former lake basin.
Artefacts of Mesolithic type were found around the margins of the lake, first visited more than 9,000 years ago.
Pollen evidence has shown human interference with the vegetation, perhaps involving the use of fire to improve grazing for game.
DI2006_0769 NPRN 401580

Microliths from Burry Holms.
Courtesy AC-NMW

Peat coring in a basin near Moel Llys-y-coed in Denbighshire. The core extracted here spans 8,000 years. It was carried out in partnership between the Royal Commission's Uplands Archaeology Initiative and the Heather and Hillforts landscape heritage project in the Clwydian range.
Courtesy Fiona Grant

The ice sheet from the last glaciation had retreated from Britain by about 13,000 years ago. Resettlement gradually took place, continuing in the interglacial period that began about 10,000 years ago and which we still experience today. The hunter-gatherers of the Stone Age therefore inhabited an environment that was changing – albeit over many lifetimes – as the climate warmed, the sea level rose and open grassland gave way to woodland. New hunting strategies and equipment were adopted. Smaller-bladed stone tools were developed, dominated by 'microliths' – a hallmark of the Mesolithic period. The hunter-gatherer way of life continued, but it is from this time that evidence is first detected of the human management of the landscape.

No Mesolithic structures of durable materials have been found. The detection of hunter-gatherers relies instead on scatters of stone tools and waste middens of shells, animal bones and other debris, arising from eroding peat surfaces, the investigation of caves or archaeological excavations of later monuments. Most known sites of the Mesolithic are in the lowlands, many around what is now the coast but they then lay some distance inland. However, several identified sites, like Waun Fignen Felen in Breconshire, are in the upland interior. Such upland sites are thought to reflect occasional seasonal activity, first by specialised hunting groups and then perhaps in response to stresses triggered by the rising sea level causing lower-lying areas to flood. They are especially valuable because they are often associated with peat deposits, which preserve stratified pollen and plant remains to provide a picture of vegetation change and possible human influences on the environment.

This is particularly relevant to the Royal Commission's long-term Uplands Archaeology Initiative, which is seeking to interpret the extraordinarily rich archaeological record of Wales's upland areas. The analysis of suitable peat cores in each area provides insights into episodes of land-use history implied by nearby archaeological remains. The timing of environmental transformations indicated in the pollen record can be determined using radiocarbon dating, and this can sometimes be related to climate change. This approach has been taken in the Clwydian hills, where the Commission has arranged pollen analysis of a peat core spanning more than 8,000 years to enhance understanding of regional landscape development.

From the pollen record it is possible to infer the presence of hunter-gatherers who opened up and

managed vegetation, sometimes using fire to improve grazing and attract game to the site. The visits of hunter-gatherers to the uplands were often of short duration but they persisted over several millennia, part of a complex pattern of movement across the landscape by highly mobile groups which made use of both upland and lowland resources.

David Leighton

008 Banc Du: The Causewayed Enclosures of Wales

Banc Du Neolithic hilltop enclosure, illustrating the irregular, intermittent ramparts which first indicated that it might pre-date the Iron Age. The two phases of ramparts on the summit and the prominent outcrop that forms the rear can be seen.

AP_2007_4216 NPRN 308024

Banc Du occupies the summit of a low hill overlooking the New Inn crossroads at the west end of the Preseli ridge in Pembrokeshire. Royal Commission aerial photography resulted in its discovery in 1990 and in 2002 raised the possibility that it was an exceedingly rare Neolithic hilltop enclosure, defined by the low ramparts having been built in short sections with gaps between. A ground survey by the Commission suggested that an original enclosure had been subsequently enlarged with an outer bank. Research at the site formed part of a landscape study of north Pembrokeshire, between Strumble Head and Crymych, by the University of Bournemouth and the Bluestone archaeological consultancy in partnership with the Commission. This included geophysical surveys to map the earthworks and other archaeological features and the excavation of an evaluation trench across the inner earthwork.

The excavation on the north side of the enclosure in 2005 revealed a rampart that was originally well-built, with a stone-walled outer face and timber lacing to the front and rear. The ground surface underneath it appeared to have been de-turfed beforehand. The rock-cut ditch in front of the rampart was 2.8 metres wide and 1 metre deep. Overlying the early collapse of the stone facing to the rampart were two dark

Right: A trench excavated by archaeologists of the SPACES project through the slight defences of the Banc Du enclosure.

Courtesy Professor Geoffrey Wainwright, SPACES

Below: A survey of Banc Du completed by the Royal Commission in 2005.

NPRN 308024

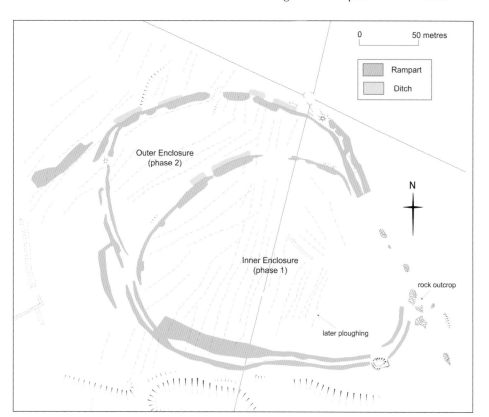

ash-rich layers containing charcoal from heather, hazel, alder and oak. Six radiocarbon dates obtained from these deposits showed that the initial silt in the ditch had accumulated at around 3,650 BC, and the middle fills of the ditch overlying the stone collapse contained material from the period 3,000 to 2,600 BC.

Banc Du is the first confirmed Neolithic enclosure in Wales and the mid-west of Britain. It is contemporary with the great megalithic tombs of the region such as Pentre Ifan, just 7.5 kilometres to the north, and the passage grave at Bedd-yr-afanc, 6 kilometres to the north-east. This was the period when fine metamorphic rocks were exploited in the area for the production of polished axes, and Banc Du – and doubtless other enclosures yet to be discovered – will have profound implications for our understanding of the area in the fourth and third millennia BC. The east end of the Preseli ridge also provided the eighty or so stones taken 250 kilometres south and east to Stonehenge soon after 2,600 BC [011]. Banc Du is therefore an important contribution to our understanding of the social context that gave birth to that extraordinary phenomenon.

Timothy Darvill and Geoffrey Wainwright

009 Neolithic Chambered Tombs

Tŷ Illtud Neolithic chambered tomb, near Llanfrynach, Breconshire.
DI2006_1886 NPRN 96

A facial reconstruction of a Neolithic skull from Pen-y-wrlod chambered tomb.
Courtesy AC-NMW

Pentre Ifan portal dolmen, near Nevern in Pembrokeshire.
CD2005_602_011 NPRN 101450

The Royal Commission's Breconshire inventory published in 1997 included the definitive account of the Neolithic chambered tombs of the county. Although less well known than the stark and picturesque portal dolmens that have survived in parts of south-west and north-west Wales, such as Pentre Ifan in Pembrokeshire, they form one of the more interesting and complex groups in the country. They show that these earliest structures were complex and well considered, exhibiting skills in planning, architecture and engineering. Half a dozen were excavated with varying degrees of care during the twentieth century and at times it can be difficult to distinguish between ancient and restored features. The Commission's study accordingly drew heavily on antiquarian descriptions by John Aubrey and Edward Lhuyd in the seventeenth century and Sir Richard Colt Hoare in the late eighteenth and early nineteenth centuries. These accounts provide records of lost features; they also demonstrate that an entire chambered tomb has disappeared from land at Bryn y Groes, south of Three Cocks.

Several chambered tombs in southern Powys are notable for their structural complexity. Gwernvale near Crickhowell, first dug by Colt Hoare and others in 1804, was excavated in 1977-8 by W. J. Britnell, who recorded its surviving dry-walled structure and elaborate side chambers in meticulous detail. Of considerable importance was the discovery of earlier activity over several thousand years, including Mesolithic occupation and a Neolithic timber-supported structure pre-dating the chambered tomb, possibly a dwelling or mortuary house. The Pipton cairn, overlooking Three Cocks, was excavated in 1949 by Hubert Savory. Its central burial chamber was originally accessed through a 4-metre-long zigzag stone passage. Tŷ Isaf at Cwmfforest was totally excavated in 1938 by W. F. Grimes. Its long mound was fronted by a 'false portal' or mock chamber entrance similar to Pipton's. It housed two lateral chambers, accessed from either side, and an impressive double-walled rotunda enclosing a transepted gallery, accessed along a passage.

Tŷ Illtud, near Llanfrynach, is one of the most rewarding of the tombs to visit. A history of digging and quarrying has left the chamber exposed in a slight hollow. Some unusual incised graffiti can be seen on the inner face of the chamber. These are accessed by crawling inside, where the visitor is confronted by a wall of crosses and chevrons, and even a carving of a five-stringed lyre. Although similar to some Neolithic tomb art from Wales and Ireland, they are probably the marks of medieval masons who quarried from the nearby flagstone outcrop. Aubrey was probably describing Tŷ Illtud when he wrote '...under this Carn is hid great treasure. The Doctor caused it to be digged; and there rose such a horrid tempest of thunder and lightening, that the workmen would work no longer; and they sayd they sawe strange apparitions'.

Breconshire's hills and deep wooded valleys have probably not yet yielded all their Neolithic tombs. One sizeable example went unnoticed at Pen-y-wrlod near Talgarth until 1972 when it was discovered during quarrying. Subsequent excavation yielded some of the best-preserved skeletal remains known from any Neolithic tomb in Wales, enabling the facial reconstruction of one of the 5,500-year-old skulls.

Stephen Briggs and Toby Driver

010 Neolithic Henge Monuments: Llandegai

The Neolithic henge complex at Llandegai, near Bangor, revealed as cropmarks in the ripening field during the summer of 1960.
The clear circles of the henges are underlain by the pattern of periglacial cracks in the subsoil.

Copyright reserved Cambridge University collection of air photographs, ABQ 30, 29 June 1960.
DI2008_0860 NPRN 93620

One of the most important archaeological sites ever to be discovered through aerial photography was the Neolithic henge complex at Llandegai near Bangor, identified on 29 June 1960 from cropmarks during a prolonged drought. The discovery was made by J. K. S. St Joseph of the Cambridge University Committee for Aerial Photography, which was then the only Britain-wide service undertaking aerial reconnaissance for geological, geographical and archaeological subjects. Its early photographs, many of which are held in the National Monuments Record of Wales, are sometimes the only aerial record of now-vanished monuments – as at Llandegai.

The most obvious features were a pair of Neolithic henges, with their characteristically neat, circular ditches broken by simple entrances. Such sites are rare in Wales, so the occurrence of two together was exceptional. Two long parallel ditches showed the site of a Neolithic cursus or ritual avenue, another rarity. The publication of the aerial photograph in 1961 caused consternation as Caernarvonshire County Council had acquired the site for industrial development and its destruction was imminent. There was no legal right of access for archaeologists and no obligation on the developer to fund an excavation, but negotiations resulted in Christopher Houlder of the Royal Commission being invited to direct excavations. This he did in 1966-7 before the field was handed back for development.

Excavations at Vaynor farm henge, Carmarthenshire, sited on a hill overlooking Llanddowror.

AP_2006_2058 NPRN 405883

Air-photo mapping of the Llandegai complex, showing the two henges (large circles), cursus (centre right) and smaller burial mounds and ancient boundaries. The whole now lies under an industrial site, shown by faint mapping.

NPRN 93620
Crown copyright: RCAHMW.
OS licence number 100017916

The rescue excavations revealed a complex where ritual and burial activity spanned several millennia. Some Mesolithic activity was recorded, but the earliest structure was an exceedingly rare Early Neolithic house, dated to around 3,900 BC. Of the henges, the earlier was that to the north, dated to the Late Neolithic, with a contemporary burial inside it. Other burials were found in a ring of pits at the single entrance. The slightly later, southerly henge had two entrances, one marked by a large burial pit. It contained several other pits with carefully laid deposits of Late Neolithic pottery. A burial mound demonstrated ritual activity continuing into the Bronze Age, while wooden roundhouses and other structures inside the first henge indicated a later prehistoric settlement. Also significant was the discovery of an early medieval cemetery of more than fifty-seven graves over the site of the Late Neolithic cursus. The full story of the excavations at Llandegai was not told until 2004, when Frances Lynch and Chris Musson published a comprehensive report in *Archaeologia Cambrensis*, based on Houlder's notes.

Early prehistory is still capable of yielding surprises. In 2006 and 2007 Gwynedd Archaeological Trust carried out major excavations at Parc Bryn Cegin, close to Llandegai, which revealed a further Early Neolithic house, more Late Neolithic pottery pits, and roundhouses of an Iron Age and Romano-British farmstead.

Another, separate, discovery was made ahead of the gas pipeline being constructed between Milford Haven and Gloucestershire in 2006, at Vaynor farm, Carmarthenshire – a substantial henge with rock-cut ditches, two opposing entrances and an oval setting of thirteen pits for stones or posts.

Frances Lynch, Chris Musson and Toby Driver

011 Carn Meini and the Preseli Bluestones

The shattered outcrops of Carn Meini, Pembrokeshire.
DS2006_070_001 NPRN 401098

The wealth of monuments and historic landscapes to be seen in the beautiful Pembrokeshire Coast National Park is outstanding. Six thousand years ago the earliest farmers extracted stone from the north of the region to make polished axes. A millennium later the connection was established between the Preseli hills and Stonehenge on Salisbury Plain with the transportation of the bluestones to form a centrepiece inside the famous henge. Surprisingly, there has been little archaeological investigation of the Preseli hills to provide a social context for the bluestone phenomenon – a substantial proportion of the sites are unrecorded, their nature and variety are unstudied, there is no chronological framework for the prehistoric period, and no environmental context has been established. To remedy this the SPACES project (Strumble–Preseli Ancient Communities and Environment Study) was begun in 2001 to investigate the archaeology of north Pembrokeshire, including the Preseli hills and the bluestone outcrops.

In partnership with the Royal Commission, surveys of the area have shed light on a number of issues. Overall, the project has demonstrated the depth and variety of settlement. Surveys and limited excavation at the hilltop enclosure of Banc Du show that it dates from around 3,650 BC, when farming was just beginning to be established in the area. Detailed recording of the megalithic tombs, stone circles and stone pairs, cairns, cists and standing stones that thickly populate the landscape has indicated that Carn Meini was a very special place in the middle of the third millennium BC. The Carn Meini crags, the

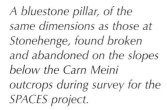

The Carn Meini outcrops from the east.

AP_2007_3703 NPRN 401098

A bluestone pillar, of the same dimensions as those at Stonehenge, found broken and abandoned on the slopes below the Carn Meini outcrops during survey for the SPACES project.

Courtesy Professor Geoffrey Wainwright, SPACES

source of the bluestones, have been subjected to several phases of exploitation, the earliest being quarry pits to extract silicified mudstone, which borders the igneous bluestone, to make polished axes. Columnar pillars were removed from the bluestone outcrops and eighty of them were taken to Stonehenge – the southern slopes of Carn Meini are littered with discarded stones, some broken in transit on their way south towards the River Cleddau below.

At the foot of the crags is a series of springs, some of which were considered to have health-giving properties until comparatively recent times. A number have cairns, megalithic tombs or cup-marked stones near where the water emerges from the bluestone rocks, and it is clear that they had a special significance in early prehistory.

The derivation of the Stonehenge bluestones from Carn Meini and the concentration of sepulchral and ceremonial monuments around the crags and springs hold the key to the enigma of Stonehenge. The bluestones were clearly of special significance as they were used throughout the structural life of Stonehenge. The archaeological evidence of bodies found around Stonehenge, together with this link to the associations of the bluestones, suggests Stonehenge was a source and centre for healing based on their presence. We have to look to the far west of Wales to understand Europe's most famous prehistoric monument.

Timothy Darvill and Geoffrey Wainwright

012 Neolithic Manufacture: The Mynydd Rhiw Axe Factory

The 1958 excavation at Mynydd Rhiw with ranging poles marking the centre of the hollows. The peaks of Carn Fadryn rise above the lowlands of Llŷn.
DI2008_0254 NPRN 302263

Dominating the south-western tip of the Llŷn peninsula, Mynydd Rhiw is a peaceful ridge clad in heather and gorse, rising to 304 metres, which offers stunning views across Snowdonia, along the coast and, on clear days, to the Wicklow mountains of Ireland. During the Neolithic period this was an important source of fine-grained stone (specifically an altered tuff) used for the manufacture of tools such as axes, knives and scrapers. The flanks of the hill were pitted and scarred with quarries that would have been visible for many miles around.

Stone axes from Mynydd Rhiw.
Courtesy AC-NMW NPRN 302263

The discovery of the Mynydd Rhiw axe factory was made by the Royal Commission in the late 1950s. In 1956 A. H. A. Hogg visited the site during fieldwork for the Caernarfonshire inventory to verify aerial photographs that had revealed a set of three hollows, interpreted as the remains of 'round huts'. The timing of Hogg's visit could not have been better, as a recent gorse fire had revealed banks surrounding the hollows which closer examination showed to be composed of debris from stone axe manufacture. It thus appeared that the 'huts' were contemporary with axe-making activity on the hill, although the source of the axe material was not immediately apparent. In order to find out more about the hollows, the Royal Commission carried out an excavation over two seasons in 1958 and

The broad summit of Mynydd Rhiw, broken by outcrops, looking south-west over Cardigan Bay.
AP_2007_2947 NPRN 302263

1959: this showed they were not huts but rather the remains of quarry pits exploiting a rock seam that dipped into the hillside. The hollows had been created by the backfilling of the exhausted quarries, though a series of open hearths placed in them suggested that they might subsequently have provided shelters for the workforce.

The 1950s excavations showed the potential of the site and provided the basis for a new programme of fieldwork that began in 2005 under the direction of Steve Burrow from the National Museum of Wales. This project followed the geological seam examined by the Royal Commission across to the other side of the hill, where abundant traces of quarrying and stone axe manufacture have been identified over a 600-metre length of hillside. Excavation has demonstrated that Neolithic people were digging into the drift deposit to extract loose blocks of stone from the soil rather than quarrying the bedrock. Radiocarbon dating suggests that the hill was visited for this purpose from 3,650 BC until about 3,050 BC and that there was later use of the stone associated with the building of cairns and possible agricultural activity.

The extent of the quarrying demonstrated at Mynydd Rhiw has caused a rethink of its role during the Neolithic. Despite the massive amount of quarrying on the hill only about a dozen axes of the material produced have been found across Wales – in Flintshire, Glamorgan and the borders. This suggests that the ridge was exploited primarily to supply stone locally rather than for long-distance trade.

Louise Barker and Steve Burrow

013 Great Neolithic Enclosures: The Walton Basin

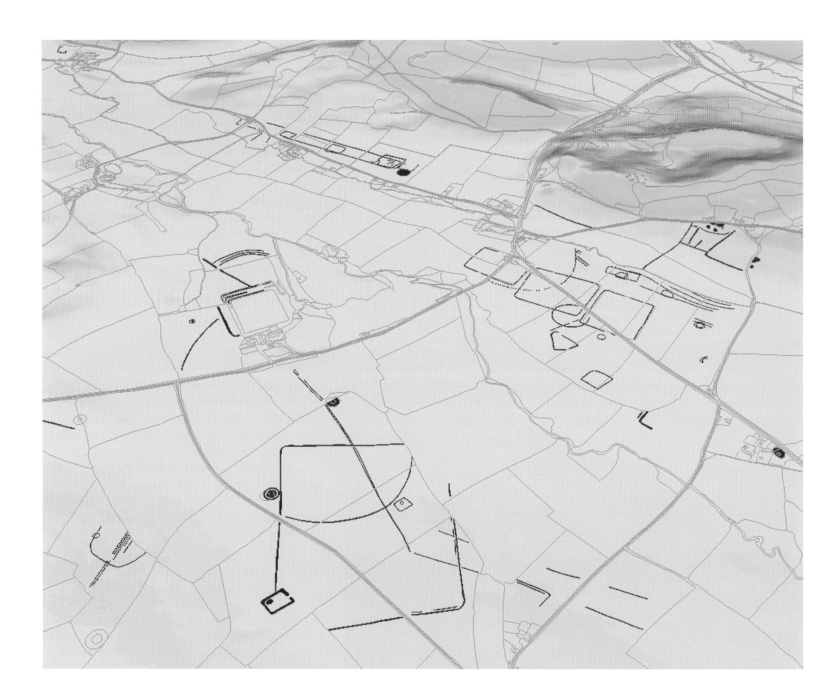

A digital view of the cropmark features of the Walton Basin from the north-west. Rectangular Roman forts and camps overlie many prehistoric monuments, including the vast oval Hindwell enclosure (centre left).

NPRN 309366
Digital Terrain/Surface Model - ©GeoPerspectives. © Crown copyright: RCAHMW. OS licence number 100017916

The Walton basin is a parcel of rich, low-lying land, surrounded by the eastern uplands of Radnorshire, where an exceptional group of Neolithic ritual monuments has been discovered. The fertility of this area seems to have been recognised as early as the Neolithic and the Bronze Age. Substantial numbers of flint scatters, standing stones, the Four Stones circle and round barrows attest to long prehistoric occupation. Continuous arable farming has meant that most monuments have been ploughed flat, but the present agricultural regime results in buried features becoming visible from the air as cropmarks. These were investigated as part of the Walton Basin Project by the Clwyd-Powys Archaeological Trust in the 1990s.

The most important discoveries are a cursus and two oval palisaded enclosures. The Walton cursus is 680 metres long by 60 metres wide and may date from about 3,000 BC. Like similar sites elsewhere, it appears to be strategically placed: at a pass from the mid-Wales uplands to the lower-lying ground of the English midlands. The smaller of the two palisaded enclosures, just to the west of Walton village, may be the earlier. It consisted originally of a wall of large posts set in individual postholes with a long entrance passage on the west. It is believed that walled spaces such as these date from around the early third millennium BC and were used for ritual activities.

The vast, second enclosure, at Hindwell, was 2.35 kilometres in circumference and enclosed 34 hectares, making it the largest Neolithic enclosure known in Britain; generally such enclosures are 3-8 hectares. It was built from over 1,400 massive oak posts, each some 0.7 metres in diameter. Trial excavations have revealed that these were sunk two metres into the ground and may have stood six metres tall. Remains have been radiocarbon-dated to around 2,500 BC. The resources involved in the construction would have been truly enormous – felling, trimming, transporting and setting 1,400 oak trees (around 6,500 tonnes of timber). The entrance way was to the west and narrow, as at Walton, suggesting that entry to the enclosure was ordered, perhaps processional. The timbers here appear to have been significantly larger than in the rest of the perimeter. Geophysical survey of the interior has not identified internal structures, though numerous pits suggest ritual depositions, perhaps of stone axes or other objects of value.

The Hindwell and Walton enclosures are overlain by Roman military remains. Although the wooden walls would almost certainly have long disappeared by this time, the monuments may have retained significance for the native populations. Digital mapping of the cropmarks, compiled by the Royal Commission from decades of aerial photography from different sources, enables the features to be seen in context. In the main image two arcs of the Hindwell enclosure are in the foreground, linked by a section of road on the same line. The nearer arc is overlain by a rectangular Roman fort. An arc of the smaller Walton enclosure is in the right background, amidst three small Roman camps. The cursus is the long rectangle at the top of the image.

Alex Gibson

Right: Cropmarks of the western end of the Hindwell enclosure. A small, square Roman camp lies just beyond.
CD2003_608_023 NPRN 309366

Below: On the eastern edge of the Walton Basin, the Womaston Neolithic enclosure was discovered from the air in the dry summer of 2006. It shows that rare and important monuments can still be discovered in intensively-researched landscapes. Excavations by the Clwyd-Powys Archaeological Trust in 2008 yielded early Neolithic pottery from its ditches.
AP_2006_2198 NPRN 404649

014 The Stone Circles of Wales

Maen Mawr standing stone and Cerrig Duon circle, Breconshire.
DI2006_1885 NPRN 95

Below: Gors Fawr stone circle in the Preseli hills, Pembrokeshire, is one of the best preserved in Wales.

DI2006_0615 NPRN 300422

Bottom: Dolgamfa cairn in Cardiganshire has complex characteristics, such as gradation in height from one side to the other. Some larger stone circles may have begun life as burial cairns.

DS2008_023_011 NPRN 303665

Stone circles, stone rows and stone settings date from the Late Neolithic and the Early Bronze Age. They are among the most enigmatic and thought-provoking of Britain's later prehistoric monuments. Revered by antiquaries since the sixteenth century, they have always excited the popular imagination. Most tend to survive in the remoter uplands, where their stark stones evoke an air of desolation and tranquillity. How far these survivors are representative of the original distribution, forms and appearances of such monuments may never be known.

The most celebrated stone circles are Cerrig Duon in Breconshire, Gors Fawr in Pembrokeshire and the Druids' Circle in Caernarfonshire, but many more survive, often as much as 15 metres in diameter.

Some were the kerbs to cairns that were subsequently eroded but others lack any evidence of cairn materials; across Britain it is unclear how many of the larger stone circles, apart from sites like Stonehenge and Avebury, may simply be unfinished burial sites.

Stone circles probably originated, like circular burial mounds and cairns, in the Late Neolithic, developing as upland, stone-built expressions of circular 'sanctuary' henge monuments that in the lowlands would have been of timber. Interestingly, the builders of Stonehenge utilised mortice and tenon joints to link the stones together, probably because they were used to working in wood. Some earthen henges, with their great circular or elliptical banks and ditches, were often enhanced later by stone circles (as at Stonehenge).

Among a handful of timber circles identified in Wales, the best-known is that excavated at Sarn y Bryn Caled on the outskirts of Welshpool in the early 1990s. A further example was discovered during Royal Commission aerial reconnaissance in 1990 at Withybush in Pembrokeshire, where a circle of thirty pits was recorded as a cropmark. The chances of similar monuments existing elsewhere are high, but if they lie under woodland or towns, or in damper ground where cropmarks do not form, they are unlikely to be discovered. The present-day distribution of henges on remoter hill tops and upland fringes is probably not representative of their original distribution, and there may have been as many lowland sites.

Cerrig Duon stone circle and its associated standing stone, Maen Mawr, lie in a constricted valley of the Black Mountain in Breconshire, alongside a minor road linking Glyntawe to Trecastle. In common with nearly all the circles known in Wales, the stones are relatively small and could easily have gone unrecognised without the bulky presence of Maen Mawr. The stone circle is approached on the east side by a narrow avenue of small stones barely visible in long grass. Although desolate today, it is probable that it was erected by Early Bronze Age communities practising agriculture in well-defined fields, of which some vestigial walls remain. If not originally intended to be filled with a massive burial cairn, the stone circle may have been a significant meeting place for communal or ritual activity. Its presence signals a well-populated landscape, while Maen Mawr has long acted as a beacon to keep travellers on their route over a dangerous pass.

Toby Driver and Stephen Briggs

015 The Origins of Hillforts

The hillfort of Llwyn Bryn-dinas in the dry summer of 1989, looking west along the Tanat valley, Montgomeryshire, with cropmarks of an Iron Age defended enclosure in the centre foreground.

DI2008_0669 NPRN 306785

The late 1960s and 1970s saw great advances in understanding Iron Age hillforts in various parts of Britain. Large-scale rescue excavations for the Rescue Archaeology Group, and later the Clwyd-Powys Archaeological Trust, at the Breiddin north of Welshpool and at Moel y Gaer, Rhosesmor and Dinorben in Flintshire contributed significantly to the debate about the character and origins of these most prominent features of the Iron Age landscape. However, a key discovery at the Breiddin was that the hilltop had been enclosed initially by a substantial timber-reinforced rampart not in the Iron Age but towards the end of the Bronze Age. Evidence from pottery, bronzes, metalwork furnaces and radiocarbon dates all suggested origins in the early ninth century BC.

It was no great surprise that some hillforts along the borderland might have begun life relatively early in the first millennium BC, when climatic deterioration probably combined with population growth to put pressure on land and bring about major social and economic changes, including a transition from largely open settlements of the Early and Middle Bronze Age to enclosed or defended homesteads in lowland and hillslope situations, along with major defended enclosures on many of the prominent hilltops. The demarcation or defence of a piece of land, and perhaps a territory around it, was beginning to create the pattern of settlement that typified Iron Age Wales from around 700 BC. However, in the 1970s the scale of the Late Bronze Age enclosure at the Breiddin (probably 28 hectares) was a revelation.

Other large hillforts had hints of Late Bronze Age origins, for instance Old Oswestry, about 20 kilometres to the north, but confirmation came in 1983 at Llwyn Bryn-dinas, a striking, isolated hillfort dominating

the Tanat Valley near Llangedwyn. Here, rescue excavations for the Clwyd-Powys Archaeological Trust showed the hilltop to have been enclosed by a substantial stone-faced rampart (in this case without detectable timber reinforcement) that was radiocarbon-dated to the ninth century BC. Although the resulting fort was much smaller than the Breiddin, around 3.2 hectares, its commanding location hinted at similar social realities in the domination and control of the valley below: visibility from a distance perhaps had as much value as military strength in averting conflicts with other groups over land, livestock or other possessions.

Chris Musson

Bronze Age defences at the Breiddin under excavation in 1971. The stony Iron Age rampart has been partly removed to reveal a row of paired postholes from the Bronze Age timber-revetted rampart.

Courtesy Clwyd-Powys Archaeological Trust
NPRN 141162

The Breiddin hillfort, looking south-east across the Severn Valley in eastern Montgomeryshire. The dolerite quarrying that prompted the rescue excavation continues to make inroads into the hill.

AP_2007_2835 NPRN 141162

Iron Age and Roman Wales

Toby Driver and David Browne

Wales at the end of the Bronze Age appears to have experienced a marked deterioration in the climate. The emerging competition for food and conflict between neighbouring peoples were among the characteristics of the Iron Age, beginning in about 700 BC, expressed most vividly in the proliferation of defended settlements. With the Roman occupation, from about AD 47 to about AD 410, enormous changes were visible in the landscape, but there was much continuity in the character of everyday life for most people.

There have been considerable advances in our understanding of the Iron Age – the crucial centuries prior to the Roman invasion. Traditionally, the period has been identified with the arrival of iron tools, the emergence of new types of defended enclosures, and the absence of the ritual monuments dominant in earlier periods. This seemed to signal greater territoriality and aggression as a response to the climatic deterioration. However, the complex changes in the landscape suggest that there was not a sudden break at the beginning of the Iron Age. This was a time of developing complexity in society, of enormous endeavour in the construction of communal settlements, and of achievements in metal working and art. Long-distance trade brought overseas contacts in Europe, including the expanding Roman empire. The term 'Celtic' is a useful shorthand, but while Celtic traditions influenced artistic expression, language and perhaps social structures and methods of inheritance across much of Europe, there was not a uniform culture. Local and regional leaders presided over well-defined territories that in some parts of Wales may have been as densely settled and farmed as they were in later times. Settlements continue to be discovered today, and those in the lowlands particularly contribute to understanding of possible population densities and territorial divisions.

Hillforts have long dominated research on the Iron Age. However, these complex structures are just the most visible of the variety of defended enclosures that date from this period; their size and character varied from ring-forts and raths in lowland Pembrokeshire to the large earthen hillforts of central Wales and the border [016 and 017] and the stone-built fortresses of north Wales and the Llŷn peninsula [018]. A. H. A. Hogg of the Royal Commission, who spent much of his life advancing the study of British

hillforts, wrote in 1975, 'No archaeologist is satisfied with the term… the enclosures may have corresponded to anything from a cattle kraal to a small town, but were seldom exclusively military.' In Wales they were usually heavily-defended hilltop enclosures with encircling earth or stone ramparts topped with timber palisades and entered through well-defended gateways. Inside there were thatched roundhouses, raised granaries, smithies and industrial areas.

The study of Welsh hillforts began in the later nineteenth century, with work on the Clwydian hillforts by Wynne Ffoulkes and S. Baring Gould's study of Pembrokeshire hillforts. The Royal Commission's early inventories described hillforts, but the monuments were still poorly understood in archaeological terms. Before the Second World War it was still assumed that they were built by invading immigrants who arrived in southern England and spread to the rest of England and Wales. It is now clear, on the contrary, that hillforts were indigenous creations, though they were influenced by developments in mainland Europe. While some have been shown to have originated in the later Bronze Age [015], the majority were probably built in the later centuries of the Iron Age as wealth

Opposite: The Iron Age field system on Skomer Island, Pembrokeshire, looking south-east towards The Neck and its promontary fort (top).
AP_2008_0285 NPRN 24369

Foel Trigarn hillfort, Pembrokeshire, investigated by Rev. Sabine Baring Gould in 1899 and surveyed by the Royal Commission with Portsmouth Polytechnic in 1988. Iron Age ramparts coloured brown and over two hundred platforms coloured green surround the grey Bronze Age cairns.
DI2006_0507 NPRN 94948

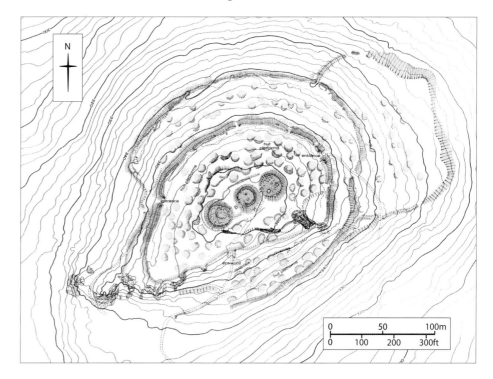

A precarious method of elevated photography developed for the excavations at Pen Dinas hillfort, Aberystwyth, directed by Daryll Forde in the 1930s. The reports were brought to publication by the Royal Commission in 1963.
DI2007_1991 NPRN 92236

from the land increased and powerful leaders consolidated their territory. Many continued in occupation and flourished in Romano-British times.

Impressive entrance defences and gateways at even small hillforts served as deterrents to would-be attackers and as statements of power and status. When freshly built, the ramparts and entrances would have been even more striking than they are today. The greatest of them were vast in scale and unprecedented in the effort invested to create them. Additional protection might be provided by *chevaux de frise*, upright stones or timber stakes outside the ramparts. These are rare in Wales, except for a handful of examples in Gwynedd and Pembrokeshire, though more may await discovery – timber examples in particular will have left few traces. However, it is still debatable whether hillforts should be viewed as military strongholds in a dangerous world or, rather, as farms and villages designed to ward off aggressors through the appearance of strength. Excavated finds and chance discoveries indicate that many hillforts were armed

with the most basic – yet effective – of ammunition, the sling-stone. In experienced hands these were accurate and deadly, with a range of 60 to 100 metres. Roman histories of the conquest of Britain, as well as archaeological evidence, indicate that Roman troops clashed with Iron Age tribes.

A useful analogy when considering the role of hillfort defences may be the post-medieval Scottish chiefdoms of the highlands and islands, for which feuding and feasting were the principal forms of display by chiefs: aggression took the form not of sustained warfare but of periodic raids on rival clans, destroying crops and stealing cattle. The existence of this kind of localised, intermittent, and unpredictable conflict in the Iron Age is supported by archaeological finds of ostentatious weaponry, chariot fittings and horse harnesses. The culture required leaders to assert their political status through investment in elaborate gates and walls, and reasonable defences for settlements and fields, but it is likely that many hillforts never experienced attack. Iron Age leaders would doubtless have worked to retain their positions

by forging alliances with rival communities, helped by impressive hillfort architecture that demonstrated their power.

Hillforts were only one form of settlement, but they have survived conspicuously by virtue of their massive engineering and their siting on marginal land. On surrounding slopes and along valley floors were a plethora of lowland forts, small defended farms and concentric corrals – specialist sites consisting of a larger outer enclosure and an inner yard for settlement. In many parts of Wales, Iron Age farmers sited their settlements on the most productive agricultural land, where farmers from medieval times to the present day have continued to cultivate. Decades or centuries of ploughing have gradually worn away defences and other traces. However, aerial photography has rediscovered hundreds of these settlements, the ghosts of which are visible in patterns of differential crop growth [019]. Many parts of pre-Roman Wales would have been busy, industrious, and cosmopolitan places. Great field systems extended across parts of the country, some first laid out in the Late Bronze Age [020]. Goats and sheep provided meat, dairy products, leather, and wool, and helped to maintain pasture against the return of forests. Woodland

management, hunting and fishing supplemented the agricultural economy and diet. Cattle were highly prized in Iron Age societies as sources of wealth and for their additional use in traction – they were celebrated as iconic beasts in art and metalwork.

Networks of trackways (precursors of historic droving routes) connected communities across the country. Salt brought from the Cheshire plain, fine ceramics, and imported goods from more distant parts indicate a lively economy. Although coastal and river transport would have been important for many purposes, there is evidence that overland routes were used. It is significant how quickly the Roman armies established bases and supply depots in the Welsh heartland and penetrated the hills through mountain passes, seemingly drawing on local knowledge of existing routes.

The advent of the Romans led to the death or enslavement of many of the native peoples. Subjugation of the tribes took about thirty years after AD 47, in the face of stubborn resistance organised by leaders such as Caratacus. However, Agricola's defeat of the Ordovician rebellion of AD 77 brought an end to large-scale campaigning. From then until Roman rule collapsed in the fourth century, tight control was exercised from strategic fortresses at Chester and Caerleon and an infrastructure of lesser installations that maintained law and order [022]. The most intense period of garrisoning followed the final conquest. Within a few years military units were being moved to the north of Britain and by the mid-second century only a few forts in mid-Wales and Segontium on the north coast were maintained

Left: Crug Hywel hillfort in Breconshire.
DI2006_1664 NPRN 92128

Below: An Iron Age farming landscape, centred on Brechfa in Pembrokeshire. The map shows three concentric enclosures, possibly corrals with central settlements, which occupy a ridge. Each map square measures 1 km.
Crown copyright: RCAHMW. OS licence number 100017916 NPRN 401988, 309502 and 401987

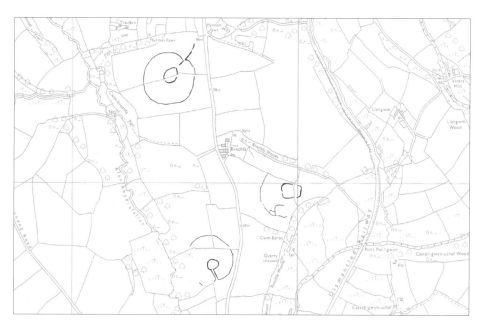

The Allt Aber-mangoed defended enclosure near the Roman mines at Dolaucothi/Pumsaint, Carmarthenshire, was discovered during winter aerial reconnaissance in 2002. It filled a gap in the prehistoric settlement of upland Carmarthenshire and is the only later prehistoric settlement recorded near the Roman mines.

DI2007_0184 NPRN 307331

Arosfa Garreg Roman marching camp, Carmarthenshire.

DI2008_0344 NPRN 84422

to control the nearby populations. The latter part of the third century saw the coast defended from seaborne marauders with a fort at Cardiff and refurbishment elsewhere. The garrison at Caerleon was probably withdrawn by the end of the century, though it may have had a skeleton force as late as the mid-fourth century. The military dispositions in the fourth century, at Cardiff, Caernarfon, Holyhead and Caerhun, seem to have been concerned with incursions by Irish bands. All recognisably military posts seem to have been abandoned in about AD 393 when soldiers were needed to counter rebellion in Gaul, though there is some evidence that troops were left to guard the towns of Carmarthen and Caerwent even into the fifth century.

The Roman armies on campaign were lodged in temporary marching camps [021]. Once an area was pacified the troops were billeted in forts of various sizes from which they could patrol and collect levies. The headquarters of the legions responsible for maintaining the 'Roman Peace' (*Pax Romana*) were the fortresses of Chester and Caerleon. These controlled the land in their vicinity: it is thought that the second Augustan legion drained the Gwent levels to supply pasture for horses. Inevitably, military bases attracted settlements of merchants, craftsmen, entertainers, and also the troops' unofficial spouses. Such settlements were called *canabae* outside legionary fortresses or *vici* outside auxiliary forts. The system of roads was constructed under army direction in the decades after the Flavian conquest [023].

The two settlements that developed into urban centres (*civitates*) for the tribes of the Silures and Demetae were Venta Silurum and Moridunum, respectively Caerwent and Carmarthen [025]. Caerwent had many of the features of Roman cities, such as a forum, temples and well-appointed houses. Carmarthen's best-known feature is the amphitheatre outside the north-east gate. Besides acting as relatively secure homes for those of the tribal aristocracy who accepted imperial rule, the cities were centres of trade, manufacture, and tax collection.

Above: Roman road near Whitland, Carmarthenshire.
DI2006_1214 NPRN 308888

Left: Caerwent forum and temple.
GTJ00143 NPRN 403922

Roadside settlements, or small towns, were a common feature of Roman Britain, but in Wales they were mainly confined to the south-east, usually developing at former army sites. Usk, Monmouth, Cardiff, Abergavenny, Cowbridge and probably Chepstow are examples. A feature common to most was the production of iron objects. There may have been two similar settlements near Ruthin, and at Ffrith in Flintshire, a small settlement produced lead and silver.

Villas, well-appointed houses with associated agricultural buildings, showing signs of acceptance of Roman values and lifestyles, are found on fertile lands and within reach of urban centres [024]. The distribution of known examples reinforces the idea that the lands of the Silures were much more integrated than the territory of the Ordovices – the settlement forms in north-west Wales appear not to have been influenced significantly by Roman styles, whether through cultural resistance or limitations of investment. Equally, in mid-Wales and the territory of the Deceangli in the north-east there is little evidence of Roman influence on rural settlement, except at Plas Coch, Wrexham. By contrast, economic conditions and the disposition of local rulers in the lands of the Demetae in the south-west seem to have favoured the building of small villas,

such as Trelissey in Pembrokeshire and Cwmbrwyn in Carmarthenshire.

The Silures, who offered the greatest initial resistance to the Romans, inflicting a humiliating reversal on a campaigning legion in AD 51, were the people that most readily embraced aspects of Roman culture once they had been defeated. The presence of the second Augustan legion at Caerleon

Below: Carmarthen amphitheatre.
DI2005_1177 NPRN 303957

Cropmarks reveal Croes Carn Einion Roman villa, Monmouthshire.
DI2006_0739 NPRN 90528

would have been a major influence, but there must have been a conscious adjustment by the ruling classes from the end of the first century. The proliferation of villas in Silurian territory reflects the wealth accumulated by a class of landowners who had thrown in their lot with Rome. Some might have been able to retain their ancestral homes and develop them in the Roman style, as at Whitton in Glamorgan. A villa estate was a world away from the constructions of pre-Roman times – with masonry buildings, imposing architectural facades, tile or stone roofs, a bath house, a hypocaust heating system, mosaics and wall paintings.

Local dignitaries would have been introduced to imported goods such as oil, wine, pottery, glass and ceramic lamps when guests of senior army officers. The introduction of coinage to Wales signalled a new system of exchange that lasted until peace and stability were undermined. Coinage was essential to pay taxes, but judging by the paucity of coin finds, non-monetary exchange persisted alongside the cash economy throughout the Roman era. The continuing presence of military and imperial officials who required supplies, the development of a money economy and the growth of new markets around towns in the south

encouraged agricultural production. In upland areas pastoral agriculture was the norm, but the balance between cattle and sheep might vary from place to place and there was localised crop growing. In the lowland valleys and coastal zones arable farming usually predominated.

Extractive and manufacturing industries operated at various times and places, encouraged by improvements in sea and road transport that enabled exports. The imperial government was interested in the extraction of precious metals, if only to offset the costs of maintaining a large army. Gold was probably mined at Dolaucothi in Carmarthenshire, though the total haul from Wales must have been disappointing. More lucrative was the extraction of silver for coinage: ingots, mines and settlements have been found at Prestatyn, Ffrith and Pentre in Flintshire. Copper mining is attested by ingots from Anglesey and Caernarfonshire and adits at Llanymynech on the Montgomeryshire-Shropshire border. However, disarming the population resulted in a decline in the production of iron until settled conditions developed.

Several manufacturing industries were stimulated by the needs of the military and the growing taste for

Roman goods, particularly in the south-east. The army needed tiles, and kilns were built near bases, for example at Holt to supply the twentieth legion at Chester. As garrisons became settled, itinerant potters set up kilns to supply army needs, while the taste of senior ranks for better quality tableware was satisfied by Rhenish and Gallic imports. Kitchenware manufactured in the west of England dominated the market during the second century and found its way to a wide range of settlements. After the mid-second century there is little sign of pottery being produced in Wales.

Classical-style art could be seen in military centres and the Romanised south-east. Stone sculpture was particularly associated with the army, especially at Caerleon, where it was in demand for burial monuments and religious objects. Fragments of statuary of imperial subjects are known from the towns, mosaics adorned villas and urban properties in Caerwent, and wall painters decorated country houses, military buildings, and private and municipal edifices in towns.

The native inhabitants possessed greater sophistication of ideology and religion than Roman propagandists admitted. Many of the deities of native religion continued to be revered, even if sometimes associated with gods of the Roman pantheon. The army introduced the principal Roman gods, headed by Jupiter; later, eastern cults popular with the soldiers gained a footing, such as that of Mithras at Caerleon and Segontium. Other cults popular in Romanised areas included those of Mercury, Fortuna and Mars. Romano-Celtic temples were built at Caerwent and Carmarthen, and a circular stone temple at Gwehelog in Monmouthshire. Isolated finds of votive objects suggest the widespread presence of small shrines, such as Llys Awel at Abergele where a statuette of Mercury and three models of dogs have been found. The evidence for Roman Christianity is not strong in Wales, but its presence was felt: there are the possible remains of a church at Caerwent. Cremation was the norm until the mid-third century, ashes being deposited in cists or pottery vessels, sometimes accompanied by personal objects; inhumation prevailed later, the bodies of wealthier individuals being placed in stone coffins. Long-term cemeteries like those near Caerleon were marked by gravestones for both soldiers and civilians, and some mausoleums. A few barrow cemeteries are known, for example at the military complex of Tomen-y-mur in Merioneth [022].

Wales shared in the Roman empire's political, economic and social tensions as it struggled against

Roman tombstone found close to the fort at Y Gaer, Breconshire.
DI2008_0837 NPRN 92001

fragmentation in the fourth century. Despite worsening conditions, urban life continued at the end of the century at Caerwent and Carmarthen. However, the threats to stability are shown starkly by defensive installations at Cardiff, Caer Gybi and Holyhead mountain and the maintenance of garrisons at sites like Segontium, almost certainly to deter and combat raiding by Irish bands. Peace and stability were essential to the limited market economy. As these were threatened and coin ceased to circulate, the Roman economic system probably broke down rapidly.

016 Surveying Iron Age Hillforts: Gaer Fawr

Gaer Fawr, Guilsfield, a virtual view closely matching the aerial photograph on page 44, looking across the Severn Valley to the Breiddin hillfort.
The Royal Commission digital survey has been modelled in 3D, allowing the prehistoric earthworks to be seen once again unencumbered by trees.

NPRN 306997
© GeoPerspectives. © Landmark Information Group Ltd.

Right: W. E. Griffiths's graphic of the south gateway of the south fort, Pen Dinas, Aberystwyth, for the 1963 publication of the excavations. The depiction at various scales and in differing projections communicates the complexity of this gateway structure and provides a definitive record.

DI2008_0426 NPRN 92236

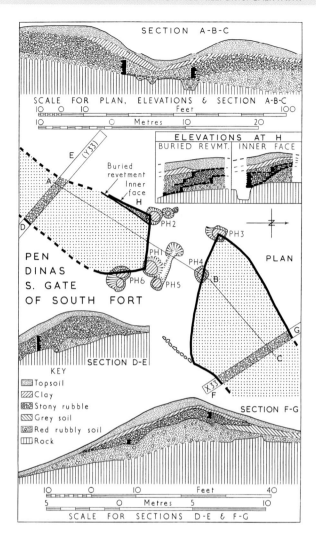

Iron Age hillforts represent an astounding communal feat of prehistoric civil engineering. The great earthworks seen in the landscape today are the ruins of ramparts originally revetted with drystone walling or timber posts and topped with palisades and walkways. Although they are associated with the Iron Age, some hillforts originated in the Late Bronze Age whilst others were reoccupied and altered in later periods.

Making an accurate measured survey of these complex monuments is crucial to the understanding of their construction and use. Differing forms can be compared, and the survey process often reveals new features and clarifies the relation of earthworks to one another, providing evidence about dating, phasing and alteration. Excavations have been carried out at only a small proportion of hillforts, so field surveys are the prime means to establish a tentative understanding of most sites. Aerial reconnaissance, excavation and remote sensing have revealed more about later prehistoric landscapes, but detailed interpretative plans of hillforts remain the lifeblood of Iron Age research.

Techniques of survey have changed. Prior to the 1980s theodolites, tapes and chains were used, in conjunction with laborious traverses and manual calculations of angles. By the time of the Royal Commission's Breconshire inventory, ortho-rectified vertical aerial photographs were used to produce basic plans to guide some of the ground surveys. Nowadays, investigators use high-grade digital survey instruments such as the total station (an electronic theodolite combined with electromagnetic distance measurement) or a global positioning system (GPS). The GPS can find its position anywhere in the world to centimetre accuracy through triangulation with orbiting satellites – this is particularly useful for hillforts in remote or wild terrain with few mapped features nearby.

Gaer Fawr, at Guilsfield near Welshpool, is one of several large, multivallate hillforts overlooking the upper Severn valley which indicate the power of communities in this area in the Iron Age. A remarkable helmet mount in the form of a bronze boar, found in the nineteenth century, conjures an impression of the people who may have commanded the site in its heyday. It covers 5.8 hectares with up to five lines of ramparts over 8 metres high. Although remarkably well preserved, it has never been excavated and dense woodland makes it impossible to appreciate its form or scale. In 2007 the Royal Commission carried out the first detailed survey of the site, using

Below: GPS survey on Pen'r-allt hillfort, Montgomeryshire.

DS2008_020_005 NPRN 400895

a total station to record thousands of points. The resulting digital terrain model allows the hillfort and its setting to be visualised stripped of woodland and makes it clear that Gaer Fawr was constructed in many phases. It originated as a small summit-fort. Additional space was enclosed later on its west side and two highly-developed entrance-ways were created with graded approach ramps and defended gateways. An annexe was also added to the south. One of the more intriguing features uncovered in the survey is a bank dividing the interior space that could be associated with early medieval occupation.

Louise Barker and Toby Driver

017 Interpreting Iron Age Wales: Hen Gaer

A reconstruction drawing by Dylan Roberts of Hen Gaer Iron Age hillfort, Cardiganshire, looking south.
GTJ00067 NPRN 92249
Courtesy of Dylan Roberts.

Reconstruction drawings are often the best way to interpret the past in the present, especially to give a sense of how the humps and bumps of an overgrown earthwork may have appeared in prehistory. The dramatic reconstruction drawing of Hen Gaer Iron Age hillfort, near Aberystwyth, by Dylan Roberts of the Royal Commission, reveals as much about changing interpretations of the Iron Age as about the archaeology of the site.

Hen Gaer is a small, well-preserved hillfort 6 kilometres north-east of Aberystwyth. Partly excavated by Christopher Houlder of the Royal Commission in 1967, it is typical of many hundreds of such defended enclosures on the slopes and hilltops of mid- and west Wales. In common with its prehistoric neighbours, Hen Gaer incorporates a puzzling choice of site: part of the rampart encloses a steep slope to the south and avoids a more level summit position to the north. This preference must have made building houses much more difficult. On the ground there are signs of the considerable human effort directed to its construction. A partly infilled, but still impressive, rock-cut ditch is topped by an earth and stone rampart that is 3-4 metres high and some 12 metres wide at its base, enclosing a total area of 1.3 hectares. Although the rampart is grassy and tree-grown, short sections of fine drystone walling can be seen at intervals, demonstrating that this fort, like others in the region, was once entirely stone-walled, rather than earth-banked as shown in the drawing. It would have been a hugely impressive sight in the Iron Age landscape.

Other hillfort reconstructions by Royal Commission

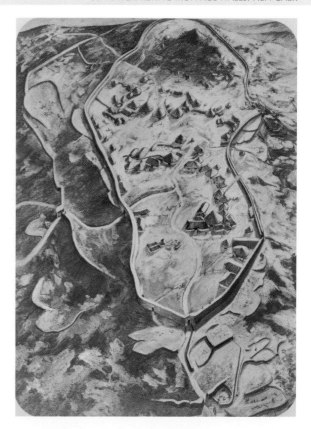

staff illustrated A. H. A. Hogg's *Hill-forts of Britain* (1975): for example, of Tre'r Ceiri in Gwynedd and Maiden Castle in Dorset. This view of Hen Gaer was drawn for the headmaster and pupils of Ysgol Rhydypennau, Bow Street, in the early 1970s. Elements such as the ditch were emphasised to show schoolchildren the massive scale of the defences. The reconstruction represents the view of the Iron Age at the time it was drawn. The round huts with their shaggy thatch and protruding sticks conjure up impressions of mud huts in Africa, but experimental reconstructions now suggest that Iron Age roundhouses were probably imposing buildings with a highly finished appearance. Excavations, field walking, and paleo-environmental work in the hinterland of Aberystwyth have indicated that the valleys around Hen Gaer were farmed and settled from Neolithic times onwards, and would have been relatively clear of forest and enclosed by fields. Nevertheless, the image remains relevant and powerful today. It conveys the formidable nature of these prehistoric defences and the massive communal effort involved in building them by hand, more vividly than can any plan or photograph.

Toby Driver

Right: A reconstruction of the stone fort of Tre'r Ceiri, Caernarfonshire, in its last phase, by Dylan Roberts for A. H. A. Hogg's Hill-Forts of Britain (1975).
CD2005_635_004 NPRN 95292

Below: The defences of Hen Gaer, showing the north-east angle of the fort (left foreground in the reconstruction).
The infilled ditch would once have been entirely rock-cut.
CD2005_621_002 NPRN 92249

018 Tre'r Ceiri and the Stone Forts of Llŷn

Tre'r Ceiri hillfort from the west, showing the fine stone fort crowning the rocky summit.
In 1960 A. H. A. Hogg wrote: 'In its present form the fortress is probably unique…'.

AP_2007_0224 NPRN 95292

Few Welsh prehistoric sites capture the imagination as powerfully as Tre'r Ceiri hillfort, which dominates the Llŷn peninsula from the easternmost of the three peaks of Yr Eifl, looking down from a scree-strewn summit 485 metres high. Tre'r Ceiri is one of the best preserved Iron Age hillforts in Britain. Roundhouses, gateways and ramparts can be seen in remarkably intact condition.

Tre'r Ceiri occupies a steeply-sloping site and encloses at the mountain summit a substantial Early Bronze Age burial cairn that was preserved and respected during the construction and life of the hillfort. The main fort is enclosed by a formidable single rampart, still standing up to 3.5 metres high in places. Parts of the rampart top are nearly intact, retaining their parapet walk reached by sloping ramps from the interior. This great wall is pierced by two main gateways, both of which funnelled people approaching the fort through narrow, restrictive passages. Three 'posterns', or minor gateways, can also be identified, one of which at least seems to have been designed to allow inhabitants down a narrow mountain path to gather water from a spring. Beyond the rampart is a partial outer wall, reinforcing more vulnerable approaches on the north and west sides.

As befits one of Britain's finest hillforts, there have been many surveys and excavations of Tre'r Ceiri. During the 1950s the Royal Commission conducted several campaigns of excavation and survey of the regional hillforts to clarify their development for the Caernarfonshire inventory. W. E. Griffiths and A. H. A. Hogg made a full survey of Tre'r Ceiri in 1956,

complete with contours and details of surrounding hillslope enclosures, building upon Harold Hughes's pioneering measured survey of 1906. The resulting record was immensely detailed and clear, and was only superseded by a modern total-station survey in 1980.

Excavations have shown that the hillfort was probably constructed in the later Iron Age and remained in use until at least the fourth century AD. Other prominent stone-built hillforts on Llŷn, principally Garn Boduan and Carn Fadrun, have stone citadels on their highest summits from later phases, thought to have been castles of medieval Welsh princes; but there is no evidence of such a structure at Tre'r Ceiri.

These stone ruins have long astounded those who have seen them, yet two thousand years of weathering and collapse, together with pressure from visitors, have taken their toll. As long ago as 1894 members of the Cambrian Archaeological Association lamented Tre'r Ceiri's condition and lack of protection: 'It would hardly be thought that in a civilised community it was possible that such a splendid specimen of a prehistoric city would be allowed to perish miserably… Yet stone by stone Treceiri is being gradually destroyed.'

In 1989 Cyngor Dosbarth Dwyfor and Gwynedd County Council began a programme of consolidation and repair of the fort with support from Cadw, under the supervision of Gwynedd Archaeological Trust. The project ran for a decade, leaving this most intriguing of hillforts consolidated, perhaps to endure for another two thousand years.

Toby Driver

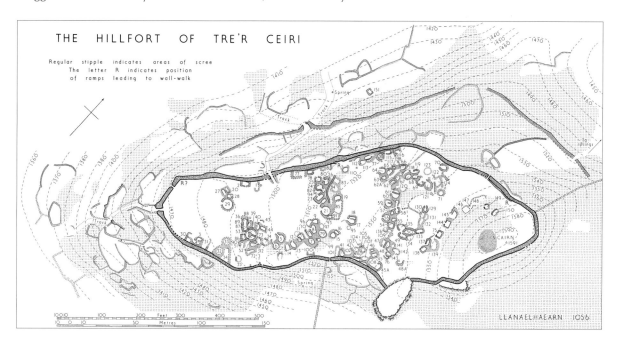

The detailed survey of Tre'r Ceiri and its surrounding slopes completed by the Royal Commission in 1956.

DI2008_0130 NPRN 95292

019 Lost Defended Enclosures

The Cawrence defended enclosure in Pembrokeshire, showing as a cropmark in 1996.
DI2005_0139 NPRN 308918

Excavation at Troedyrhiw defended enclosure, north of Cardigan, by Dyfed Archaeological Trust in 2005. The site was discovered during Royal Commission aerial reconnaissance in 2003 as a faint cropmark. The excavation discovered rock-cut ditches up to 3.4 metres deep. The field beyond shows how comprehensively the site had been ploughed, with only 20-30 centimetres of soil remaining above the shale bedrock.

DS2005_109_002 NPRN 309072

The plough-levelling of a prehistoric defended farmstead rarely eradicates all traces of rock-cut ditches and rampart foundations. Such buried remains affect the way a crop grows and ripens in a drought year, giving rise to cropmarks.

Many prehistoric remains have been denuded by subsequent agricultural activity: large parts of the country have been enclosed by fields and ploughed since medieval times, and since the Second World War mechanisation and the pursuit of higher yields have had a marked impact. After two millennia of agricultural activity, scores of prehistoric monuments have vanished from the landscape, reduced to barely perceptible earthworks or invisible below-ground traces.

Before the advent of archaeological aerial photography in the twentieth century prehistorians drew conclusions about settlement density, population and land-use in the Iron Age from an uneven sample of sites that depended on their survival as upstanding earthworks. Prior to the 1950s it seemed that large areas of lowland, for example in Montgomeryshire, Glamorgan, Monmouthshire and Cardiganshire, were devoid of smaller, enclosed prehistoric settlements, being characterised as exclusively 'hillfort country'. However, pioneering archaeological aerial photography by Cambridge University and others after the Second World War began to suggest the extent of plough-levelled prehistoric farms and forts that might survive below ground.

The awareness of the smaller farms and specialist stock enclosures that results from aerial reconnaissance has altered perceptions of Iron Age society. The wealth of evidence now suggests a busy, well-settled and intensively farmed pre-Roman landscape. Powerful ruling hierarchies and centralised economies are implied by the existence of large hillforts, while some autonomous settlements, perhaps in the control of wealthy individuals, are indicated by small, strongly defended hillforts and ring forts. The Cawrence defended enclosure in Pembrokeshire is an example of the concentric defended farms common in Wales: a funnelled entrance-way gave access to the interior, where there were close-packed roundhouses; livestock may have been penned in the outer enclosure. Cawrence was discovered from the air in 1995 and photographed again a year later as a remarkably clear cropmark. The main gate is to the left, facing downslope, with a 'back door' on the right of the outer enclosure. The road shows the large scale of the monument.

Aerial reconnaissance has made considerable progress in rediscovering patterns of prehistoric settlement where the growth of arable crops and drought conditions in grassland and hay fields reveal cropmarks in dry summers. Yet this technique is not as successful inland, where the effects of drought on

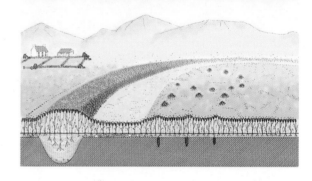

grassy hillslopes and pasture are less marked, and regions like Radnorshire and Breconshire retain an appearance of hillfort-dominated mountainous country without much sign of significant lowland settlement.

The Royal Commission and the Welsh Archaeological Trusts have investigated the plough-levelled settlements that have been discovered from the air by using ground-based geophysics and excavation. Partnership projects have been particularly successful on the Llŷn peninsula, where cropmark discoveries have been followed up, and in south Cardiganshire, where many years of cropmark reconnaissance charted an unusual concentration of square Romano-British defended settlements on the fertile coastal plain.

Toby Driver

020 Surviving Landscapes of the Prehistoric Farmers: Cors-y-gedol

Cors-y-gedol ancient field system, Merioneth.
DI2008_0318 NPRN 401827

It is difficult to appreciate the deep antiquity of the Welsh landscape, yet at intervals along the coast and in upland areas, where land is generally more marginal and less cultivated, fragile traces of ancient settlements and fields survive – fragments of the houses, farms and trackways laid out by Iron Age people or by Bronze Age or Neolithic people before them. Such remains are vulnerable to ploughing, land drainage and stone clearance, particularly in the fertile, well-drained lowlands of south and central Wales. However, early farming landscapes can be well preserved in parts of the uplands, on islands like Skomer and Ramsey, and on heath-grown coastal headlands in Pembrokeshire, Gwynedd and Anglesey. Welsh examples rank among the finest in western Europe.

The Cors-y-gedol field system, near Dyffryn Ardudwy in Merioneth, is particularly impressive. Although the ancient fields here have long been known to archaeologists, only during the 1980s and 1990s did sustained programmes of ground survey, aerial reconnaissance and air-photo mapping by Snowdonia National Park and the Royal Commission begin to reveal their complexity and quality. The major oval and rectangular field enclosures and roundhouse foundations probably belong to the Iron Age and Romano-British periods. However, Neolithic origins can be postulated for at least part of this farming landscape (something that is rare in Britain), indicated by its association with a chambered tomb. Burnt mounds also survive in the fields – mounds of fire-cracked stones thought to have been used in communal cooking or bathing, usually of Bronze Age date. Settlement, farming and replanning of these fields continued after they were brought within the Vaughan estate of Cors-y-gedol in the seventeenth century. On the ground the stony, gorse-grown banks are disorientating, but with a map or guide one can seek out substantial foundations of Iron Age roundhouses and walk along an embanked trackway between field plots in the footsteps of countless prehistoric farming families.

Cors-y-gedol is one of the better researched parts of the Dyffryn Ardudwy coastal strip, but the area has other remarkable survivals, including Muriau'r Gwyddelod (Irishman's walls), above Harlech. This is a tract of hillside where Romano-British huts and paddocks are divided by sinuous walls from neighbouring homesteads, just a few hundred metres from the sprawling houses of modern Harlech. Other such landscapes no doubt remain to be discovered along footpaths and on open hills across Wales. Each new example provides a tangible and potent link to the prehistoric past.

Toby Driver

The Iron Age or Romano-British farming landscape at Muriau'r Gwyddelod, above Harlech. A double hut group is enclosed in a curving paddock (centre foreground) with radiating field walls. Some of the walls still in use fossilise the lines of boundaries probably laid out in prehistoric times.

AP_2005_0072 NPRN 401818

021 The Roman Army on Campaign

Aerial view of Y Pigwn Roman marching camps, Breconshire.
DI2006_0230 NPRN 92004

The Roman army left a rich archaeological legacy of its campaigns in the province of Britannia. Field works carried out during the conquest are particularly interesting. Among the products of these are temporary 'marching camps' in spectacular locations, such as at Y Pigwn on the summit of Trecastle mountain in Breconshire, about 400 metres above sea level. Here, two consecutive camps overlap one another. The earthwork remains of the rampart and ditch of both camps are clearly visible, though one side has been partially destroyed by later quarries for tilestones. Such defences were constructed to enclose a large area for the tents of the military commanders and their troops and all their accoutrements. Most Welsh camps are detectable through the presence of the perimeter rampart and ditch, but in lowland arable areas often all that can be seen are the cropmarks to indicate the buried remains of ditches. Marching camps are usually square or rectangular in plan, with rounded corners, and often with entrances in each side.

The two camps at Y Pigwn were the first to be recorded in Wales, being described by the antiquarian Thomas Rees in the 1850s. They represent different campaigns by the Roman army in southern Wales in the first century AD – camp prefects tended to prefer to build their camps from scratch rather than refortify old ones. The larger, earlier camp encloses 15 hectares and the later, which more or less fits inside it, 10 hectares. A distinctive feature found in both camps is the semicircular arc of ditch guarding each of the entrances, known as a *clavicula*. These funnelled

Aerial view of the camp at Twyn-y-briddallt, Glamorgan, looking south-east along the ridge.

CD2003_647_012 NPRN 301354

Pen Plaenau camp in Denbighshire.

AP2004_0994 NPRN 308852

visitors sideways, exposing their unshielded flanks to the soldiers guarding the gate. Once inside the camp, visitors would have been confronted by rows upon rows of tents, regularly laid out with a unit (*contubernium*) of eight men sleeping in each tent.

Some thirty marching camps (as well as twice as many practice camps) are now known in Wales, from the Marches to Caernarfonshire, with further examples across the English border. Many of these have been recorded during aerial reconnaissance by the Royal Commission and through the detailed examination of vertical air photographs during the preparation of county inventories. Examples include a group in the Walton basin [013] and the unusual camp at Twyn-y-briddallt, shaped to conform to the profile of the ridge on which it is sited, above the Rhondda valley in Glamorgan. This was recorded by Commission staff in 1958, along with two other camps in Glamorgan, providing valuable details about the movement of the Roman army during its attempts to control the Silures.

Sites continue to be recorded: for example the stunning earthwork camp at Pen Plaenau in Denbighshire was discovered by Hugh Toller and recorded by the Royal Commission in 2003. The location of this camp indicates a route of march taken by armies in the first century AD and further develops the picture of the campaigns of the Roman army in Wales.

Rebecca H. Jones

022 Advances in Roman Military Studies:
Tomen-y-mur

Tomen-y-mur, Maentwrog, Merioneth: a Roman fort with a Norman motte superimposed.
DI2008_0386 NPRN 95476

Knowledge of Roman military archaeology has been transformed since the Royal Commission was established in 1908. While the character of the military presence was known at that time, little was understood about the dates of the occupation and even less about the period of campaigning prior to the conquest. Facts now taken for granted, such as the presence of a Roman auxiliary fort on the site of Cardiff Castle, were recent discoveries. The journal *Archaeologia Cambrensis* showed interests focused on the medieval period, with some inquiries into prehistory but few into Roman Wales.

Some significant detail was added in the first part of the twentieth century, for example by investigations at Caerleon, Brecon Gaer and Segontium (Caernarfon); but the period after the Second World War brought fresh impetus to Roman military studies with the first edition of Nash-Williams's *The Roman Frontier in Wales* in 1954. This summarised existing knowledge and acted as a stimulus to further research. By the time Michael Jarrett produced a revised edition in 1969 he could point to additional discoveries of nine auxiliary forts, fourteen marching camps and nine practice camps.

Nor did the pace of work slacken thereafter with, for example, W. H. Manning's work on the early legionary fortress at Usk dramatically enhancing knowledge of the conquest period. The Commission played its part in this evolving picture. Prior to the

introduction of a structure for rescue archaeology, work in advance of quarrying recorded the auxiliary fort at Pen Llystyn, Caernarfonshire [003]. At the same time the potential of aerial photography to add previously undiscovered sites to the record and enhance knowledge of those already identified was being demonstrated. The Royal Commission's aerial photograph of Tomen-y-mur, taken by Chris Musson in 1996, provides a wonderful overview of one of the best-preserved Roman military complexes in Britain. This has been used with ground observation to produce interpretative mapping of the landscape. Geophysical survey could reveal yet more.

This Roman auxiliary fort stood in a prominent position on the road from Brithdir near Dolgellau to Segontium, overlooking the Vale of Ffestiniog. It was probably founded around AD 70 and abandoned by about AD 130: a snapshot of half a century of intense activity can be read in the landscape. The playing-card plan of the fort (A) is clear; less so is the line of defence to reduce the size of the fort, which lies beneath a Norman motte (B). The headquarters building (C) and barrack blocks can be seen, but the most unusual features lie outside the fort. It is rare for a parade ground (E) to be visible from surface evidence. Although other sites survive with practice camps (J), an amphitheatre (D), a bathhouse (G), an annexe (K), water-supply leats (I) and bridge abutments (H), this concentrated suite of classic military structures is exceptional. The tribunal (F) from which officers oversaw the troops on the parade ground may have originated as a geological feature.

The aerial photographs and mapping vividly recreate the scene of 1,900 years ago.

Henry Owen-John

Right: Castell Collen, Radnorshire, Roman fort: the trenches visible are the early excavations in the central range of buildings.

GTJ00160 NPRN 95708

Below: Computer mapping of features associated with the Roman fort at Tomen-y-mur.

CD2003_606_055 NPRN 95476
© Crown copyright: RCAHMW.
OS licence number 100017916

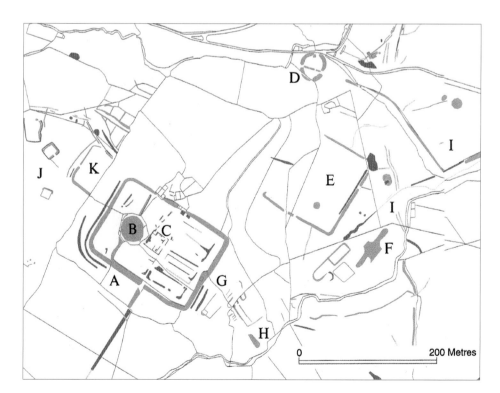

023 Roman Roads

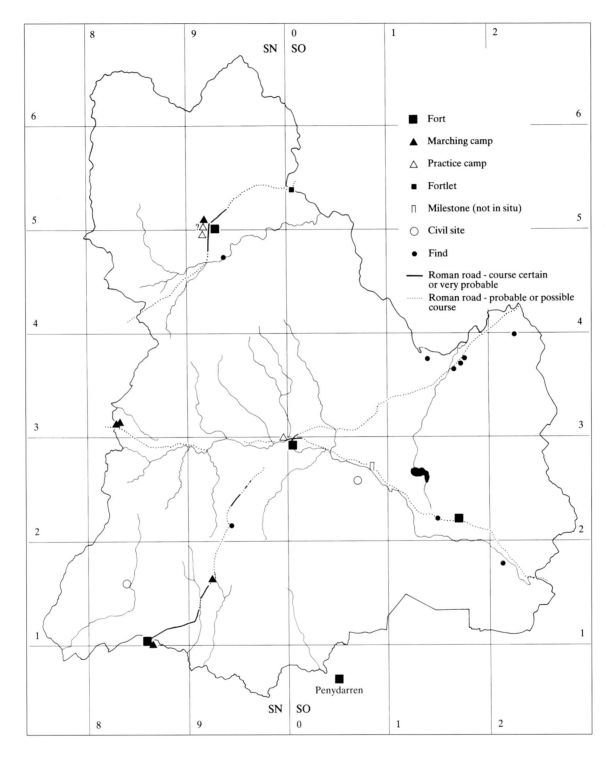

8 9 0 1 2

SN | SO

Fort ■

Marching camp ▲

Practice camp △

Fortlet ■

Milestone (not in situ) ⊓

Civil site ○

Find ●

── Roman road - course certain
or very probable

····· Roman road - probable or possible
course

?

Penydarren

SN SO

8 9 0 1 2

*Map of Roman remains in Breconshire, including roads, prepared for the inventory published in 1986.
Y Gaer is the fort in the centre.*

DI2008_0838

Above: A reconstruction of Brecon Gaer.

DI2005_1152 NPRN 92001

Top right: A well-preserved length of Roman road running north from Coelbren fort to the important base at Y Gaer near Brecon.

DI2008_0320 NPRN 275611

The system of Roman roads was a palimpsest of different routes drawn onto the landscape during successive phases of conquest and consolidation. Much of it would have been constructed using forced labour under military supervision before the early second century, though some elements probably remained unfinished. Roads were used by troops, by the *cursus publicus* (the imperial messenger service), for the movement of tribute and taxes, and for trade in consumables. Part of the system is likely to have remained under military control throughout the occupation, but considerable sections were devolved to the civil authorities when garrisons were redeployed beyond Wales.

Roman roads can be identified through several kinds of evidence, of which the clearest are excavated structural remains, characteristic *agger* paving, and milestones (not necessarily *in situ* but often found nearby). More circumstantial evidence comes from forms of terracing and the existence of long, straight alignments between changes of direction at sighting points. Clustering of early medieval inscribed stones may also indicate Roman route ways.

In compiling the Breconshire inventory in the 1980s the Royal Commission reconsidered the network of supposed Roman roads in the county. Earlier authorities had suggested a multiplicity of routes – far in excess of the likely number of engineered ways. The same writers had also made modern Brecon the focus of the system, though there was no evidence of Roman occupation there, and the large fort at Y Gaer, four kilometres to the west, was a far more likely destination. Exhaustive documentary study and fieldwork pushed forward knowledge of the roads of the county. It became clear that Y Gaer was the focal point of the Roman road system in Breconshire. The Abergavenny to Llandovery road was a major arterial route, following the Usk valley for most of its length. Y Gaer was also at the end of an arterial route from Kenchester in Herefordshire, to the north-west. Other routes

traversed uplands between major valleys.

Five routes were confirmed in Breconshire and in two cases extensive lengths of the actual line (with *agger* and excavated remains) were demonstrated – between Coelbren and Y Gaer, and between Caerau, Beulah and Castell Collen in the north. The first kilometre of the road north-eastwards from Y Gaer had been verified by excavation, though its course beyond was hypothetical. The general route along the Usk from Abergavenny to Y Gaer and on to Llandovery was demonstrated by milestones and short lengths of probable ancient road (and excavation confirmed a section of this in 2006). This arterial route would have placed Y Gaer only a day's march from Abergavenny. The milestones provided evidence of its refurbishment in AD 258-62, AD 296-306 and some time between AD 317 and 340. However, it was not possible to indicate with certainty a direct course from Y Gaer to the forts in the north, and the evidence did not confirm the anticipated connection in the opposite direction, southwards from Y Gaer to the fort at Penydarren, Merthyr Tydfil.

David Browne

Right: Milestones found at Millbrook Farm near the line of the Roman road from Abergavenny to Y Gaer.

DI2008_0322 NPRN 404239

024 Villas: Llantwit Major

Llantwit Major Roman villa: the opening between rooms 8 and 9, from the north-east, with floor mosaics.
DI2008_0279 NPRN 301356

Above: Stone statuette of the goddess Fortuna.
DI2008_0281 NPRN 301356

Right: Drawing of the mosaic pavement in room 8.
DI2008_0280 NPRN 301356

Below: Plan of the Roman villa, Llantwit Major.
DI2008_0266 NPRN 301356

The Roman villa system of land-use and lifestyle in south Wales is the main evidence for the adoption of features of Roman civilisation by the upper echelons of native society. The building complex at Cae'r Mead, near Llantwit Major in the Vale of Glamorgan, is an excellent example of a well-appointed villa belonging to a wealthy landowning family. It was discovered and trenched by J. Storrie in 1887-8. A more detailed examination was made by V. E. Nash-Williams in 1938-9 and 1948. The Royal Commission re-excavated a small area in 1971. Its plan shows the buildings as they would have been in the fourth century, when the prosperity of the owners was probably at its height.

Nash-Williams's excavations revealed features typical of a villa establishment. It consisted of an inner courtyard on the west, enclosed by ranges of buildings, and an outer courtyard on the east (extending beyond the area of the plan). The building stone was local limestone and sandstone, with Bath stone used for architectural details and Pennant sandstone for roof slabs. Glass was used for some of the windows, whilst internal walls were plastered and living-room floors were of *opus signinum*, the

characteristic Roman paving of concrete mixed with crushed tile or brick. The main apartments seem to have been in the north range of the inner courtyard where some rooms had patterned mosaic floors and painted wall-plaster, and one had under-floor heating. In the adjacent west range was a complete baths suite and more rooms with under-floor heating. The basilica-shaped building on the south side of the courtyard is thought to have been the quarters of the house servants and estate workers. Other buildings may have been barns, stables and workshops.

After the Royal Commission's investigations clarified the complicated chronology of the villa, A. H. A. Hogg was able to claim that its 'structural history now seems reasonably certain'. The earliest occupation was by a pre-Roman ditched enclosure. In the early Roman period a timber villa was built, to be replaced in the mid-second century by a simple rectangular masonry structure with no corridors (the later north range). About AD 270 the east end of the masonry building was enlarged and the nucleus of the west wing was probably put up. About thirty years later the two separate blocks were linked and provided with a corridor, and the basilican building and a block on the north-east were built. The villa was at the height of its prosperity in the mid-fourth century when mosaics were laid and there was replastering and new wall painting. Soon after, however, the basilican building and the baths were disused, with the baths furnace given over to iron-working.

The date when the villa was abandoned is uncertain. Storrie's nineteenth-century excavations revealed two groups of skeletons. One set belonged to a band of about thirty people, mainly men, who seem to have been killed at the site, perhaps a century or more after its desertion. The other was part of a later Christian cemetery, begun when the site would have been no longer recognisable as the wealthy country seat it had once been.

David Browne

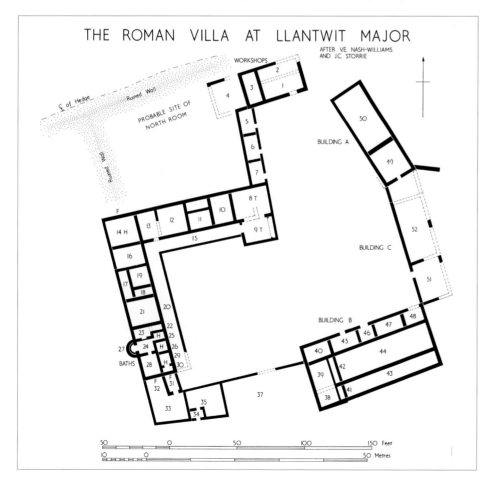

THE ROMAN VILLA AT LLANTWIT MAJOR

AFTER V.E. NASH-WILLIAMS AND J.C. STORRIE

025 Roman Towns

Caerwent Roman town from the south-east. The road through the village follows the line of the Roman road.
The town walls enclosed 18 hectares with the forum-basilica in the centre.

AP_2005_1209 NPRN 93753

Above: The inscription to Tiberius Claudius Paulinus, commander of the Second Augustan Legion, on a statue base found in 1903. It states that the Silures tribal council (ordo) met in the town of Venta, making it one of the key inscriptions found in Britain.

Courtesy AC-NMW

Right: Extensive excavations took place in Caerwent between 1899 and 1913.

Courtesy AC-NMW NPRN 93753

Below: Caerwent has the best preserved defences of any Roman town in Britain. The town walls were a source of civic pride and status.

AP2004_0367 NPRN 93753

For the Romans an ideal province was one with a stable, peaceful population, based in villa-type rural settlements or towns. The town was a key element in provincial organisation, since administration, commerce, trade, amenities and entertainment had an urban focus. The Romans regarded it as the centre of civilised life.

This was the model presented to the Britons. Most tribes developed a centre where the tribal council could meet, law courts could be set up and other administrative duties were carried out. In Wales only the Silures in the south-east and the Demetae in the south-west established such towns: Venta Silurum (Caerwent) and Moridunum (Carmarthen). Both flourished, set in areas of prime agricultural land with good communications. Other settlements, such as Cowbridge, Usk, Monmouth, Abergavenny and Chepstow – most of which began as a *vicus* outside a fort – had the potential to develop as towns but did not, suggesting an element of official direction in the emergence of Caerwent and Carmarthen as tribal capitals. The absence of urban development elsewhere in Wales (though Wroxeter and Kenchester were on its eastern fringes) was largely because upland terrain made communication difficult and there was insufficient momentum from agriculture or mineral extraction.

Venta Silurum – market of the Silures – was once the largest centre of civilian population in Wales. Excavations have shown Caerwent to be a bustling market town with shops, houses, baths, temples and a *forum-basilica* (market place and civic hall). Although at only 18 hectares it was one of the smallest tribal capitals in Roman Britain, it contained most of the buildings associated with such a centre. Research excavations between 1981 and 1995 by the National Museum of Wales and Cadw uncovered a large

courtyard house in the north-west corner of the town, a Romano-Celtic temple and part of the *forum-basilica*. Venta seems to have emerged as a tribal capital in the earlier part of the second century when the Silures were granted a form of self-government under their own elected council. The town seems to have developed slowly and it may not have reached the full extent of its street grid until late in the second century. By this time it was defended by a ditch and an earthen bank topped with a timber palisade. Later, perhaps towards the end of the third century, an impressive stone wall was built in front of the bank. The town probably started to decline in the later fourth century, but it continued into the fifth, even though many buildings were ruinous.

Moridunum covered only 13 hectares. Since the name did not incorporate the tribe's, its status as the capital of the Demetae is assumed from a regular street layout, defences and Roman-style public buildings (including an amphitheatre). A fort was founded about AD 75 west of the later town. Its garrison was withdrawn in the early second century, probably coinciding with the time when the Demetae were granted self-government. Large-scale excavations between 1978 and 1993 produced evidence of a temple and Roman domestic and commercial buildings. Locating the *forum-basilica* would confirm Moridunum's status as a tribal capital but the central area is now covered by modern buildings.

Richard Brewer

Early Medieval Wales

David Browne and Mark Redknap

The seven centuries between the breakdown of Roman imperial authority and the Norman conquest have been difficult to understand historically given the scant documentary record and the few investigated archaeological sites. Yet this was a period during which Wales acquired an identity and a distinctiveness in language and culture. It was a time of fundamental change: the consolidation of Christianity as the religion of the people, new settlements, and diverse influences from west and east as Romano-British culture decayed and the impact was felt of Anglo-Saxon hostilities and then Viking incursions. There was a transformation of tribal groupings into larger, more stable kingdoms, and fleetingly the idea of Wales was translated into a political unity.

Wales shared in the Roman empire's political, economic and social vicissitudes as it struggled against fragmentation in the course of the fourth century. As peace and stability waned, the economic system, particularly that of Romanised south-east Wales, would have changed once coinage ceased to circulate. With the collapse of central Roman administration during the early fifth century a new social order developed with independent regional kingships. There is no reason to believe that power was seized by force from the Roman authorities. It is more probable that, in the absence of effective central government, authority was assumed by local elites accustomed to civic rule or running large estates. Some new elite groups may have emerged with the aid of remnants of the Roman army. Leaders of early medieval kingdoms probably legitimised their standing by laying claim to continuing Roman authority, as is suggested by the practice of erecting stones inscribed with Roman terms.

While some new rulers may have considered themselves to be heirs of Rome, and titles like 'protector', magistrate', 'prince' and 'king' continued to be used by Latin writers, there were conspicuous changes. Secular power shifted to new locations. Although the walled town of Caerwent (Venta Silurum) near Chepstow, in the most Romanised part of Wales, seems to have given its name to the early medieval kingdom of Gwent, it probably failed to

Opposite page: Bardsey Island or Ynys Enlli was one of the most important pilgrimage centres of 'the Age of the Saints'. Tens of thousands of pilgrims must have landed at the narrow neck of land and walked the path across Mynydd Enlli to the abbey beyond.
GTJ00234 NPRN 402783

Caerwent in Monmouthshire collapsed as a town after the departure of the Romans but became the location for a monastery within the Roman walls.
GTJ22615 NPRN 33166

operate as a town beyond the early fifth century.
Like the late Roman fort at Caer Gybi near
Holyhead, it became the location of a monastery, while
many Romano-British settlements were abandoned.

Throughout the British Isles the fifth century was a
time of migrations and invasions. In Wales many
kingdoms developed, and as the years passed the
more energetic and warlike ones overcame weaker
neighbours. The foundation of the kingdom of Gwynedd
has been attributed to a war leader, Cunedda, who
migrated from north Britain to Gwynedd in the early
fifth century and is supposed to have expelled Irish
invaders from north-west Wales. However, the
authenticity of the Gwynedd foundation story is
questionable: many scholars consider it to be a later
invention to justify a contemporary ruling house of
Gwynedd and its expansion. In particular, the house
of Merfyn of Gwynedd ('glorious King of the Britons',
died AD 844) manipulated pedigrees to justify the
rise to power of Merfyn Frych in the ninth century.
He may have been from the Isle of Man, and one
aspect of legitimising his foreign origin may have
been to assign the foundation of Gwynedd to Cunedda
as an earlier immigrant.

There is debate as to when the immigration of Irish
tribesmen to south-west Wales began. They were
raiding the area in the second half of the fourth
century but it is unlikely they were allowed to settle
under Roman supervision. Dyfed was a kingdom of
Irish origin: in the fifth century the Déisi, a tribal
group driven from the Waterford area, crossed to
south-west Wales, and their leaders replaced native
elites to rule the Demetae there. There is strong
evidence of the Irish presence in ogam inscriptions
[026], genealogies and place names of Irish origin.
The ruling dynasty of Brycheiniog seems also to have
been partly of Irish origin.

The kingdom of Powys emerged in the fifth
century and extended far into what later became
Shropshire; Wroxeter, east of Shrewsbury, was
probably an important early centre. To add lustre to
their triumph over the Anglo-Saxon Mercians in the
early ninth century, Powys's genealogists claimed the
Roman Magnus Maximus and perhaps the Briton
Vortigern as their ancestors, a tradition denied by
their arch-rivals in Gwynedd in the *Historia Brittonum*.

South-east Wales was the most Romanised part of
the country. It is possible that Roman estates in the
area survived as recognisable units into the eighth
century. The kingdom of Gwent is likely to have
been founded by direct descendants of the Silurian
ruling class. Another kingdom in the region, Erging,

*Offa's Dyke: the section
south of Pen-y-bryn to
Orseddwen, Denbighshire.*
DI2006_0437 NPRN 275764

was dominant around 500 to 600. However, in the
seventh century the kingdom of Glywysyng to the
west (the forerunner of Morgannwg) gained control
of both Erging and Gwent.

Despite the fragmented political geography of
Wales, a common language emerged, distinct from
the ancestral Brittonic, attested by the end of the
eighth century in a few surviving literary works and
inscriptions [033]. The upper echelon of society in
the petty kingdoms was formed by the king and his
kin, supported by a warrior class. They were
maintained by levies on the agricultural products of
the mass of the population, whose mobility both
geographically and socially was tightly restricted, and
who lived in small dispersed settlements or *maerdrefi*.

During the seventh century the Welsh kingdoms
confronted Anglo-Saxon aggression. On occasion
they formed temporary alliances with individual
English kingdoms against a common foe. For example,

Dinas Powys ringwork, Glamorgan: the inner bank and ditch looking west.
DI2008_0814 NPRN 301314

when Northumbrians attacked Powys in a campaign that was probably aimed at all of north Wales and Mercia, in about 633, Cadwallon of Gwynedd and Penda of Mercia formed an alliance. Northumbria was repulsed by Cadwallon, who took the fight to the aggressor but was killed in 634, and the Gwynedd-Mercia alliance was eventually successful in about 642. Soon afterwards, Mercia started to expand its own borders into Powys and began a long period of intermittent border warfare.

After a century of Mercian expansion, Powys under King Eliseg [034] regained enough strength to defeat Mercia in about 750, but King Offa of Mercia (757-96) responded with vigour. The dyke that takes his name was at least initiated by him. It was a forceful statement of demarcation and was capable of acting as a control on organised movement of people and goods. One of the great achievements of construction before the Industrial Age, the earthwork is the most impressive early medieval field monument in Britain. Seen as a tribute to the power of the Welsh rulers, it has shaped our view of the extent and identity of Wales.

The ninth century saw far-reaching changes in the British Isles that had serious consequences for the Welsh kingdoms – the raids of the Viking warbands, the collapse of some of the old Anglo-Saxon kingdoms and the rise of Wessex to leadership among the English. Unsettled conditions allowed some Welsh kingdoms to extend their power. The achievement of Rhodri Mawr (the Great) of Gwynedd (died 878) in uniting for the first time the three largest kingdoms of early Wales was inspirational. He is said to have acquired Gwynedd from his father (844), Powys from his mother (855), and Deheubarth through his wife (874); by his own efforts he defeated a Danish force on Anglesey (856). His sons completed his conquests in south-west Wales, and henceforth the line was split into two: the northern descended from his son Anarawd and the southern from his son Cadell. King Alfred of Wessex (died 899) claimed overlordship of Wales, which Gwynedd resisted, but some Welsh kings found it convenient to win Alfred's support against the Vikings and other Welsh rulers in order to protect themselves from Anglo-Saxon aggression. Welshmen appeared at Alfred's court, such as the cleric and scholar Asser. In 893 Gwynedd acceded to Alfred's authority.

In the next century Hywel (later know as Dda, the Good) consolidated Deheubarth. He too had to confront the Vikings and the kingdom of Wessex and was prepared to accept the overlordship of Anglo-Saxon kings to strengthen his position. As a result, he was able to invade Gwynedd and annex Brycheiniog, giving him control by the time he died in about AD 950 of most of Wales except the south-east. Known as 'the head of glory of all the Britons', Hywel's name is forever associated with codifying Welsh Law, which had developed over centuries as, among other things, a sophisticated regulation of relationships between kin groups.

Ultimately, these territorial achievements sprang from the personal qualities of individual kings rather than from marriage and inheritance, and so they had a fitful existence – and still did so on the eve of the Norman conquest, when Gruffudd ap Llywelyn (died 1063) made himself king of Gwynedd, Powys and Deheubarth, and even took Morgannwg. Yet, even for the two centuries before the Norman conquest, knowledge of the material history is meagre.

While historical records highlight the activities and interests of the powerful, remarkably little is known about settlements or population. Archaeological evidence is frustratingly elusive – though it certainly exists hidden from view. In many areas timber was favoured over stone for building, leaving less visible remains, and substantial earthworks were rare apart from the great linear dykes. The lack of a strong tradition of using ceramics also means that the scattered fragments of pottery that indicate settlement in other periods are absent. The rate of finding new sites is low compared with other periods, but hunting them down has been made easier through aerial reconnaissance by the Royal Commission.

Most early medieval settlements have been discovered in the coastal lowlands. Among these, several distinct types can be recognised. Defended sites are most clearly identified on the ground, such as the small promontory hillfort at Dinas Powys near Cardiff. This was the first such site to be comprehensively

Hen Gastell, Glamorgan, during excavations in 1991.

DI2005_0691 NPRN 401406

vessels from Anglo-Saxon England and the continent, and metal scrap for recycling. Since this important excavation, similar sites have been excavated, such as the hilltop fort near the mouth of the River Neath at Hen Gastell. Other investigations have confirmed long-standing views that many hillforts occupied during the Roman period were refurbished as royal or aristocratic strongholds between the fifth and seventh centuries. Among those investigated have been the multivallate promontory fort at Carew in Pembrokeshire and the imposing hillforts at Degannwy and Dinas Emrys in Caernarfonshire. Rhuddlan in the north-east is somewhat different in character, generally being thought to be the Anglo-Saxon burh known as Cledemutha, established in 921 by Edward the Elder to bring the surrounding area under English political control. It may have been a regional centre or a small enclave dependent on its port, border traffic and nearby estates.

investigated, and excavations between 1954 and 1958 revealed the residence of a local ruler and the trappings of power that surrounded him. There were traces of several buildings encircled by four banks and ditches, numerous artefacts, and evidence of economic activity. Imported goods included pottery from the Mediterranean and France (the amphorae probably containing wine and olive oil), fine glass

On a smaller scale, the coastal promontory fort at Castell on Anglesey, excavated in 1991, has been compared with Viking promontory forts on the Isle of Man and tentatively associated with eleventh- and twelfth-century links between the kings of Gwynedd, particularly Gruffudd ap Cynan, and the Vikings of Dublin and Man. Defended economic centres in coastal lowlands are known from the enclosed coastal settlement at Llanbedrgoch on Anglesey [030], while one artificial island settlement, or crannog, at Llan-gors

Dinas Emrys, Caernarfonshire: a hillfort that became an early medieval stronghold and the site of a medieval castle.

AP_2005_0494 NPRN 95284

has been identified as a royal site associated with the kings of Brycheiniog [032]. Undefended high-status settlements also existed, such as Longbury Bank in Pembrokeshire, occupied between the late fifth and seventh centuries. Early medieval sites may be suggested by concentrations of artefacts, as at Kenfig and Twlc Point in Glamorgan and at Linney Burrows in Pembrokeshire. Evidence for small-scale activities of various sorts has also been found at some enclosed hut groups dating from the late Roman period and a few caves in south Wales, such as Minchin Hole in Gower and Lesser Garth cave north of Cardiff, which was perhaps associated with a settlement on the ridge above.

Even where major elements of the early medieval landscape are highly visible, such as the Offa's Dyke and Wat's Dyke systems along the borders with England, or the cross-ridge dykes attributed to this period [031], there is hardly any knowledge of their contemporary environment. What little is known points to a rural economy based on subsistence farming with small-scale production, exchange and trade. New discoveries, such as the recently excavated corn-drying kilns and iron-smelting furnaces at Herbranston near Milford Haven, may illuminate resource management and specialisation.

Artefact production was at a craft scale, supplying local requirements, with the possible exception of some metal working. Activities identified include

Castell, the coastal promontory fort of Tre-Fadog, Anglesey.
AP_2004_0284 NPRN 95571

leather working, textile weaving, bone and antler working (particularly to make combs), iron working (to make tools and weapons), manufacturing of copper-alloy objects such as penannular brooches, stone working to produce querns and whetstones, and timber working (for buildings, palisades and boats). No pottery was produced locally.

Archaeological evidence shows that coastal Wales retained links directly or indirectly with the Mediterranean from the fifth to seventh centuries. There is clear Gallic influence on some early inscriptions. During the fifth and sixth centuries amphorae and fine red-slipped tableware were imported from the eastern Mediterranean and north Africa; during the sixth and seventh centuries ceramic wares were imported from western France. It is thought that metalwork and raw material were used for exchange by Welsh rulers, whose power was reinforced by trade with west Britain, Ireland and the continent. Much of this may have been in response to initiatives from outside. There was also limited importation of glassware, beads and metalwork from Anglo-Saxon England in the sixth and seventh centuries, some by overland routes – perhaps through travel or diplomatic or marital gifts rather than sustained trade.

The period after 500 has been called the 'Age of the Saints', and the rise of a local form of Christianity and Church was one of the characteristic features of these centuries. The persistence of traditions and dedications suggests that some religious leaders – Dewi, Padarn, Teilo, and Deiniol – created such

Stray finds, such as the penannular brooch found inside one of the huts at Pant-y-saer, Anglesey, suggest that sites built in the Roman period were used at various times.
Courtesy AC-NMW NPRN 93857

Right and below: Excavations at the monastic hermitage at Burry Holms in north Gower in the 1960s revealed a shrine and burials.

DI2008_0813 and DI2008_0815 NPRN 94719

strong impressions that tales of them were transmitted down the generations. Dewi (St David), who came from a Ceredigion dynasty in the sixth century, was the leading Christian ascetic of his day. Others were abbots ruling monastic communities, one of the most renowned being Illtud, abbot of the monastery of Llanilltud Fawr or Llantwit Major. Early Christian centres included Bangor and St Davids, renowned as important ecclesiastical lordships that suffered at the hands of Viking raiders, as did a string of others: Caer Gybi and Penmon on Anglesey, Tywyn in Merionethshire, Clynnog Fawr in Caernarfonshire, St Dogmael's in Pembrokeshire, Llanbadarn Fawr near Aberystwyth, and Llantwit Major and Llancarfan in the Vale of Glamorgan. By the ninth century monasteries had become important landholders and were centres of learning and political influence. The landscape would also have been dotted with small churches, and in many localities Christian communities built enclosures or *llannau* for their burials.

The physical remains of early churches have proved elusive. Aerial photography and field observation have identified a growing number of cemeteries – recently excavated examples include Brownslade Barrow in Pembrokeshire and Tywyn y Capel on Anglesey. While ecclesiastical centres are referred to in saints' lives, charters, Welsh Annals and the Anglo-Saxon Chronicle, and their locations

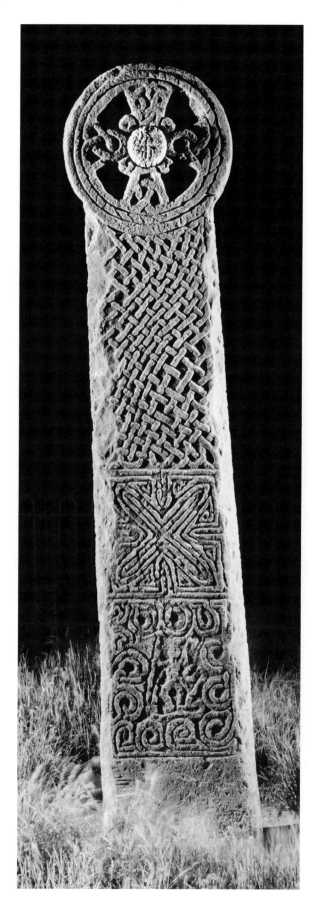

are suggested by concentrations of inscribed stones and stone sculpture, little is known of their original appearance. Their size and layout, their relationship to secular settlements and the peripheral sites within their pastoral spheres are often unclear. A rare exception is Burry Holms in Gower, excavated in 1965-8 by the Royal Commission, whose survey of the early Christian period in Glamorgan (published in 1976) suggested it was a pre-Norman hermitage or retreat. Some islands became monastic enclaves. Centres such as Caldy received imported goods from Gaul and the Mediterranean during the fifth to seventh centuries, implying contact with the outside world and probably with secular settlements. Aerial reconnaissance by the Royal Commission has revealed a handful of defended enclosures related to smaller circular or curvilinear churchyards, though the significance of the associations is not yet clear [035].

Inscribed stones and stone sculpture provide the most prolific evidence for the period, and they are crucial to our understanding of the evolution of the Welsh kingdoms, languages, literacy and the Church. Cross-carved stones and more ambitious sculpture, including freestanding crosses (sometimes with inscriptions), date from the seventh century onwards. Variations point to a number of workshop traditions or groups, often centred on monasteries [029]. They allow us to identify a range of early medieval ecclesiastical sites and trace the patronage of the Church by the secular elite. The Royal Commission included detailed entries on many stones in their first county inventories (for example, the tenth-century cross known as Maen Achwyfan in the 1912 volume on Flintshire), and its records and photographs have enriched the new *Corpus of Early Medieval Inscribed Stones and Stone Sculpture*, the first two volumes of which appeared in 2007 [028].

Much remains to be learned about early medieval settlement in Wales – from identifying and dating sites to understanding more complex issues [027]. For example, how were older sites reused and new ones constructed? How did they function within a changing society? What impact did settlement have on the landscape? What variations existed in agriculture and animal husbandry? Many of the high-status sites may have provided security in times of turmoil, but where did most of the population live (estimated at two or three hundred thousand)? The archaeological archive of the Royal Commission is an essential tool for those wishing to understand six centuries of shadow-like history.

Among the achievements of early medieval art in Wales is Maen Achwyfan cross, Flintshire.

DI2008_0433 NPRN 94449

026 Early Inscriptions and their Language

The Latin inscription at Penbryn, Cardiganshire, reads 'CORBALENGI IACIT ORDOUS'.

DI2008_0439 NPRN 304135

The stonework surviving from early medieval Wales is of particular importance owing to the near-total disappearance of more perishable materials such as wooden buildings, fabrics and manuscripts. Stonework shows us styles of decoration and calligraphy that may once have been common in many materials. Inscriptions tell us a good deal about the languages of Wales and their development in sound and spelling.

In the immediate post-Roman period, from about AD 400 to 600, the most striking monuments – shared with Ireland and the Atlantic seaboard from Brittany to Argyll – are the so-called 'Early Christian' inscribed stones. Only some of these are explicitly Christian, but it seems probable that most of them were erected within Christian communities.

An early photograph of the inscribed pillar at Llanerfyl church, Montgomeryshire.

DI2008_1826 NPRN 154091

Typically they commemorate the dead, sometimes specifying the deceased's social status, for example as bishop, priest, priest's wife, king, 'protector', 'leader' (*tovisaci*), magistrate or doctor (*medicus*). Some, as one would expect, follow the tradition of sub-Roman Christian memorial stones: an example is the pillar now in the church at Llanerfyl, Montgomeryshire, commemorating Rustica, daughter of Paterninus, aged thirteen, in horizontally inscribed Roman capitals, and ending with the formula IN PA[CE], 'in peace'.

A surprisingly high proportion, however, are inscribed vertically and include little more than the name of the deceased and his father. In this they resemble the contemporary ogam stones of Ireland and it is likely that many of them were erected by Irish settlers or by native Welsh people responding to Irish practices. This explains both their concentration in the areas most open to Irish influence (for example, there are thirty-six in Pembrokeshire but none in Monmouthshire) and the predominance of Irish personal names on them. In Pembrokeshire twenty-five early inscriptions use ogam script and/or Irish names, as opposed to a single inscription with only Welsh names (plus a number with only Latin names, which could have been used by both communities).

Some inscriptions use both Roman and ogam letters, as if to assert the equal status of the two scripts and the communities who used them. An example is the Crickhowell stone, now in Brecknock Museum, Brecon. The Roman letters commemorate Turpillus, 'boy' of Trilunus Dunocatus (an early form of the Irish name *Dúnchad*). The Roman name *Turpillus* created a problem, as the ogam alphabet originally lacked a symbol for P, a sound absent from early Irish. Hence an X-shaped ogam symbol is used instead, as also on the dual script Pumpeius Carantorius stone in Margam Stones Museum. An impressive example of an inscription solely in Roman letters but with an Irish name, *Corbalengas*, is the pillar stone from Penbryn, Dyffryn Bern, Cardiganshire, as photographed in raking light by the Royal Commission. Originally the stone stood on a cairn covering an earlier Roman cremation burial overlooking the sea. Corbalengas is styled *Ordous*, a spelling of *Ordovix*, suggesting that his family had been established in Wales long enough to identify itself with the native tribe of Ordovices.

Patrick Sims-Williams

027 An Early Medieval Settlement: Gateholm Island

The numerous cells on Gateholm Island, Pembrokeshire, looking south-west.

DI2006_0616 NPRN 102906

The intriguing traces of settlement on the small tidal island of Gateholm, at the western extremity of Marloes Bay in Pembrokeshire, were studied by the Royal Commission in the 1960s to provide a more detailed account of a field monument of national significance that was densely obscured by coarse tussocky grass. The remarkable aerial photographs revealed what could not be seen with clarity at ground level: the whole plateau was filled with the turf-covered walls of a large number of buildings (about a hundred compartments or cells), many joining up to form strips or rows – perhaps as many as thirty of them.

Excavations in the 1930s had produced a wide range of datable objects – Neolithic, Roman, early medieval and medieval – pointing to activity and occupation over a long period. One of the buildings, constructed after AD 340-400, produced an early medieval ringed pin and shale finger ring and perforated whetstone, suggesting settlement at some point between the fifth and ninth centuries.

Gateholm was once interpreted as a Welsh religious settlement on the basis of the apparent similarity of its buildings to those at Tintagel in Cornwall, whose building clusters were long held to be monastic cells. This famous Cornish site is now considered to be a secular citadel rather than a monastic site and doubts have been cast on a religious identification for Gateholm. As at sixth- to seventh-century Tintagel, perhaps early medieval Gateholm was once a post-Roman promontory citadel, defended by bank or ditch on the landward side, now eroded. It has been suggested that the house and circular enclosure on the western slopes of the island represent some kind of early medieval farmstead. Further fieldwork would refine our knowledge of the development, growth and decline of the whole complex.

Mark Redknap

Right: Finds from Gateholm in the 1930s: a ringed pin, a fragment of a shale finger ring and a whetstone.

Courtesy AC-NMW
NPRN 102906

Below: A plan of the Gateholm cells by Royal Commission staff, published in Archaeologia Cambrensis *in 1971.*

DI2008_0730 NPRN 102906

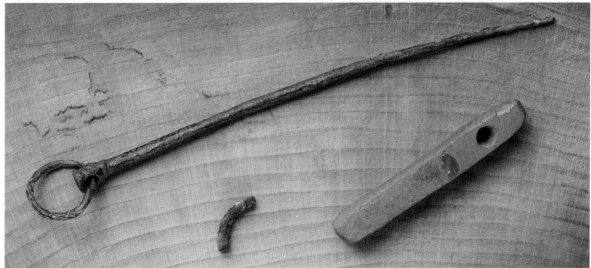

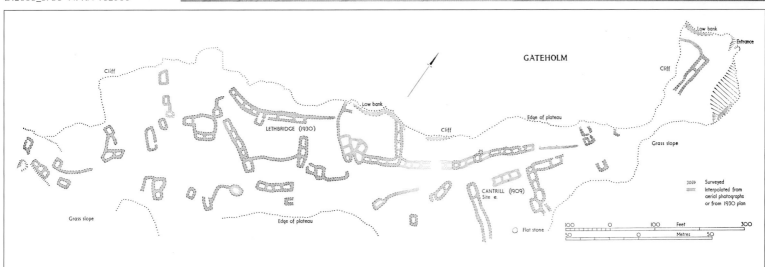

028 Recording Early Medieval Inscribed Stones

Night-time photography of an inscribed stone using directional light: the Fishguard South stone, Penwaun, Dinas Cross, Pembrokeshire.
DI2008_0446 NPRN 276068

Above: Carew high cross, Pembrokeshire.

DI2006_1322 NPRN 103458

Top right: Blaen-awen farm inscribed stone, Nevern, Pembrokeshire.

DI2008_0429 NPRN 404576

Right: Penwaun, see left.

DI2008_0445 NPRN 276068

Work by the Royal Commission on the systematic recording of early medieval inscribed stones started in 1987 for a revised edition of V. E. Nash-Williams's *Early Christian Monuments of Wales*, first published in 1950. The original photographers and illustrators had often used chalk to highlight the inscriptions as they perceived them. By 1987 it was felt that a more objective approach would be to photograph what was visible with the aid of directional lighting. This has often enabled detail not previously visible to be recorded, as in the Fishguard South (Penwaun) stone.

The best approach was found to be working at night with tungsten lighting. This had two advantages: the stone would be separated visually from its background and the lighting could be controlled much more precisely than in daylight. Different camera formats have been used over a period of twenty years – 5x4-inch sheet film, 6x7-cm roll film, and now digital capture. The 5x4 format was particularly good as it enabled the image to be positioned easily on the ground glass of the camera-back in darkness and allowed retouching of the film emulsion to remove unwanted artefacts from the background. The digital camera permits a similar approach.

To show carving, light is projected onto the stone at an oblique angle to give a tone difference between the untouched stone surface and incisions;

the shallower the incisions, the more oblique the light needs to be. In addition to being oblique to the surface it is important that the direction of the illumination does not coincide with the direction of incised lines, which would render them invisible. Ideally, powerful light sources are used, as they can be positioned further from the monument to reduce variation in fall-off from one side of the stone to the other. The image appears more natural if it is possible to position the lights high up, making the effect more like daylight. Stones with multiple facets or very coarse texture pose problems. Where facets are in different planes, additional lights are needed to pick them out individually. Counterbalanced boom arms allow fine control of the light's position.

Working with tungsten lighting requires the use of generators, and in isolated locations this presents considerable problems, particularly since the work is carried out in darkness. Recently, tungsten lighting has been replaced by powerful portable flash units incorporating modelling lights, while the use of radio control has greatly simplified synchronisation problems.

The usual first consideration for photography is the position of the sun; working at night solves this at a stroke, leaving only the weather to consider. With large lighting rigs, wind is as much of a problem as rain, sleet or snow.

I. N. Wright

029 Early Medieval Sculpture

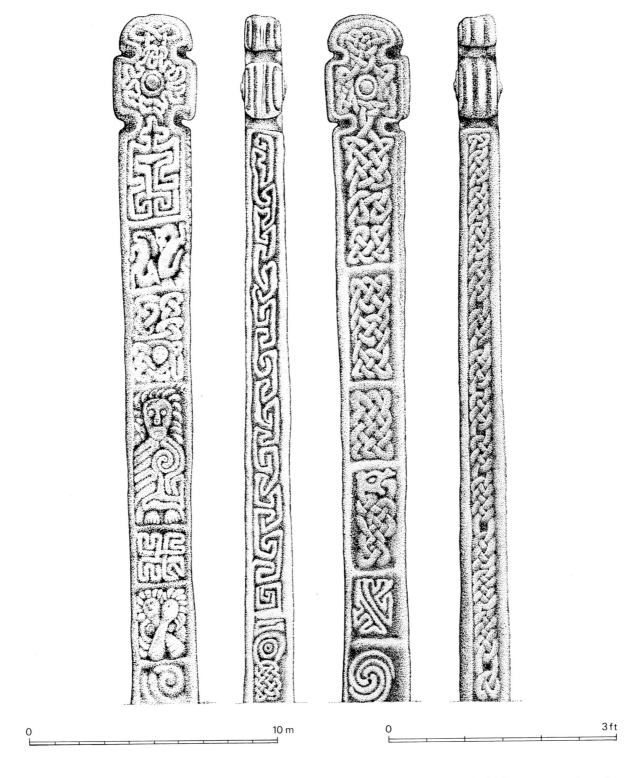

A drawing of the four faces of the tenth- or early eleventh-century cross at St Padarn's Church, Llanbadarn Fawr, Cardiganshire.

DI2005_1199 NPRN 308695

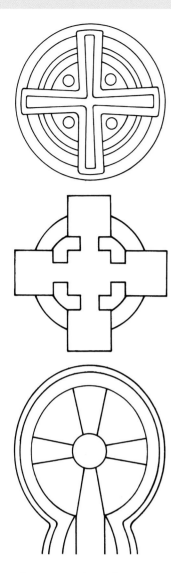

Above: Cross-head forms of (from top) ring and circle, ring, and circle type.

Above right: Nevern Cross, Pembrokeshire.

DI2006_0444 NPRN 304393

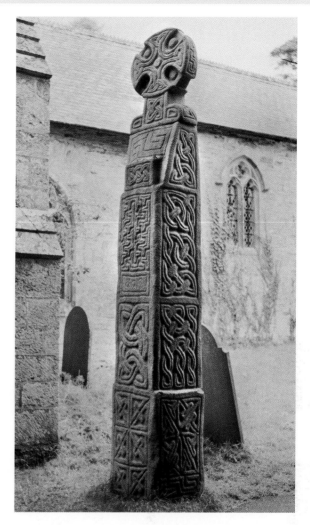

One consequence of the ravages of war, change and decay during many centuries has been the loss of much of the artistic output from early medieval Wales, particularly of perishable materials such as wood, textile and parchment. More durable works in stone provide one of the most important sources of information about early medieval art, supplemented by decoration found on small, usually personal, items of metalwork like brooches, pins and mounts. The interplay of ideas between different materials is illustrated by the occurrence on some sculpture of boss-like or rivet-like designs (taken from metalwork), interlace and fret patterns (resembling manuscript ornament) and mortice and tenon joints (appropriating wood-working techniques).

Surviving early medieval sculpture occurs in a wide range of sizes and shapes. At one end of the spectrum are cross-carved stones, from the seventh century onwards. Many of these are simple modifications of boulders, pillar-shaped stones or slabs, with pecked designs. At the other end are tall, elaborate, freestanding crosses, demonstrating an expansion of techniques, forms and motifs from about AD 800 onwards, and the growing patronage of the Church by secular elites.

Recent analysis of the relationship between form, ornament and function, and of the local distribution of styles, has led to the identification of regional groups and local clusters of sculpture. For example, in Breconshire a western, upland group can be contrasted with the Llan-gors ring-cross group. Two late groups of Glamorgan crosses, west and east of the River Ogwr, may echo political and geographical influences and the established kingdoms from which the monuments sprang. Other groups include the Monmouthshire cross-slabs, the large crosses in Penmon priory on Anglesey, the tall composite crosses of the Carew-Nevern group in Pembrokeshire, and the ninth- to eleventh-century regional group centred on St Davids.

Some sculpture belongs to a wider tradition of monuments found in other parts of Wales and further afield, in Ireland, the western islands and highlands of Scotland, and the Isle of Man. The precise processes by which common features were transmitted are open to speculation. The appearance of new motifs that remained undiluted by local imitation points to the continuing importance of maritime contacts around the Irish Sea. Irish craftsmen may have worked on sculpture in Wales, for instance the crosses of the interlaced type, ninth-century slabs that use the *crux christi* formula at Margam, Llantwit Major and Llangyfelach in Glamorgan, and sculpture in south-

west Wales. It seems likely that some ideas were transmitted through the developing monasteries of the coastal lowlands. Well-defined regional distributions of sculpture dating from between the ninth and eleventh centuries often appear to be focused on monastic centres, such as Bangor, Penmon on Anglesey, St Dogmaels and St Davids in Pembrokeshire, Llanbadarn Fawr in Cardiganshire, and Llantwit Major in Glamorgan.

While many stylistic characteristics reflect the transmission and incorporation of ideas from Ireland, the Irish Sea zone and Anglo-Saxon England, most sculptures are presumed to have been made and erected not far from their geological source. Inscriptions on upright crosses make it clear that the intentions of their donors varied. Most represented an act of piety by a named donor or commissioner. Some, like the Pillar of Eliseg [034], named members of ruling dynasties.

Mark Redknap

030 Defence against the Vikings: Llanbedrgoch

The location of the trading settlement of Llanbedrgoch, in the centre of the photograph, on a ridge overlooking Red Wharf Bay, Anglesey.
AP2007_0119 NPRN 405456

Above and right: Excavations in progress at Llanbedrgoch, Anglesey.

Courtesy AC-NMW
NPRN 405456

Given the geographical position of north Wales it was inevitable that its coastal population would engage in some manner with Scandinavians operating around the Irish Sea. Relationships were influenced in particular by the movements of Viking bands and the eventual establishment of Viking Dublin.

The historical framework provided by the Welsh annals and other documentary sources records the presence of Vikings in the Irish Sea from 795, but the first recorded attack on north Wales and the kingdom of Gwynedd is not until 854. Finding evidence for Vikings in Wales has been elusive and, until recently, heavily reliant on place-name evidence, much of it late in date. Excavations conducted at Llanbedrgoch, near the east coast of Anglesey, by National Museum Wales between 1994 and 2004 have revealed remarkable evidence for a farming settlement that developed into a rich Viking-age market centre closely linked to this Scandinavian world.

During the seventh and eighth centuries the settlement at Llanbedrgoch had wooden dwellings – one small circular roundhouse and at least one large rectangular hall – encircled by a ditch and earthen bank, presumably with a wooden palisade. The dark line of this ditch was shown in aerial photographs taken by the Royal Commission in 1995. In the mid-ninth century, however, the enclosure boundary was upgraded into a defensive system with a massive dry-stone wall of sufficient height and width to carry a wall walk. This was substantially larger than any other enclosure walls known on the island and may be interpreted as both an expression of power and a deterrent to potential raiders.

The period of activity that produced the new defences coincided with the reigns of Rhodri Mawr ('the Great', 844-78) and his sons. According to the Welsh annals, Rhodri led initial resistance to Viking attacks on Anglesey in the 850s. His successes were noted in Ireland and at Liège on the continent. The

Hack-silver and silver waste from Llanbedrgoch.

Courtesy AC-NMW
NPRN 405456

temporary presence of hostile Vikings on the island seems likely during the later ninth century, and it is known to have occurred in 902/3 when the Viking Ingimund attempted to settle with his followers after their expulsion from Dublin.

The ninth-century defensive wall encircled an array of rectangular buildings of different sizes, including a large hall. Occupants engaged in a wide range of craft activities, including leather and antler working, casting objects in bronze and silver, and ironworking. They also farmed, cultivating barley and rearing domesticated animals. The rich array of finds illustrates trade (hack-silver, coins and lead weights) and home life (dress accessories, jewellery, food waste, baking).

Llanbedrgoch became a strategically-sited, fortified centre operating within the Hiberno-Scandinavian political and commercial world of the late ninth and tenth centuries. Its demise, probably in the later tenth century, may have been associated with the raiding activities of the Vikings from the Isle of Man during the 960s and 970s.

Mark Redknap

031 The Mysterious Dykes of Early Medieval Wales

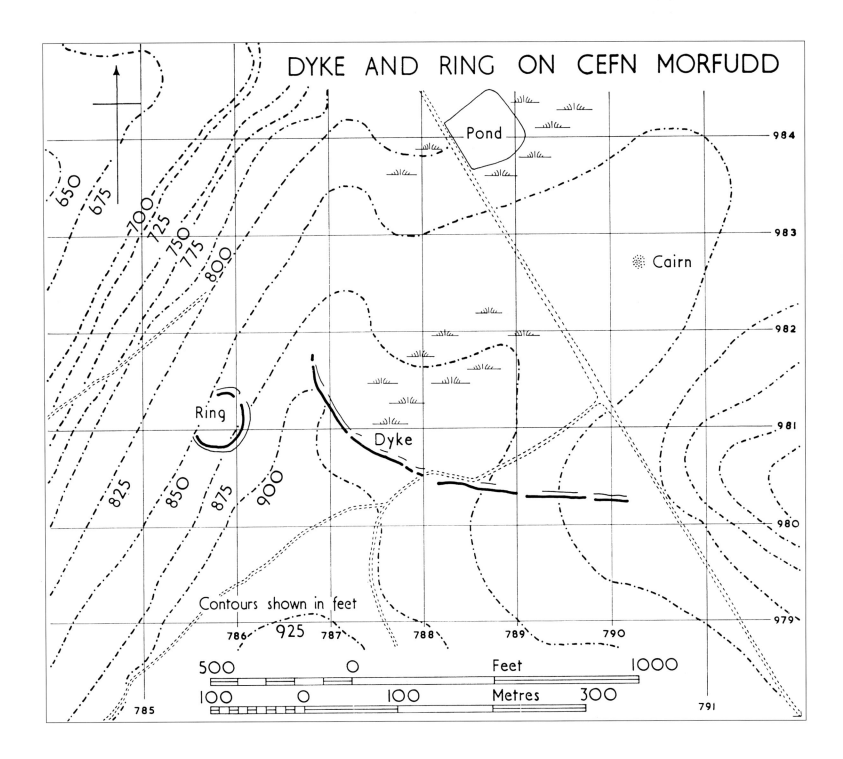

DYKE AND RING ON CEFN MORFUDD

A plan of a short dyke and ringwork on the ridge east of Neath, from the Glamorgan inventory (1976).

DI2008_0729 NPRN 301282

Wat's Dyke at Mynydd Isa, Flintshire.

DI2007_0644 NPRN 309593

Field remains attributable to the centuries between the end of Roman rule and the Norman conquest are sparse in Wales. Offa's Dyke is emblematic of the era, as are similar linear earthwork 'dykes' (ditches and accompanying banks) that are found primarily in eastern Wales and the border country beyond.

Offa's Dyke is one of the two great dykes in the Welsh Marches. Asser's statement in the ninth century that Offa, king of Mercia from AD 757 to 796, built 'a great bank' from 'sea to sea' means that this huge earthwork can be attributed to the later eighth century, but this dating has never been confirmed archaeologically. It runs from the Severn estuary near Chepstow northwards to Holywell, a distance of 225 kilometres, although there are long breaks in its course and only 130 kilometres of earthwork can be identified. While the height of any dyke is best appreciated at ground level, it is the bird's-eye view that provides the best guide to a dyke's scale and its course through the landscape. The Royal Commission and other organisations have contributed to the study of the dykes by regularly photographing them from the air. First studied in its entirety by Cyril Fox in the 1920s, and more recently by David Hill, some details of the structure of Offa's Dyke still remain to be established, and the general view that it defined a boundary between the Mercians and the Welsh rather than acting as a barrier is not universally accepted.

Offa's Dyke is not unique as a boundary along the Welsh borders. Lying east of it is Wat's Dyke, an earthwork just 65 kilometres in length but of only marginally smaller dimensions. It has long been argued that Wat's Dyke was earlier than its more westerly counterpart, probably a barrier from the north coast at Basingwerk to tributaries of the River Severn in Shropshire thrown up by Aethelbald, Offa's predecessor in Mercia. Excavations in 2006 near Oswestry have cast doubt on this, as dates from the lower silts in the ditch suggest that it was filling up in the ninth century. This may imply a construction date in the 820s.

Similar in form to these two great dykes is a group of smaller earthworks varying from less than a hundred metres long to more than a kilometre. Known as short dykes, they cluster in two regions. The dykes that form the first group were found in the uplands of northern Glamorgan by Cyril and Aileen Fox in the 1930s and by the Royal Commission during the preparation of the Glamorgan inventory. The other group is in Montgomeryshire and Radnorshire and across the border in Shropshire and Herefordshire. One Shropshire example has a prehistoric Bronze Age

The tree-lined route of Offa's Dyke striding across Chirk Castle estate.

DI2007_0646 NPRN 306866

radiocarbon date, but recent Cadw-funded work has demonstrated convincingly that many of the Welsh examples are of the early medieval period, peat from beneath five of the dykes producing dates in the sixth and seventh centuries. Some of these smaller dykes may have formed ineffective barriers, while others are thought to have defined tribal territories.

R. J. Silvester

032 A Royal Site: Llan-gors Crannog

Llan-gors lake, in the rich lands of Brycheiniog, seen from the south-east, with the royal llys set in the lake on the far right.

AP_2005_1878 NPRN 32997

A recent breakthrough in understanding high-status settlement in south Wales during the ninth and tenth centuries has been the archaeological investigation of the crannog or artificial island situated in the shallows of Llan-gors lake, the largest natural lake in south Wales. The man-made nature of the island – constructed out of brushwood, stone and wood, and surrounded by palisades of oak planks – was first established in 1867 by Henry Dumbleton and his brother Edgar when the water level of the lake was lowered. The date and full significance of the site remained uncertain until they were revealed by a programme of survey and excavation by the National Museum and Cardiff University between 1988 and 1994.

Tree-ring analysis of samples of oak planking from the palisade showed a felling date of the summers of 889 to 893. It was clear that the crannog was constructed within a very short period. Artefacts found during the investigations included a very fine textile of linen and silk, exquisitely decorated with small lion and bird motifs, parts of a small portable reliquary shrine, pins, brooches (some in Irish style) and bone combs. That occupants of the crannog patronised craftsmen or engaged in economic activities is shown by fragments of furnace lining, moulds and failed castings. Recent studies of remains of domesticated animals found on the island, including cattle, sheep and pigs, point to livestock-rearing or possibly the taking of tribute in the form of food, while bones from wild animals such as red deer, roe deer and wild boar point to hunting.

The date, form, size and location of the crannog, the high quality of the artefacts recovered and the economy of its occupants support its identification as a royal llys or court associated with the ruling dynasty of the inland kingdom of Brycheiniog. The destruction of the crannog by a Mercian (Anglo-Saxon) army after a very short period of occupancy

Excavations on Llan-gors crannog, July 1990.
GTJ25670 NPRN 32997

Underwater investigation in progress.
Courtesy AC-NMW
NPRN 32997

is documented in an entry in the Anglo-Saxon Chronicle for the year 916: 'Æthelflæd sent an army into Wales and destroyed Brecenanmere ['Brecknockmere'] and captured the king's wife and thirty-three other persons'.

The site is so far without parallel in Wales. The closest comparable sites of similar date are found in Ireland, where they are among the most evocative and remarkable features of the country's early medieval landscape. The sophisticated construction of Llan-gors crannog may have been directed by an Irish master craftsman, and the unusual choice of site may have been an experiment in proclaiming the status and lineage of its inhabitants. Perhaps it helped to reinforce the legitimacy of the ruling dynasty via the origin legend of the local Welsh kingdom: rulers of the kingdom of Brycheiniog claimed descent from Brychan, son of an Irish father and a Welsh mother. Irish metal-working styles are reflected in some of the artefacts, while other objects manufactured on the island reveal artistic responses to local tastes. The assemblage reveals both the high status and the particular tastes of its occupants, and much about court life and culture in the early medieval period.

Mark Redknap

033 Later Inscriptions and the Use of Languages

The Houelt cross at Illtyd's church, Llantwit Major, photographed in 1964.

DI2008_0556 NPRN 171

Above: The inscription at Llanwnnws, Cardiganshire.
DI2008_0440 NPRN 275652

Right: The Elmon stone, Llanarthne, Carmarthenshire.
DI2008_0430 NPRN 100711

Below: A Royal Commission drawing of about 1914 of the inscription at St Cadfan's, Tywyn, Merioneth.
DI2008_0545 NPRN 43861

By the early ninth century Irish names recorded in inscriptions had disappeared, since the settlers had adopted Welsh names and merged with the local population. A cross-carved stone in the church of Llanwnnws, Cardiganshire, bears a Latin inscription, lettered in a form of manuscript-influenced 'minuscule' (small cursive script): it asks 'Whoever reads this, may he give a blessing on the soul of Hiroidil son of Carotinn'. The father's name seems to be Irish but he has given his son a definitely Welsh name: *Hirhoeddl*, 'he of long life'.

Inscriptions like this show that the carvers of Welsh inscriptions and their patrons were familiar with manuscripts. Unfortunately, nearly all contemporary Welsh manuscripts have perished – the few exceptions left Wales at an early date and were preserved in Anglo-Saxon England, being valued there for their Latin contents rather than for the incidental marginalia in Old Welsh considered so important by modern linguists. Any manuscripts written mainly in Welsh would be unlikely to be preserved abroad. It might be hoped, therefore, that Wales's stone inscriptions would make up the deficiency. Unfortunately, the grip of the Roman and Christian epigraphical tradition was so strong that stone memorials used the Latin language exclusively for many centuries. The one remarkable exception is the inscription in Tywyn church, Merioneth, possibly dating from the early ninth century, commemorating Tengrumui, wife of Adgan, and Cun, wife of Celen, with a poetic phrase in Old Welsh: *tricet nitanam*, 'the grief-loss remains'. Was the mother-tongue used because the deceased were female?

In the later inscriptions Roman names die out (apart from those that had become wholly naturalised

in Wales) and native Welsh names predominate, with the occasional English name and possibly even a Norse name in runes, as perhaps on the cross at Corwen in Merioneth. Sometimes the names can be identified with historical figures. Thus, a cross in the church at Llantwit Major, Glamorgan, records that 'Houelt prepared this cross for the soul of his father Res'. This must be Hywel ap Rhys, king of Glywysing, who allied himself with Alfred, king of Wessex, in the 880s. The imposing cross is typical of this later period, when major sculpture is concentrated in the prosperous south-east. A later and debased example, in the church at Llanarthne, Carmarthenshire, reveals further sociolinguistic changes in Wales round about 1100. The inscription is damaged (in 1833 the cross was used as a stile), but on the mid-left the English name of the sculptor, *Elmon*, can be read and at the right there is a French formula, *merci et g[ra]ce*.

Patrick Sims-Williams

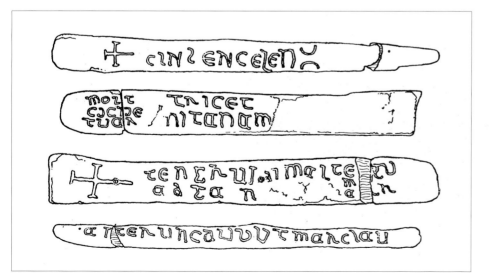

034 Commemorating a King: The Pillar of Eliseg

The Pillar of Eliseg, Llangollen, Denbighshire.

DS2008_022_003 NPRN 165274

Above: A reconstruction by Cadw of the complete Eliseg Cross as it may have appeared.

Courtesy of Cadw NPRN 165274

Right: The re-erected pillar showing the inscription added in 1779.

DS2008_022_008 NPRN 165274

The appearance of this broken stone pillar is very different from the prominent cross that would have been familiar to the Cistercian monks of Valle Crucis. Erected in the ninth century by Cyngen to commemorate his great-grandfather, Eliseg (or Elisedd), the cross was toppled in the 1640s, prey perhaps to the Puritan iconoclasts of the Civil War. Its prostrate, broken form and its inscription, worn even then almost to the point of being indecipherable, were recorded by the antiquary Edward Lhuyd in 1696. Were it not for Lhuyd we would have lost one of the most important early medieval inscriptions in Britain, so weathered is the carving. Today, even expert photography in raking light indicates no more than where the lines of text once were.

The pillar was re-erected by a local landowner, Trevor Lloyd, in 1779 as a picturesque feature visible from his abbey summer-house. By this time the cross head that would have surmounted the pillar – to judge from similar monuments in the early medieval kingdom of Mercia in the English Midlands – had been lost. We have no knowledge of the appearance of the cross, but the moulded collar and swags at the top of the rounded pillar mark the transition to a quadrangular shaft. Lloyd's mason reset the remaining pillar in its square socket stone, placing it on a new dry-stone plinth on top of the mound to enhance its visibility from his summer-house bay window.

All landscapes evolve, as do their component features, and this monument is no exception. The mound with its stone kerb is the earliest part, raised some four thousand years ago, probably for the burial of an important Bronze Age leader. However, a skeleton found lying in a box of blue stones during Lloyd's eighteenth-century excavations was later in date, set within a stony capping added to house a new interment in the early medieval period. Was this the body of Eliseg, the eighth-century ruler of Powys, laid to rest on the prominent mound? Excavations elsewhere suggest that prehistoric monuments were often selected as fitting burial places for early medieval heroes.

Later still, Eliseg's great-grandson and the last of his family's line, Cyngen (died 854), commemorated the achievements of his illustrious ancestor by raising the inscribed cross (though its original position cannot now be proved). The inscription, written in Latin in thirty-one horizontal lines, was broken into paragraphs separated by small crosses. It glorified Eliseg and Cyngen, proclaiming their lineage from Emperor Magnus Maximus and his son Vortigern (Gwrtheyrn), both celebrated figures from the end of Roman

Britain. Eliseg, the inscription asserted, drove the English from the area after they had laid this borderland waste for nine years. The text transcribed by Lhuyd thus gives a unique insight into the rulers of this area, their political achievements, and the tensions along the border. Unusually, the mason who carved the inscription – Cynfarch – is also named.

Clearly visible on the reverse of the stone is the Latin inscription recording the final modification, that of the restoration and re-erection of the cross in the eighteenth century. Though now only about half its original height, the cross is still an evocative element in this celebrated landscape.

Sian Rees

035 Discovering Early Medieval Religous Sites

The present church of St Mary Magdalene, Llanfair Nant-y-gof, south of Trecwn in north Pembrokeshire was built in 1855,
replacing a medieval church, but the subcircular churchyard hints at an early medieval origin.
Earthworks and a large recumbent limestone slab in the churchyard indicate a long history of activity.
AP_2006_1130 NPRN 230

A rare group of early medieval square barrows discovered as a parchmark next to a Roman road at Druid, Corwen, during the drought of 2006. Up to four barrows are visible on a ridge of parched ground, but any features in the remainder of the field are obscured.

AP_2006_3977 NPRN 404711

The religious sites of early medieval Wales are elusive. Early medieval communities frequently reused Iron Age defended enclosures for their church sites and Bronze Age barrow cemeteries for their typical square barrows – hence religious sites may lack obvious characteristics and the continuity of burial places often makes them difficult to recognise.

Clues to an early medieval date for church sites include defended enclosures in close association with circular or curvilinear churchyards, churches housing early Christian monuments, and early dedications. In the 1990s Terry James of the Royal Commission undertook research and aerial reconnaissance on this subject in west Wales, with notable results. Flights to identify potential early church sites in low winter light and summer droughts were guided by documentary and map research linked to place-name studies. Place names that proved to be potential indicators of early medieval religious sites include *llan* (originally an enclosure or graveyard, with or without a church), *eglwys* (church), *bedd* (grave) and *mynwent* (cemetery or graveyard). James reinterpreted ditched or palisaded curvilinear enclosures in the light of this documentary evidence, overturning a long-held notion that all cropmarks of defended enclosures were of Iron Age or Roman date. Continuing Royal Commission aerial reconnaissance has identified further defended

Cropmarks of ditched enclosures surrounding St Baglan's Church near Caernarfon.

AP_2005_1621 NPRN 403370 and 43690

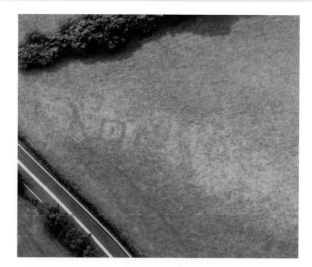

enclosures paired with isolated or early church sites, notably in Gwynedd. A striking complex of ditched enclosures revealed as cropmarks was found surrounding the isolated coastal church of St Baglan near Caernarfon. Although the earliest datable feature of the present church is the late thirteenth- or early fourteenth-century north door, the church houses a later fifth- or early sixth-century inscribed stone. The enclosure complex may have been an early medieval settlement.

Square-barrow cemeteries of late Roman or early medieval date can be far more readily identified during aerial reconnaissance, though the full extent of potential buried remains may not be revealed. While a number of square-barrow cemeteries have been excavated, they are still relatively rare. However, several have been discovered during Royal Commission reconnaissance, each a valuable indicator of potential early medieval burial and religious activity. Patterns can be discerned in their discovery. One group lies close to an Iron Age defended enclosure and spring at Ffynnon near Aberporth in Cardiganshire. Another single square barrow has been found in the vicinity of the Roman fort at Segontium, Caernarfon. A notable group of square barrows has also been discovered alongside a Roman road at Druid, near Corwen in Denbighshire. Together with ongoing ground prospection and excavation by other organisations, the Royal Commission's reconnaissance programme continues to add to our understanding of early medieval Wales.

Toby Driver

The Middle Ages

Ralph A. Griffiths

The four and a half centuries between the start of the Anglo-Norman conquest of south-east Wales in 1070 and the union of Wales with England in 1536 have left a legacy of buildings and archaeological sites that help us to visualise the lives of medieval people more clearly than is possible for earlier ages. As a result, historians have reconstructed a society – or rather a number of societies – of fascinating complexity: rural folk and townsfolk, hill dwellers and valley and coastal communities, native and immigrant peoples, some rich and others very poor, some known to us by name but the majority now quite anonymous. At the end of the Middle Ages Wales had a population of about 300,000, perhaps double what it had been in 1070 – and yet still hardly the size of the city of Cardiff in 2008. As elsewhere in western Europe, the population had grown steadily for more than two centuries, but between 1310 and 1370 famine, disease and plague of a sort never experienced before cut it by at least a third, and it was not until the sixteenth century that it again reached the level of 1300.

These changes had profound effects on Welsh society: on agriculture and the use of the landscape, on the number and size of towns, and on the growth or decay of local communities. Meanwhile, developments in politics, war and ways of government in the British Isles had a lasting impact on Wales, creating a complex pattern of lordships and counties, administered from courts (or llysoedd), castles and houses whose remains still dot the landscape. Medieval society was, too, a universally Christian society that experienced periods of intense religious enthusiasm. This enthusiasm and spiritual devotion inspired much church and monastery building, sculpture and painting, many examples of which (like Tintern Abbey) enrich our culture today. The small number of Jews who settled in Welsh towns in the wake of the Norman conquest all but disappeared after 1290, when King Edward I expelled the Jews from both England and Wales.

The Welsh experience had much in common with that of other countries in the British Isles and western Europe during the Middle Ages, yet it had a marked social and cultural distinctiveness. In many ways, medieval society was militaristic in tone and violent in action. The patchwork of Welsh kingdoms, some of which (in Powys and Gwynedd) resisted the Anglo-Norman conquest for two hundred years, encouraged their rulers' rivalries and caused political instability. At the same time population growth and social mobility produced other tensions and conflicts. Groups of English, Normans, Bretons and Flemings advanced into Wales in the wake of William the Conqueror's invasion of south-east England in 1066; William himself travelled as far as St David's in 1081. This migration continued for centuries and, of course, there have been few periods in Wales's modern history that have not witnessed waves of immigrants. From 1070 to 1282 English and French lords and kings and their descendants struggled with the ruling Welsh lords for dominance in Wales. The organisational changes and influences which the migrants brought with them affected all aspects of Welsh society: they

Opposite: Detail of the Tree of Jesse in the sumptuous east window (1533), north nave, St Dyfnog's Church, Llanrhaeadr-yng-Nghinmeirch, Denbighshire. Here Kings Solomon and David rise from the sleeping Jesse.
DI2007_1988 NPRN 165239

Below: The graceful west front of Tintern Abbey, Monmouthshire, built about 1300 in classic Decorated style.
DI2008_0287 NPRN 359

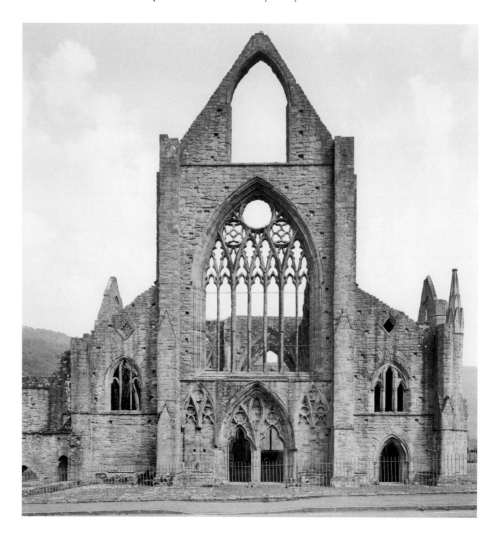

St James's Church (foreground) and castle, Manorbier, on the Pembrokeshire coast. Both probably date from the mid-twelfth century, the church enlarged during the Middle Ages and the castle much altered in more modern times – and the outer ward largely obscured. No town developed alongside them.

DI2008_0289 NPRN 94195

built castles in the landscape, stimulated town life, and gradually formed a parish system for the Church. The imprint of Wales's medieval past is all around us.

The social impact of migration was lasting. Many incomers intermarried with native inhabitants and settled alongside them, and some of these families provided migrants onwards to Ireland after 1170. In the opposite direction went Welsh folk from the borderland with England (what had become the lordships of the Welsh March) to the English midlands and the West Country. In the lowlands and wider valleys of eastern Wales, and along the southern and northern coasts, these processes gave rise to communities that might be bi- or tri-lingual and developed a distinctive, cosmopolitan culture, for all the tensions that accompanied English and French colonisation. A sense of Welsh identity persisted most strongly in Gwynedd, the last region to feel the full effect of these cultural influences.

Economic life was boosted by migration and closer relations with England, Ireland and the continent. The *Itinerary of Wales*, written by Gerald of Wales (died 1223), who was born of mixed Welsh and Norman parentage in Manorbier Castle, provides a snapshot of the changes that were taking place.

Roman roads were still used in the Middle Ages but were gradually supplemented by newer routeways, and ferries crossed the main rivers and straits (including to Anglesey). The fertile lowlands of the east and south supported villages and English-style manors, with arable fields and pastoral spaces for animals. The fields were arranged according to a field system common in lowland England, with strips of land cultivated by individual tenants and their families; such 'open fields' may still be seen at The Vyle in Gower [036] and in Pembrokeshire. In upland areas pastoral agriculture prevailed, and as time passed sheep runs became increasingly common, centred on farmsteads run by lay landholders and a score of new religious houses, as at Hen Ddinbych and Strata Florida Abbey's grange at Penardd, whose remains at Troed y Rhiw have been recorded by the Royal Commission. Along what is a very extensive coastline and in the Severn and Dee estuaries, punctuated for most of the distance by a host of anchorages, fishing was common and some of the fish-traps that have been located are thought to be of medieval date [042]. A more dramatic change occurred between 1070 and 1330 with the emergence of almost a hundred towns, the majority

of them situated on or close to the coast or on navigable rivers [041]. Some (like Carmarthen) developed from earlier communities, the more important of them (like Brecon) were given charters as boroughs by their lords or the English king, and all of them, from Chepstow to Caernarfon, Pembroke to Flint, were the focus of a money economy and of trading through markets and fairs. In the thirteenth century many of the towns set about protecting their interests and controlling their commerce by building stone walls (and a few, like Monmouth, stone bridges). Some of the larger islands around the coast were inhabited and modestly developed too – Lundy with its church, Cardigan Island with its animal pens, and Bardsey, the supposed resting-place of countless saints.

The stages by which these conquerors and colonisers advanced in Wales were marked, first, by the speedy erection of mottes of impacted earth with baileys and wooden buildings (as at Tomen-y-mur), designed to overawe localities and act as springboards for further advances. A minority of these fortresses were still needed later as invasion turned into colonisation

and settlement, and they were converted into stone castles at places like Abergavenny and Builth. Even Welsh lords saw the need for strong castles as at Dinas Brân. All in all, by 1300 Wales had more castles per square mile than almost any other comparable region of the British Isles, and examples of the most primitive of the earliest mottes are still being identified today by the Royal Commission's aerial photography programme.

The new rulers revitalised religion in Wales as they did in England, along lines familiar in France and with a direct link to Rome. The traditional centres of St David's, Bangor, Llandaff and, later, St Asaph became the focus of new dioceses, though under the oversight of the archbishop of Canterbury. Existing churches and monasteries (like Llanbadarn Fawr) were complemented by new religious houses, at first built close to the invaders' castles and towns, as at Abergavenny and Brecon, and then in wilder country to meet the aspirations of the international Cistercian Order of monks at places like Valle Crucis and Strata Florida [040]. Only a small number of

A mid-twentieth century photograph of Caernarfon Castle, from the south-east. This part of Edward I's fortress, from the Queen's Gate (right) to the Eagle Tower (left), with distinctive polygonal towers, was built quickly between 1283 and 1292 (though never finished). In the angle between the River Seiont (foreground) and the Menai Strait, it was the Crown's headquarters in north Wales.
DI2008_0288 NPRN 95318

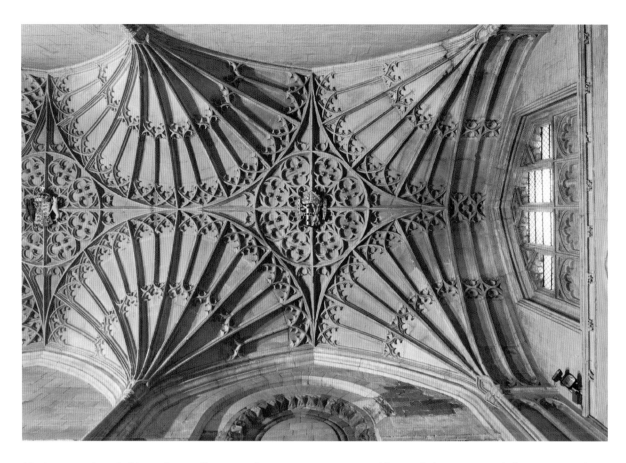

The fan vaulting of Bishop Vaughan's Chapel at St David's Cathedral, Pembrokeshire.

DI2007_0733 NPRN 306

friaries were founded in Wales to offer pastoral care to comparatively large centres of population like Cardiff and Haverfordwest. By the thirteenth century even small churches were being rebuilt in stone, often (as in Gower and at Hodgeston in Pembrokeshire with defensive bell-towers of local or regional style sponsored by the communities themselves [039].

The years between 1260 and 1295 were a turning-point in Wales's history. In Gwynedd Llywelyn ap Gruffudd created a sophisticated state which expanded its power eastwards to the River Dee and southwards to Carmarthenshire and almost to Brecon. To complement his grandfather's castles at Cricieth and Dolwyddelan, he built a massive new fortress at Dolforwyn, just a few miles from the king's own castle of Montgomery. He encouraged the little towns of Pwllheli and Nefyn, and he patronised the Church, including Penmon Priory in Anglesey. At Rhosyr, overlooking the Menai Strait in Anglesey, the site of one of his residences has recently been excavated [133].

In 1267 Llywelyn became the first Welsh ruler to be acknowledged as prince of Wales by an English king. This remarkable achievement provoked the new monarch, Edward I (1272-1307), to curb Llywelyn's pretensions. In two sharp wars between 1277 and 1283, the principality of Gwynedd was

conquered by English armies; and despite several uprisings soon afterwards it was incorporated into a new royal principality of six counties that covered most of north and west Wales. The rest of the country consisted of numerous marcher lordships, mostly ruled by English nobles. This political and governmental

Right: Dolwyddelan Castle, Caernarfonshire, from the west. Sited on a ridge overlooking the Lledr valley, it was built by Prince Llywelyn ab Iorwerth in the early thirteenth century. One of its two square keeps was renovated (with battlements) in the mid-nineteenth century.

DI2006_1686 NPRN 95299

The earthen motte with its ditch and levelled bailey that was the home of Owain Glyn Dŵr at Sycharth, Denbighshire.

DI2006_0979 NPRN 306999

structure was the culmination of two centuries of military conquest and colonisation in Wales, and it lasted for a further 250 years. It also hastened economic, religious and cultural changes that were already in train, yet without obliterating earlier features of Welsh society. Moreover, communication within the British Isles and with western Europe was strengthened, and the peoples of England and Wales grew closer while acknowledging ethnic and social differences.

This did not, however, guarantee a more peaceful Wales. Edward I was responsible for the greatest castle-building programme ever attempted in the British Isles. Its aim was to ensure English control of Gwynedd and the surrounding country: it began in 1277 with castles like Aberystwyth and ended with Beaumaris, which was completed after the king's death. In 1986 four of Edward's most imposing fortresses – Harlech, Caernarfon, Conwy and Beaumaris – were designated by UNESCO as Wales's first World Heritage Site. Some of the castles, and others that were built or rebuilt in marcher lordships like Denbigh and Newport, became seats of government supported by boroughs that were intended to exploit the wealth of the countryside. Other castles were mainly garrison centres and in more peaceful times they fell into disrepair. The archbishop of Canterbury had visited Wales in 1284 to enforce discipline in Church and society, to restore damaged monasteries and churches

(like Bangor Cathedral) and to promote reconciliation between the Welsh and immigrant populations. For a time the policies worked.

Yet social integration was not a smooth process. In the fourteenth century life's uncertainties were increased by worsening weather across England and Wales in the 1310s that caused cattle murrain and famine, by economic dislocation and hardship, and by a series of devastating plagues. 'The great mortality' or 'the great pestilence' (later known as the Black Death) quickly spread from the Severnside ports in 1349 through the southern lowlands, the Severn valley and the borderland – and it reappeared in later decades. Manors, villages and towns were more seriously affected than scattered upland farms. The disasters disrupted the lives of individuals and families, urban and rural communities, lords as well as clergy; towns like Radnor shrank and several villages (like Runston [036]) began to wither – to be rediscovered by aerial archaeologists in our own day.

Such experiences increased the possibility of unrest in a volatile society where rulers and ruled faced greater hardships and uncertainties and where, especially in northern Wales, the memory of conquest was greenest. The most spectacular outburst was the revolt of Owain Glyn Dŵr (1400-10). Aside from Owain's own grievances as a prominent Welsh landowner in north-east Wales, his revolt was so

Above: Medieval tiles at Strata Florida

CD2003_625_021 NPRN 95764

127

Pembroke Castle and the medieval burgh protected by it.

DI2005-0919 NPRN 94945

serious and lasted so long because it tapped into broader resentments in Church and state and the economy which prompted Owain and his supporters to attack the Anglicised towns of the north-east (like Ruthin and Welshpool), to descend into southern Wales to attack Brecon, Cardiff, Kidwelly and Carmarthen with devastating effect, and to besiege Grosmont and Coity castles. His forces won as many battles as they lost, though the sites of these encounters (even at Pilleth in 1405) can rarely be pin-pointed precisely [100]. Owain had ambitious plans for an independent state, but the revolt never struck a universal chord among the peoples of Wales and ultimately it was unsuccessful.

Where the armies marched, the revolt was destructive: the fabric of towns and rural houses and mills suffered, especially in central and southern Wales, and the experience interrupted the evolution of a peaceful society. Yet from the 1430s there are signs of recovery, with population levels more stable, commercial life reviving in places like Haverfordwest and Oswestry, and the cloth and cattle trades with English towns across the border and in the Severn valley flourishing. Progress was made in refurbishing town buildings and, as the Royal Commission's survey of Radnorshire has shown, reconstructing rural halls [043].

Some of those who weathered the turbulence of the fourteenth century and the great revolt grasped the opportunities presented by any volatile society, buying vacant properties or moving elsewhere, and realigning their loyalties. Enterprising peasants laid the foundations for family estates or started sheep farms, or prospered by providing craft and retail services in the larger towns [044]. Welsh labourers found seasonal work on English estates, just as construction workers and craftsmen had been enlisted on either side of the border when castles and town walls were being built; after their work was done, some of these workers and craftsmen had put down roots in and around towns like Harlech and Beaumaris. The Welsh-born ancestors of Sir William ap Thomas were so successful that their family became one of the most powerful in fifteenth-century Wales, building a magnificent castle at Raglan [038]. The Bulkeley family was English in origin, but they too seized their chances, this time in the commercial world of Beaumaris and the Anglesey countryside.

Successful gentry families, whether of Welsh or immigrant stock (and few of the latter did not intermarry with Welsh families during the fifteenth century), were needed by monasteries as protectors, by poets and artists as patrons and, above all, by the king and marcher lords as administrators of their lordships. They came to dominate local society and exploited civil war in England (the Wars of the Roses). Some of them acquired town houses (like the Kemeyses of Newport) or built large manor houses (like the Vaughans of Tretower), and they arranged to be buried in style, just like English lords and gentry (as the Herbert tombs in Abergavenny Priory testify [045]. Although they were admired by Welsh poets, the culture of the age was increasingly cosmopolitan and multilingual. After centuries of alien rule self-government by such families was common throughout Wales before the arrival of the Tudors, so that union with England aroused little opposition.

Above: The cruck truss at Hafodygarreg, Erwood, Breconshire has been tree-ring dated to 1402. The absence of any earlier houses in Wales may indicate the extent of destruction during the wars of 1400-10.
CD2005_611_001 NPRN 301421

Above, left: A reconstruction of the hall at Bryndraenog near Beguildy in Radnorshire, tree-ring dated to 1436. It was an imposing hall-house built probably by a Welsh uchelwr or gentleman.
DI2005_0884 NPRN 81056

036 The Humane Landscape

The Vyle medieval field system, Rhosili, Gower, photographed from the air in 1995.
The small medieval village and church, now ruined, lay just beyond the open fields.
RCAHMW: DI2006_0508 NPRN 24333

*Above: Rosemarket,
Pembrokeshire: the planned
village behind its Iron Age rath.*

DI2006_1228 NPRN 305262

*Below: The site of Runston
village and its ruined church,
Monmouthshire.*

DI2006_1440 NPRN 15511

The countryside of medieval Wales was varied and dynamic rather than static, and highly sensitive to changing external circumstances. This gave rise to a variety of settlement patterns and land uses that can still be seen. Their fossilised remains have been revealed, often spectacularly, through the Royal Commission's aerial photographic programmes.

The Vyle at Rhosili in south Gower is a rare survival of an open field system, a relict of an early kind of communal agriculture which integrated arable and pastoral resources. The layout took the form of bundles of narrow, individually-held, strip fields of one to one-and-a-half acres each. Instead of being defined by hedgerows, the strips were separated from each other by low grassy banks, or baulks, giving the system its open appearance. The cultivated strips were not allocated to individual tenants as compact blocks but were scattered across the field system. This arrangement ensured not only an equitable distribution of different qualities of land amongst the landholders, but also that everyone participated in communal grazing after the harvest, manuring the land in readiness for the next crop. Despite becoming largely enclosed, the overall pattern is clear today. Though not the only kind of medieval farming, fields like these were once

widespread in the lowland landscape. Rhosili had a history of monastic settlement prior to the Norman conquest, so both village and fields may have originated in pre-Norman systems of social organisation.

The same cannot be said of Rosemarket, near Neyland. Under Anglo-Norman rule the Pembrokeshire landscape underwent great change, particularly in the south where large numbers of peasant settlers, many from Flanders, colonised the area in the twelfth century. New villages were planned. Rosemarket is one of several around Milford Haven founded on such lines, typically laid out along a main street, with a church, village green and nearby open fields, which have since been enclosed. It was sited close to a circular fort dating from the Iron Age which was possibly refortified at this same time.

Not all medieval villages have survived as settlements; many became deserted. Runston, occupying a small hill near Chepstow, is one example. Possibly referred to in the tenth century, the building of the church relates to the Anglo-Norman settlement of Gwent from the late eleventh century onwards. The village reached its maximum extent in the medieval period, when around twenty-five buildings lay along a series of tracks, close to a village green, a church and possibly a manor house. Thereafter the number of occupied houses dwindled until, by the late eighteenth century, the landlord allowed the remaining buildings to fall into disrepair, apparently in order to dislodge lawless tenants.

It was not just the lowlands that were exploited. The attractions of upland pastures were recognised by religious houses that were often granted vast tracts by secular authorities. Hen Ddinbych on the Denbighshire moors is thought to have been the focus of an upland grange. The enclosed area contained several long-roofed buildings, possibly sheepcotes enabling flocks to be over-wintered for wool and other produce. The grange was probably established before the Edwardian conquest but seems to have gone out of use during the fourteenth century when its pastures were leased to the local community.

David Leighton

037 Castles and Courts

The great keep at Pembroke Castle, the tallest cylindrical keep in Britain.
DI2006_0438 NPRN 94945.

Above: The excavated llys site at Rhosyr, Anglesey. Remains of the thirteenth-century court of the princes of Gwynedd are visible.

AP_2005_0150 NPRN 306904

Right: Dinas Brân, Denbighshire, from the east.

AP_2006_0942 NPRN 165276

Below: The motte at Tomen-y-mur, Merionethshire, sits in the rectangle of the Roman fort.

AP_2005_0134 NPRN 95476

The Norman invasions left a distinctive mark on the landscape of much of Wales in a large number of earthwork castles, most of them mottes, often with a bailey attached. They are typified at Tomen-y-mur, a motte built within the walls of a Roman fort that may have served as the bailey. This is one of only a few monuments in Gwynedd that reflect the advances made into the kingdom from Chester and recorded in Domesday Book in 1086. For the Norman presence here was brief, terminated by a Welsh resurgence that gave Gruffudd ap Cynan authority over an extensive territory; although Henry I's advance brought him to Tomen-y-mur in 1114, the castle by then had ceased to be of any value to the invaders.

Pembroke Castle, by contrast, depicts a more enduring Anglo-Norman presence. A stronghold of immense strategic importance was built at Pembroke following an advance into Deheubarth from a base at Montgomery, even as the Normans were being forced to withdraw from Gwynedd; its importance was later enhanced by the needs that arose from the extension of Anglo-Norman power into Ireland from south-west Wales. The present structure was the work of William Marshal, earl of Pembroke (died 1219). The site originally chosen proved to be an ideal location for a major castle built at the upper end of a ridge that also accommodated the town of Pembroke. A gatehouse controlled entry to an outer bailey, with an inner bailey enclosing a cylindrical tower or keep that formed the core of the fortification.

Round keeps fashioned in the likeness of Marshal's great tower are found in some number, including at Skenfrith and Bronllys in the March of Wales, and at Dynevor and Dolbadarn in the Welsh princes' lands. During the thirteenth century, however, the princes' residences, and the places where many of their

documents were written, generally remained the timber-framed halls that stood on stone foundations at their courts (or llysoedd), one llys normally located in each commote. Their remains have consequently proved elusive, but the site at Rhosyr, the centre of the commote of Menai in Anglesey, was excavated in the 1990s to reveal impressive evidence of a court characteristic of those that feature in medieval Welsh law texts and poetry.

Nonetheless, the princes also invested in strategically-placed stone castles for the defence of their territories. Some, like Dolwyddelan and Dolbadarn, consisted of a single structure that formed a keep within a curtain wall. Conspicuous among the more extensive structures was Castell Dinas Brân, almost certainly the work of Gruffudd ap Madog (died 1269), the last prince to rule Powys Fadog in its entirety. Built in a commanding position at the heart of his dominion, the castle had a gatehouse leading to an extensive rectangular-curtained courtyard, with a rectangular keep and – a distinctive feature of Welsh masonry castles – an apsidal tower. 'There is no stronger castle in Wales, nor has England a greater', declared Henry de Lacy, earl of Lincoln, when his army reached Dinas Brân in the war of 1277. The division of Powys Fadog among the sons of Gruffudd ap Madog, and their virtual extinction in the war of 1282-3, spelled the end of a fine exemplar of Welsh military architecture.

Beverley Smith

038 Later Castles and Residences

The imposing new gatehouse of Raglan Castle, Monmouthshire, from the south-east.
It was built of pale Wye valley sandstone by William Herbert, later earl of Pembroke, in the 1460s.

DI2006_1137 NPRN 93387

The military character of twelfth- and thirteenth-century castles meant that domestic considerations came a poor second to defence: the keep had limited potential in terms of space and design. The construction of Edward I's 'ring of stone' (at Flint, Rhuddlan, Aberystwyth, Conwy, Caernarfon, Cricieth, Harlech and Beaumaris) was intended to subdue the princes of Gwynedd, but it also offered more palatial accommodation than almost anything previously known in Wales: Beaumaris could provide space for up to eleven separate households.

After Edward's conquest there was demand for more space and greater comfort. His architects piloted the courtyard castle, where domestic ranges were integrated in the design, and other castles were modified along similar lines. Militaristic features such as gatehouses and mural towers persisted and symbolised economic and political power, but their role in a more domestic scheme reflected a change from the imperatives of war and defence to those of settlement and control. Grosmont Castle dates from the early thirteenth century but was redeveloped in the fourteenth. The north range provided comfortable apartments and is dominated by a delicate octagonal chimney with cusped openings and an elaborate, coroneted and gabled top.

A castle's social heart continued to be the great hall, but ancillary rooms and private apartments were also provided. There were better facilities, including large fireplaces for superior heating and larger windows lighting the chambers. Improved sanitation meant that the latrine pits of an earlier period gave way to private garderobes. Tretower, or 'Tower homestead', originated as a shell keep in the mid-twelfth century, and a circular tower keep was built in the early thirteenth to improve the domestic accommodation. A century later the site's focus shifted a short distance to a new court, which was

Right: The ceremonial entrance porch (1506) to the great hall of Carew Castle, Pembrokeshire, from a nineteenth-century photograph. The ivy has since been removed to reveal the coat of arms of the builder, Sir Rhys ap Thomas.
DI2008_0183 NPRN 92709
Courtesy Howarth-Loomes collection

Below: An interior of the court at Tretower, Breconshire, in 1934. The upper floor of the north range was reconstructed for greater comfort in the late fifteenth century by Sir Roger Vaughan and his family.
DI2008_0158 NPRN 16305

extended over the next 150 years: comfort and restrained splendour, without much pretence of defence, mark the great hall and the high-quality roof trusses.

Carew Castle, Pembrokeshire, was transformed in successive generations. At the end of the thirteenth century, Nicholas de Carew rebuilt the castle to a courtyard design: its west wing with first-floor hall is flanked by two massive drum towers, and the semi-octagonal chapel tower has a first-floor chapel with a fine, cross-rib vaulted ceiling. Sir Edmund de Carew sold the castle to Rhys ap Thomas, who enjoyed royal favour under Henry Tudor. Rhys converted the site into a lavish home worthy of an influential knight: a fine hall porch was built in 1506 at the time of celebrations to mark his election to the Order of the Garter, and twentieth-century conservation has revealed heraldic arms over the doorway. In 1558 Carew was rented to Sir John Perrott, who completed its conversion into a residence of the highest quality: his great north range was lit by large mullioned windows, all glazed, and its top floor housed a long gallery.

Raglan, one of the last castles to be built in Britain, is one of the finest. A courtyard castle of the fifteenth century in the newest design, it combines fortification with sumptuous accommodation, juxtaposing an imposing gatehouse with twin hexagonal towers and a range of state apartments. The evolution of residential accommodation at Carew and Raglan marks the transition from castle to fortified manor and, ultimately, to grand country house.

Susan Fielding

039 Religious Life and Churches

The fifteenth-century wall painting of St Christopher and the Christ child in St Saeran's Church, Llanynys, Denbighshire.
Its vibrant colours and detail – watchman, windmill, fish, flowering staff and the Virgin's monogram – are remarkable.

DI2008_0286 NPRN 155246

Above: Hodgeston Church, Pembrokeshire.
DI2007_0630 NPRN 403981

Right: The central tower at St David's Cathedral, Pembrokeshire.
DI2005_0788 NPRN 306

Below: The rood screen at Partrishow, Breconshire, photographed in 1930.
DI2008_0157 NPRN 163422

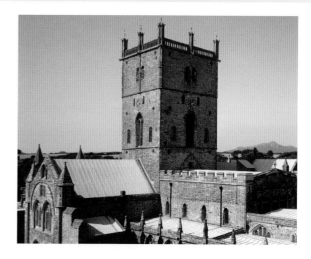

Wales has a particularly rich religious heritage from its medieval past: from large-scale monasteries to small parish churches, from vibrant cathedrals to ruined chapels. The Royal Commission has striven to investigate and record them all, their structures and their furnishings, whether the buildings are sited in modern towns or rural villages or stand isolated in the countryside. In so doing, it has employed a range of techniques, including investigation in its own and others' archives, detailed surveys on site, and aerial photography. By the beginning of 2008, its centenary year, the Royal Commission had placed on Coflein more than 1,000 digitised images from its archive of these buildings, and the number continues to grow.

The cathedral of St David is the largest and most important ecclesiastical building in Wales and is a fine example of the heights that medieval people were willing to scale to show their Christian faith. The present cathedral mostly dates from 1180-1220, although alterations and additions continued through the centuries: for instance, the original main central tower collapsed in about 1220, and was rebuilt with pointed arches to form the current structure; recent dendrochronology by the Royal Commission has confirmed its rebuilding in the fourteenth century. By 1869 further work was carried out to strengthen the dangerously faltering tower and a restoration of ceilings and roofs was undertaken.

The Royal Commission's archive contains many examples of smaller but equally fascinating sites. One such is the medieval free chapel at Hodgeston Church, Pembrokeshire. Although restored in the nineteenth century, this is largely a medieval church, which boasts an impressive, unusually slender, west tower. Inside the church is a thirteenth-century vaulted nave and an important fourteenth-century chancel with sedilia (decorated seats) and piscina (stone wash basin) of the same period.

Medieval wall paintings have been the subject of special investigation by the Royal Commission. They rarely survive today and where they do they are frequently fragmentary or in poor condition; but they can enhance our historical understanding of Welsh art and religion. The typical medieval church was full of vibrant colours; paintings might cover every available wall, sometimes spreading to the ceilings and vaults. The main purpose of these paintings was simple: to illustrate to a largely illiterate populace the teachings of the Bible. One such example dating from the fifteenth century is the large painting at St Saeran's Church, Llanynys, which depicts St Christopher carrying the Christ child across a river.

Some buildings illustrate the phases of development that religion underwent in the Middle Ages. St Ishow's Church in Partrishow is one example: although containing fragments from an eleventh-century church, most of its interior dates from the fourteenth and fifteenth centuries. Most strikingly, St Ishow's contains fixtures and fittings that demonstrate the radical changes which took place in the liturgy; they include pre-Reformation stone altars, a rood screen of about 1500 and a number of post-Reformation wall paintings. The Christian faith and religious devotion of medieval people still leave their mark in every corner of Wales.

Christopher Nicholas

040 Monks and Pilgrims

One of the earliest photographs in the National Monuments Record:
a salt paper print of Valle Crucis Abbey, Denbighshire, by John Forbes White in 1855.
DI2006_0430 NPRN 95205

Above: Stone corbel at St Winifride's well, Holywell, Flintshire.

DI2008_0349 NPRN 32328

Below: A reconstruction plan of the priory at Brecon, now Brecon Cathedral.

DI2008_0350 NPRN 96574

After the Norman conquest change came quickly to the communities of Christian monks in loose groupings of cells and churches which had been established in Wales, as in Ireland, from the sixth century onwards. Wave upon wave of new religious foundations, based directly or indirectly on St Benedict's rule, swept across England and into Wales. Religious reform was central to the conquest, and monasteries and friaries were part of the outcome.

One of the earliest Norman monasteries was at Brecon, where a priory was built as a daughter house to the Benedictine abbey founded by William the Conqueror at Hastings. It was never within the walled area of Brecon, but it confirmed the importance of the settlement and its place on the pilgrim route to St David's. The priory was enlarged in the centuries before the Reformation, and in 1923 became the cathedral church of the new diocese of Swansea and Brecon. In 1994 the Royal Commission published its detailed survey of the church to mark the 900th anniversary of the priory's foundation.

From the twelfth century the Cistercians, who followed a stricter interpretation of Benedict's rule, became the most prolific order of monks in Wales, and their remote locations became an attraction. They founded thirteen abbeys, from Margam and Tintern in the south to Whitland and Strata Florida in the west, and Valle Crucis in Denbighshire. These abbeys had large churches in precincts the size of a small town – a physical presence that must have seemed awesome to local inhabitants. They also revolutionised the economy by farming on an industrial scale. Outlying farms (or granges), often best located today from the air, might be many miles from the parent monastery. The administrative hub of these enterprises was the abbey's chapter house: at Margam the delicacy and dignity of the ruined chapter house still impress.

From the thirteenth century the growing towns were served by the preaching orders of friars. Their friaries were more modest in scale and fewer in number: the only Carmelite friary (founded in 1289) was at Denbigh, though the Dominicans (or 'Black Friars', from their robes) had houses at Rhuddlan, Haverfordwest and elsewhere. Few of their remains have survived urban developments since the Middle Ages, but at Brecon the Dominican friary's church is now part of Christ College, Brecon.

Religion as much as trade was a reason for travelling in the Middle Ages. Large numbers of both religious and lay folk went on pilgrimage, which was an essential part of the journey of life: religious houses offered food and drink at their gates and even provided lodging. Many monasteries and churches housed sacred relics, like the holy taper in Cardigan's priory, the Virgin Mary's image at Penrhys in the Rhondda, and St Winifride's holy well in Flintshire, where a surviving stone carving depicts a porter carrying a sick pilgrim. The saint's shrine at St David's, which William the Conqueror visited, was one of the most venerated pilgrim destinations in the British Isles.

Peter White

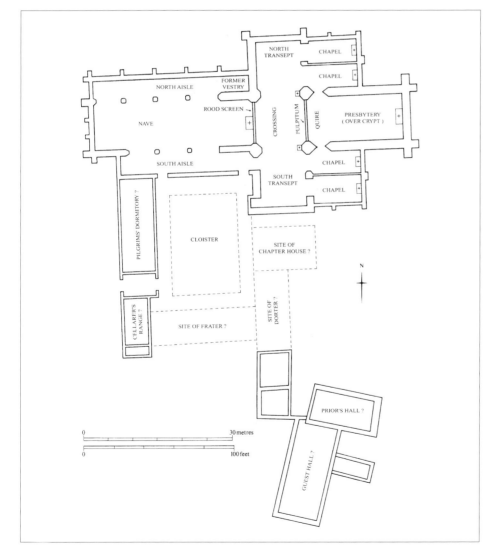

NORTH TRANSEPT
CHAPEL
CHAPEL
NORTH AISLE
FORMER VESTRY
ROOD SCREEN
CROSSING
PULPITUM
QUIRE
PRESBYTERY (OVER CRYPT)
NAVE
SOUTH AISLE
CHAPEL
SOUTH TRANSEPT
CHAPEL
PILGRIMS DORMITORY?
CLOISTER
SITE OF CHAPTER HOUSE?
N
CELLARER'S RANGE?
SITE OF FRATER?
SITE OF DORTER?
PRIOR'S HALL?
GUEST HALL?

0 ———— 30 metres
0 ———— 100 feet

041 Towns

Conwy's superbly preserved walls contain the medieval layout of the town at the end of the thirteenth century.
Aberconwy House is at the corner of the street, bottom left.

DI2008_0416 NPRN 95280

*Above: The fortified bridge
at Monmouth.*
DI2006_1147 NPRN 24219

*Right: Tenby town wall and
gateway, Pembrokeshire, in 1979.*
DI2006_1714 NPRN 127

*Below: Aberconwy House,
Conwy, Caernarfonshire.*
DI2006_1481 NPRN 25978

Although many of Wales's towns originated in the Middle Ages, there is no Welsh Siena among them, nor even a medieval 'shambles' like that at York. Often the only reminder of a town's medieval past is the street plan, and even that may not always be immediately obvious to us today. At Montgomery and Llanidloes the regular, grid-like pattern of medieval streets and a market square have been respected by later builders. However, some medieval urban buildings other than churches and castles do survive.

A number of the larger towns were defended by stone walls. Many of these have long since vanished but substantial defences remain at Caernarfon and Conwy, where they were integrated with the massive Edwardian castles, and also at Chepstow and Tenby, where the thirteenth-century walls are punctured by an elaborate medieval gateway known as the Five Arches. At Denbigh the walls surround an open space because of the gradual removal of the original borough to another site, while further remains may still be seen in other towns, such as Pembroke, Brecon and Beaumaris. At Monmouth the medieval bridge across the River Monnow is still protected by the town's West Gate; this is the only surviving medieval fortified bridge in Britain and it dates from the latter part of the thirteenth century.

Few medieval administrative buildings are left, but in Ruthin the former courthouse of the marcher

lordship of Dyffryn Clwyd, now a bank, probably dates from the third quarter of the fifteenth century, having been built after the Glyn Dŵr revolt. The town hall at Bangor, begun in about 1500, was originally the bishop's palace. Ruthin has other medieval buildings, but most towns that have any such structures at all can only boast scattered houses rather than complete streets. One of the outstanding medieval town houses in Wales is Aberconwy House in Conwy, so often overshadowed in the town by the late sixteenth-century Plas Mawr. Aberconwy House is a fine example of a late-medieval merchant's jettied house, with a stone-built trading basement; it was built about 1420 near the quay of Conwy. A similar example is the early Tudor Merchant's House in Tenby.

It is particularly tantalising that so many towns once had buildings of this kind – like the original Bulkeley family's house at Henblas in Beaumaris – which were swept away in the nineteenth century. But recent documentary and dendrochronological research at the Royal Commission is indicating that houses assumed to date from the sixteenth or seventeenth century are, in fact, sometimes older, and that the medieval built environment in some of Wales's towns (Denbigh and Ruthin are but two examples) is richer than was once thought.

Antony Carr

042 Sea and Coast

Seasick pilgrims in a boat, carved on a misericord of about 1500 in the choir of St David's Cathedral, photographed in 1948.
DI2008_0016 NPRN 306

Above: Stone corbel, in the shape of a mermaid, for the roof of St Giles's Church, Wrexham. It probably dates from the late fifteenth century.

DI2008_0015 NPRN 162808

Right: The medieval fish weir at Newlands, Anglesey.

AP_2005_0266 NPRN 405412

Below: Excavation of the large fifteenth-century ship found at Newport, Monmouthshire, in 2002.

DI2008_0018 NPRN 307059

The twelfth-century traveller Giraldus Cambrensis wrote that the Welsh had little interest in shipping, but other accounts and archaeological evidence suggest Welsh involvement in coastal trade, sea transport and naval expeditions throughout the Middle Ages. Ships and sailors were recruited in Welsh ports by English kings and Welsh princes for service in war. In 1212 King John sent a fleet to destroy Llywelyn ab Iorwerth's ships, galleys and boats, and, some forty years later, Llywelyn ap Gruffudd assembled a fleet to counter an English threat.

The twelfth-century charters establishing regular markets in Cardiff, Neath, Pembroke and Swansea are evidence for the development of maritime trading centres. The liberties granted to the merchants of Swansea to build ships are of similar date. Trade across the Irish Sea was well established by 1260 and there is still an area of Dublin known as Villa Walensis (Welsh town). Tenby's prominence in trade with France, Ireland and Bristol Channel ports was supported in 1328 by Edward III's grant of a landing stage in order to bring supplies to the castle and town.

Archaeological finds like the Magor Pill boat, discovered in the Severn Estuary in 1994, are physical evidence of the types of vessels (cogs, hulks and galleys) involved in trade. Artistic representations also provide clues. The twelfth-century and later seals of the towns of Monmouth and Haverfordwest show contemporary craft, as does a carved seat or misericord from St David's Cathedral. The Magor Pill boat had overlapping planking (clinker-built), a side-steering oar and a primitive forecastle which can be seen in medieval depictions of 'hulks'. The misericord (photographed in 1949 as part of the National Building Record) may depict a story relating to St Nicholas, patron saint of sailors, or a scene from everyday Pembrokeshire life – seasickness was one of the hazards of sea travel then as now.

One of the major maritime discoveries in Wales is the fifteenth-century ship unearthed on the banks of the River Usk in 2002 during building works for Newport's Riverfront Arts Centre. Photographs and reports from the excavation are held in the National Monuments Record. Research by the Glamorgan–Gwent Archaeological Trust has found a reference in the papers of Richard Neville, earl of Warwick, that may be to the Newport ship. In correspondence in 1469 with Thomas Throkmorton, receiver of the lordship of Glamorgan and Morgannwg, Neville authorised various payments for work carried out on a ship at Newport. Shoring timbers, used to support the vessel in its mud berth, have been dated by dendrochronology to 1468 and 1469.

The records of religious houses such as the Cistercian abbeys of Margam, Neath and Tintern reveal that they were using sea transport for trade and were ship-owners in their own right (Neath Abbey is reported as owning a hulk in 1235). They also show that abbeys were keen to establish ownership of foreshore and rights to wreck material: in 1198 Aberconwy Abbey was granted exclusive rights to wreck by Llywelyn ab Iorwerth. Other legal documents relating to the foreshore provide evidence of the great number of fish weirs in daily operation, and coastal aerial photography by the Royal Commission continues to locate similar sites.

The sea could also represent a threat. The religious settlement on Bardsey Island (Ynys Enlli) was exposed to the piracy rife in the Irish Sea: in 1346 thirty well-armed men in two boats took away 'much of the food and drink and much other goods'.

Deanna Groom

043 Houses and Homes

Heritage in danger: the cruck frame of the derelict Denbighshire house, Ty-draw, photographed in 2003.
DI2008_0374 NPRN 35439

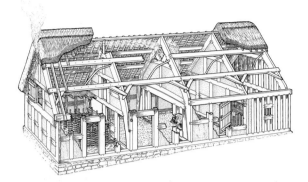

The modern study of medieval houses in Wales by the Royal Commission began at Ty-draw, Llanarmon Mynydd Mawr. This isolated, uninhabited but virtually complete, cruck-framed house (discovered by Bernard Mason, the National Buildings Record photographer) was surveyed by Peter Smith and Douglas Hague. Survey showed that this small dwelling, like early houses observed by Fox and Raglan in Monmouthshire, was hierarchically planned like a medieval great house, complete with cross-passage, open hall and dais. The open hall with its central hearth was set between storeyed inner and outer rooms. Stone walling had replaced the original timber-framed walls. The sophistication of the carpentry was recorded in an explanatory drawing, the first of many such reconstructions by the Commission.

The wide distribution of the smaller, mostly cruck-trussed medieval houses was subsequently charted on distribution maps. They show the dominance of the medieval timber-building tradition over the greater part of Wales, except in south Glamorgan and Pembrokeshire, the region of early Anglo-Norman settlement. However, the chronology and relative status of these houses remained mysterious. Fortunately, tree-ring dating has now revolutionised the study of medieval houses. No standing medieval house built

Right: A cutaway reconstruction drawing of the peasant hall at Tyddyn Llwydion, Pennant Melangell, Montgomeryshire.

DI2005_0042 NPRN 3020

in Wales before 1400 has yet been identified; the earliest known house was built from timber felled in 1402. Houses formerly regarded as fourteenth-century in date, including Ty-draw, are now known to have been built in the fifteenth and sixteenth centuries. The absence of fourteenth-century houses is explained, tentatively, by destruction during Owain Glyn Dŵr's revolt.

Where precise dating is possible, it establishes that people with greater resources built earlier and to a larger scale than those with lesser resources. Greater houses (the centres of lordship administration and monastic halls among them) were built in the first half of the fifteenth century. Houses of gentry status, like Ty-draw, usually with an ornate central truss in the hall, were mostly built in the second half of the fifteenth century: as witnessed by the reconstructed cutaway of the hall at Bryndraenog (page 129). Peasant halls, the dwellings of the free tenants of a lordship, were characteristically built after 1500, and especially in the mid-sixteenth century; the reconstruction drawing of that at Tyddyn Llwydion gives an impression of what they looked like.

In the towns, fifteenth-century hall and cross-wing dwellings differ little from their counterparts in the countryside. Perhaps as many as 1,000 medieval houses survive in Wales today: the work of discovery and interpretation continues. There is growing appreciation of the exceptional nature of this Welsh historical resource, for the durable house was the exception rather than the rule in medieval Europe. Moreover, the interconnections between building and literary culture help to contextualise Welsh houses to an unusual degree. They present serious conservation issues (as the once-derelict Ty-draw shows), but the more we understand medieval houses, the more we value them. Against the odds, Ty-draw has been restored.

Richard Suggett

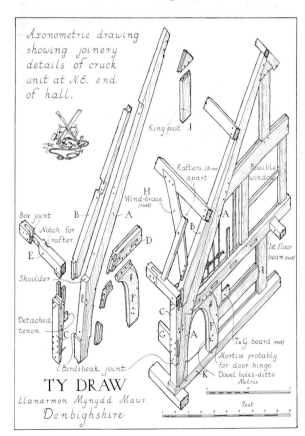

Axonometric drawing showing joinery details of cruck unit at N.E. end of hall.

King post J

Rafters 18ins apart

Possible window

Wind-brace (rest)

H

Box joint

Notch for rafter

A

B

A

B

D

1st floor beam (rest)

E

Shoulder

F

Detached tenon

C

C

G

A

F

T & G. board (rest)

Mortise probably for door hinge

Birdsbeak joint

K

Dowel holes-ditto

Metres

TY DRAW
Llanarmon Mynydd Mawr.
Denbighshire

Feet

Right: The Royal Commission's drawing of the fifteenth-century crucks at Ty-draw, Llanarman Mynydd Mawr, Denbighshire.

DI2008_0371 NPRN 35439

044 The Worlds of Work and Leisure

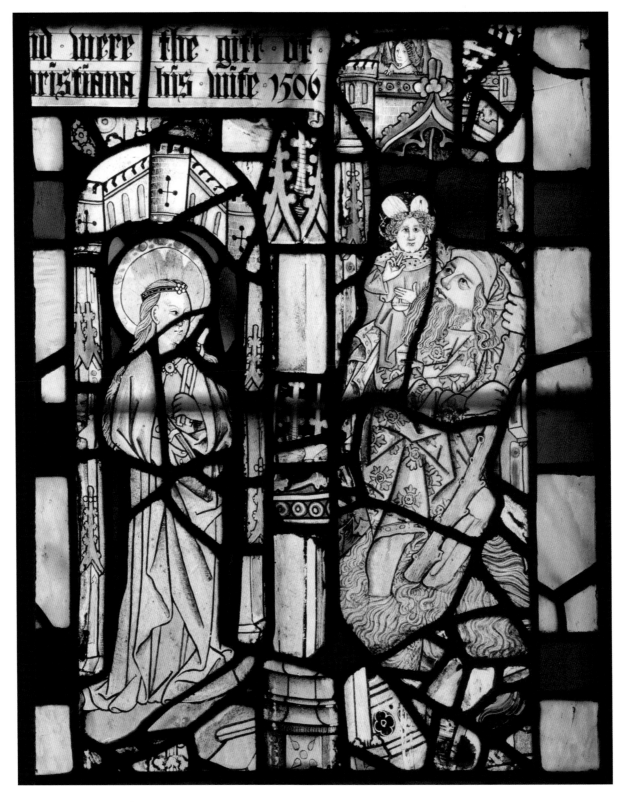

St Appolonia, left, bears a dentist's tools in the east window of the north aisle of All Saints Church, Gresford, Denbighshire.

DS2008_042_007a NPRN 165221

Above: Shipwrights shown at work on a misericord of about 1500 in the choir at St David's Cathedral, Pembrokeshire.

DI2008_0162 NPRN 306

Right: An angel playing bagpipes in the roof of St Giles's Church, Wrexham. Representing the Heavenly Host, it dates from the late fifteenth century.

DS2008_043_009 NPRN 162808.

Below: Ceramic tiles from Neath Abbey showing a hunting scene. They date from the mid-fourteenth century.

NPRN 133
Courtesy AC-NMW

Although the worlds of work and leisure do not figure prominently in the iconography of medieval Wales, the many ways of earning a living and the amusements and entertainments available to the well-born as well as to a broad swathe of the population may sometimes be glimpsed in surviving buildings and on monuments and brasses. The skills of the carpenter and wood carver have best survived, and are most readily appreciated, in the intricate rood screens of medieval churches like Bettws and Partrishow in the south-east, or in the gloriously-fashioned roof structures of ecclesiastical and domestic buildings which the Royal Commission's staff have reconstructed. They are here represented by the depiction of carpenters at work on building a ship, an image found on one of the misericords of late-medieval date which survive in the choir of St David's Cathedral – an illustration which reflects the numerous calls on the wood carver's expertise and the varied demands made on the country's timber-supply. Even more vital to the physical well-being of many Welsh folk were the skills of medical practitioners, though relatively little is known of their identities or their availability to the inhabitants of rural and urban communities. The need for medical services is illustrated by the representation in stained glass at All Saints Church, Gresford, of St Apollonia, tortured (according to legend) by having her teeth smashed with a club and by the later Middle Ages revered as the helper and patron of those afflicted by toothache. Armed with pincers, her image was a popular one in several late-medieval churches and reflects the devotion accorded by lay-folk in the cults of the age to saints blessed with particular powers of healing.

The worlds of work and leisure were not, however, entirely separate and frequently overlapped. The subjects in the designs of medieval floor and wall tiles, like those found at Neath Abbey or at Strata Florida, is often a valuable index of the secular and religious mentalities of the period. Some of the surviving examples portray a hunting scene, illustrating the delights of the chase enjoyed by the aristocracy and the well-born. But for numerous families, hunting in the forests, parks and warrens which dotted the medieval landscape was far more than a leisure activity: it was a necessity and an important means of augmenting their diets (although many seignorial regimes, jealous of their privileges within their domains in the fourteenth and fifteenth centuries, sought to curtail the rights of their tenants in this respect). The fifteenth-century roof bosses found in the church of St Giles at Wrexham, in an area remarkable for its fine fifteenth- and early sixteenth-century churches, show angelic musicians playing their instruments within an ecclesiastical and liturgical setting. Itinerant harpers and minstrels and those who practised the *crwth* for a living were also a common sight and a source of entertainment in numerous medieval communities, albeit an element often viewed by the authorities as a nuisance and a scourge, and even a source of sedition.

Llinos Smith

045 Commemoration and the Arts

The carved memorial to King Pabo at Llanbabo, Anglesey, of about 1380.
Similar figures at Llaniestyn, Anglesey, and in Bangor Cathedral may be by the same craftsman.

DS2007_440_002 NPRN 91214

Above: The finely carved alabaster tomb effigy of Sir William ap Thomas of Raglan, in St Mary's Church, Abergavenny, Monmouthshire.

DI2006_1154 NPRN 377

Right: The sleeping Jesse, a detail from the Tree of Jesse in St Mary's Church, Abergavenny.

DI2006_1153 NPRN 377

Below: Wall painting of the mocking of Christ, formerly in St Teilo's Church at Llandeilo Tal-y-bont, north Gower.

DI2005_0794 NPRN 94698

A rt forms in the Christian world of the Middle Ages were mainly inspired by individuals' beliefs and the desire of families and institutions to proclaim their devotion to God. They also celebrated families and their ancestors. Painters, sculptors in wood and stone and metal workers drew inspiration from the human condition and nature, from legend and chivalric romance, and they portrayed their subjects sometimes with realism, sometimes as grotesques, and often with humour. A carved stone grave slab of about 1380 in the church of Llanbabo, Anglesey commemorates the legendary fifth-century King Pabo, patron saint of the church, and it may have been commissioned by a notable local family. The image is one of many contributed by the Royal Commission to the *Buildings of Wales* series.

Churches, monasteries and Wales's four cathedrals were pre-eminent patrons of the arts. Much was destroyed after the Reformation, when monasteries were dissolved and puritans removed Christian ornamentation. Some items were transferred elsewhere, though the Royal Commission's dating of carpentry by dendrochronology at Llanidloes Church shows that the ceiling was not, as tradition has it, brought from the former abbey of Cwm-hir. If castles and manor houses of lords and gentry had survived other than as ruins we might have more examples of secular art than those that can be seen today in museums and roofless buildings. Townsfolk constructed public buildings such as town halls and private residences (like the Merchant's House in Tenby) that would have been richly decorated. Finally, families of the well-to-do patronised craftsmen in their homes and commissioned elaborate tombs for themselves. In the Hastings Chapel in Abergavenny Priory stands the tomb-chest with life-like effigies of Sir William ap Thomas (died 1446) and his wife Gwladys (died 1454). Its opulent alabaster carving

reflects the ambitions of this Welshman, who was knighted by King Henry VI and transformed Raglan Castle into a palace. It stands comparison with the best of gentry tombs in England and Wales.

The art forms were many: decorated fonts, carved screens and ivories, and roof bosses. In Strata Florida and Neath abbeys floor tiles were decorated with flowers, heraldry and hunting scenes. In St David's Cathedral misericords on the fifteenth-century stalls show comic human and animal figures. Wall paintings at Llandeilo Tal-y-bont and Llantwit Major were intended to impress as well as instruct. A painting of about 1500-1530 depicts the New Testament's description of the Mocking of Christ during the Passion: it is part of a series of evocative paintings recorded by the Royal Commission in the derelict church at Llandeilo Tal-y-bont, near Pontardulais, before its removal to St Fagans for restoration. The luxuriant stained glass at Gresford had similar purposes and in addition has Renaissance features. The stunning window in the nave of St Dyfnog's Church, Llanrhaeadr-yng-Nghinmeirch, near Denbigh (page 122), shows the figure of Jesse at the base of a complete Tree of Jesse, with the Virgin and Child at the top, supported by figures of prophets amid rich foliage. It is dated 1533, on the very eve of the Reformation that elsewhere destroyed much of the work of the medieval craftsman.

Ralph A. Griffiths

Early Modern Wales

Richard Suggett

Historians generally judge processes that continue over many years to be more important than single events. However, the beginning of early modern Wales may be said to date effectively from one action: the passing of the Act of Union in 1536. The end of the period is more indistinct: it could be said to wane as the Industrial Revolution gathered pace after the mid-eighteenth century.

The 1536 Act created the thirteen historic counties out of a patchwork of marcher lordships and the principalities of north and west Wales. The new shire administrations, the quickening pace of the economy and an increasing population all promoted a flowering of the principal towns. Almost simultaneous was the pivotal moment in the Reformation in Wales – the suppression of the monasteries, which was completed in 1539. This resulted in the decay of many great abbeys and their estates but at the same time the consolidation of great private landholdings that would dominate Welsh rural life until their own breakup in the nineteenth and twentieth centuries. The Reformation also fundamentally changed the ordering and decoration of the parish church and led to the first examples of a new building type, the nonconformist chapel. All these changes were reflected clearly in the buildings of Wales.

The shires created by the Act of Union survived as administrative units until the later twentieth century; they still have a lively presence reflected in vigorous county history societies and ongoing county history projects. They created a new administrative role for the principal towns in each county, where the shire hall became the focus of county administration. By contrast, while the previous symbols of seignorial authority, the castles, might retain a residual role as shire gaols, most continued their long decline into ruin. Welsh towns were generally small: research indicates that few had populations of over a thousand at the start of the early modern period. John Speed's town plans of the early seventeenth century not only show how restricted they were in size but suggest that some of those without new functions were in a state of decay. The Royal Commission's work in a range of towns has shown the importance of surviving architectural remains in telling the story of Welsh urban history, but suggests there is much still to be discovered.

It is easy to underestimate the vitality and influence of the new county towns. They were like vessels that filled and emptied for quarter sessions, assizes (or great sessions) and markets. A new building type made an appearance – the shire hall – where court

Opposite: The porch, Old Beaupre, Glamorgan, dated 1600 by an inscription:
'SIR THOMAS JOHNS KNIGHT / BWYLT THIS PORCHE WITH / THE TONNES [chimneys] IN ANO 1600 / HIS YERES 65 HIS WIFE 55'.

DI2006_1602 NPRN 19488

Below: The timber-framed courthouse at Llanidloes, Montgomeryshire, with an aerial view showing its location at the intersection of the principal streets.

DI2006_1969 and DI2008_0400 NPRN 32039

Above: Plas Mawr, Conwy:
the 1595 entrance from
High Street, photographed in
the mid-twentieth century by
Una Norman.
DI2007_0242 NPRN 16754

Right: The end elevation of the
shire hall at Denbigh: a survey
drawing showing the phasing.
DI2002_0242 NPRN 23423

sessions were regularly held. These were built and regularly rebuilt throughout the early modern period, but there are some precious and representative survivals. The timber-framed 'market hall' at Llanidloes, with a first-floor courthouse raised on timber piers above a covered market area, illustrates the first phase of courthouses. The replacement of timber civic buildings in stone is represented by the shire hall at Denbigh of 1572, rebuilt through the patronage of the earl of Leicester. Eighteenth-century redevelopments, which tended to exclude markets from the ground floors, are represented by Beaumaris courthouse, where a dedicated courtroom is preserved.

The columned space beneath many shire halls was often occupied by a shambles which provided a focus for the market. Weekly markets and seasonal fairs were a key trading activity that periodically filled the main streets of the early modern town and spilled into the churchyard. In some cases it is possible to reconstruct distinct areas associated with certain trades, as at Haverfordwest. The layout of many towns still reflects their historic market function, with wide streets that could be used for temporary stalls. Machynlleth retains a weekly street market with some claim to continuity from the medieval period, whereas at Denbigh the market area was partly infilled with buildings.

The survival of early modern buildings in towns has been very uneven [048]. A few very substantial town houses have survived, notably Plas Mawr in Conwy, but generally there has been continual attrition of the housing stock through redevelopment. Towns in early modern Wales were predominantly timber-built, and timber-fronted houses have been identified even in areas outside the main concentrations of timber building, as for example at Haverfordwest. However, the prevalence of timber is sometimes difficult to imagine today. Towns were vulnerable to fires that could destroy large areas, as happened at Builth and Presteigne. The approximate area of the catastrophic fire that consumed Presteigne in 1681 can be traced today from the absence of medieval buildings.

Many early modern and medieval buildings were destroyed by late Georgian or Victorian urban redevelopment, without any visual record being made. Some towns, like Aberystwyth, are almost wholly Victorian and later, even though their layout is more ancient. Nevertheless, older urban buildings can be identified behind later facades, especially in less-developed towns or those that retain their historic centres. The Royal Commission's survey of

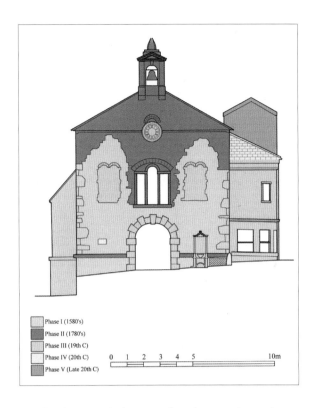

Phase I (1580's)
Phase II (1780's)
Phase III (19th C)
Phase IV (20th C)
Phase V (Late 20th C)

0 1 2 3 4 5   10m

Cowbridge revealed twenty-four houses dating from before 1700 in the High Street. Surveys of Presteigne, Haverfordwest and Denbigh have revealed similar concentrations of early-modern buildings.

Some distinctively urban building types, such as guild buildings, have disappeared entirely (although the symbol of the glovers' guild survives at Denbigh [048]). Relatively unaltered examples of other types are rare. Historic taverns often have a domestic or semi-domestic plan but they can be detected by their tendency to add specialised rooms, as at the Spread Eagle Tavern in Cowbridge where an eighteenth-century meeting room survives above a brewhouse dating from about 1740. Shops and commercial buildings, too, are scarce, while evidence for the booths and stalls typically used in market areas is purely documentary. Royal House in Machynlleth, first visited by the Commission in 1909, is notable for its continuity as a mercer's dwelling and store for some 400 years [047].

Shops thrived as trade and disposable incomes increased, helping to support the growing population of towns as well as the demand for consumer goods in surrounding areas. Trade was supported by a growing infrastructure: facilities at ports and creeks among the most important. Coastal trade has left a legacy of quays and wrecks as well as some specialised buildings, including warehouses like the extraordinary fortified tobacco store at Aberthaw [051.

Port books show the range of traded commodities, from ovens of imported Devon fireclay (still to be seen in some Glamorgan farmhouses) to exported bar iron. There was industry in Wales before the Industrial Revolution, not only mining for coal and metals but also lesser-known commercial undertakings, including several coastal salt works, one of which has been excavated at Port Einon in Gower. Iron, copper and lead were exported from furnaces established in the sixteenth and seventeenth centuries, there were important wireworks in Monmouthshire, and a mint was established at Aberystwyth, though it did not

survive the Civil War. Timber for charcoal was essential to these undertakings: ore was brought by sea to the Ysgubor-y-coed iron furnace established in a well-wooded part of north Cardiganshire, where the furnace and charcoal barn are in the care of Cadw.

A new elite emerged, beneficiaries of the Act of Union and the Reformation, and they favoured great houses of an architectural type that could be found across England and Wales. From these houses 'Leviathan' estates were consolidated in the seventeenth and eighteenth centuries. The houses of the Welsh squires, the new magistrates and county

Ysgubor-y-coed iron furnace and charcoal store, north Cardiganshire.
DI2006_0785 NPRN 93938

Bachegraig house and gate-house built by Sir Richard Clough, and prominently dated 1567.

DI2008_0444 NPRN 35642

officials who were also substantial landlords, are an interesting group. In the later sixteenth century open-hall houses were rebuilt with wings and upper floors [053]. They generally had a parlour at the entry and a first-floor great chamber above the hall and displayed a profusion of chimneys. Numerous examples have survived and topographical drawings

The enriched carriage arch of the great stable at Tredegar House, Newport, of 1684-8.

DI2008-0075 NPRN 20907

(especially those commissioned in the eighteenth century by Thomas Pennant) provide a visual record of many lost houses of this type. The earliest of them, like Monaughty in Radnorshire, were probably built in the first decades after the Act of Union. The Royal Commission's thematic volume on the greater houses of Glamorgan charts the themes and variations in plans and detailing. Some Welsh houses stand out as truly innovative in their Renaissance inspiration, notably Bachegraig in Denbighshire, built of brick and influenced stylistically by the high-roofed urban houses of the Low Countries. The verticality of these new houses (sometimes called towers by the poets), with their important first-floor chambers, provides a telling contrast with the long and low houses of sub-medieval type of the farmer.

The Civil War and interregnum interrupted elite building during the mid-seventeenth century; the dated addition to Uwchlawr'r-coed by John Jones, the regicide, is a telling exception. A new confidence after the Restoration prompted the rebuilding of several great houses, including Tredegar House near Newport and Newton House at Llandeilo [052]. These were advanced houses designed by professionals – though it has proved difficult to identify the architects concerned. The anonymity of architects continues to the mid-eighteenth century, even with regard to important houses like Nanteos, Ynysymaengwyn, Erddig, and many others. It is only from the later eighteenth century that the professional architect living

Rhosson-uchaf: the last relatively unaltered round-chimneyed farmhouse of the St David's area.

DI2006-1597 NPRN 30144

and working in Wales and the borders can be properly studied: most notably John Nash (page 186-7).

Other indications of status of the great house included dovecots, lavish stables, deer parks, fishponds, gatehouses, and heraldic ornament (features mapped in the Glamorgan inventory). There is growing appreciation of the number of early modern gardens surviving as earthworks, sometimes dramatically revealed by aerial photography, and spectacular painted representations survive of those at Newton House and Llannerch, but they are best appreciated from the recreated garden at Tredegar House. These mannered gardens seem to express a concern for order after the dislocation of the Civil War, and new lodges and gated entrances of growing elaboration maintained social distance architecturally.

The trend towards national tastes and styles in the squire's house may be contrasted with the growing regional character of farmhouses and cottages. One conventionally thinks of post-medieval domestic architecture as becoming more uniform, but the reverse was true in early modern Wales. In the sixteenth and seventeenth centuries a uniform hall-house plan, generally built using cruck frames, was replaced by an astonishing local diversity of types nuanced by region and class.

Peter Smith's classic map of regional house-types in *Houses of the Welsh Countryside* shows the varied geography of vernacular architecture [004]. The work of exploration on which the map was based, involving the classification of many hundreds of houses, made an enduring contribution to Welsh archaeology. It reveals some major contrasts in planning between west and east, and north and south. The mapping of architectural detail reveals some remarkably localised features: notable examples of this local distinctiveness are the round-chimneyed farmhouses of Pembrokeshire and, more particularly, the conical chimneys of the St Davids area.

The maps in *Houses of the Welsh Countryside* present a series of overlapping regional contrasts not only in terms of architectural detail but also in building materials. Stone versus timber was a fundamental contrast, with concentrations of timber buildings on the eastern side of Wales (though much timber building is disguised today behind later façades). Brick building before 1700 was largely restricted to north-east Wales. The Royal Commission's recording of vernacular buildings has investigated this contrast through intensive surveys of Glamorgan in the south and Radnorshire in the east, while it has shown that Caernarfonshire houses combined

The Snowdonian house: an explanatory drawing by Peter Smith published in Houses of the Welsh Countryside *(1975).*

DI2008_0441

timberwork of high quality with robust stone walls. The Commission's recording of clay (clom) buildings features in contributions to the Cardiganshire County History and its forthcoming volume on cottages.

Several new plan-types emerged, defined according to the diagnostic feature of the position of the main doorway in relation to the fireplace. The lobby-entry type was characteristic of Clwyd and north and central Powys, and the longhouse or hearth-passage type was characteristic of southern Powys, upland Glamorgan, upland Gwent, Carmarthenshire and Cardiganshire. Both types derived from the hall-

house plan and preserved the hall (now with a ceiling), with its bench and table at the upper end.

In the hearth-passage house, house and cowhouse were frequently combined under one roof. There has been considerable interest in this 'longhouse', sometimes claimed as the quintessential Welsh house. Recent research has shown that the longhouse had a wide distribution but that it was by no means found throughout Wales. It was concentrated in the pastoral areas of the centre, west and south but not in all areas of pastoral farming: it is noticeably absent from the north-west. The Commission's study of Radnorshire houses advanced the thesis that the longhouse was characteristic of areas that saw endemic cattle stealing in the later sixteenth and early seventeenth centuries [046]. It is probable that these combined ranges were not just convenient agriculturally but a prudent response to the crime of the period.

The early rejection of the hall-house plan in north-west Wales was remarkable. Within two or three generations open halls had been replaced by fully storeyed houses with enclosed fireplaces at ground and first floors. The Caernarfonshire inventory charted the remarkable ubiquity of the 'Snowdonian' house, which is also dominant across Merioneth. The earliest example dated by an inscription on the building is 1585 but dendrochronology carries the story back to about 1540. The cross-passage and the lower service-rooms of the medieval plan were retained but the hall was replaced by a kitchen with a large gable-end fireplace as its focus. A stair, frequently sited alongside the fireplace, led to the upper chambers that had replaced the old inner rooms.

A process of make do and mend can be identified in farmhouses, which were often altered piecemeal rather than rebuilt, with a surprising number retaining medieval fabric. However, in the early modern period there was considerable investment in new farm buildings, whose vernacular character is strongly marked. The earliest that survive in quantity are barns. Survey in Glamorgan has revealed a wide range in size and chronology from great sixteenth-century and seventeenth-century barns to smaller upland examples. The earliest barns dated by inscription were built in the seventeenth century. In Radnorshire the development of innovative combination ranges (integrating barn and cowhouse, often at different levels) can be charted through eighteenth-century date inscriptions, but other combinations (especially stables, carthouses and granaries) are later, dating from the late eighteenth century or more usually the nineteenth. The outline of a chronology of farm buildings has been established, but they remain under-recorded and among the vernacular buildings most at risk. Many types of farm building and architectural detail are highly localised or pleasingly idiosyncratic. The circular pigsties of south and west Wales are good examples of relatively minor buildings of regional character [055]; the dovecot constructed in a cave at Culver Hole, Gower, is unique.

The impact of the Reformation on religious buildings was profound. Its strictures were enforced by the new magistrates through the assizes and quarter sessions. The religious houses were swept

away, creating a supply of building materials for robbing within a large radius of a dissolved house, such as the now fragmentary Abbey Cwm-hir. The dissolution involved the destruction of centres of craft patronage as well as of religious life and it terminated a long period of beautification and renewal of church fabric, best illustrated by the ornate timber roofs and rood screens of the late Middle Ages [039]. Llanidloes parish church shows the often contradictory nature of the Reformation process. It has been argued that the church took advantage of the dissolution of Abbey Cwm-hir in

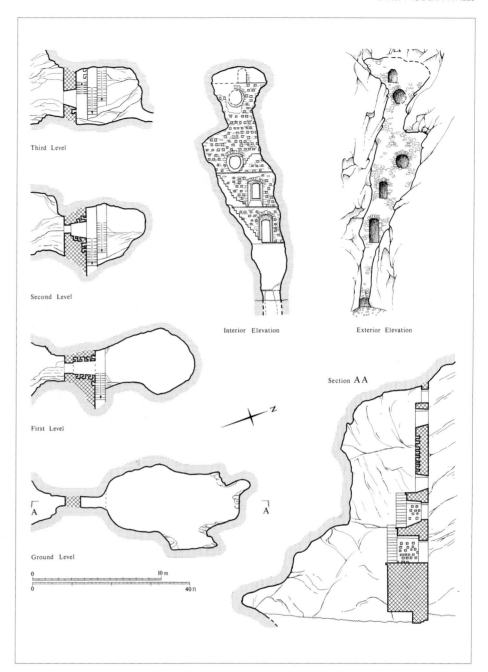

Survey record of the dovecot construction in a cave at Culver Hole, Gower.

DI2008_0442 NPRN 37514

Gresford parish church: the reclining effigy of John Trevor (1589), builder of Trevalyn Hall.

DS2008_042_011 NPRN 165221

1536 to retrieve an arcade from the abbey and reuse it to enlarge and re-roof the church. However, the 1542 completion date on one of the shields has now been confirmed by tree ring dating to show that this was a new hammer-beam roof complete with its winged angels; it was the last of its type.

Within a few years the interiors of parish churches had changed almost beyond recognition. Church goods were seized, images were destroyed or defaced, wall paintings were whitewashed over and sometimes replaced by black-letter texts and the royal coat of arms [049]. Occasionally, there is evidence for iconoclasm, as at Llandeilo Tal-y-bont, where a face

appears to have been obliterated deliberately. Some chapels of ease were permanently closed and converted to domestic use: the Commission has recorded three chapels in Glamorgan that were converted to houses in the early modern period. The Welsh gentry's support of the Anglican settlement is readily appreciated from their monuments and hatchments, which increasingly cluttered parish church chancels or special chapels. Some monuments are of considerable historical and artistic interest, for example the Stradling and Aubrey monuments in Glamorgan.

The post-Reformation reordering of parish churches is difficult to chart and has been overlaid by nineteenth-

Leicester's Church, Denbigh: the ruins photographed before the First World War.

DI2005_0752 NPRN 93307

century restorations. Very few new churches were built, but they included the extraordinary Leicester's Church begun in 1578 – first given serious attention in the Denbighshire inventory. This was a Protestant preaching hall of extraordinary size (55 metres long); the largest church erected in Britain between the Reformation and the seventeenth-century rebuilding of St Paul's Cathedral. The most important surviving example of seventeenth-century reconstruction is Mallwyd parish church, which was rebuilt according to Laudian principles by an intellectual clergyman, Dr John Davies, and included an extraordinary timber tower with Latin inscriptions [050]. Estate chapels at Rug and Gwydir, the latter recorded in the

Caernarfonshire inventory, preserve interiors of high craftsmanship.

The most significant purpose-built religious buildings of the period are the early nonconformist chapels. They are vernacular in spirit and low-key: despite the Toleration Act intended to protect them, chapel congregations did not want to draw attention to themselves. Internally the chapels were arranged according to Protestant principles. Maesyronnen in Radnorshire [054] and Capel Newydd at Llangian in Caernarfonshire are the best examples. From these unobtrusive buildings a very visible national religious architecture was to develop in the nineteenth century.

046 A Welsh Longhouse: Nannerth-ganol

Cutaway drawing of Nannerth-ganol showing the cruck-trussed longhouse after the insertion of the fireplace in the late sixteenth century.

DI2005_0027 NPRN 81416

Above: Nannerth-ganol before restoration.

DI2008_0403 NPRN 81416

Right: Nannerth-ganol after restoration.

DI2007_0381 NPRN 81416

Below: Reconstructed plan and elevations of Nannerth-ganol from Houses and History in the March of Wales.

DI2008_0402 NPRN 81416

The longhouse, combining dwelling and cowhouse in a single range, is often regarded as the quintessentially Welsh upland house. Iorwerth Peate coined the term 'longhouse'. He also discovered Nannerth-ganol, near Rhayader, which, as a classic longhouse, occupies a prominent place in the literature.

The Royal Commission's survey of Radnorshire houses provided the opportunity to reassess Nannerth-ganol and place it in its historical context. The cutaway drawing by Geoff Ward shows the essential features of the house. Nannerth-ganol was a substantial stone-built range with thick walls and an intercommunicating house and cowhouse that could be secured from the inside. The house is cruck-framed and these great arcing timbers, still smoke-blackened in places, belong to the first building phase. Later a fireplace was inserted against the cruck. The unusually tall and slender chimney expressed the pride of the owner of Nannerth-ganol in his new, heated house.

This homestead, it must be emphasised, was not a poor man's house. The builder of Nannerth-ganol could probably have afforded to build a house of a different type if he had wanted to. The longhouse needs to be understood in terms of its historical context, but who built it and when was it built?

Dendrochronology has established that the timber used for the cruck-trusses was felled in the mid-sixteenth century: building work was well under way

in spring 1556, and a construction date towards the end of the sixteenth century is probable for the inserted fireplace.

Documents show that Nannerth-ganol was held on a long lease by Bedo (or Maredudd) ap Steven, whose sons were indicted in 1557 at the Radnorshire great sessions on three separate counts of cattle stealing: Thomas as principal and Edward as accessory. They failed to answer the charges and were outlawed. Both must have 'fled to the woods' and were only able to return when a general pardon was declared at the beginning of Elizabeth's reign. Nannerth-ganol was still a new-built house when Thomas and Edward returned to plead their pardons and to be bailed for their future good behaviour.

It is extraordinary that these accusations of cattle theft should have coincided so closely with the construction of Nannerth-ganol. Cattle theft was a risky but obvious short cut to capital accumulation and it may be, of course, that it helped to finance the large, professionally-built house-and-byre homestead. The capacious and secure cowhouse of a longhouse might be used not only to safeguard cattle but also to conceal them. The exact circumstances at Nannerth-ganol are not recoverable but it is clear that the longhouse has to be understood in part in relation to a pastoral economy in which cattle rustling was common.

Longhouses were the products of particular historical circumstances. They offered additional security for over-wintered stock in areas prone to livestock theft. Indictments for cattle theft actually increased during the second half of the sixteenth century, reaching a peak at the beginning of the seventeenth. The house-and-byre homestead may be understood as a prudent response to these conditions.

Richard Suggett

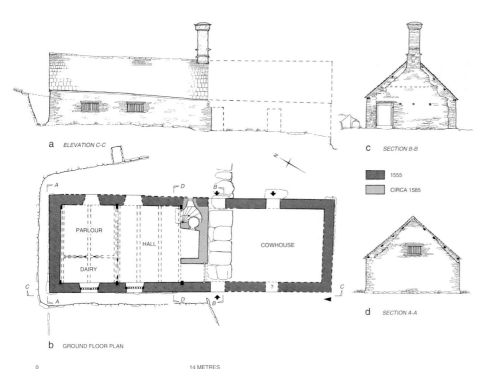

a *ELEVATION C-C*

c *SECTION B-B*

1555

CIRCA 1585

PARLOUR

HALL

COWHOUSE

DAIRY

d *SECTION A-A*

b *GROUND FLOOR PLAN*

14 METRES

50 FEET

047 Royal House, Machynlleth

Royal House, Machynlleth, and the draper's shop at the front, photographed before the First World War.
DI2008_0398 NPRN 29929

Decorative plasterwork at Royal House.
DS2006_116_039 NPRN 29929

Painted decoration on the post-and-panel partition in the hall.
DS2006_116_029 NPRN 29929

The sixteenth-century principal room (hall) at Royal House after restoration, with the doorway into the addition.
DS2006_116_021 NPRN 29929

Surviving pre-Georgian town houses are rare in Wales, and early shops or commercial premises are exceedingly rare. Royal House is an example of a relatively unaltered mercer's dwelling and storehouse. It has some claim to be one of the oldest shops in Wales. When it closed in 1988 there had probably been a shop in the same location for 400 years or so. It was recorded as part of the Royal Commission's emergency recording programme, and after a period of great uncertainty it has been exemplarily restored.

Machynlleth was founded in the late thirteenth century and the town still preserves its T-shaped plan around the intersection of roads from the north, south and east. Its heart is the crossroads where the clock tower (erected 1873) stands on the site of a market hall and courthouse like that which still survives at Llanidloes. At regular intervals hundreds of people would flock to Machynlleth for the markets and the courts. Space was at a premium nearest the market hall, and characteristically urban buildings were located here that were not only dwellings but shops and storehouses. Royal House occupied a prime position in the town, between the parish church and the market hall.

It miraculously survived the nineteenth-century rebuilding of the town. Its long and low sub-medieval elevation contrasts with the adjacent tall nineteenth-century buildings. By the second half of the nineteenth century Royal House was so obviously different that some interesting historical claims were attached to the building. Postcard views advertised it as the oldest house in Wales, and of course maintained that King Charles I had stayed there – hence the name 'Royal House'.

How old is Royal House? It occupies an old 'burgage' plot that probably dates back to the origin of the town. The elongated range has three parts, with a dwelling set between an upper shop and a lower store. Some excellent vernacular detail survives, including a corbelled fireplace, a post-and-panel partition with traces of painted decoration, a double-ogee doorhead and decorative plasterwork. The architectural detail suggests a sixteenth-century date of building, and the relatively unaltered roof produced tree-ring dates of spring 1561 for the front range and 1576 for the lower range. Town houses are difficult to document but, remarkably, a series of deeds relating to Royal House (then called Tŷ-yn-y-lon) has been preserved. They show that it has been occupied by a succession of mercers since the seventeenth century. The lower unit was a store and referred to in 1628 as 'Sgubor Newydd', or the new barn. Mercers were the linchpin of the economy of a town like Machynlleth. Cattle were exported from its market but in return Machynlleth imported goods (primarily textiles but also books, sugar, spices, and other foodstuffs) that were redistributed from the shop to the surrounding countryside.

Royal House is one of very few early, truly urban buildings in Wales. It is not a grand piece of architecture but it typifies Machynlleth's trading history. Its importance lies in its continuous use on the same spot for the same purposes – shop, dwelling, store – for four centuries. The original house has never been demolished but it has been repeatedly adapted to new circumstances. Every alteration has successively left its mark on the building's fabric.

Richard Suggett

048 Hidden Architectural Detail in Denbigh

The stair at The Bull Hotel displaying the gloved hand on the newel-post.

CD2005_627_033 NPRN 26894

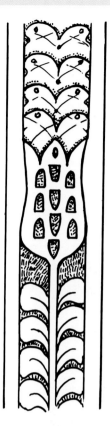

Above: The tulip motif on the stair at 1 Park Street.

DI2008_0407 NPRN 27620

Right: The elaborate mid-seventeenth-century well-stair at the Forum Restaurant, High Street.

CD2005_627_031 NPRN 27338

The 1643 heraldic overmantel displaying the double-headed eagle may have prompted the naming of The Eagles Hotel.

CD2005_628_002 NPRN 26773

The Royal Commission surveyed a selection of Denbigh town houses after the emergency recording in April 2002 of Bryn-y-parc, a timber-framed courtyard range of the sixteenth century that had been badly fire-damaged. The work was complementary to the recently established Denbigh Townscape Heritage Initiative (THI). A selective survey informed the THI's work and enhanced the National Monuments Record with new information about historic town houses, which often preserve older detail behind nineteenth-century façades. Some fine architectural detail was lost in the fire at Bryn-y-parc, including an important mid-sixteenth-century carved armorial panel, which fortunately had been photographed some years before. However, the Commission's survey revealed hidden features in many of Denbigh's older town houses.

Urban houses, even those of medieval origin, are storeyed and sometimes have three floors with attics, and many of these tall town houses preserve attractive stairs, often of seventeenth-century date. Well-stairs, where flights were arranged around an open space or well, created opportunities for architectural display. The early sixteenth-century example at The Bull Hotel rises to the attic and has carved and moulded balusters, a strap-work moulded string, a moulded hand-rail and square newel-posts, formerly with finials and pendants, one of which survives at the base. Each newel-post displays the carved motif of a gloved hand, related to the town's guild of glovers, which may well have met in an upper room of the inn.

The full potential of the well-stair for impressive display is realised at 29 High Street (The Forum Restaurant). The building's elaborate mid-seventeenth-century well-stair extends from cellar to attic. It has moulded and pierced splat-balusters, carved lozenges to the strings, a moulded handrail, carved strap-work newel-posts (formerly with elegant finials) and surviving pendants.

Two later seventeenth-century stairs with barley-twist balusters survive at 2 Hall Square and 1 Park Street. Newel-posts provided a convenient surface for decoration. Continuity of motif between the

earlier and later seventeenth century is shown by the use of vertically linked 'S' motifs at The Bull Hotel, 1 Park Street, and The Crown Hotel. However, the bottom newel at 1 Park Street prominently displays a motif that was novel at the time it was carved – the tulip – an early Welsh expression of the 'tulipomania' that swept Europe from the Netherlands in the seventeenth century.

The decoration found in these stairs may be compared with other contemporary details, especially plaster overmantels and date inscriptions. At 15 Vale Street a diagonally-set fireplace inserted into what was formerly an open hall has an overmantel with the interlinked initials 'PTA' below the date '1639'. The slightly later overmantel at The Eagles Hotel, Back Row, is more elaborate, having a double-headed eagle on a shield with flanking initials, 'IFP 1643', with linking strap-work and fleurs-de-lys. Many more buildings might be mentioned, but these few examples highlight the hidden seventeenth-century architectural delights of Denbigh, which have their counterparts waiting to be discovered in other historic Welsh towns.

Geoff Ward

049 Post-Medieval Church Wall Paintings

*Llanynys parish church, Denbighshire: an accomplished painted panel (oil on canvas) dated 1661
with the arms of Charles II, the newly restored monarch.*

DI2005_1090 NPRN 155246

Above: Memento mori (restored) in Llaneilian parish church, Anglesey.
DI2005_1082 NPRN 32283

Below: Creed in elaborate cartouche in Llangybi parish church, Monmouthshire.
DI2006_1710 NPRN 220654

The Reformation had as great an impact on the decoration of churches in Wales as it had in England. Orders in Council of 1548 required the obliteration of all images, whether in the form of statuary, painted glass or wall paintings, and, as in England, the local clergy and people obeyed more or less diligently. While few statues survived the iconoclasts, in most cases paintings were simply covered by lime-wash, and many have been rediscovered and recorded by the Royal Commission.

The Orders in Council gave specific instructions to replace pictures by texts from the reformed Prayer Book and 'chosen sentences' from the newly-translated Bible. The standard suite of the Lord's Prayer, Apostles' Creed and Ten Commandments would have been found in almost every church from the late sixteenth century onwards, in English or Welsh depending on the locally dominant language. In some cases (such as Eglwys Gymyn, Carmarthenshire, and Llandeilo Tal-y-bont, Glamorgan) a succession of texts shows a shift in language. They were copied from printed examples using the same black-letter script (and incorporating the printer's variants of spelling). They were usually bordered in imitations of picture-frames or sculpted tablets – a Paternoster at Llandeilo Tal-y-bont of about 1600 even hangs from a painted 'picture-wire'. The 'chosen sentences' include psalm texts such as the Psalm 84.9-10 at

Cilycwm, Carmarthenshire, and didactic or hortatory verses such as John 14.15 at Partrishow, Breconshire, and Matthew 26.6-8 at Myddfai, Carmarthenshire. There is a notable series, possibly of Commonwealth date, at Rhuddlan, Flintshire.

After the Restoration there was a change in style and content. The Royal Arms became a standard item, sometimes associated with overtly pro-monarchist political texts. It is interesting to note that in at least two cases (Llandeilo Tal-y-bont, Glamorgan, and Llangelynen, Caernarfonshire) these were in English, while contemporary liturgical texts were in Welsh. Lettering changed to reflect new printing styles. Figures again became acceptable, though limited in number: Moses and Elijah might accompany the Ten Commandments (as at Cilycwm), and the emblematic figure of Death replaced St Christopher opposite the main door (as at Llangar, Merioneth). Sometimes the composition became quite complex, as at Pennant Melangell in Montgomeryshire, where the Ten Commandments on two panels were flanked by the Creed and the Lord's Prayer as well as figures. Occasionally the painter might leave a signature or a monogram, such as 'J. Cartwright de Aberedw' of 1733 at Colva, Radnorshire. Otherwise, his identity may be identified in parish records (such as Thomas Jones, who was paid £3 for painting the Ten Commandments at Pennant Melangell in 1791) or by a stylistic similarity with other artistic work such as monumental tablets.

Inscriptions continued to be part of the decoration of churches and nonconformist chapels in the nineteenth century, with the paradoxical situation that while new Gothic revival churches were being decorated with inscriptions (as at Llanfrynach, Breconshire, 1855), seventeenth- and eighteenth-century texts were scraped off the walls of medieval churches in the name of ecclesiology (as at Llanbadarn Fawr, Cardiganshire). For any type of painted decoration, changes in taste mean the loss or concealment of the old, which is only to be revealed during later restoration. Hence the National Monuments Record contains many fragments of inscriptions, such as the possible Lord's Prayer and frames of two others at Llanbister, Radnorshire, concealed for a while but hinting at the richness of many post-medieval church interiors.

A. J. Parkinson

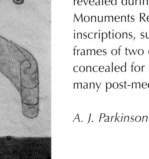

050 Dr John Davies of Mallwyd and his Tower

The porch and tower of Mallwyd parish church, Merioneth, in 2002.

DI2007_0353   NPRN 43907

Above: Unicorn and fleur-de-lis of the royal coat of arms carved on the chancel roof truss.
DI2008_0496 NPRN 43907

Right: Cutaway drawing showing the timber construction of the tower.
DI2008_0428 NPRN 43907

Below: Pont-y-Cleifion, the dramatic single-arched bridge built by Dr John Davies in the first half of the seventeenth century.
DI2007_0350 NPRN 24201

D r John Davies (died 1644) is today regarded as the greatest scholar of the later Renaissance in Wales. His contemporaries admired him as a builder or architect as well as a scholar. During a long period as rector of Mallwyd in Merioneth, John Davies rebuilt the rectory, established a garden and built three bridges of increasing difficulty, culminating in Pont-y-Cleifion, a single-span bridge over a chasm. However, his most ambitious work was the comprehensive rebuilding of the parish church, a task that preoccupied him for three decades.

The old parish church at Mallwyd was a single chamber and John Davies extended the chancel and added a new west tower and south porch. He completely re-roofed and reordered the church, and in the process destroyed most of the surviving late-medieval detail. Several building phases may be distinguished, but they were unified by a distinctive ovolo moulding.

The new timber tower dominated the west end of the church. The Royal Commission's drawing shows its timber framework in perspective. The structure is cleverly engineered with a complex system of posts and braces. It is not free-standing but takes advantage of the masonry of the west gable to lend it rigidity. There are three floors. At the base of the tower a special chamber was partly screened from the nave by a system of braces. The bell-ringers' stage above is framed by massive braced posts, which rise to the top of the tower and frame the bell chamber. Prominent, pious, Latin inscriptions were made on each face of the belfry in perforations of the weatherboarding that helped carry the sound of the bells.

The room at the base of the tower was in effect a 'baptistery' with a screen and canopy. John Davies was evidently concerned to provide the church with a 'baptismal room' that matched the new chancel or 'communion room'. The focus at the west end was

the font; the focus of the chancel was the altar placed in the traditional way at the east end. In Dr Davies's church the spiritual progression from baptism or rebirth to communion was deliberately and strongly marked architecturally for the congregation, which gathered in the body of the church between font and altar.

The rebuilding of Mallwyd church belonged to a general phase of early Stuart church restoration which assumed increasingly ideological importance, signalled especially by the position of the altar. In the 1630s until the Civil War hundreds of parish churches were repaired and reordered according to traditionalist (Laudian) principles, new domestic chapels were built by landed proprietors for the use of family and tenants, and Archbishop Laud himself initiated the restoration of St Paul's Cathedral, soliciting contributions from the English and Welsh county and clerical elite, which Dr Davies himself collected in Merioneth. Little is known about the majority of these re-edified churches, probably reordered rather than rebuilt, and now disguised by later restorations. Dr Davies's church assumes a special architectural significance because its interior ordering can be reconstructed and its seventeenth-century fabric is largely intact.

Richard Suggett

051 Marsh House: A Fortified Warehouse

Marsh House in the shadow of Aberthaw power station, Glamorgan, photographed in 1982 shortly after partial demolition.
DI2008_0395 NPRN 19309

Above: Musket loop at Marsh House.

DI2008-0393 NPRN 19309

Right: Ground plan of the Marsh House complex.

DI2008_0405 NPRN 19309

The maritime trade of seventeenth-century Wales was carried on from dozens of small ports and creeks along the western seaboard. These traded not only coastally but with continental ports and as far afield as the West Indies. Archaeology provides constant reminders of the importance of this trade in the form of imported ceramics and the innumerable bottles and clay pipes from which imported wines and tobaccos were consumed. The architectural remains of this trade are slight.

However, fieldwork by the Royal Commission brought to light a fascinating legacy of seventeenth-century trading on the coast of Glamorgan. Marsh House is situated near the small port of Aberthaw, in the shadow of Aberthaw power station. It comprised a fortified compound containing a storehouse, later extended outside its perimeter, and what was once a small but imposing lime-plastered house.

The compound was defensible, with a single entrance on the north side. It was bounded by a stone wall 2.5 metres high, pierced at regular intervals by musket loops. The storehouse, too, was provided with musket loops: one was sited to defend the entrance to the compound.

What was its function and why was it defensible? Marsh House is unique in Wales but it belongs to a class of fortified compounds scattered across the western seaways from Ireland to New England. It resembles some of the 'bawns' or fortified enclosures recorded in County Down and elsewhere, some associated with English and Scots planters. This type of structure, developed in Elizabethan Ireland, was transplanted to Virginia in the early seventeenth century at the pioneering Martin's Hundred plantation.

Who built Marsh House and when? Documentary evidence suggests that the storehouse and compound were built around 1636 by Thomas Spencer, a wealthy and ambitious merchant trading through Aberthaw in the first half of the seventeenth century. Spencer was involved in the West Indies trade, and between 1636 and 1640 was importing tobacco shipped from St Kitts. The tobacco trade was dominated by Crown-appointed monopolists and was supposed to enter London through the Custom House Quay.

Thomas Spencer was involved in an illegal trade and required the security provided by Marsh House to protect his enormously valuable cargoes. A single shipload of tobacco could be worth several thousand pounds and was stored in the warehouse for resale when the time was favourable. Spencer's foray into this tricky trade was short-lived and came to an end with the loss in 1639 of his largest ship, the 'Great

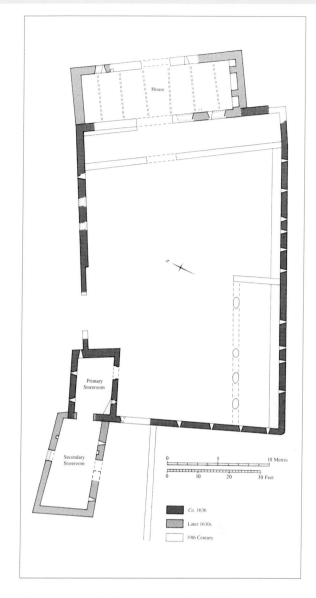

Thomas', to Turkish pirates, and with the onset of the Civil War.

Marsh House survived until the 1980s when, not long after discovery by the Royal Commission, it was partially demolished before its importance was fully appreciated. An interim building preservation notice was placed on the building but the site was eventually used as a dumping ground for ash from the power station, now the major user of the port of Aberthaw.

This is an edited version of the accounts by Matthew Griffiths and Howard Thomas in Morgannwg *26 (1982), 84-8, and Howard Thomas and Jack Spurgeon in* Archaeologia Cambrensis *146 (1997), 127-37.*

052 Newton House, Llandeilo

The house and gardens at Newton House depicted not long after completion.

DS2007_163_002 NPRN 17603
Courtesy The National Trust.

Above: The great stair at Newton House.

DS2007_163_025 NPRN 17603

Right: One of the spectacular Restoration ceilings at Newton House.

DI2006_0822 NPRN 17603

Below: Aerial view of the present Newton House with the inner (service) and outer (stable) courtyards.

DI2006_0924 NPRN 17603

The Royal Commission's involvement with Newton House dates back to 1917. The Commission was then perhaps more interested in the archaeology of Dynevor Park, in which the house is set, than in the house itself: the castle, the medieval borough, and the lost manor house are described in an inquisition of 1532. In the Carmarthenshire inventory of 1917 the house was described as 'completely rebuilt'. This was a mistake, but an understandable one, as the inspecting officer seems not to have ventured inside, presumably deterred by the exterior, which had been recast in baronial style in 1856.

The sixth Baron Dynevor later pointed out that Dynevor Castle incorporated the earlier Newton House and retained much seventeenth-century detail. Apparently a date of 1660 had been seen in the roof. On entering the house one immediately has the impression of a Restoration house. In plan there is a double-pile arrangement, with a spine wall between entrance hall and great stair. The hall was no longer a significant room – as in the medieval hall-house. It was simply the ante-room before the parlour (saloon) and the withdrawing room: rather grand rooms with some spectacular ceilings which still survive.

The great stair is the major architectural feature of the house. It rises through three storeys and is a constant delight of bulbous balusters, a continuous, broad handrail, thick newel-posts, and carved pendants and finials. In houses lacking a gallery the stair could perform the function of a picture gallery. This was probably the case at Newton House. Miraculously, four seventeenth-century paintings survive depicting the house and parkland as they were not long after the house was built. Buildings are shown that can still be identified in the courtyards – a stable and barn. The meticulously ordered gardens seem to express the craving of the landed class for order after the uncertainties of Civil War and Commonwealth.

Who built Newton House? Traditionally the rebuilding has been ascribed to Sir Edward Rice (died 1663/4). Unfortunately, the '1660' date in the roof cannot now be verified; it was almost certainly a misreading of a nineteenth-century inscription in the plastered underside of the Victorian roof. The architectural detail could perhaps date to 1660, but the date seems impossibly early for the completion of a building project only recently made possible by the new conditions of the Restoration.

The National Trust and the Royal Commission decided that the only certain way to establish the building date was through dendrochronology. Fortunately, a sample with complete sapwood was obtained from the original oak roof-trusses. This gave a felling date of the summer of 1664 and establishes that, even if Newton House was started by Edward Rice, it can only have been completed by his brother Walter, who inherited the estate in 1664 and lived for another ten years. Recently discovered documents reveal that Walter Rice died in debt owing at least £3,500; his fortune had presumably been squandered on building Newton House. His dying words addressed to his importunate wife have been preserved: 'Ffye, will you not let me dye in quiett!'

Richard Suggett

053 'Painted Tapestries': Discoveries at Ciliau

A detail of the painting at Ciliau, Radnorshire, showing the agitated bird and the complacent cat. A tracing (left) reveals details that are not readily visible.

DS 2007_024_023 NPRN 81106

When the Royal Commission prepares a reconstruction drawing the emphasis is on revealing the structure of a building. Interiors can look rather empty and plain, as in the cutaway of Ciliau, a remarkable mid-Tudor gentry house that was designed with a traditional open hall but heated by a newly-fashionable lateral fireplace. It is probable that most sixteenth-century dwellings did not have much hall furniture beyond a table and benches, and any decorative scheme is usually lost forever; but vernacular houses do sometimes reveal their past in surprising ways. After the Commission completed this cutaway drawing, Roger Capps discovered that the plaster over the screen at the dais end of the hall concealed an extensive painted scheme.

The dominant motif of the painting is a freehand leaf-and-flower trail. Nevertheless, the painting is consciously structured to show a frieze above a main panel. The frieze initially appeared to be a repetitive design of luscious fruits, but careful cleaning revealed that these were bold acanthus leaves. The panel below has a lamp-black ground covered by trails of leaves and exotic flowers that flow unconstrained by the posts and panels making up the structure of the partition. The elongated and serrated leaves are depicted as folded or curling, with the back and front given different colours – brown-fawn and orange respectively. Interspersed among the foliage are several creatures. After cleaning it was apparent that a bird was confronting a rather complacent cat, the

Right: The painted screen at Ciliau revealed by the removal of plaster but before conservation.
DI2006_1740 NPRN 81106

earliest surviving depiction in Wales of this ubiquitous household pet. Elsewhere are another bird and a collared hound following the scent of an unseen quarry.

The painting was designed to imitate textiles of 'verdure' style, which were rich with depictions of vegetation. Tapestries, especially figurative tapestries, were an aristocratic taste but few survived in the long term. The problems of preservation are illustrated by the will of Bishop Rawlins of St Davids (who died in 1536), which describes his wall-hangings as gnawed by rats and eaten by moths. Contemporaries were aware of the vulnerability of expensive fabrics. It was more practical to paint the tapestry designs directly onto walls and partitions. Further discoveries at Ciliau have shown that three, and perhaps all four, walls of the hall were covered by these painted hanging imitations.

The painting must date from the period before the insertion of the hall ceiling in the early seventeenth century because the design runs behind the wall beams. Stylistically it belongs broadly to the period 1575-1625 and may be paralleled by a number of wall paintings in the Welsh Marches that employ the three-part divisions of the wall into dado, main panel and frieze, which have been analysed by Kathryn Davies, partly from material in the Royal Commission's wall paintings archive. The scheme can probably be more closely dated from documentary sources. There were two changes in ownership in the later sixteenth century. Ciliau was inherited in 1574 by John ap Robert (son of its probable builder, Robert ap Gwilym). Five years later he sold it to Edward Daunce of Hereford, gentleman. The new owner of 1579 is likely to have redecorated Ciliau in fashionable style.

Richard Suggett

Below: Reconstruction drawing of Ciliau showing the open hall; (a drawing prepared for Houses and History in the March of Wales, *2005, before the discovery of the wall paintings.*
DI2005-0051 NPRN 81106

054 Maesyronnen Chapel, Glasbury

*The interior of Maesyronnen Chapel showing the seventeenth-century and eighteenth-century furniture,
and the late-medieval cruck-truss embedded in the wall between house and chapel.*

DI2008_0392 NPRN 81403

The complexities of changing culture in the eighteenth century are illuminated in an unexpected way by Maesyronnen, one of the earliest and best-preserved nonconformist meeting-houses. As a chapel the building has been precisely dated to 1697, when it was registered at the assizes as a place of worship under the terms of the Toleration Act of 1689. However, the Royal Commission's study of Radnorshire houses showed that it was converted from a longhouse of medieval origin.

Maesyronnen is a substantial but low-key vernacular building that does not advertise its presence. Its seclusion is partly explained by the closed fellowship of the nonconformist Independents but also by the prejudice against members of the denomination, who were regarded as 'king killers' after the execution of Charles I. Its conversion was an example of the prevailing attitude of 'make do and mend', which led to the adaptation of buildings rather than demolition and new building. The original farmhouse was

Below: Reconstruction drawings, plan and elevation of Maesyronnen Chapel as built (prepared for Houses and History in the March of Wales *(2005).*

DI2008_0401 and DI2008_0474 NPRN 81403

replanned as a chapel-house with a central doorway, while the downhouse (for the animals) was thoroughly rebuilt as a meeting-house. A medieval cruck-truss has recently been exposed, still embedded in the rear of the chimney stack between house and chapel.

Externally the meeting-house was an early attempt at a symmetrical frontage. The windows were set between two end doorways which were provided with diminutive ornamental gables to provide visual balance with the gabled dormer windows that then existed on the house. The Royal Commission's perspective sketch shows a reconstruction of the front of the buildings at the time of their conversion, including a covered walk from house to chapel which is now lost. There was no attempt to make the rear symmetrical.

Internally the arrangements of the meeting-house provided a radical contrast to an Anglican place of worship. It was dominated by a pulpit in the middle of the long wall, facing the entry. Timber supports embedded in the wall show that the pulpit was originally cantilevered out at a higher level than it is now. There was no altar in this Calvinist plan but a substantial communion table was placed in the centre of the meeting-house – the original table with six turned legs has been superseded by a plain table flanked by two benches, one inscribed 'AP 1728'. Several early box pews survive, as well as some simple benches.

Two important points emerge from this early meeting-house, whose congregation was drawn from farming families. First, although its materials were local and vernacular, the planning was consciously radical, and indeed transnational, having its roots in the new religious practices coming from Geneva. Second, although the meeting-house is not externally ostentatious, internally it was full of furniture and artefacts of good craftsmanship. These included the multi-paned mullioned and high-transomed windows, the pulpit, the box pews, the communion table, and the pewter communion vessels of porringer type. In the chapel, as in the farmhouse, an attitude of make do and mend in building coexisted with an increasing interest in furnishings and other items of consumption.

The chapel remains in use and is cared for by its congregation in association with the Landmark Trust.

Richard Suggett

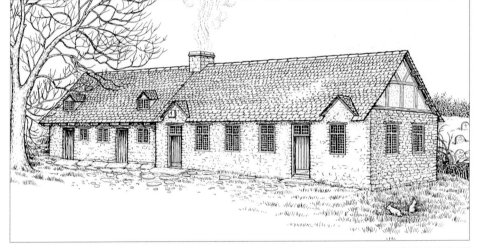

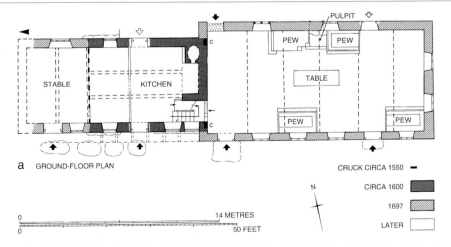

055 The Corbelled Pigsty: 'A Palace for Swine'

The corbelled pigsty at Pencaedrain, Gelligaer, Glamorgan, photographed in its complete state by the Royal Commission in 1972.
DI2008_0404 NPRN 37632

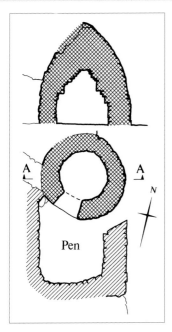

Above: A plan and section of the corbelled pigsty at Pill House, Llanmadoc, in Gower.

DI2008_0406 NPRN 37656

Right: The rear of the corbelled pigsty at Penddeugae-fach, Bargoed.

DI2008_1029 NPRN 37634

Below: The distribution of known corbelled pigsties in Glamorgan.

DI2008_0408
© Crown. Ordnance Survey.
100017916

Round, stone-built structures, some with corbelled roofs, have been recorded throughout Europe, both archaeologically and as standing buildings. Many examples are of uncertain date and function. Their persistence can be traced through circular dovecots of the medieval period to the later eighteenth century, when corbelled structures were built in parts of south Wales to provide a palatial home for one of the mainstays of the cottage and farm economy, the humble pig.

In his study of *The Welsh House* (1940) Iorwerth Peate noted thirty-five examples of corbelled pigsties in south Wales, and this geographically restricted distribution was later confirmed by the studies of Eurwyn Wiliam. There are few dates to allow their chronology to be understood. They were first noted as a curiosity by late eighteenth-century travellers, while the latest example dated is of 1856 at Llanover, Monmouthshire; they continued an archaic building tradition into the industrial age.

Whatever its origins, this type of pigsty was a ubiquitous feature of Glamorgan farms from the later eighteenth century or earlier. However, by the completion of the Royal Commission's inventory of Glamorgan farmhouses and cottages in 1988 only twenty-two survived. Corbelled pigsties were distributed throughout the county. All appear to have been drystone, with courses set sloping slightly downwards to the outside to shed water. Above the cylindrical base the diameter of each course diminished to produce the conical top. In upland parts of south Wales most examples were built with thin courses of stone or reused stone tiles, as found in the make-up of the sties at Hendre-Prosser, Pontypridd, and near Pencaedrain, Gelligaer. A few

had a ventilation slot, as at Hendre-Prosser and at Tŷ-draw, Welsh St Donats. All identified examples had a low, square-headed entry into the circular chamber. The floor in the sty was usually of earth, although a few were stone cobbled, and one at Pensianel, Dyffryn Clydach, was lined extravagantly with ceramic tiles. A few sties were built into the walls that bounded the farmyard.

There were regional differences in the external appearance of the structures, although all were similar in size – approximately two metres in width and height. In Gower the two surviving examples, Jane's Grove at Pennard and Pill House at Llanmadoc, have a distinctive rounded beehive shape, and all those found around the Swansea Valley had a tendency to be of this form. The pigsty at Pensianel in Dyffryn Clydach is unique in form, having a rendered top set out on a projecting string-course. The tallest pigsties, such as Hendre-Prosser, Pontypridd, and Penddeugae-fach, Bargoed, are in the eastern uplands – all capped by a flat circular stone that supports a pointed finial shaped from a similar conglomerate stone, which may suggest the work of a single builder. Most of the other sties also have a capstone of some form.

Most of these remarkable structures, which provided dry accommodation for their original porcine occupants, have long since fallen into disuse. A few have found new uses, but most remain as rather enigmatic monuments to long-past farming practices and building traditions.

Harry Brooksby

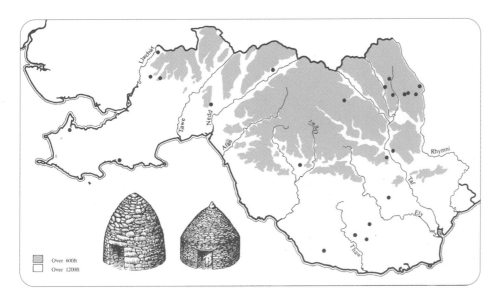

Over 600ft
Over 1200ft

The First Industrial Nation

Stephen Hughes and Peter Wakelin

Between the mid-eighteenth and mid-nineteenth centuries the economy was transformed. Wales was at the heart of the Industrial Revolution, innovating in technology and organisation, and experiencing novel social changes and major alterations to the landscape. These developments have left a legacy of sites and landscapes that are, in their way, as precious as the remains of Renaissance Italy or Ancient Greece. By the 1851 census Wales had become the first country to count more people employed in industry than in agriculture. It was one of the leading industrial exporters of the world, and everyday life for most people had changed fundamentally. During the same period increasing wealth led to unprecedented urbanisation, movements to improve agriculture, and large investments in architecture.

A driving force was the unprecedented growth in population, which more than doubled between 1780 and 1851, reaching 1,189,000. War in Europe, especially with France from 1793 to the fall of Napoleon in 1815, created demand and raised prices, encouraging investment in industry and the exploitation of marginal land for agriculture. There was even an invasion: the minor incursion of French troops at Fishguard in 1797.

While the effects of industrialisation were felt in all parts of Wales, industry was localised, notably in Swansea, the heads of the south Wales valleys, and the Greenfield valley of Flintshire. In the ironmaking towns of Glamorgan and Monmouthshire the population grew faster than in almost every other part of Britain as a result of rising birth rates and large-scale migration, primarily from rural Wales. A distinctive working-class society emerged which was to remain largely Welsh-speaking, even in the new industrial towns, until the end of the nineteenth century. Rural areas saw a decline in population, especially in the marginal uplands, as people pursued the opportunities offered by wages and urban communities [062]. In both town and country there was a rapid expansion in nonconformity and chapels became familiar features of the Welsh landscape.

The essential material for many industries was coal, found abundantly in the south and the north-east. Its prime use was in the metals industries; while

Left: Libanus chapel, Llansadwrn, Carmarthenshire, built in 1788 and rebuilt in 1841.
DI2005_0200 NPRN 6580

Opposite: Pontcysyllte Aqueduct on the Ellesmere Canal is recognised as one of the outstanding monuments of the world [058].
AP_2006_0914 NPRN 34410

Below: Horseshoe Falls weir near Llangollen, built in 1804-08 to supply water to the Ellesmere Canal.
DS2007_081_003 NPRN 403685

export of coal began in the late eighteenth century, its boom time as an independent industry was a century later. The earliest Welsh industries to become internationally important were connected with non-ferrous metals. Mining for lead, copper or silver ore had taken place in most parts of Wales at one time or another. The scale of activity increased and during the Industrial Revolution the lead mines in upland Cardiganshire, Montgomeryshire, Denbighshire and Flintshire employed thousands of people. Thomas Williams developed Mynydd Parys on Anglesey into the world's biggest copper mine in the late eighteenth century and the port at Amlwch, which served it,

Right: The characteristic crowsfoot waste tips at an upland lead mine on Esclusham mountain in Denbighshire.

GTJ26392 NPRN 33927

grew to be briefly the second largest town in Wales, with over 5,000 people. To process his Anglesey ore Williams developed a chain of smelting and manufacturing works, including water-powered mills in the Greenfield valley at Holywell and the Middle and Upper Bank copperworks at Swansea.

The industrial-scale smelting of copper was introduced to Britain from Germany in 1584, in the form of a new works near Neath in Glamorgan. From 1717 it was centred on the River Tawe above Swansea, using ore brought across the Bristol Channel: it concentrated on the Swansea side because the quantities of fuel used were greater than the quantities of ore and ships could return to

Devon and Cornwall with coal. Thirteen works were established by the early nineteenth century, and soon 90 per cent of Britain's copper smelting capacity was located within twenty miles of Swansea [056]. There were also smelters for zinc, lead, silver and other metals. Eighteenth-century copperworks did not employ more than a hundred but those established in the early nineteenth century had workforces of over a thousand. At the time of the 1841 census the lower Swansea valley was the largest concentration of population in Wales, housing some 40,000 people divided equally between the mercantile town and its industrial settlements. The valley filled with poisonous fumes and smouldering slag tips.

The second of the internationally important metals industries of Wales was iron. Blast furnaces were established in Glamorgan and Monmouthshire in the late sixteenth century to exploit local charcoal supplies and ore from the rims of the south Wales and Forest of Dean coalfields. All of the early ironworks were small, charcoal-fuelled and water-powered, and they were distributed widely, the only cluster being in the Wye valley. The discovery in 1709 by Abraham Darby of Coalbrookdale of how to smelt iron with coked coal rather than with charcoal paved the way for a revolution in the iron industry,

Right: The great opencast at Mynydd Parys copper mine, Anglesey, with the ruined windmill tower near the centre indicating its enormous size.

DI2006_1353 NPRN 33752

but the method was taken up only slowly at first. In 1713 Darby planned an iron furnace at Dol-gun, east of Dolgellau, and his fellow Quaker, Charles Lloyd, built a furnace at Bersham near Wrexham in 1717 which he converted to coke in 1721. The use of coal allowed furnaces to be larger and grouped together and a burst of new works helped transform the iron trade of Britain. Hirwaun furnace was the first in south Wales to use coke, in 1757, followed by Dowlais two years later. Along the heads of the valleys vast territories rich in coal, ironstone and lime were leased to new enterprises and all the latest methods were applied on a grand, coordinated scale. The works of the new generation were multi-furnace, coke-fired, mainly steam-powered, and usually integrated with puddling furnaces to make wrought iron. By 1830 south Wales produced 40 per cent of all British pig iron and had a greater capacity than any other ironmaking region in the world.

Merthyr Tydfil, with an agglomeration of huge ironworks, became the capital of the iron trade and the biggest town in Wales – its population reached 46,378 by 1851, when Cardiff had only 18,351 inhabitants. Merthyr's Cyfarthfa Ironworks was the largest in the world by the 1790s, with 2,000 workers; thirty years later neighbouring Dowlais was the largest, with a workforce of 6,000. Pig iron and wrought-iron rails were the mainstays of the trade. Richard Crawshay at Cyfarthfa was the first ironmaster to make use of Henry Cort's 'puddling' process to make wrought iron with coal fuel, developing it in multiple forges and rolling mills: it became known as 'the Welsh method'.

Wales was also of international importance in the tinplate industry. Mechanical rolling of iron plates for tinning was invented at Pontypool around 1720 and south Wales led the industry for two centuries. 'Tin cans' acquired importance as containers for the preservation of food. Some tinplate works were established in the eighteenth century in south-west Wales, for example at Carmarthen, Castell Malgwyn near Cardigan, Kidwelly, and Ynyspenllwch in the Swansea Valley. After the mid-nineteenth century the heartland of the industry was a belt from Port Talbot to Llanelli.

Other industries also contributed to the transformation of the economy. The long-established woollen industry burgeoned in the early nineteenth century, though it was still largely a domestic industry and most factories were built after 1850. At Newtown in Montgomeryshire the number of handloom weavers grew rapidly from the 1790s and

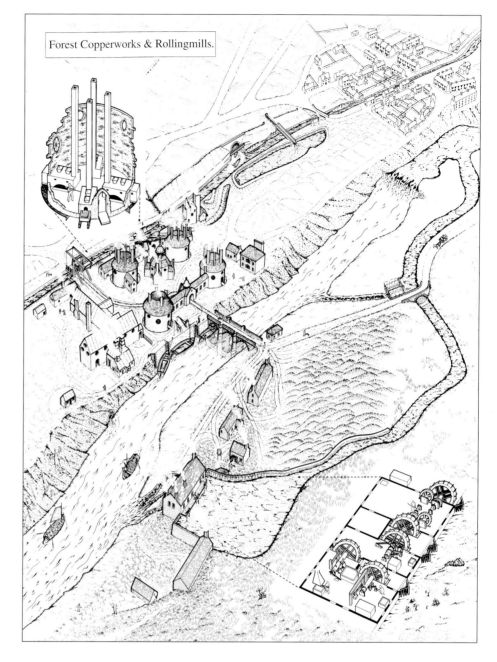

Forest Copperworks & Rollingmills.

a new suburb of houses with loom-shops above was laid out at Penygloddfa. Brewing quenched the thirst of the new urban and industrial workforce. Brick-making grew to supply the needs of smelting and building. Limestone quarrying and lime-burning expanded to provide mortar and lime fertiliser. The spectacular rise of the slate industry in north-west Wales began in the late eighteenth century, though it reached its greatest scale in the late nineteenth, roofing buildings as far away as South America and Australia [069].

The territory of the mineral fields posed major challenges for entrepreneurs. Shipping connected

A Royal Commission reconstruction of the Forest copperworks at Swansea in the late eighteenth century.
DI2007_1276 NPRN 300874

Right: William Edwards's Bridge, Pontypridd, photographed in the late nineteenth century.

CD2005_612_013 NPRN 24145

Below: Hill's tramroad, built in 1817-18 to carry iron from Blaenavon ironworks to Garnddyrys forge and the Brecknock and Abergavenny Canal, winding along a route cut into the mountainside before dropping to the canal by counterbalanced inclines.

DI2006_1719 NPRN 85860

harbours around the coasts and was of great importance in bringing ore to Swansea, taking finished copper to brass mills in Bristol, distributing slates, exporting iron, and carrying imported consumer goods [063]. Improvements to harbours and lighthouses were made to assist this flourishing exchange by sea [064]. On the other hand, penetration of the hinterlands was arduous. The uplands were agriculturally poor and improved turnpike roads arrived late by English standards, though some impressive bridges were built, most notably William Edwards's at Pontypridd in 1756, for two generations probably the largest masonry span in the world.

Canals and horse-worked railways were a joint solution to the transport problems of industry [057]. Canals were promoted by companies of small shareholders during the investment mania of the 1790s, climbing up strategic valleys in south Wales and crossing from the English lowlands to Denbighshire. The railways fed coal, iron and limestone to these waterways from the hillsides: south Wales probably possessed the densest networks of horse-worked railways ever built, perhaps extending for more than 1,000 miles. Other early railways brought slate from the mountain quarries to the ports of north-west Wales – from Penrhyn in 1801, Dinorwic and Nantlle in the 1820s and Blaenau Ffestiniog in 1836. Such facilities transformed the economics of production by lowering transport costs: new mines and quarries opened wherever they reached mineral reserves. In 1809 Walter Coffin opened Dinas level in the Rhondda, providing the first glimmer of the enormous growth to come in the central coalfield. In 1841 the Taff Vale Railway became Wales's first completely locomotive-hauled public railway and its penetration of the lower Rhondda, following the completion of the Bute West Dock in Cardiff in 1839, created further opportunities for coal exporting.

The designers and entrepreneurs in Welsh industry and transport were innovators: they are credited with the earliest all-iron rails, the first railway viaducts, the first recorded use of a locomotive to haul a load (by Richard Trevithick in 1803) and the first railway passenger service, in 1807. At Bersham John Wilkinson developed a boring-machine to make cannon and steam-engine cylinders. Thomas Williams led important innovations in copper manufacture that improved the sheathing of ships' hulls [063]. The capabilities of locally-trained engineers such as Watkin George at Cyfarthfa produced numerous innovations: George built the first ever iron aqueduct and railway bridge in 1793 and some of the first large-span iron roofs. These prototypes informed the design of Pontcysyllte aqueduct [058], which in turn influenced aqueduct construction in many countries. Through his work on the Ellesmere Canal and the Holyhead Road, Thomas Telford developed important techniques for iron engineering, earthwork construction and project management that were to influence engineering internationally.

The end of the eighteenth century and the beginning of the nineteenth was an age of 'improvers'. The idea of progress was in the forefront of the minds of landowners who promoted the improvement of agriculture and the infrastructure of the countryside. The enthusiasm reached its height during the Industrial Revolution and especially the French Wars, when population was growing rapidly, corn prices were exceptionally high and

Enlightenment thinking challenged the status quo. The improvers, singly or in companies, built roads and bridges, enclosed fields, drained land, and developed and disseminated better agricultural techniques, such as planned farm buildings and the use of lime to improve the soil. Enclosure by Act of Parliament had a major impact on the landscape after the 1760s, imposing regular field boundaries on open commons [060].

The Industrial Revolution was a period of enormous growth in the number and size of towns. The rate of growth was phenomenal in mining and manufacturing areas – towns like Merthyr Tydfil and Tredegar – but resorts like Tenby, county towns like Abergavenny and Wrexham, and ports like Caernarfon and Newport also expanded. Of course, many towns functioned on several levels and so grew especially fast: Swansea was a resort, mining town, manufacturing centre, regional centre and port. Other towns without important functions stagnated. Most towns grew in an unordered way, as in ironmaking settlements like Blaenavon [061]. Houses followed the lines of horse-worked railways and fitted between mines, furnaces and tips: streets with names like Tram Side, Cinder Hill or Furnace Row were commonplace across the heads of the south Wales valleys.

The web of hardships and opportunities presented by the Industrial Revolution was apparent in

The regular field boundaries of parliamentary enclosure of the wastes: Cellan, Cardiganshire.
CD2003_643_002 NPRN 402564

Sir Richard Colt Hoare's view of Blaenavon Ironworks in about 1798, when it was only ten years old.
DI2008_0859 NPRN 34134

185

Above: One of the two defensive towers built by the owners of Nantyglo ironworks behind their mansion as a refuge in times of unrest.

DI2008_0845 NPRN 54623

Right: Bute Town near Rhymney, which was laid out for ironworkers as a Palladian set piece in 1802-4.

DI2007_0464 NPRN 18180

industrial towns more than anywhere. They seldom had sanitation adequate to the densities of people crowded into them, and periodic epidemics could decimate them – the hilltop cemetery at Tredegar is an evocative reminder of the cholera epidemics to which settlements were vulnerable. Housing conditions were poor by later standards, but they compared favourably with the hovels of the rural poor. Some industrialists offered an education for the children of their employees in works schools, but child labour remained ubiquitous. Works schools contributed to the spread of English (making Wales largely bilingual by the mid-nineteenth century), while the Methodist revivals starting in industrial communities stimulated and supported Welsh. Wage-earners had far more disposable income, but dependence on industrial masters was a cause of strife, expressed in the grain riots of the 1790s and reaching a crescendo in the Merthyr Rising of 1831 and the Chartist riots of 1839, during which at least twenty demonstrators were killed. When the ironmasters of Nantyglo built defensive towers next to their mansion it was out of genuine fear that their workers might turn upon them.

New towns or elements of them were planned from time to time, as at Tremadog in Merioneth [060], Aberaeron in Cardiganshire, Bute Town near Rhymney, or the copperworks village of Morriston, Swansea. Probably the largest planned town was Pembroke Dock [059]. Such set pieces were examples of greater investment in buildings of many types. The Georgian style became the preferred architectural language of the period, dominating townscapes from Denbigh to Haverfordwest and

Montgomery to Cowbridge as houses, shops and guildhalls were refronted or rebuilt. Its symmetry, proportion and simplicity represented the triumph of Renaissance principles over vernacular traditions. However, the late eighteenth and early nineteenth centuries also saw a profusion of architectural fashions, including a pervasive neo-classicism, the first experiments in reviving Gothic architecture in the form of the picturesque 'gothick' style, and a brief Egyptian revival.

Landed estates were enriched by agricultural and mineral incomes and colonial trade, and great houses were created according to the latest tastes. Penrhyn Castle near Bangor was designed by Thomas Hopper in a brutal Romanesque style in the 1820s as an expression of vast wealth and conspicuous consumption. Margam Castle was an exercise in gothick in 1830. The most important architect working in Wales was John Nash. in just a decade from 1788 Nash designed public buildings for the improving Georgian towns and a series of innovative villas for the gentry of south-west Wales, learning how to relate buildings to landscape in a picturesque way.

Right: Montgomery was among many medieval towns made 'polite' by Georgian rebuilding. The town hall was designed by William Baker in 1748. The upper floor was raised by Thomas Penson in 1828 and the open ground floor was closed in.

DI2006-1963 NPRN 32055

of the landscape: among many that still delight the eye are the Derry Ormond monument in Cardiganshire, the shell grotto at Pontypool Park, and the tower at The Kymin, high above Monmouth.

Houses and grounds like Piercefield on the Wye, Wynnstay on the Dee and Hafod on the Ystwyth became essential destinations on the tour of Wales. It may seem ironic that at the same time that Wales was experiencing its Industrial Revolution it became a magnet to early tourists. However, many visitors who sought the magnificent scenery celebrated by the Romantic movement were fascinated by man's impact on nature in the mining and manufacturing districts. Tourism transformed the architecture of coastal towns, and Aberystwyth, Swansea and Tenby (towns of medieval origin) had become significant seaside resorts by the turn of the nineteenth century. Aberystwyth preserves some fine town houses and an assembly room of this era, and contemporary newspapers list the gentry who visited. Their presence had an effect on the way that country houses and estates developed. Many saw Wales, with its surviving language, as representing ancient British culture. This was paralleled by a revival of interest among Welsh people in their own past, expressed most notably in the works of Iolo Morganwg, who reinvented ogam script, the Gorsedd of Bards and the idea of stone circles. It was an excursion into interpreting the past based on invention more than analysis, but it promoted an interest in the ancient monuments of Wales that continues to this day.

Hundreds of houses were built or rebuilt, many in the Nash style. Although the wealth to be invested in country houses was less in Wales than in many parts of England, there was a notable effect on buildings and the wider landscape. The grounds of many houses were replanned according to the English parkland style, and walks and prospects were laid out in accordance with the aesthetics of the Picturesque movement, which had a spiritual home in Wales thanks to the explorations of the Wye valley by William Gilpin and the work of Uvedale Price and Thomas Johnes. Nash built Emlyn Cottage, a gothick dower house at Newcastle Emlyn, Castle House, a marine villa for Price at Aberystwyth, and the famous Hafod for Johnes [065]. This was the great age of follies, designed to embellish prospects

Above: Paxton's Tower, the triangular belvedere outside Carmarthen designed by S. P. Cockerell in 1808. Carriages could enter through the great arches. Above were a banqueting chamber and a 'prospect room'.
DI2006_0784 NPRN 32666

Above left: The 'Bardic' complex of Y Gareg Siglo, Pontypridd. The rocking stone at the centre was used by Iolo Morganwg for druidic rituals around 1814. The stone circle and mystic avenue in the shape of a serpent were added by his disciple Evan Davies (Myfyr Morganwg) in 1849.
AP2007_1663 NPRN 275888

Left: Aberystwyth seafront before the arrival of the railway, with Castle House (right), designed by John Nash in 1794 for a pioneer of the Picturesque movement, Uvedale Price. In 1864 it was subsumed within the buildings of the railway hotel, later to become the University College of Wales.
CD 2003_646_012
NPRN 23303/96582

056 Uncovering a Swansea Copperworks

An aerial view of the excavations at Upper Bank in March 2008.

AP_2008_0113 NPRN 40465

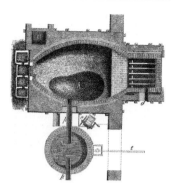

Above: Plan of a coarse-metal melting furnace.

DI2008_0714

Top right: Gas producers and gas-fired zinc smelters found in the last phase of excavations.

AP_2008_0713 NPRN 40465

Right: Section of a calcining furnace.

DI2008_0717

Below: Elevation of an idealised Swansea copperworks, 1852.

DI2008_0713

Swansea was the world centre of copper smelting during the Industrial Revolution, but most of the physical structures of this great industry have long been demolished or hidden by later development. The Royal Commission investigated copperworks sites at the time of large-scale demolition and land reclamation in the 1960s, but much disappeared forever. During the 1980s it identified previously unrecognised remains and began research that led in 2000 to the publication of *Copperopolis: landscapes of the early industrial period in Swansea*.

A new housing development on brown-field land in 2007 and 2008 gave an exceptional opportunity to reveal the hidden heritage of the copper industry at the site of the Upper Bank smelting works, established in 1755. The Commission had previously identified Swansea's last standing copper-smelting hall here and it advised that substantial remains of early furnaces would be found below ground. Glamorgan-Gwent Archaeological Trust accordingly requested an archaeological watching-brief during development. As the buildings were cleared all that was visible to Oxford Archaeology, the contractors employed by the developer, Barratts, were the concrete substructures of later buildings. However, when these were cut through they revealed something resembling a hidden city, consisting of numerous structures from the early copperworks and zincworks.

The Commission's aerial photograph taken in March 2008 shows a large area of the site uncovered. On the right the quays along the River Tawe, paved with cast slag blocks, were where copper ore that came by sailing ship from Cornwall, Anglesey and Chile was stockpiled, then distributed on radiating narrow-gauge railways. The most prominent features across the site are the nine furnaces dating from its conversion from copper- to zinc-smelting after 1890, each with four parallel gas flues. The three circular structures midway up the right-hand side produced gas to fuel them.

At the left-hand side towards the bottom are four pits (crossed by a concrete ramp) that were the bases of the earlier copper furnaces. Copper-smelting at

Swansea was carried out by 'the Welsh method', which involved at least twenty successive roastings of ore. The reverbertory-type furnaces drew the heat through and reflected it off vaulted roofs, allowing the metal to be uncontaminated by the coal. Their stoking holes, the pits into which waste from each furnace was cleaned and the bases of chimneys all survived.

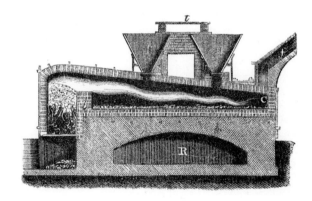

Remains were also excavated of granulation pits where the molten copper from the furnaces was dropped into water so as to solidify as granules that were taken for further processing. Interlocking cast-iron barrowing planks were found: it is known from records that a woman labourer called Mrs Matthews barrowed 23 tons of copper ore in a single day here (she was said to be 'too tired to attend chapel'). At the centre of the site is the base of a large calcining furnace, marked by two oblongs and an archaeologist in a yellow jacket lying with arms and legs outstretched. This was where the initial drying and roasting of the ore took place. The contents were extracted through rectangular slots, the workers using long rakes and covering their mouths to reduce their exposure to the sulphur.

Other sites in the Swansea valley may yet produce further significant remains of 'Copperopolis'.

Stephen Hughes

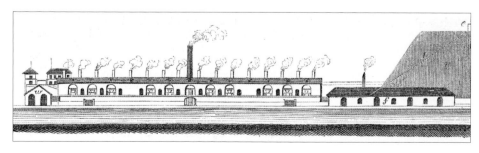

057 Industrial Transport:
The Swansea Canal and its Railways

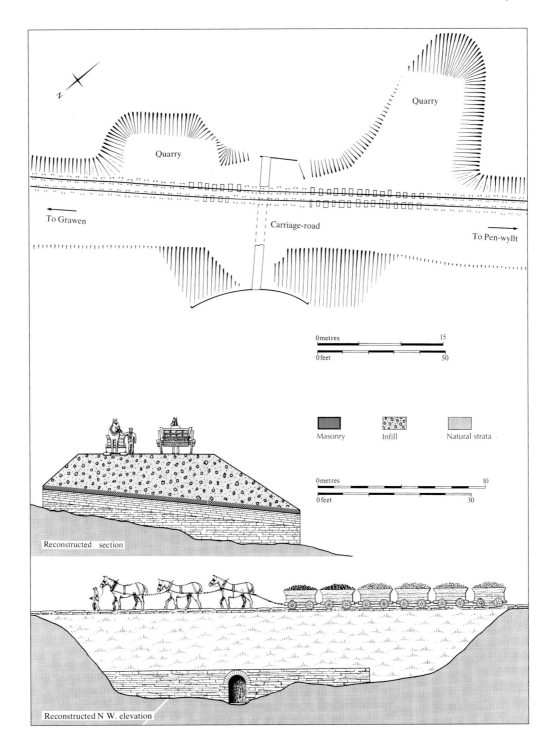

*A Royal Commission plan and reconstruction drawing of a culvert and embankment
on the Brecon Forest Tramroad at Grawen, built in 1821-5.*

DI2008_0856 NPRN 406575

Above: A typical Swansea Canal over-bridge, Ynysmeudwy.
DS2006_230_001 NPRN 34508

Right: Iron plates and stone sleepers excavated in a stream bank near Abercrave Ironworks.
DI2008_0857 NPRN 34028

If canals were the arteries of the Industrial Revolution, horse-worked railways were its capillaries. The 17-mile Swansea Canal was connected to almost 140 miles of early railways. An Act of 1794, like other Acts of the period, provided statutory powers to compulsorily purchase land for railways within an eight-mile corridor of the waterway. The powers were used by the canal company, or by local landowners or industrialists with its agreement, to create what was effectively an integrated transport network.

The canal was promoted by local merchants and landowners principally to exploit the mineral riches of the upper Swansea valley, bringing them to the harbour and the smelting works of the lower valley. Some primitive wooden railways had existed to link mines to the river wharves on the Tawe since the 1750s, but the canal began a rapid growth of new infrastructure. The railways were built to a variety of forms and gauges, but most used cast-iron plates about 3 feet apart, laid on stone sleepers which can still provide clues to the former routes.

Short railways connected to mines on the eastern side of the valley and others over two miles long were built into the two western side-valleys of Cwm Clydach and Cwm Twrch. In 1803 the leading coppermasters, the Morrises, wanted to build a private canal to link coal reserves on land along Swansea Bay to the Swansea Canal, but the company insisted on a railway instead. The resulting Mumbles or Oystermouth railway in 1807 began the first paying passenger service on any railway in the world. Further railways were added in the first thirty years of the nineteenth century on both sides of the canal.

At the top of the Swansea valley over 16 miles of railways were built to exploit limestone, silica-sand and rottenstone reserves. It had been hoped to extend the Swansea Canal northwards to cross the watershed to Sennybridge in the Usk valley, doubling its length, but the costs would have been prohibitive. In 1821-3 a railway was built by John Christie, an East India merchant who had purchased the Fforest Fawr estates. Christie's railway initially went northwards from his limestone quarries on the mountain peaks to his new farmlands, but the coal to burn the lime was only available further south, near the canal, so he created a through-route. There was an explosion in the number of substantial ironworks alongside the canal in the upper Swansea valley in the 1830s when the introduction of hot blast allowed anthracite, the coal available locally, to be used in smelting. A second substantial line was added at the head of the valley to take coal and limestone to Ynyscedwyn ironworks near Ystradgynlais.

Ironworks, tinplateworks and copperworks eventually clustered around the canal, served by a dense web of railways. Locomotive railways only penetrated the upper Swansea valley in the 1860s and the canal and some of its railways continued to be used intensively until the end of the nineteenth century.

Stephen Hughes

Below: The Swansea Canal and its railways.
DI2007_0157

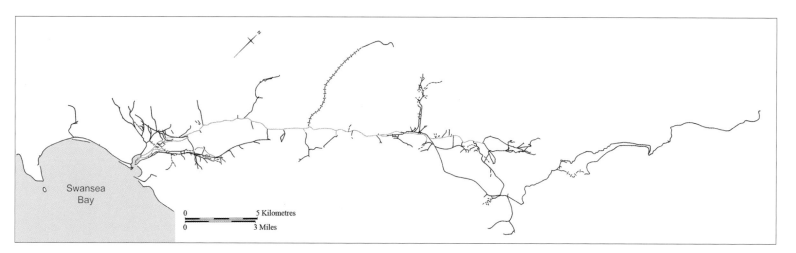

Swansea Bay

0   5 Kilometres
0   3 Miles

058 An Engineering Masterpiece: Pontcysyllte Aqueduct

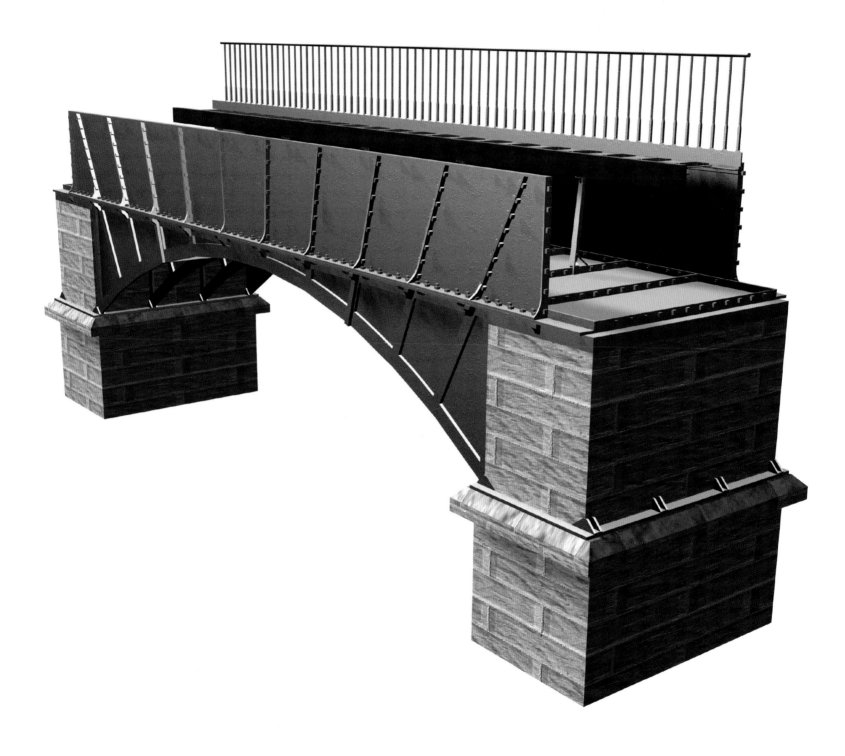

The Royal Commission's digital model of the upper section of Pontcysyllte Aqueduct showing the construction of the piers, ribs and towing path.
NPRN 34410

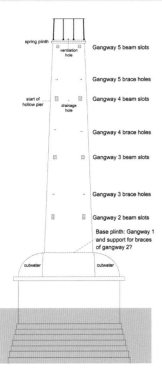

spring plinth

ventilation
hole

Gangway 5 beam slots

Gangway 5 brace holes

start of
hollow pier

drainage
hole

Gangway 4 beam slots

Gangway 4 brace holes

Gangway 3 beam slots

Gangway 3 brace holes

Gangway 2 beam slots

Base plinth: Gangway 1
and support for braces
of gangway 2?

cutwater

cutwater

Above: Detailed analysis of each pier has identified irregularities in the otherwise standard stonework. These provide evidence of how the piers were constructed, verifying contemporary paintings.

NPRN 34410

Upper right: Pontcysyllte Aqueduct from the banks of the River Dee.

DI2005_0878 NPRN 34410

Right: Small blocks level with the drain hole mark where gangway beams were removed. Two further pairs of holes are where diagonal braces for the deck above were fixed.

DS2008_208_001 NPRN 34410

Pontcysyllte Aqueduct has been described as one of the world's greatest engineering achievements. It was built between 1795 and 1805 to carry the Ellesmere Canal across the Dee valley, linking the coal mines of Denbighshire to the national canal system and the heartlands of the Industrial Revolution. The mountainous terrain presented many obstacles to the engineers, William Jessop and Thomas Telford, and when it was completed the stretch of canal between Trevor basin and the English border was said to be 'composed of works more difficult of execution than can perhaps be found anywhere within an equal distance of canal navigation'. The greatest challenge was the crossing of the Dee valley. The initial plan was for a series of locks on either side with a low, masonry aqueduct crossing the river at the bottom. Enormously time-consuming to operate and costly to build, the lock staircases were eliminated by a high-level crossing of daring innovation and virtuosity.

With its nineteen spans and height of 38.4 metres above the bed of the Dee, Pontcysyllte Aqueduct was the tallest and longest navigable aqueduct yet built. It was to remain the tallest aqueduct in the world for some 200 years. This spectacular achievement was made possible by the pioneering use of cast iron, and the aqueduct became famous as one of the symbols of the new industrial age. The height of the stone piers made it necessary for Telford and Jessop to devise ways of reducing the volume and weight of the stonework – tapering the piers and constructing the top sections hollow.

Studies of the surviving clues in the structure have revealed the methods by which the huge construction project was achieved. The location of the quarry and construction yard on the north side of the river determined the sequence for building the piers. They were raised in stages of between six and eight metres at a time, moving south to north across the valley.

Five successive levels of timber gangways were constructed to transport materials from the north bank, probably by railway. Each gangway was supported from the stonework of the piers by two timber beams and diagonal braces held in cast-iron shoes. Subtle evidence of these features can still be detected in the stonework of each pier.

The arches and trough of the aqueduct are entirely of cast iron, produced at a newly-established forge near the construction yard at Plas Kynaston. Each of the eighteen spans is composed of four cast-iron ribs that support a trough of bolted cast-iron plates. In order to maintain flexibility, the trough is not fixed to the ribs but is prevented from lateral movement by brackets and lugs and by the load imposed by the water inside it. The appearance of the structure harks back to earlier traditions, with the outer ribs designed to give a sense of solidity and the raked side plates imitating a stone arch. A German visitor, Prince Hermann von Pükler-Muskau described it in 1832 as 'a work which would have done honour to Rome'.

Louise Barker and Susan Fielding

059 A Royal Dockyard and New Town: Pembroke Dock

Looking over the ordered grid of Pembroke Dock down Pembroke Street to the deep water of Milford Haven (before 1905).
DI2008_0842 NPRN 30298

Pembroke Dock was probably the largest of the planned towns built in Wales, built as a result of enormous government investment from 1812 to create a secure place for naval shipbuilding in the protected waters of Milford Haven. The dockyard itself produced some remarkable buildings. It continued in operation until 1926, though its creation was the result of accidents.

The relationship of Admiral Nelson with Sir William Hamilton gave birth to a small naval facility at Milford, on the north bank of the Haven: the land belonged to Hamilton, Nelson promoted it as a location, and Hamilton's nephew, Charles Greville, was entrusted with making a new town and port. The Navy began a neo-classical crescent in 1809 but Greville died and negotiations to buy the site failed. So in 1812 the Navy decided to look elsewhere, specifically at land the government already owned at Paterchurch, on the opposite shore.

The site was inspected by the eminent engineer John Rennie and by 1813 the assistant architect to the Navy, Edward Holl, was in charge of building the encircling wall and shipbuilding slips. The first warships were begun before any buildings: the first four houses for the workforce came in 1814, houses for dockyard officers in 1817-18, and storehouses and offices from 1822. The dockyard built timber warships until it moved to iron from the 1860s. As the Navy's principal building yard, it had more slips than any other dockyard – thirteen in all – but fewer buildings, as the ships were fitted out and serviced elsewhere. It was the only Royal Navy yard to specialise exclusively in building. The workforce was around 2,000.

Right: Number 1, The Terrace, built inside the dockyard walls by Edward Holl in 1817-18.
DI2008_0843 NPRN 30298

The town consisted of a regular grid of broad streets with two-storey houses, but it filled out gradually and ribbons of single-storey cottages extended beyond it. The buildings of the dockyard included the shipbuilding slips, which began to be roofed from the 1830s. Sir Robert Sepping's slip roof of 1841 spanned 100 feet in timber, while the pioneer cast-iron roofs of 1844-5 by Fox and Henderson, who were to make their name building the Crystal Palace for the Great Exhibition of 1851, were 80 feet wide, clad with the novel material of corrugated iron. All thirteen slips were roofed eventually.

The Navy buildings inside the dockyard's 12-feet-high wall embodied late Georgian elegance and structural ingenuity. The officers' houses in The Terrace designed by Holl in 1817-18 and his storehouse of 1822 have iron roof structures of experimental form, and the storehouse has fireproof iron and stone floors. The Captain Superintendent's office of 1847, by Fox and Henderson, is also iron-roofed.

The defences of the dockyard were part of the mid-nineteenth-century fortification of the entire Milford Haven waterway. The town usually contained more Army personnel to protect the dockyard than Navy ones as the workforce was largely civilian. The Defensible Barracks of 1842-5 are a barrack-square on a dry-moated gun-platform. Set high above the town to command the sea approach, the barracks are imposing, but a fossil of military architecture – the last European fort built to Vauban's seventeenth-century corner-bastion plan. Just offshore from the dockyard's south-west and north-east corners are two superbly-built gun towers of 1848-51, the guns above barrack-rooms that are in turn above basement ammunition stores.

Julian Orbach

Below: An aerial view of Pembroke Dock Defensible Barracks reveals the plan of the dry moat and bastions and the elegant Georgian square enclosing the parade ground.
DI2005_0929 NPRN 34323

060 The Age of Improvement

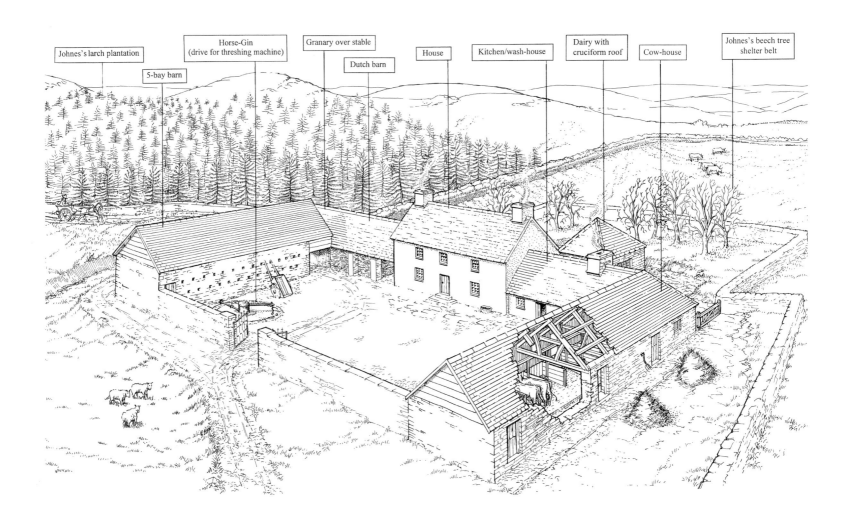

Johnes's larch plantation

5-bay barn

Horse-Gin
(drive for threshing machine)

Granary over stable

Dutch barn

House

Kitchen/wash-house

Dairy with
cruciform roof

Cow-house

Johnes's beech tree
shelter belt

A reconstruction drawing by Geoff Ward of Gelmast model farm in Cardiganshire, built in 1803.

GTJ00066 NPRN 3073

In an age of 'improvers' one of the most visionary was William Maddocks, who developed a grandly ambitious private scheme at the mouth of the Afon Glaslyn in Caernarfonshire between 1798 and his death in 1828. His central project was to drain the marshes known as Traeth Mawr and create farmland by building a causeway dam almost a mile long, finished in 1811. The causeway carried the coast road, which met the road from the east at the town he laid out. Tremadog, as he called it, was neat and orderly, and his ambitions for it to become a staging post on the route to Ireland were indicated by his naming of the main streets after London and Dublin – before Telford's great Holyhead Road was built on a more northerly route. Maddocks's impetus to improvement led him to build a woollen factory and enhance the harbour that would become Porthmadog. Later, this became the terminus of the Festiniog Railway: millions of slates would come down the valley, cross Maddocks's embankment and be shipped from his harbour.

More typical of the spirit of widespread improvement was the building of new farms and the enclosure and drainage of marginal land on heaths and hills. Better agricultural methods were promoted by model farms and by newly-formed agricultural societies, and progress was reflected upon in a series of county reports published by the Board of Agriculture. When Thomas Johnes inherited the Hafod estate in Cardiganshire [065] its farms were occupied by poverty-stricken tenants unaware of current agricultural methods and the land was regarded as essentially unproductive. He developed

Right: One of the many farms bought and developed by Thomas Johnes was Bodcoll, Cardiganshire.

DI2005_1194 NPRN 403857

Below: A detail of a painting showing the Traeth Mawr causeway, built by William Maddocks at what became Porthmadog.

DI2005_1083 NPRN 34165

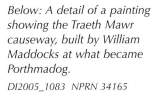

the home farm, Pendre, and bought many more farms across the hills, improved them and let them to tenants. He built Gelmast, or New Farm, in about 1803 to showcase his ideas on grassland management, stocking and dairying. It exploited the sheep grazing on the vast upland tracts and introduced dairy farming on ground that was newly enclosed and drained. The grazing and tree plantations amounted to more than 450 acres.

Gelmast was intended to supply milk, butter and cheese to the locality, and its buildings relate primarily to the dairying enterprise. The Royal Commission's reconstruction, prepared for an interpretation panel at the site, shows the farmstead's orderly and rational courtyard layout. The house was symmetrical and spacious, with sash windows either side of the central doorway. A free-standing dairy with a pyramidal roof stood at the rear. Along the east side of the yard was a large cowshed. The west side was flanked by a large barn which may originally have been intended, optimistically, for substantial grain production, and there is some evidence for a horse-powered threshing mill. The stone-pillared Dutch barn was an innovation, allowing hay to be stored more conveniently than by ricking or in a traditional loft above a cow-house.

Anna Skarzyńska and Peter Wakelin

061 The Iron Towns: Blaenavon

Stack Square at Blaenavon Ironworks in 1983, before it was conserved.
The court was built in 1788 to house key workers and, in the centre, the company shop.
DI2005_0035 NPRN 20853

Above: The viaduct houses as recorded by Sir Richard Colt Hoare in about 1798.

DI2008_0858 NPRN 302129

Right: St Peter's Church, built by the Blaenavon ironmasters in 1804.

DI2006_0003 NPRN 96484

Below: The creation of Blaenavon Ironworks (far left) brought housing, a mansion in wooded grounds, a works school and a church to the curving line established by the railway that served it. The new town centre of the 1840s was above the church (far right).

CD2003_629_016 NPRN 33165

The uplands at the heads of the Glamorgan and Monmouthshire valleys were hardly populated before the Industrial Revolution but by the 1840s some 150,000 people lived there. A string of new ironworks appeared between the 1750s and the 1830s on the rim of the coalfield, where iron ore, coking coal and limestone were found in close proximity. These were vast enterprises by the standards of the day and people flooded in – for example Cyfarthfa Ironworks at Merthyr Tydfil employed 2,000 people in the 1790s. The workers were housed initially by the iron companies in scattered terraces, but in time towns began to appear. Some were planned by the ironmasters, like Butetown near Rhymney, but most grew haphazardly as the iron industry expanded. Most early ironworkers' housing disappeared during clearance schemes in the twentieth century, but examples were recorded by Jeremy Lowe, whose database is held in the National Monuments Record of Wales. The Blaenavon World Heritage Site is one of the best places to see how the early industrial settlements evolved.

There were only scattered hill farms around the head of the Afon Lwyd until 1787, when three Midlands businessmen chose it as the site for a new ironworks and began negotiations to lease a tract of 4,855 hectares of mineral-rich land. By 1792 they had laid out three furnaces blown by a steam engine, mines for coal and iron ore, limestone quarries and interconnecting railways. A courtyard of houses built in 1788 still overlooks the furnace yard at Blaenavon Ironworks, now in the care of Cadw. These four-room

houses were of a standard to attract skilled workers who would establish the ironworks. The middle row of the court contained the company shop, an institution vital to support a new community in such an isolated location. Terraces of smaller company houses were placed near the ironworks, mines and quarries, and such was the pressure on accommodation that the ten arches of a railway viaduct were infilled with dwellings. It was more than a decade later that the nucleus of a town began to develop through the addition, along the curving line of the railway that carried the products of the ironworks to the Monmouthshire canal, of a mansion for the managing partner in 1800, a church in 1804, a works school in 1816 and further terraces of company housing.

However, the town really came into existence only between the 1840s and the 1860s, when a new centre appeared on privately-owned plots of land north-east of the church, breaking the iron company's stranglehold on the supply of food, drink and accommodation. Features typical of the ironmaking towns of south Wales can still be seen – chapels, pubs, shops and ranks of houses built by speculative builders. The numerous shops sold the full range of products that a prosperous industrial community wished to buy, including food, clothes, boots, jewellery and glasswares. By the late nineteenth century there were eighteen places of worship and some forty pubs. Having come from nothing, the town reached a population of 13,000 before halving in size in the twentieth century as the iron, steel and coal industries declined.

Peter Wakelin and Tom Pert

062 Depopulation in the Uplands: Penblaenmilo

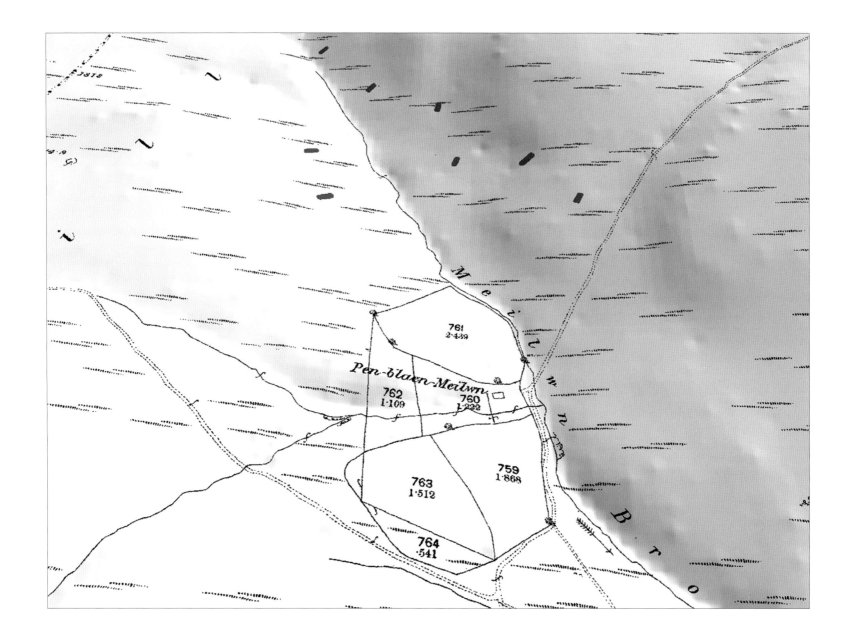

*The farmstead at Penblaenmilo, Radnorshire, was already roofless by the time of the Ordnance Survey map of 1891,
but the boundaries of its small enclosure remained. This image has been rendered in three dimensions to show the valley topography
and the pillow mounds identified by fieldwork (added in red).*

NPRN 81460
© Landmark Information Group Ltd. © geoPerspectives

Above: A ruined upland farmstead: Pen-castell, Aberedw, in 2004.

DI2006_1959 NPRN 81463

The abandoned farmstead of Penblaenmilo is high on Aberedw Hill near Builth Wells. It is one of many abandoned homesteads scattered across the rural landscape, memorials to an agricultural society that reached its zenith at the beginning of the age of industry. According to local tradition the house stood on one of the main droving routes running eastwards from Builth Wells to the English cities. Drovers could stop for a break on their long journey, their animals being penned in the fields around the house.

The 1841 census shows that 'Penblaenmilon' was then the home of William and Anne Meredith and their five young children. William, like many men in this wholly agricultural community, was employed as a labourer. The 1841 census marked the high tide of population in many rural parishes. It recorded 345 people in Aberedw, almost all making their living from the land. The 1842 tithe survey recorded that Penblaenmilo was owned by the Boughrood Charity Trust, founded in the seventeenth century to assist poor children in Radnorshire. The rents paid by the tenants at Penblaenmilo would have contributed to the fund.

From the 1840s onwards the increasing attraction of better wages and living conditions in towns and industrial areas, particularly in the south Wales valleys, drew more and more of the rural population away. By 1871, the last census to record people living at Penblaenmilo, the parish population had fallen to 306. By the 1880s Penblaenmilo was one of thousands of upland farmsteads and cottages that had been abandoned. Farmers were finding it increasingly difficult to retain younger farmhands on the land. Low wages, long working hours, often miserable conditions and the ill-health endured in damp, poorly-thatched homes made life in an industrial community an attractive proposition – stone-built, slate-roofed terraced houses were a step up for most rural people. Employment

in industry or commerce also meant a regular wage, usually much higher than could be earned on the land, and brought opportunities for further advancement. The 1891 census reflects this trend: by then Aberedw parish had a population of 197.

It is still possible at Penblaenmilo to make out the shape of the inglenook fireplace and the position of the front door, but the building is a complete ruin. Nearby are some of the other features of the working landscape: the small enclosures from the common land, evidence of former ploughing up to an altitude of 400 metres, and a group of pillow mounds used by earlier generations to farm rabbits for meat and fur, clustered around the stream above the house. Other farmsteads were spread across the hill, each now marked by small enclosures. Remains of a small kiln for drying grain have been found at one of them. Aberedw Hill must have seemed a very different place when large families lived and farmed on its slopes.

The Royal Commission's Uplands Archaeology Initiative has succeeded in recording the existence of a great number of abandoned cottages and farms similar to Penblaenmilo. In the uplands the ruins of such places have usually been left undisturbed. On lower farmland, away from the commons, they have almost always been swept away during the twentieth century by land improvements and more intensive farming methods.

Jenny Hall and Paul Sambrook

Below and right: All that remains of Penblaenmilo.

NPRN 81460
Courtesy of Trysor

063 Marine Transport

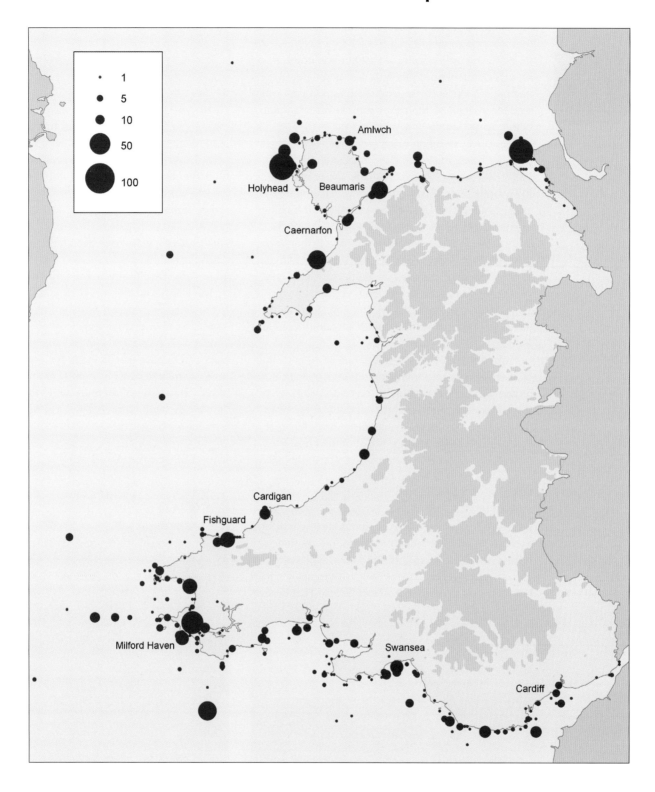

Known shipping losses around the Welsh coast between 1750 and 1850.

The Royal Commission has a remit to compile information about maritime archaeology, including shipwrecks, downed aircraft, submerged prehistoric landscapes and monuments in intertidal areas. Part of the work to enhance the maritime record involves searching written sources for shipwrecks. The early industrial era produced much documentation of shipping and maritime casualties: for example, the grouping of insurance underwriters that was to become Lloyds of London published a newspaper of shipping intelligence in 1741 and its first *Register Book of Shipping* in 1764.

The 7,000 identified wrecks and shipping losses recorded in the Royal Commission's databases indicate where some of the greatest hazards lay: the Llŷn peninsula, Anglesey and the Menai Straits, St David's Head and Strumble Head. Shipping losses concentrated in the approaches to the most successful ports. A map of the 1,245 that date from between 1750 and 1850 reveals the importance in the Industrial Revolution era of Cardiff (especially for the growing iron trade from Merthyr Tydfil), Swansea (the copper trade), Milford Haven, Fishguard, Cardigan, Caernarfon, Holyhead and Beaumaris. It shows the growing importance of the transatlantic trading routes to Liverpool and Bristol bringing sugar, tobacco, cotton and slaves. The losses include brigs, sloops, schooners, galiots, snows, full-rigged ships, packet ships working to and from Ireland, and several early paddle steamers and steamships.

Right: Meadow Mill, Greenfield valley, the site of Thomas Williams's copper mill.

DI2008_0844 NPRN 408131

Below: Amlwch harbour in the nineteenth century, showing the shipyard and graving dock to the left, the working quayside, warehouse and ore storage bins to the right, and three trading schooners.

DI2007_1760 NPRN 41244

One concentration of losses highlights Amlwch in the north of Anglesey. With the rapid expansion of copper mining at Mynydd Parys after 1768 this small fishing village experienced a boom and the numbers of ships working in and out of the small inlet made improvements necessary. After 1793 the channels and berths were deepened and two piers were built, each with a small whitewashed lighthouse. The eastern side of the harbour was quarried back to create a wide quay with a warehouse and bins for the storage of ore, coal and scrap iron, and the western side was dedicated to shipbuilding and repair. The town's first recorded shipyard belonged to Nicholas and Francis Treweek, who launched their first vessel, the 68-ton Unity, in 1825. A northerly gale could still wreak havoc, as witnessed in 1889 when five damaged vessels broke free from their moorings, including 'the schooner Emporer which was in the dry dock floated and came out and knocked against the backing of the pier head and went to pieces'.

Copper ore from Amlwch was transported to smelting works at Ravenhead in Lancashire and Swansea, and copper goods were manufactured at Greenfield in Flintshire. Anglesey's 'Copper King', Thomas Williams, produced copper sheathing and innovative copper bolts to fix them to ships' hulls to prevent damage by marine organisms such as the teredo worm. This gave important protection to wooden ships sailing to warmer waters and was found to discourage barnacles and weed, helping them to maintain speed and manoeuvrability. Sheathed ships were marked with the abbreviation 'Y M' for 'yellow metal' in Lloyd's Register. The rivalry between masters to complete fast passages in their 'coppered bottoms' became an intrinsic part of the spirit of the wooden sailing ship era.

Deanna Groom

064 Protecting the Shipping Lanes: Lighthouses

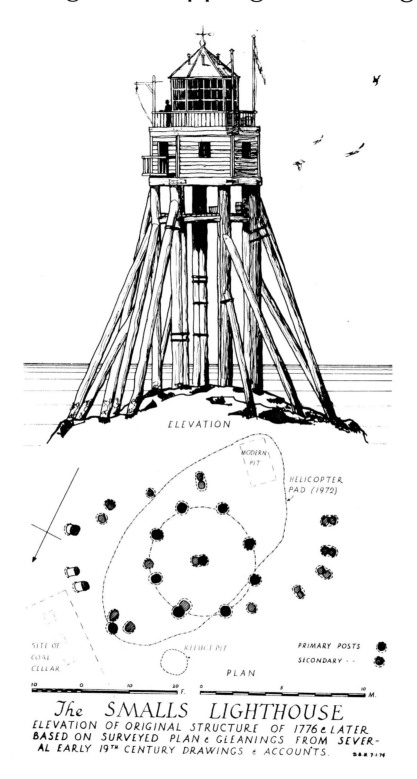

ELEVATION

MODERN PIT

HELICOPTER PAD (1972)

SITE OF COAL CELLAR

REFUGE PIT

PRIMARY POSTS

SECONDARY

PLAN

The SMALLS LIGHTHOUSE
ELEVATION OF ORIGINAL STRUCTURE OF 1776 & LATER
BASED ON SURVEYED PLAN & GLEANINGS FROM SEVER-
AL EARLY 19TH CENTURY DRAWINGS & ACCOUNTS.   D.B.H. 7.1.74

*Douglas Hague's drawing of the original Smalls lighthouse and the archaeological remains
of what was the first piled-light to be built in Britain.*

DI2006_0587 NPRN 34350

Above: James Walker's graceful tower of 1858-61 stands on the exposed rock of the Smalls.

DI2008_0797 NPRN 34350

Below and right: Diagram showing the development of the castellated tower at the Skerries, Anglesey. The Skerries lighthouse is one of the notable rock-towers off the Welsh coast.

DI2008_0798 and AP_2004_0275 NPRN 41287

Welsh lighthouses played an important part in ensuring the safe carriage of the products of the world's first industrial revolution and the goods and materials that came to Britain in return. Liverpool and Bristol, at either end of Wales, became principal ports for rapidly expanding transatlantic trade in the eighteenth and nineteenth centuries. Milford Haven and the great coal, iron and copper ports of south Wales also generated large amounts of maritime traffic. Between 1770 and 1870 about twenty new lighthouses were built and many older ones were reconstructed to light the Welsh coast as a result of rising shipping losses and pressure from merchants, owners and seamen.

The Smalls lighthouse, far out to sea beyond the western tip of Pembrokeshire, and the Skerries lighthouse, off Anglesey, were crucial in lighting the sea lane southwards from Liverpool. Both were privately owned until they were bought by Trinity House in the mid-nineteenth century. Light dues were claimed from ships at every port and huge revenues were available from lighthouses on prime routes as trade grew. John Phillips, the master of St George's Dock in Liverpool, obtained a lease to build a lighthouse on the Smalls Rock in 1773. Henry Whiteside, a musical-instrument maker, designed the lighthouse for Phillips. Rather than build a massive masonry tower to defy the elements, he adopted the ingenious plan of a piled structure through which the fury of the sea could pass. His design, completed in 1776, was the forerunner of all pile-lights of the nineteenth century. It was of composite construction with a number of timber piles and three cast-iron ones – a pioneering use of

cast iron structurally. It was replaced in 1861 by a stone tower built for Trinity House by the prolific engineer James Walker.

The danger of the Skerries rocks was recognised as early as 1658, when Henry Hascard appealed to Oliver Cromwell's Council of State to build a beacon. The first lighthouse, erected in about 1716, was rebuilt in about 1759 as a stone tower capped by a coal fire. The early eighteenth-century detached keeper's house may be the first such residence ever built. In 1804 it was raised and an oil-burning lantern was installed. James Walker then extensively restored it in a lavish style in about 1848 for Trinity House. The tower exhibits two of Walker's design characteristics – a decrease in diameter from bottom to top and a solid parapet.

By 1852 the dues paid to the Smalls and Skerries lighthouses were far greater than those of any other in the British Isles. When the Skerries was purchased by Trinity House in 1844 it was for a record price of £440,984. The original Smalls lighthouse, with its economic method of construction, was almost certainly the most profitable in the world.

The National Monuments Record contains a wealth of information about lighthouses, much of it from the work of Douglas Hague, investigator with the Royal Commission from 1948 to 1981, who wrote the book *Lighthouses* with Rosemary Christie, published in 1975. The Commission published *Lighthouses of Wales* in 1994, a compendium of Hague's research illustrated by his scale-drawings and photographs.

Angharad Williams

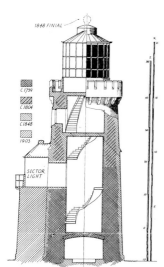

1848 FINIAL

C 1759
C 1804
C 1848
1903

SECTOR LIGHT

SECTION LOOKING SOUTH-WEST
The SKERRIES Anglesey

065 Picturesque Wales and the Early Tourists: Hafod

A mansion in the mountains: Hafod was designed by Thomas Baldwin and added to by John Nash and Anthony Salvin.
DI2008_0841 NPRN 5577

Jane Austen knew all about tourism. In *Pride and Prejudice* (1813) Elizabeth Bennet's 'touring' visit to Pemberley with her uncle and aunt illustrates a well-established practice among the aspiring social classes that permitted them to see both the countryside and how their betters lived. Such visits were undertaken when the owner of a country house was not at home, so that there should be no likelihood of the faux pas of Austen's novel. For those of matched social standing there was the house party: a fashion that had an impact on the architecture of houses by placing emphasis on ground-floor reception rooms that opened directly onto surrounding gardens or parkland. All visitors, invited and uninvited, would 'take in' local landmarks and beauty spots.

Such tourism was confined to those with connections and sufficient funds. By 1800 it had accelerated, aided by the growing network of turnpike roads and the curtailing of the fashionable European grand tour by the wars with France. The remoter parts of the United Kingdom became attractive substitutes for the continent, and Wales especially so. The Cambrian Mountains and Snowdonia provided natural scenic beauty together with physical and linguistic challenges, which were described in published tours and guides such as Thomas Pennant's *Tours in Wales* (1778-81), Revd Richard Warner's *A Second Walk through Wales* (1799) and B. H. Malkin's *The Scenery, Antiquities, and Biography of South Wales* (1804).

Right: A fountain mask photographed in Hafod's gardens in 1951.
DI2005_0904 NPRN 5577

Below: Hafod Arms Hotel.
DI2007_0107 NPRN 108359

Some estates were managed actively to create a picturesque landscape and provide amenities to attract visitors. Notable among them was Thomas Johnes's Hafod estate in the upper Ystwyth valley, Cardiganshire. Johnes inherited Hafod in 1780 and chose to settle there rather than in his native Herefordshire. In an area considered a remote wilderness he spent the next thirty-five years and his fortune improving the estate [060]. He had a 'gothick' mansion built and then employed the architect John Nash to add a long conservatory and an eye-catching octagonal library. He laid out extensive grounds, built walks among the waterfalls and precipices and is believed to have planted more than three million trees. He positively welcomed visitors: his 'invited' guests included distinguished people of the day, whose letters, notes and sketches give fascinating insights into Johnes's activities. He also keenly 'advertised' Hafod to a wider audience, for example convincing William Gilpin to describe the recently laid out Lady's and Gentlemen's Walks for the second edition of his *Observations on the River Wye, and Several Parts of South Wales etc. relative chiefly to picturesque beauty* in 1789. In 1795 he went even further and provided accommodation, building the first Hafod Arms at Devil's Bridge.

Hafod's interest as a tourist attraction was sustained long after Johnes's death in 1816. During his tour in 1854 the author of *Wild Wales*, George Borrow, stayed at the Hafod Arms 'to view the wonders of Wales, of which this region close by is considered amongst the principal'. He was the only visitor at the inn but noted that 'in the summer [it] is thronged with guests'.

Peter White

Gardens

266
4·737

269
2·761

TYLER STREET

BOOKER STREET

FOX STREET

RICHARDS TERRACE

ROAD

B.M. 38·5

B.M. 36·9

MAUD STREET

THEODORA STREET

B.M. 38·3

Hotel

BROADWAY

HAROLD STREET

BERTRAM STREET

CECIL STREET

HELEN STREET

B.M. 36·3

B.M. 36·8

B.M. 38·6

B.M. 39·2

B.M. 38·0

B.M. 36·6

Steam
Joinery
Works

Chapel
(Bible Chr¹)

Victorian Society

Penny Icke[1]

In 1918 Lytton Strachey wrote, in *Eminent Victorians*, 'The history of the Victorian Age will never be written: we know too much about it. For ignorance is the first requisite of the historian – ignorance, which simplifies and clarifies, which selects and omits, with a placid perfection unattainable by the highest art.' The Victorian Age was a tumultuous period about which we know a great deal, but some of its most important themes are still being explored. The buildings and landscapes of Wales are an important resource for understanding the processes that transformed the country.

The reign of Queen Victoria from 1837 to 1901 saw an astonishing speed of social, intellectual and technological development. It was an age of industry, wealth and social reform. A dramatic increase in the population together with mass migration changed the face of town and countryside. New-found wealth from industry and international trade led to the growth of the middle classes as the economy was transformed from one based primarily on agriculture to one driven by capitalism and entrepreneurship, while the identity of the new industrial working class was consolidated. The valleys of south Wales drew in tens of thousands to work in the coal and iron industries, and slate-quarrying communities in the

north also expanded rapidly [069]. Locomotive railways aided the boom in Welsh industry and by the 1870s the new networks enabled all classes to enjoy travel and tourism [075]. Such fundamental change inevitably had its downside, and Victorian Wales also witnessed social distress and exploitation. In the middle of the century legislation began to regulate the atrocious working conditions. Reforms followed, directed at public health, social conditions and education. Such measures were seen as an antidote to the popular unrest that had broken out previously in the shape of the Rebecca Riots, the Merthyr Rising and the Chartist movement.

The rapid growth of the south Wales coalfield was the outstanding feature of Wales's development in the second half of the nineteenth century. Although coal had been mined for many years on the coalfield rims to fuel iron or copper smelting, the 1840s and 1850s saw the exploitation of the central coalfield and the beginnings of the international trade in steam coal, supported by the coming of the railways and the building of docks at Cardiff, Newport and Swansea. Output from the valleys rose from approximately 4.5 million tons in 1840 to 8.5 million in 1854 and over 50 million by 1912. The Rhondda valleys especially became synonymous

Above: Historic photograph of about 1915 showing a locomotive at the Ocean Deep Navigation Colliery, Treharris, Merthyr Tydfil.
GTJ28935 NPRN 80489

Opposite page: First edition (1881) 25-inch Ordnance Survey map (enlarged) of Cardiff showing the later nineteenth-century process of laying out workers' terraced housing around the main railway in Roath, Splott and Adamsdown.
GL MMXXXVII.12 DI2008_0541

Left: Crumlin Viaduct under construction in 1856.
DI2008_0532 NPRN 34959
Courtesy Howarth-Loomes collection

[1] With a contribution on country-house architecture by David McLees.

Above: Early photograph from the John Cornwell collection showing the Ferndale Collieries in the Rhondda which were sunk by David Davies for the extraction of steam coal. The terraces overlooking the mines were built to house the influx of miners and their families.

DI2008_0535 NPRN 80496

slate, non-ferrous metals, iron and tinplate, and was a significant steelmaking country. Supporting industries such as brick and tile manufacturing, engineering, transport and brewing also flourished. Industrialists, merchants and landowners ploughed much of their wealth back into the infrastructure of railways, docks and towns.

Wealthy Victorians also sought to satisfy their own tastes and interests, and for many of them money was no object. They could indulge their flights of fancy to build lavish country houses – the marquis of Bute's Castell Coch remains a prime example [073]. The years from 1855 to 1875 saw country-house building at its peak. No single style dominated and architects felt free to experiment. Victorian house design ranged stylistically through Italianate classicism at Penoyre (Breconshire), French Renaissance at Wynnstay (Denbighshire), French Gothic Revival at Hafodunos (Denbighshire), Spanish at Soughton Hall (Flintshire) and Queen Anne Revival at Kinmel Park (Denbighshire), with its high mansard roofs and dormer windows.

with black coal tips, colliery headgear and row upon row of miners' terraces. Workers flooded in from all over the British Isles but especially from the Welsh rural hinterland and agricultural areas across the Severn estuary. Between 1851 and 1910 the population of the Rhondda soared from perhaps 1,000 to more than 150,000. Other industries grew alongside mining. For much of the Victorian period Wales was the world's most important producer of

The grade I listed Hafodunos was built in 1861-8 for a wealthy Liverpool merchant, H. R. Sandbach, by Sir Gilbert Scott, who was also famed for the design of St Pancras Hotel and the Foreign Office in London. Though he dominated the mid-Victorian Gothic Revival, Scott designed only this one country house in Wales. He employed a sober, late thirteenth-century French style, as shown by the symmetrical garden front, though he added extravagant touches with the octagonal structure to the gable end

Hafodunos, built to the design of Sir Gilbert Scott in 1861-8.

DI2005_0768 NPRN 27268

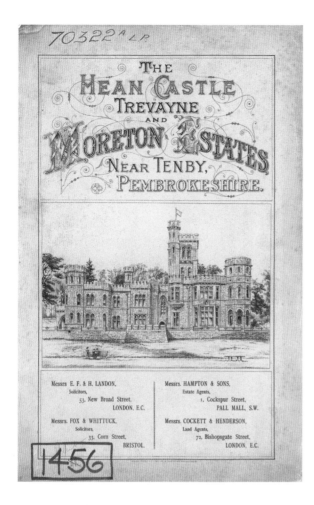

(suggestive of a medieval kitchen like Glastonbury's but actually a top-lit billiard room) and an openwork spire over the clock tower to the rear. The house has suffered from serious dilapidation and was devastated by a fire in 2004, adding to the importance of the photographic archive held by the Royal Commission.

The landlords of large estates spent much of their capital on improvements, not only of their grand houses and gardens but of farms, estate villages, roads and bridges. Their estates were seen as an outward symbol of their aspiration to social eminence, and some overstretched themselves financially [074]. After his Gothic Revival house at Leighton near Welshpool was completed in 1851 the banker John Naylor went on to build a model farm where he experimented with many of the new technologies of the age [072]. His neighbour, the earl of Powis, spent almost a quarter of his rents on improvements to his own estate between 1859 and 1875, helping to sustain it through the agricultural depression of the late nineteenth century when many landowners were hit badly by poor harvests and the growth of imports from North America and Australasia. The

National Monuments Record of Wales holds a collection of estate sales particulars from this period that demonstrates both the scale of such estates and the effects of the slump. Many tenants and labourers moved to the towns and industrial areas in search of work.

In the eighteenth century the iron districts had seen families like the Crawshays in Merthyr Tydfil build cheap housing for the people who flooded to industrial work. In 1866 the Sanitary Act compelled local authorities to improve conditions by providing sewers, supplying water and cleaning streets. It defined overcrowding for the first time and appointed sanitary inspectors. This Act, combined with local by-laws, meant that most workers' housing built from the 1870s onwards was far better designed and constructed than the cottages associated with the iron industry a century earlier, or the primitive dwellings of the rural poor [066]. In south Wales most of the workers' housing in the Victorian era was not built by industrial employers but by private building firms. Building clubs were set up to help families save to buy their houses, but many people rented from private or industrial landlords. As wages increased, for the first time ordinary people were able to save or spend their surplus on things other than the basics of life. The better-paid aspired to a detached house or villa with a private garden – suburbs were built with leafy parks and open spaces in places such as Roath, Pontcanna, Victoria Park and Penarth around Cardiff, and Sketty and Morriston at Swansea.

Left: Sales particulars of the Hean estate in 1898. A series of bad investments led to the breakup of the estate only twenty years after this grand castellated Tudor gothic mansion had been built.
DI2008_0544 NPRN 22044

Above: Terraced housing in Splott, Cardiff built during the 1880s to house the steel workers and their families.
DI2006_1810 NPRN 309003

Below: Victoria Park, Cardiff, was built in 1897–8 to celebrate Queen Victoria's Diamond Jubilee. It was the first municipal park in Cardiff and one of the first in the country.
AP_2006_1815 NPRN 301658

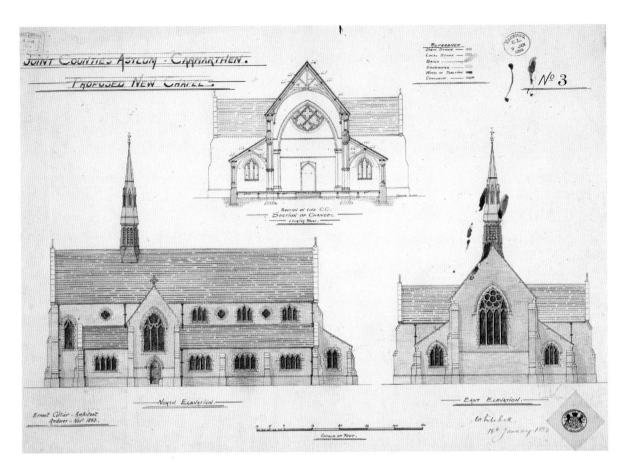

Designs by Ernest Collier (1883) for the proposed new chapel at Joint Counties Asylum, Carmarthen.

DI2005_0791 NPRN 100196

Although the Victorian era saw moves towards state involvement in social welfare, its institutions were desperately inadequate by modern standards. Its workhouses, asylums, prisons and hospitals kept their inhabitants separate from the rest of society. Workhouses were the only source of food and shelter for many of the old and the sick [076] but conditions were punitive and families were split up. After the 1834 Poor Law Amendment Act parishes established workhouses instead of dispensing poor relief as money, food and blankets, but the process was gradual. As late as 1845 the Poor Law Commissioners recorded that seventeen of the forty-seven Welsh Poor Law unions still had no 'efficient workhouse in operation'; it was not until 1879 that Rhayader complied with the legislation and built a workhouse for its poor. With regard to hospitals, *The Builder* in 1858 commented that in most the care of inmates was by no means a priority and people would have more hope of cure by 'lying in the open air'. Asylums were used as a dumping ground for the poor and sick and in the mid-nineteenth century were still open for inquisitive visitors to gawp at the afflicted. As late as 1844 the Commissioners in Lunacy were finding men and women in dark cells strapped to beds or chairs, although the extreme brutalities of

the previous century had largely disappeared. As the Victorian period progressed therapeutic activities, industry and patience became approved approaches. The new paternalistic notions were manifest in monumental architecture: some institutions appeared more like stately homes than medical facilities, having attached farms, lodges and chapels [093].

The first half of the nineteenth century saw an enormous popular growth in religion, predominantly marked in Wales by nonconformist chapels. By 1851 the religious census noted 2,813 chapels in Wales – over the preceding fifty years one chapel had been built every eight days on average [071]. Most parish churches were far from the new industrial communities. The established Church was slow to adapt but there was a gradual upsurge in church building [070]; however, the chapel was the choice of the majority in Wales. Chapel services emphasised the individual, were highly charged and allowed the layperson to play a prominent role, giving individuals a sense of self worth they could not find in the established Church. It was claimed in the middle of the nineteenth century that 'The Non-conformists of Wales are the people of Wales'. They came to dominate all aspects of life. The 1852 general election saw the first Unitarian Member of Parliament, Walter

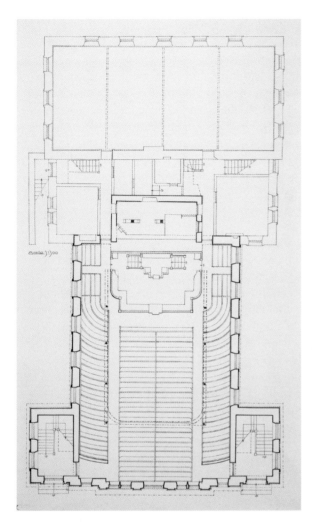

opposite the entrance, some of the more wealthy congregations built an imposing organ.

Externally chapels varied enormously; for although chapel designers such as Thomas Thomas, William Beddoe Rees and Richard Owens had distinctive styles it was frequently the minister and congregation who chose the style of their building having consulted design catalogues or viewed other chapels. This led to strange juxtapositions from architectural history. Compendia of Gothic, Lombardic, Classical and Greek were created that generated many unfavourable comments from architectural critics. The rivalry of denominations combined with the revivalist fervour during the nineteenth century meant that chapels underwent many alterations, ranging from a new façade to a complete redesign. The chapel fabric was not seen as sacred; it was merely a meeting house to be altered, enlarged or demolished. Most chapels have plaques recording their establishment, rebuildings, enlargements and renovations.

Pupils in the mid-nineteenth century were segregated by gender, class and religion. Relatively few girls received any formal instruction. The wealthy educated their sons at home or at private school. Middle-class boys tended to go to small, local fee-paying schools. Sons of the poor were

Coffin, elected to a Cardiff constituency. Nonconformity became integral to attitudes to the individual's worth, support for education and the politicisation of Wales.

Many of the larger chapels were complexes containing schoolrooms, a vestry, a minister's house, meeting rooms, library and stables as well as the chapel itself – an example is Moreia Calvinistic Methodist Chapel in Llangefni, Anglesey. Such chapels became focal points of their communities, not just filled on Sundays but used throughout the week for meetings, instruction and eisteddfodau. In layout they differed from Anglican churches in that each was seen as an auditorium where the congregation gathered to listen to the word of God rather than to practise liturgical rites. Nonconformists were unconcerned about the orientation of their buildings and did not require the pulpit at the east end: it tended to be placed on the back wall of the chapel with the *sedd fawr* or 'big seat' for the chapel elders directly in front. Frequently there was a three-sided gallery to maximise capacity. On the fourth side,

Above: Seion Independent Chapel, Aberystwyth, originally built in 1814-15 and then rebuilt in 1876-78 to the designs of Richard Owens of Liverpool. It is a grade 2 listed building with a particularly fine arcaded and galleried interior.
DI2006_0268 NPRN 7147

Above left: Plan of Moreia Calvinistic Methodist Chapel, Llangefni, Anglesey, surveyed as part of the Chapels Recording Project. It was erected as a memorial chapel to the preacher and minister John Elias to the designs of Owen Morris Roberts of Porthmadog. The large chapel complex includes a vestry, various schoolrooms and minister's rooms, and a chapel house.
GTJ00013 NPRN 8783

restricted to charity schools, Sunday schools or no schooling at all. Charity schools such as those run by the National Society for Promoting the Education of the Poor in the Principles of the Established Church and the British and Foreign Society were founded to further elementary education, and the first half of the century saw a great many of these schools being built [068]. Progress was still slow, however, as the *Blue Books* suggested controversially in 1847 in a damning report on education in Wales. The Welsh were painted as 'ill-educated, poor, dirty, unchaste, and potentially rebellious'. This was mainly attributed to the Welsh language and nonconformity. The majority of the working classes were still monoglot Welsh speakers, yet lessons were held in English. Teachers received no training and few government grants for schools had come to Wales. It was noted in the 1840s that literacy in Wales was so bad that barely half of all bridegrooms could sign their name on the marriage register.

By 1870 Wales had experienced a huge change in attitudes towards elementary education. Even in south Wales, where children working in industry brought vital income to their families, 102 British schools were built between 1853 and 1860. Schools tended to have a distinctive architecture with high windows and a bell tower, as can be seen on the British School at Corris. Gothic was deemed to be

the appropriately solid and imposing style, as recommended by Henry Kendall in his *Designs for Schools* in 1847.

Some industrialists provided schools where their employees could send their children, but few boys or girls would remain in them for more than a year or two as parents withdrew them to start work. It was not until the Factory Acts Extension Act of 1867 that children aged between 8 and 13 were prohibited from night work and compelled to attend school half-time. This, combined with the Education Act of 1870, created a network of elementary schools across Wales. For the first time education was seen as a state responsibility rather than the remit of voluntary effort, and the country was divided into districts to build the new board schools. British schools were incorporated into the school board system but national schools remained independent. In 1889 the Welsh Intermediate Education Act led to county schools being built in a flurry. By 1902 Wales had 95 intermediate schools with most pupils originating from lower middle-class and working-class backgrounds. The period also saw the introduction of higher education to Wales with the University of Wales set up in 1893 as a degree awarding body. By the end of the nineteenth century, as the historian John Davies has said, 'there were more opportunities to receive an academic education in Wales than in England'.

Corris British School, Merioneth, built in 1872. It has since been converted into a youth hostel.

DS2008_179_004 NPRN 406767

Lytton Strachey was right in identifying the vast amount known about the Victorian period. The developments that took place can be charted through numerous surveys, censuses, investigations and commissions in the latter part of the century that were designed to assess trends, abuses and injustices. By the end of the century the majority of male adults could vote, there was regulation of working conditions, there were some social services and there were laws to protect the populace. The state had begun to adopt the principle that it should take responsibility for the welfare of society. These social and economic developments had a huge impact on the environment as new institutions were commissioned. Hospitals, prisons, town halls, museums and libraries multiplied and grand architectural styles reflected their dignity and importance. Victorian architecture not only served structural and functional needs but had a didactic mission and reflected the unprecedented social, intellectual and technological changes the age wrought. The last decades of Victoria's reign saw Britain reach the zenith of its industrial and economic dominance in the world and an optimism and confidence unrivalled in British history.

The Workingmen's Hall and Institute, Blaenavon, was opened in 1895 having been funded by a halfpenny weekly subscription from workers' wages. It was designed by E. A. Lansdowne of Newport and housed a library, billiards and reading rooms, and a large hall. Over a hundred such institutions were built in Wales.

DI2005_1057 NPRN 31951

066 The Victorian Cottage

Top: Troedrhiwfallen, Cribyn, prior to restoration and, below, after restoration.
Top: DI2007_0391. Below: DI2007_0088 NPRN 3079

Above: Apex of a scarfed cruck-truss supporting the thatched roof at Coed-weddus, Llangadog, Carmarthenshire.

DS2006_001_020 NPRN 17230

Right: Straw rope underthatch at Ty'n Cwm, Llansantffraid, Carmarthenshire.

DI2008_0512 NPRN 35341

The Industrial Revolution had as much of an effect on the countryside as it did on towns. A rapidly-growing population demanded more food. As more land was taken into agriculture many of the rural poor had to resort to illegally enclosing common land and building homes there for themselves; the number of cottages blossomed. By the middle of the nineteenth century, however, more and more food was being imported and increasing mechanisation on the farm meant there was less need for farm labour. A great exodus from the countryside began and the number of cottages fell: in the 1890s there were only 35,000 left in Wales, and only a fraction of those survive today. Troedrhiwfallen at Cribyn in Cardiganshire is a good example.

Early cottages were built with whatever was at hand and often display great skill and ingenuity in their construction. Turf might be used for both walls and roof but was not very long lasting. Many cottages of earth or clay ('clom' as it was known locally) survive in west Wales, sometimes combined with stone. Earth walls demanded a stone footing to prevent decay from damp and had to be protected from rain by being lime-washed. The walls of Troedrhiwfallen are unusually high – it may have been raised at some time.

A particular type of roof-truss is often associated with the earth walls of west Wales: the jointed or scarfed cruck, in which the blades of the truss sit on wooden uprights placed in the walls, pegged to them for extra security, as is the case here. Many rural cottages throughout Wales were thatched. In

the western areas branches were laid or woven around the roof timbers, and on these was laid an under-thatch of gorse, broom, heather or whatever was available locally. Similarly, the thatch could be of wheat, barley, or moorland grass; separated into handfuls, it was knotted at one end and thrust into the under-thatch with a forked implement. Hazel rods were pegged into the roof to keep vulnerable areas from being lifted by the wind. The chimney consisted of a wicker framework, also thatched, but as these were prone to catch fire many were replaced by brick stacks. When the thatch decayed, or if cottages were used for other purposes, it became usual to cover the roof with corrugated iron.

Most cottages have a very simple plan: the earliest would have been of one room only but those that survive usually have two downstairs rooms. Partitions were of wattle and daub, lath and plaster, or wooden boards. By the mid-eighteenth century it was common to have a *croglofft* or *taflod* (a mezzanine) above the smaller room, accessed by a ladder as at Troedrhiwfallen. Fully-lofted cottages had a central staircase. The room with the main, or only, fireplace was open to the roof. In west Wales particularly the chimney hood was of wattle. The open fire was later replaced with a brick fireplace and an iron grate or stove.

Troedrhiwfallen shows a welcome development – it has been sensitively restored and is now available for holidays.

Eurwyn Wiliam

Pebbled stone floor with herringbone borders in the kitchen of Hen Felin Cottage, Cwm Mabws, Cardiganshire.

DI2008_0435 NPRN 5600

067 Welfare and the Workhouse: Albro Castle

Warden and Mrs Nugent with staff and orphans at Albro Castle workhouse in 1927.

DI2008_0248 NPRN 3041

Above: Entrance front, Albro Castle workhouse, Cardigan.
DI2008_0246 NPRN 3041

Right: Aerial view showing the airing courts and central observatory at Llanfyllin workhouse, Montgomeryshire.
AP 2004 0601 NPRN 32044

Below: Rear elevation of Albro Castle workhouse showing the H-plan.
DI2008_0247 NPRN 3041

Albro Castle was the workhouse for the twenty-five parishes that joined together to meet the requirements of the Poor Law by forming the Cardigan Union. After it fell out of use, its remote rural location on the border of Cardiganshire and Pembrokeshire helped to protect it from alteration or demolition, unlike most urban workhouses. It belongs to the first phase of workhouse construction after the 1834 Poor Law Amendment Act. Workhouse design was dominated by a small number of architects. Initially, George Wilkinson of Oxford was approached by the Board of Guardians, but the final designs for a workhouse housing 120 paupers were by a local man, William Owen of Haverfordwest.

Owen's design was a version of the 'cruciform plan' recommended by the Poor Law Commissioners to segregate different types of pauper. This workhouse was an H-plan with airing courts arranged around the central spine and rear wing. An octagonal observatory (or 'panopticon') with windows in the corners of each wing provided a view of the courts. The wings housed separate male and female day-rooms and dormitories.

There were competing architectural styles for workhouses just as for mid-nineteenth-century religious, educational and public buildings. Albro Castle was in the Tudor style – expressed in the drip-moulded windows, twin Gothic entrance doorways to the gabled entrance front and brick chimney clusters. These details were more akin to George Gilbert Scott's Elizabethan-style workhouses than the severe neo-classical style favoured by Wilkinson and other architects. The different associations of architectural style were vividly depicted in A. W. N. Pugin's book

Contrasts (1841), which compared the neo-classical panopticon design unfavourably with an ancient poorhouse. However, the neo-Tudor style, which mixed the 'old English of the Elizabethan era' and the 'simpler Gothic of earlier ages', had positive connotations. *The Welshman* in 1841 considered the new Aberystwyth workhouse, which resembled Albro, 'picturesque, domestic and somewhat collegiate'.

Albro Castle remained largely as built from its completion in 1840 until it closed in 1948, apart from the addition in 1884 of vagrants' cells with stone-breaking grills. The Board of Guardians was abolished in 1929 and in its last phase before wartime requisition Albro Castle housed orphans rather than paupers and vagrants. The National Monuments Record has copied an evocative photograph of the warden and other staff with orphans.

Albro Castle belongs to a small group of early workhouses in Wales dating from around 1840. Llanfyllin and Hay are closest to it in design, with cruciform plans complete with octagonal observatories – best appreciated from the air. Rhayader is considerably later (about 1880) and is less characteristic in design. Most surviving workhouses in Wales have been incorporated in hospital complexes, as at Penrhyndeudraeth, Haverfordwest, Aberystwyth, Cardiff, Holywell and St Asaph. Rhayader has been adapted as a hotel and an energetic trust is seeking new uses for Llanfyllin. Albro Castle has been converted to flats since it was recorded by the Royal Commission but it remains a poignant reminder of early Victorian welfare provision.

Richard Suggett

068 Victorian Schools

Photomontage of school plaques and date-stones from the Malcolm Seaborne Collection.

The National School, Llanengan, Caernarfonshire, was built in 1847-8 with ornate Jacobean-style gables. It was converted to a dwelling in about 1980.

DI2007_1560 NPRN 23226

The British School, Llangollen, was built in 1846. It was converted to a Calvinistic Methodist chapel after 1882 and later became the Penllyn Evangelical Free Church.

DI2007_1565 NPRN 7726

The National School, Abergele, Denbighshire, was built in 1869 to the designs of G. E. Street. It embellishes the standard Gothic double-gabled school type with some wonderful Victorian flourishes: the octagonal stone bell-turret with spirelet, zig-zag patterned slating, and a myriad of mock-Tudor chimneys.

DI2007_1561 NPRN 23348

During the nineteenth century the population of Wales rose from under half a million to over two million. Industrialisation, particularly in south Wales, was accompanied by a rapid growth of schools. The Church of England (as it was before Welsh disestablishment in 1920) built numerous 'National' Schools. They multiplied rapidly in Wales, where there was very little educational opportunity for the poor, and by 1833 there were 146 national schools instructing over 13,000 pupils. However the Anglican principles of these schools were seen as coercive by nonconformists and many refused to send their children to them. The British and Foreign Society set up non-denominational schools in an attempt to offer a more acceptable elementary education. Without state backing such schools struggled; it was not until 1833 that the government offered grants to both societies for the building of schools.

Following the Education Act of 1870, which authorised the setting up of boards financed by local rates, the building of elementary schools increased considerably in both urban and rural areas. During the late Victorian and Edwardian period, when the Welsh coal industry reached its peak, the rate of school building in Wales exceeded that in England.

In secondary education, too, Wales was in some respects ahead of the field. The old grammar schools were reformed, secondary schools for girls were established at Llandaff, Denbigh and Dolgellau, and under the terms of the Welsh Intermediate Education Act of 1889 nearly a hundred other secondary schools were established, supported by local rates and Treasury grant – anticipating by more than a decade the Balfour Education Act of 1902. These in turn stimulated the growth of university colleges.

Late Victorian Wales was largely dominated politically by Liberal nonconformists, an important part of whose programme was to provide non-denominational schools controlled by elected bodies and financed from public funds at secondary level. This policy triumphed with the passing of the Welsh Intermediate Education Act of 1889. By the end of the nineteenth century as many as ninety-four county intermediate (secondary) schools had been established throughout Wales. These soon came to be called 'county' or 'grammar' schools until they became in most cases the nuclei of comprehensive schools after the Second World War. Even today only two per cent of Welsh children attend private schools, compared with seven per cent in Britain as a whole.

The montage of plaques and date-stones depicted here illustrates the huge campaign of school building during the Victorian period.

Malcolm Seaborne

Malcolm Seaborne donated his large photographic collection to the National Monuments Record after his book, Schools in Wales, 1500-1900, was published in 1992. The collection includes images of many National and British schools as well as some of the larger post-1889 grammar and county institutions. It provides a remarkable resource for the study of school architecture.

069 The Slate Industry

Penrhyn slate quarry, Caernarfonshire, has remained in continuous production since the eighteenth century. The old quarry faces and working terraces (bottom right) are partly overwhelmed by tipping but the remains of mills, splitting workshops and inclines can be seen.

DI2007_1578 NPRN 40564

Above: Discarded track at Penrhyn slate quarry.
DI2008_0002 NPRN 40564

Right: Ynys-y-pandy slate mill, Dolbenmaen.
DS 2007_280_002 NPRN 40572

Below: Slate splitting at Penrhyn Quarry.
DI2008_0003 NPRN 40564

Although industrial Wales in the nineteenth century is chiefly associated with the mining of coal and the processing of copper, iron, steel and tinplate, it also sustained a remarkable industry, which is still active on a much-reduced scale, in the quarrying and processing of slate. This metamorphic, compacted mudstone with fissile properties was made predominantly into roofing material, but also into slabs for architectural and other uses – floors, sills, brewery vats, cisterns, urinals, electricity switchboards. Wales was the major supplier throughout the world in this period: the slate industry's archaeological remains are to be found quite literally from China to Peru.

Though slate has been quarried at well over 400 locations in Wales, the industry has been dominated by four main areas, all in Caernarfonshire and Merioneth: Dyffryn Ogwen, where in the eighteenth century the huge Penrhyn quarry reaped the benefit of reinvestment from its owner's West Indian sugar plantations; Llanberis, dominated by the Dinorwic quarry; Nantlle-Moel Tryfan, where quarrying dates from the medieval period; and Blaenau Ffestiniog. There were smaller, outlier groups of quarries elsewhere in the north-west, such as around Porthmadog, in the Conwy valley and its tributaries, and at Talyllyn, Corris and Dinas Mawddwy. There were also small slate quarries elsewhere, such as the Dee valley and parts of Pembrokeshire. Although methods of extraction varied considerably, including

stepped gallery workings at Penrhyn and Dinorwic, open pits at Nantlle and mining underground at Blaenau Ffestiniog, what is apparent in all but the very smallest workings is their sheer landscape impact, particularly in the form of the tips where unworkable rock was dumped. In the still active Penrhyn quarry, pictured in a Royal Commission aerial photograph, modern dumper-truck roads serve working galleries and the scale of present-day methods is beginning to efface the traces of the railway inclined planes, which were introduced from 1800 to take the raw blocks from the face to the processing areas (at the bottom right of the picture).

Through most of the nineteenth century the industry was characterised by low levels of technology. Hand-processing remained important in the production of roofing slates, though mechanised mills, initially to saw and shape slabs, gradually came into general use. Most remarkable in the archaeology of technical investment is the extraordinary (and untypical) Ynys-y-pandy slate mill, erected in 1856-7. A representation of the diffusion of technology from outside Wales is the iconic Cornish pumping engine installed at Dorothea quarry in the Nantlle area in 1904. Rail transport, both for movement within the quarries and to take the finished product to navigable water or a main-line railway, was all-important until lorries and bulldozers began to take over in the mid-twentieth century, leaving an archaeological record in the form of discarded track components and fragments of pointwork.

The slate industry and the quarrymen who earned their living in this difficult environment have long been icons of Welshness and the struggle for social justice. This distinctive industry has been studied intensively, by historians, sociologists and, increasingly, by archaeologists, often benefiting from the knowledge of those who have worked in the industry.

David Gwyn

070 Victorian Churches

Interior of Holy Trinity Church, Pontargothi, Carmarthenshire, with wall paintings by Alfred Stansell of Taunton.

DI2005_0773 NPRN 192

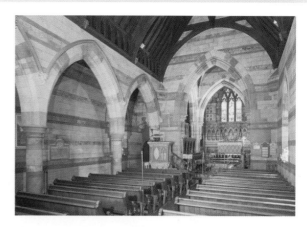

Right: St Catherine's Church, Baglan, Glamorgan, was built for the valleys industrialist, Griffith Llewellyn in 1882 to the designs of John Pritchard. The polychrome interior is of Bridgend stone of a greenish hue, banded with Forest of Dean red and white/pink Penarth alabaster.

DI2007_1765 NPRN 13664

The church of Holy Trinity at Pontargothi in the Tywi Valley contains an interior of exceptional beauty and completeness. It was built between 1865 and about 1870 for a Swansea industrialist, Henry James Bath, on his country estate, and was dedicated in his memory in 1878. The architect was Benjamin Bucknall, best known for his translation of the works of Viollet-le-duc, the French architectural historian and theorist. At Pontargothi Bucknall imitated Viollet's free Early Gothic idiom. This is a richly colourful setting for worship, with wall paintings by Alfred Stansell of Taunton and stained glass in every window by the leading London firm of Clayton and Bell. Paintings and glass together illustrate a complex programme of Old and New Testament subjects, culminating in the Crucifixion, Resurrection and Ascension depicted in the east window.

Most landowning families, whether long established as aristocracy and gentry or newly enriched through commerce or industry, adhered to the established Church, and many of them felt a social obligation to restore medieval churches on their estates and build new ones where they and their tenants could worship. Many new churches, like Pontargothi, were intended to provide impressive family burial places. Much building was also initiated by parish clergy, many of whom raised funds energetically for new churches as well as for schools and other community buildings in towns and industrial settlements.

This wave of new church building was inspired and given character by a renewed interest in medieval architecture and art. Here the guide and prophet was A. W. N. Pugin, in his writings from 1836 and in the cathedrals and churches he designed in the 1840s for newly-emancipated Roman Catholics. He preached the need to grasp the spirit as well as the forms of medieval buildings, and to make new churches worthy of a revived ritualism that would appeal to all the senses. In Wales, where Anglicans wanted to define themselves in contrast to growing nonconformity, Pugin's message was especially attractive.

Two outstanding ecclesiastical architects made their marks in Wales. John Pritchard of Llandaff trained under a pupil of Pugin's father and shared Pugin's vision, which he realised most dramatically in his magnificent recasting of Llandaff Cathedral. From the 1850s to the 1870s Pritchard built a series of beautifully crafted churches in Glamorgan, at first in partnership with the London architect J. P. Seddon. In the north-west the dominant figure from about 1860 was John Douglas of Chester. He represents a gentler, more inventive late-Victorian style and his best churches have richly detailed fittings and fine stained glass.

Time and changes of fashion have eroded the character of many churches. The Church in Wales has its own system of control, the Faculty Jurisdiction, which prevents unauthorised changes, so secular authorities such as the Royal Commission have refrained from interfering. However, as churches are steadily declared redundant there is a need to record them and their fittings before dispersal and reuse. The Royal Commission aims to record the most important buildings before their closure. In the last few years outstanding churches have also been recorded by the Commission's photographer for the Pevsner Architectural Guides.

John Newman

Below: St Mary's Church, Halkyn, Flintshire, was built by John Douglas of Chester in 1878 at the expense of the duke of Westminster.

DS2008_041_005 NPRN 308780

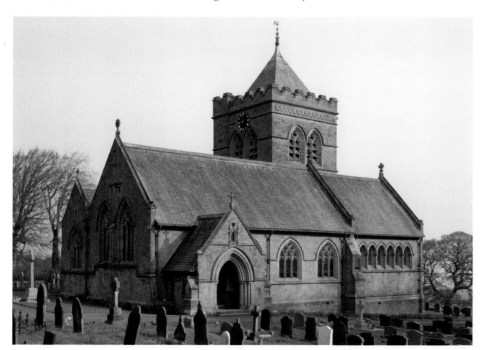

071 Nonconformist Chapels

Tabernacl Independent chapel, Llanelli
DI2006_0297 NPRN 6429

Above: Gosen Calvinistic Methodist chapel of about 1844 with the spectacular backdrop of Henry Robertson's Cynghordy railway viaduct, Carmarthenshire.

DI2006_0305 NPRN 6475

Right: Destruction of the interior of Ebenezer Welsh Calvinistic Methodist chapel, Tumble, Carmarthenshire, as the pews, fixtures and fittings are cut up for resale.

DI2005_1069 NPRN 6570

Below: Interior of Tabernacl Welsh Congregational chapel, Morriston, Swansea, showing the beautifully crafted curved gallery, pews, sedd fawr and pulpit.

DI2007_0794 NPRN 8993

In late eighteenth- to mid-nineteenth-century rural Wales the long-wall form was the dominant chapel layout, in which the entrance façade is one of the two long elevations rather than the gable end. Gosen chapel, built in about 1844 for the Calvinistic Methodists at Cynghordy, Carmarthenshire, is typical of this simple, attractive form and retains its round-headed windows with small-pane glazing, the tall centre window lighting the pulpit.

Wales's population increased four-fold between 1780 and 1901, and its economy ceased being largely rural. Of the people enumerated in the religious census of 1851, 80 per cent were nonconformist. As Geraint Jenkins has put it, 'Considerable funds and energy were now expended on building massive chapels', intended as 'ornaments to the locality'. The simple long-wall chapel was left behind by a flowering of inventive architecture. One of the finest examples is Tabernacl Welsh Congregational chapel in Morriston, Swansea. Built in 1872 by the local tinplate entrepreneur Daniel Edwards, Tabernacl's designer was John Humphrey of Morriston, a carpenter and joiner by training who had recently redesigned the nearby Mynydd-bach chapel where he was deacon. Tabernacl's interior sits 1,450. The spectacular four-sided gallery dips down to the pulpit and has space for the choir around the organ. Known as the cathedral of Welsh nonconformity, Tabernacl remains in frequent use for services and concerts.

Chapel building continued: by 1905 there were 4,280 chapels compared with the 2,813 that had existed in 1851. But in the twentieth century, especially since 1945, there has been an inexorable decline in

religious observance, with disastrous effects on the fabric of chapels. Amid widespread dismay at the dwindling of chapel heritage, the Royal Commission has been undertaking a long-term project to co-ordinate the recording of Wales's nonconformist buildings, assisted by the chapels heritage society Capel and local photographic groups. It has gathered a massive resource of drawings, photographs and other information that is currently being analysed. Ebenezer chapel in Tumble was one of many recorded by the Commission shortly before demolition.

Llanelli was one of the largest of the towns whose culture remained strongly Welsh-speaking into the twentieth century, thanks to the success of local industrialists in tinplate manufacture. The wealth that these indigenous entrepreneurs spent on their nonconformist religious life produced one of the finest and most elaborate groups of chapels in Wales. Some talented local designers emerged, such as the Baptist carpenter/architect Henry Rogers, but the most prominent architects of each denomination were attracted from far afield to exercise their vision in Llanelli. Thomas Thomas of the Independents designed Siloah, Capel Als [001], Ebenezer and probably Trinity for the Calvinists. George Morgan of the Baptists designed Calfaria and Owen Morris Roberts was drawn from as far as Porthmadog to redesign Capel Als in the latest fashion. John Humphrey, designer of Morriston Tabernacl, built Capel-y-Doc and Tabernacl (1873) for the same denomination. Humphrey's three-arch designs, from Italian inspirations such as the Florence Baptistery, are among the most sophisticated masterpieces of this 'national architecture of Wales'.

O. M. Jenkins and Stephen Hughes

072 Leighton Park Farm

Leighton Park model farm.
DI2007_1401 NPRN 80542

Above: Cil Cewydd mill.
DI2008_0127 NPRN 80538

Above: Upper cable house for the funicular railway.
DI2008_0126 NPRN 85843

Right: Leighton Park farm from the air.
AP_2007_2450 NPRN 80538

Below: The Poultry House.
DI2008_0847 NPRN 85876

It was inevitable that the new industrial technologies of the Victorian period should be applied to agriculture. Improvements in husbandry and agriculture – such as livestock breeding, mechanisation and planned farm layouts – which developed in the eighteenth and early nineteenth centuries evolved during the Victorian period into attempts to industrialise farming.

The Leighton Park estate is one of the most impressive manifestations of this trend. It was presented to John Naylor as a wedding gift by his uncle in 1846-7, together with £100,000. Its modernisation extended over the next two decades. Between 1848 and 1856 £200,000 was spent on the project, and work continued well into the 1860s. Numerous buildings were erected, including modern barns, root houses for animal feed production, a bone-grinding mill, a sawmill, engineering works, a gasworks, a corn mill on a truly industrial scale, and improved accommodation for the large workforce. Power was provided by water turbines served by a sophisticated water-management system. An innovation was the installation of a manure-supply system for part of the estate: liquid manure, enriched by bone meal, was fed by gravity from a header tank on Moel y Mab through mains to a system of temporary perforated pipes and stop valves that enabled different areas to be fertilised as required.

The hub of the estate was the home farm. Probably designed by the Liverpool architect W. H. Gee and J. W. Poundley, the complex was intended to impress. The nucleus was the stockyard at the top, built in 1849 and followed shortly afterwards by the other three yards. Prominent features are the two circular buildings: one a piggery and one for sheep (page 302). These had been added by 1855 together with a four-storey mill. By the end of the decade, the

detached fodder shed had been built and a tramway installed to carry hay and straw the length of the axis formed by the barns. The last building, in the 1860s, was a mechanised root processor and store.

The estate corn mill, Cil Cewydd mill, was built away from the home farm so that water could be taken from the River Severn and a railway siding could be laid. The main building, of five storeys, was erected in 1862 and powered by two turbines set in a brick-arched chamber beneath. A three-storey extension was added in 1868, spanning the original tailrace and powered by an additional pair of turbines.

One idiosyncrasy of the estate was the provision of a double-track funicular railway with architecturally flamboyant cable stations. It may originally have been built as part of a more extensive system connecting the home farm with the higher hill slopes, but by the end of the nineteenth century its sole role seems to have been for pleasure. Like most other things at Leighton it was turbine-powered.

Many buildings and structures of the estate were recorded between 1986 and 1989 by postgraduate students of the Ironbridge Institute under the supervision of staff from the Royal Commission.

David Percival

073 William Burges and High Victorian Architecture

The octagonal drawing room at Castell Coch.
DI2006_1486 NPRN 93112

Above: The highly Romantic chimney-piece within the banqueting hall at Cardiff Castle.

DI2008_0460 NPRN 33

Right: The banqueting hall at Castell Coch, the first of what Burges called the castellan's rooms, with early Christian imagery.

DI2005_0669 NPRN 93112

Below: Cardiff Castle with its playfully eclectic and highly individual towers. Burges built the clock, guest and tank towers, and heightened the existing Herbert, octagonal and Bute towers during the sixteen years he was employed by Lord Bute.

DI2008_0879 NPRN 33

The marvellous vigour of High Victorian architecture reached its climax with the 'medievalising' fantasies of Lord Bute and William Burges at Cardiff Castle and Castell Coch. The creative relationship of client and architect was an enchanting accident. It was also the most compelling achievement of Victorian house design.

The project for Cardiff Castle began with a rush in 1866 when Burges presented a report showing how it could be enhanced by a great tower and a moat garden. His client, the youthful third marquis of Bute, was the richest man in Britain. He possessed houses and estates throughout the country and an unquenchable interest in antiquities, theology, languages (including Welsh) and medieval design. His patronage of Burges's scholarly designs to recreate imaginatively his south Wales mansion resulted in massive masonry facades, parapeted walkways, outlook turrets, timber pentices and an unparalleled silhouette punctuated by highly individual towers. These are enriched by painted figure sculpture, especially noteworthy on the clock tower overlooking the city, and architectural borrowings from Welsh sources like the arcades at St Davids Bishop's Palace. There are sumptuous interiors to the bachelor apartments in the clock tower and the reception rooms in the western apartments.

The vast banqueting hall occupies the space of three former bedrooms within the late-medieval courtyard wall. The spectacular timber roof, with open-winged angels to the hammer-beams and fan-vaulted coving, is modelled on late-medieval English antecedents. The colourful two-level scheme of wall paintings depicts military exploits and courtly and religious ceremonies in the life of Robert of Gloucester, lord of Glamorgan, who built the first masonry castle in the twelfth century. Earl Robert is carved in full armour on horseback within the portcullised arch of a fantastic chimney-piece, with trumpeters on the battlements and a lady dropping her handkerchief. Ogee-headed door cases with copious heraldic and carved figures and linen-fold panelling complete the picture.

The Royal Commission took the laudable step of analysing and reporting on all seven building phases of Cardiff Castle for the publication on *The Early Castles of Glamorgan* (1991). This major achievement was continued with *The Later Castles of Glamorgan* (2000), which included an all-period account of Castell Coch. Prior to Burges's project of 1872 onwards, Castell Coch had been a fragmentary ruin. The Commission made a strong case for the military importance of the thirteenth-century hall range overlooking the Taff gorge and for the high achievement of the Victorian re-creation, including the vaulted drawing-room. The drawing-room is a magical Gothic space under a heavenly octagonal vault with a galleried upper level and a bold chimney-piece containing seated sculptures of the Three Fates from Greek mythology. The theme is Creation: stars and birds in the firmament, butterflies on the vault ribs, luxuriant foliage and animals from Aesop's Fables in the wall paintings, and the three ages of man on the corbels of the chimney-piece. The contrast is visible between the muscular Gothic of the main structural parts, completed in Burges's lifetime, and the later Aesthetic movement influences on the decorative surfaces.

The Royal Commission's ground-breaking research and accessible presentation are of lasting benefit for the interpretation, maintenance and repair of these two monuments of European significance – in the care of Cardiff Council and Cadw respectively. Its archives are vital for the informed care of such great architectural structures throughout Wales.

David McLees

074 The Short Heyday of the Victorian Mansion

PLAS-YN-DINAS, DINAS MAWDDWY (Copyright)

Top: The ruined Plas yn Dinas after the fire of 1912.
Below: A postcard showing the house before the fire with its eye-catching mansard-roofed tower

DI2007_1977 and DI2007_1978 NPRN 96601
Courtesy Thomas Lloyd collection

Aerial photograph showing where Plas yn Dinas once stood.

DI2008_0534 NPRN 96601

Plas yn Dinas set above fine terraced gardens.

DI2007_1979 NPRN 96601

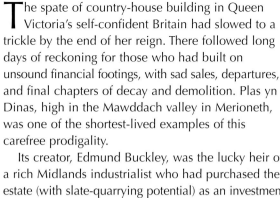

The spate of country-house building in Queen Victoria's self-confident Britain had slowed to a trickle by the end of her reign. There followed long days of reckoning for those who had built on unsound financial footings, with sad sales, departures, and final chapters of decay and demolition. Plas yn Dinas, high in the Mawddach valley in Merioneth, was one of the shortest-lived examples of this carefree prodigality.

Its creator, Edmund Buckley, was the lucky heir of a rich Midlands industrialist who had purchased the estate (with slate-quarrying potential) as an investment in 1856. In the classic Victorian way, Edmund wished to distance himself from the smoke and set up as a gentleman. His new house of 1864-7 was designed by James Stevens of Macclesfield, with lavish interiors by leading Manchester house fitters Bird and Hull. It cost a massive £70,000, but this was only the beginning. Another £40,000 went to build the Mawddach light railway to his quarries and for public use. This brought him a baronetcy. He also secured a parliamentary seat in the Midlands. The Dinas Mawddwy Hotel followed in 1873, made innovatively from concrete. A large home farmyard and nursery with much concrete and glass was under construction when he crashed into bankruptcy in 1876. Changing conditions had diminished his income and his son had run up vast debts. No buyers wanted such grandeur in the wilds. Short-term tenants came and went until finally,

with gruesome irony, Dr Walker of Hereford set up a Home for Inebriates from 1901 to 1911. In 1912 it was consumed by fire when empty.

James Stevens was principally a commercial architect. His *plas* was grand enough but run-of-the-mill as a high Gothic design in British terms. Yet there was great attention to detail – good stone that was well cut, constructed and carved, heavily ornamental fittings and terraced gardens. The loss of so much craftsmanship is much to be regretted. Buckley was one of a surprisingly large number of northern industrialists who lavished escapist dreams upon the cheaper fields and bracing air of Merioneth, leaving an architectural legacy that is now being explored.

Old-established gentry sometimes tried to keep pace, rebuilding plain homes as castles, as at Bronwydd in Ceredigion, in a doomed attempt to stay at the head of the pecking order. Few of these grand Victorian palaces now remain in anything like pristine condition. The travails of the early twentieth century made such lifestyles impossible. Grandiose establishments built by old Welsh families that could not be supported include Llawrenny Castle in Pembrokeshire, Margam Castle in Glamorgan and Llys Dulas in Anglesey, while homes of the new industrialists and bankers in Wales proved equally vulnerable: huge Glanusk Park in Breconshire and Pantglas in Carmarthenshire were among those that succumbed.

The invention of the camera, one of the greatest Victorian discoveries, allows us to see what the passage of time has denied. The photograph of Plas yn Dinas entrance front shows the house brand new in the 1870s. Two more images result from the Edwardian craze for picture postcards and were taken just before and after the fire. Copies of these views are filed in the National Monuments Record, along with thousands of others showing the buildings of Wales over the last hundred years or more. These are added to constantly by the Royal Commission's own photographers and by loan and copying of older material in private hands.

Thomas Lloyd

075 The Rise of Mass Tourism

The Royal Pier, Aberystwyth, originally built by Eugenius Birch in 1865.
CD2005_635_031 NPRN 34175

Above: Aerial view of Llandudno Pier showing the broad promenade deck, pavilions and steamer landing-stage.
DI2005_0775 NPRN 34159

Right: Tenby.
AP_2005_0905 NPRN 33213

Below: Postcard showing the large hotels of Llandrindod Wells.
DI2007_1433 NPRN 33222

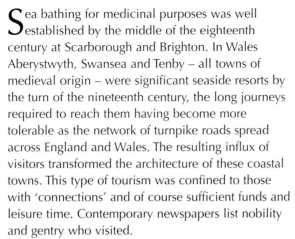

Sea bathing for medicinal purposes was well established by the middle of the eighteenth century at Scarborough and Brighton. In Wales Aberystwyth, Swansea and Tenby – all towns of medieval origin – were significant seaside resorts by the turn of the nineteenth century, the long journeys required to reach them having become more tolerable as the network of turnpike roads spread across England and Wales. The resulting influx of visitors transformed the architecture of these coastal towns. This type of tourism was confined to those with 'connections' and of course sufficient funds and leisure time. Contemporary newspapers list nobility and gentry who visited.

The mid-nineteenth-century expansion of the railway network encouraged mass tourism, but still only for those who could afford the time and money, as holidays remained unpaid until the twentieth century. Initially, the established Welsh resorts were too remote from the growing urban centres to benefit. The architect Seddon saw a future for Aberystwyth in seaside apartments instead of grand hotels, where well-to-do families could stay for some time (Aberystwyth's first grand hotel, inspired by the railway, failed within months, but was later to become the kernel of the University College of Wales). On the other hand, Wales's long channel coastlines were accessible for day-trippers. In the south the valleys railways, primarily constructed for coal haulage, enabled mining communities to reach the seaside quickly.

The north coast benefited from rail and sea connections to the expanding urban population of Lancashire. Here resorts were developed for a spectrum of social classes in enormous numbers. Foremost among them was Llandudno, carefully planned by the Mostyn estate in anticipation of the railway's arrival. The estate retained control of the town, providing for the development of its impressive promenade and rake of grand hotels. Nearby at Colwyn Bay developments were quite different. In 1865 the railway had already arrived, almost too close to the shore for comfort, and the Pwllycrochan estate was bought by Sir John Pender, a Glasgow industrialist, who had the ambition to develop a resort. Despite the appointment of an architect, John Douglas, to oversee the design of the resort, including the construction of the Colwyn Bay Hotel in 1872, the railway line inhibited the development of an impressive promenade and over the years Colwyn Bay became increasingly a residential resort.

In 1865 a new type of structure first appeared at Aberystwyth, soon followed by the other resorts. This was the seaside pier, essential for embarkation to the new pleasure steamers. Often daringly constructed using iron, piers came to characterise the seaside, providing in addition to their landing-stage a promenade, always a feature of the resort but now extended 'over the water', and spacious theatres and dance halls in pavilions.

Also enabled by the railway, Wales witnessed the modest and rather late arrival of an inland spa town at Llandrindod Wells. Here, deep in the hills, a rural townscape remains to this day dominated by a series of very large hotel buildings. Fittingly, their impact is well illustrated in the National Monuments Record by a postcard.

Peter White

Early Twentieth-Century Wales

Brian Malaws

The death of Queen Victoria in 1901 brought to a close the longest reign in British history. It had been a period of extraordinary industrial achievement, technological development and social reform. In the Edwardian era, from 1901 to 1910, optimism and confidence continued and Britons could claim world leadership in politics, commerce and social change. Many developments important to Britain today date from this period, such as the introduction of motor cars and aeroplanes, the rise of new political parties and welfare provision for children, the sick, the elderly and the unemployed. However, the shock of the 1914-18 war brought an abrupt end to optimism. During the two decades before war broke out again, Britain entered a period when the old certainties were challenged constantly: by radical changes in the technology of everyday life, new principles of modernism in planning and architecture, the increasing

dominance of America, and severe economic crises, social unrest and strife.

By 1900 industry and commerce were fundamental to the Welsh economy. The 1901 census showed that the numbers employed in agriculture had continued to fall to around 8.5 per cent of the population. 1913 was the year of peak production and manpower in the Welsh coal industry, with over 600 collieries and about 233,000 men producing nearly 57 million tonnes of coal – a fifth of the United Kingdom's production. In that year the port of Barry gained the record for the most coal exported, eleven million tons. Such frenetic production came at a price: at Senghenydd near Caerphilly an underground explosion on 14 October 1913 killed 439 men and boys – the worst mining disaster ever to have occurred in Britain. Other industries were also developing: in 1907 Port Talbot steelworks was established and the hydro-

Opposite page: Aerial view of Cardiff Docks taken by Aerofilms in 1929. The site is now occupied by the Wales Millennium Centre and the Senedd of the National Assembly for Wales. The photograph on page 271 provides an interesting comparison.
DI2006_0742 NPRN 91412

Port Talbot Steelworks.
GTJ25867 NPRN 91392

*Newport transporter bridge,
built in 1906.*

DI2006_1626 NPRN 43157

*Elan water scheme:
Garreg Ddu dam and the
replacement church under
construction in 1899.*

GTJ63724 NPRN 752

electrically powered Dolgarrog aluminium works
opened in the Conwy Valley. Alongside the
dependency on heavy industries, new technologies
were being developed. In 1912, at Waunfawr near
Caernarfon, Marconi set up the first successful long-
wave radio transmitting station, which was for some
twenty-six years the most important in Britain,
handling imperial and international communications.

The social unrest so frequent between the wars
was apparent earlier, most notably in the slate and
coal industries. There was a measure of recovery in
farming communities in rural Wales before the First

World War, but conditions of life in the industrial
regions were harsh. The strike at Penrhyn slate quarry
in Caernarfonshire, which began in November 1900,
was to become the longest dispute in British history;
the quarrymen were locked out for three years. The
community was divided and thousands left the area,
never to return. In south Wales the Tonypandy riots
of 1910, sparked by a colliery lockout, resulted in
the troops being sent in, and between 1910 and
1914 there were numerous strikes by miners, dockers
and railway workers. The economic slump after the
war brought further strife; miners struck in 1924 over
wage reductions. After the 1926 General Strike miners
were forced to return to work on reduced wages and
for longer hours. The following year desperation
brought about by widespread unemployment triggered
the first hunger march from south Wales to London.
The worldwide depression from 1929 until 1933
was disastrous. Mass unemployment was not to reach
its worst until 1930, when south Wales was
particularly hard hit.

Although the great railway-building age had long
gone, there was one final, major project: the creation
of Fishguard harbour and a main-line railway link,
between 1902 and 1906, in a bold attempt not only
to create a shorter route to Ireland via Rosslare but
to capture transatlantic liner traffic. Less ambitious
improvements to transport around that time included
the Vale of Rheidol railway from Aberystwyth to
Devil's Bridge and the Great Orme tramway at
Llandudno, both in 1902, the Welshpool and
Llanfair railway in 1903, and the vehicular Newport
transporter bridge in 1906. Before the First World
War Britain's railways were at their peak; certainly
in south Wales they were never more busy, carrying
coal for export. In 1908, for example, the Taff Vale
railway moved in excess of eighteen million tonnes
of coal over its tracks. The docks at Cardiff, Barry
and Newport dealt with huge tonnages: in one year
over ten million tonnes of steam coal were handled
by Cardiff alone, which had become the largest
coal-exporting port in the world.

Other civil engineering projects would continue
to be important. In 1904 the Elan water scheme was
opened by King Edward VII and Queen Alexandra,
after eleven years of construction [078]. This
monumental undertaking supplied clean water to the
city of Birmingham. It was followed by more projects
to flood Welsh valleys in order to provide drinking
water to English cities and to growing centres of
population in Wales, such as Cardiff, Swansea and
Newport. The most controversial was to come two

generations later: the Liverpool scheme at Tryweryn near Bala, which drowned the village of Capel Celyn in 1965.

The increasing recognition of Welsh nationality from the mid-nineteenth century led to the granting of the title of city to Cardiff in 1905, although it did not become officially the capital of Wales for another fifty years. The grand civic buildings in Cathays Park that dominate the city centre express the wealth derived from the export of coal and the rapid growth of Cardiff's importance and size over the previous half-century [076, 077]. Swansea did not grow at the same rate, despite the international significance of its major heavy industries, especially non-ferrous metal production, and it was not until 1969 that it was awarded city status.

These were years of Liberal ascendancy in national and local politics, though the Independent Labour Party made headway. The religious revival of 1904-5 sustained the cultural vitality of the late Victorian years, and by the time war loomed in 1914 moves were afoot to disestablish and disendow the Anglican Church, effected in 1920. The year 1907 was significant for the creation of national cultural institutions: it saw the founding of the National Museum and a Welsh department of the Board of Education and, following thirty-five years of deliberation, the Royal Charter establishing the National Library which, shortly after construction commenced at Aberystwyth, became one of the six British legal deposit libraries, entitled to claim a copy of all publications produced in the United Kingdom. The following year saw the establishment of the Royal Commission on the Ancient and Historical Monuments of Wales, along with sister bodies for Scotland and England. Such was the rising confidence in Wales that a home rule bill was introduced in Parliament in 1914, though it was soon abandoned due to the First World War.

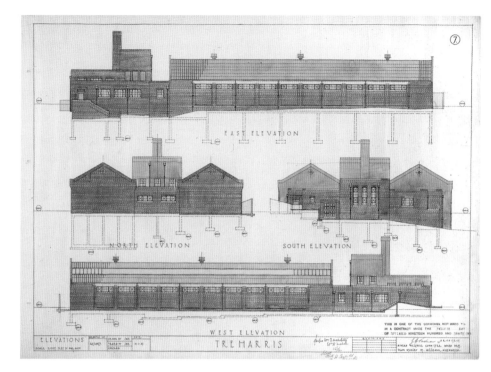

The 1914-18 war brought profound changes and swept away the old order in many spheres. Young men responded eagerly to the call to arms and some 35,000 Welshmen did not return. Part of the preparation for fighting at the front involved practice trenches at various locations, with notable remains surviving at Penally in Pembrokeshire and Bodelwyddan in Denbighshire [081]. Under the direction of David Lloyd George, minister of munitions, later secretary for war and eventually prime minister, Welsh industry contributed to the war effort, making steel, meeting the need for shells and satisfying the navy's voracious appetite for steam coal. New munitions factories were built along the north Wales coast. Margam Steelworks near Neath was established in 1916. Investments were also

Pit-head baths were built by the Miners' Welfare Committee from the 1920s onwards in modernist style: original design drawing for the 1932 baths at Deep Navigation Colliery.
DI2006_0242 NPRN 80489

Photograph of Gresford Colliery in 1975 by Terry James.
DI2008_0712 NPRN 301580
Courtesy Heather James

The new Llandarcy Oil Refinery, Glamorgan, in 1923.
AEROFILM AFL03 8769
NPRN 91695

made at collieries. The first pit-head baths in Wales opened at Deep Navigation colliery, ironically based on designs developed in pre-war Germany, unlike the modernist baths designed by the Miners' Welfare Committee from the 1920s onwards. The Deep Navigation baths were recorded by the Royal Commission as part of its survey of the rapidly-contracting coal industry in the 1990s, shortly before they were demolished.

The First World War continued a process of decline in country houses and grand estates that had begun in the later Victorian period as rising costs of labour and the introduction of death duties threatened owners' finances. In 1909 Cyfarthfa Castle in Merthyr Tydfil, for long the home of the Crawshay dynasty of ironmasters, had been

purchased by the local council to become a museum and art gallery. With so many men called away during the war, the country-house style of life seemed incompatible with the harsh demands made of men in the conflict, and afterwards it was difficult to recruit workforces and continue large estates and households as before.

The garden village movement had become established before the war, with villages begun at several locations, notably Barry garden suburb in south Wales and Rhiwbina in Cardiff [080]. After victory in 1918 demobbed soldiers expected more than a return to pre-war ways and were promised by the government that there would be no more slums but instead 'homes fit for heroes.' Although concern turned naturally to the future, almost every town and village in Wales had its own war memorial, commemorating the vast numbers of men who gave their lives in the 'war to end all wars' [082]. The loss of life hit Welsh-speaking communities hard and caused a precipitous decline in the language. Some concluded that the way to preserve the culture, and further the aims of nationalism, was through political action by the formation of Plaid Cymru, the national party of Wales. For others, the future lay with organised labour and a resurgent Labour Party locally and at Westminster.

The 1920s were years of contrasts. Although labour relations and the traditional heavy industries were in increasing difficulties and considerable numbers of workers left for English towns and cities, it was for some a time of prosperity, when new technologies were introduced and a leisure industry was developing. The BBC started radio broadcasting from Cardiff, Llandarcy oil refinery opened near Swansea, Shotton steelworks in Flintshire, geared for massive production during the war, turned to supplying the nascent automotive industry. Huge water supply schemes were in various stages of construction: for example at Alwen, Denbighshire, opened in 1921 to supply Birkenhead, and in the Brecon Beacons at Talybont (commenced 1923) and Llwyn-on (completed 1926) to supply Newport and Cardiff respectively. Improvements in education were represented by the founding, in 1920, of Swansea university college and in 1927 Coleg Harlech, Merioneth, as a residential college for adults. Although the coal industry was in difficulty, new, more efficient mines were being developed, such as Taff Merthyr Colliery in Glamorgan [083]. A major improvement in conditions for miners was brought about by the rapid construction of pit-head baths at most of the larger collieries.

By the mid-1930s Wales was emerging from the economic depression. Cardiff aerodrome was established on Pengam Moors to provide the city with the most up-to-date international links. In 1933 agriculture was given a modernising boost by the formation of the Milk Marketing Board. The Board transformed the production and marketing of milk-related products, a development of particular significance to the great dairying region of south-west Wales, where its first new dairy was completed at Pont Llanio [084]. As the decade progressed, there were signs of the promised post-war new housing: the 1930 Housing Act allowed local authorities to demolish unfit properties as long as the tenants were found alternative accommodation, thus leading to

Caerwent Ordnance Factory in 1999, six years after its closure.
GTJ26940 NPRN 96062

the mass provision of council housing. For some, the increasing prosperity and confidence brought more recreational and leisure time and the first holiday camps began to appear (such as Pontin's at Prestatyn on the north Wales coast [098]), to cater for the holidaying masses from Britain's industrial centres. The first radio programmes to be broadcast in Welsh were made by the BBC from its studio in Bangor.

In September 1934 another tragedy in the coal industry was caused by a massive explosion that ripped through Gresford colliery near Wrexham. The disaster took the lives of 266 miners. In south Wales the government's response to the still-declining coal industry and consequent lack of jobs, especially in

Swansea town centre in 1949, during the post-war clearing after the heavy bombing raids of February 1941.

AEROFILMS AFL03 R10837
NPRN 33145

areas that depended solely on coal production such as the Rhondda, was to stimulate employment by establishing the South Wales and Monmouthshire Trading Estate (later Treforest Industrial Estate) near Cardiff, the first of its kind in Wales, introducing light manufacturing industries.

No sooner had Wales emerged from the darkness of the Depression than war again cast a shadow. War

material facilities that had been dismantled or wound down since 1918 were hurriedly recommissioned and additional capacity was provided, with major Royal Ordnance Factories at Hirwaun, Bridgend, Cardiff, Newport, Caerwent and Wrexham. A series of 'shadow factories' was built, duplicating parent factories already given over to war production in the English engineering districts; there were examples at

Hawarden and Broughton in north Wales, Newtown in mid-Wales and Abergavenny in the south-east. In the knowledge that fighting might reach British soil, extensive air raid precautions and defensive measures were put in place, such as the network of radar stations along the south Wales coast at Strumble Head, Manorbier, Rhosili, Oxwich and Margam; the anti-invasion Rhos-Llangeler stop line across south-west Wales; and numerous reinforced-concrete pill boxes at strategic locations all over the country, such as bridges, docks and railway installations [085]. Some of the munitions works, the sprawling army camps, including prisoner of war camps (such as Island Farm at Bridgend), and the airfields (for example at Brawdy in Pembrokeshire), were on a huge scale.

In 1940 the National Buildings Record (NBR) was created to record photographically important architectural monuments at risk of aerial bombing and ordinary buildings of many kinds that might be threatened by an invasion. The NBR was eventually subsumed into the National Monuments Records of England, Scotland and Wales, held by the three Royal Commissions. The industrial south, with its strategic industries, vital transport routes and docks, suffered most from enemy bombing: Cardiff was severely hit and Swansea was attacked for three consecutive nights in February 1941, resulting in the destruction of much of the city centre.

Following victory in 1945, Britain elected a modernising Labour government. Nationalisation plans abounded, notably for the transport, docks, coal and iron industries, and the establishment of new industrial estates was encouraged by government subsidies and loans, many on converted military sites. There was a grim determination that, this time, there would be a break with the past and no repeat of the mass unemployment of previous decades.

The 1944 'Shadow factory' at Fforest Fach, near Swansea, built for the Mettoy company of Northampton.
AEROFILMS 235501
NPRN 300189

243

076 National Institutions

A civic centre laid out for a nascent capital. The National Museum, Cardiff City Hall and the Law Courts are at the top, with university and government buildings below.

GTJ00047 NPRN 401617

The growth in Welsh national consciousness in the later nineteenth century proved the mainspring in establishing many familiar national institutions at the beginning of the twentieth. The development of a distinctively Welsh political and cultural outlook was mirrored by the formation of public organisations, many of whose functions had hitherto been subsumed within the British establishment. The list of bodies founded in the period is a testament to this upsurge in national confidence and marks Wales's birth as a modern nation. They included the National Eisteddfod (1880), the University of Wales (1893), the National Museum (1907), the National Library (1907) and the Royal Commission (1908). In the political sphere the nascent nationalist movement Cymru Ffydd (Young Wales) was established in 1886 and Plaid Cymru by 1925. The period also saw the birth of specifically Welsh labour organisations, such as the South Wales Miners Federation in 1898. The grant of city status to Cardiff in 1905 was politically significant in cementing its position as *de facto* capital, though this standing did not become official for another fifty years.

In addition to cultural and political foundations the late nineteenth century saw the establishment of official bodies for that other cornerstone of modern national identity: sport. The Football Association of Wales (the third oldest in the world) was in place by 1876, and 1881 saw the foundation of the Welsh Rugby Union, heralding the formal arrival of Wales's national game and, in the eyes of many, its national obsession. By 1908 the Welsh rugby team had recorded its first Grand Slam, indeed the first ever

The National Library of Wales, Aberystwyth.
DI2006_0298 NPRN 23293

A design drawing by Lanchester Stewart and Rickards, 1899, for the Law Courts, Cathays Park.
DI2008_0299 NPRN 31806

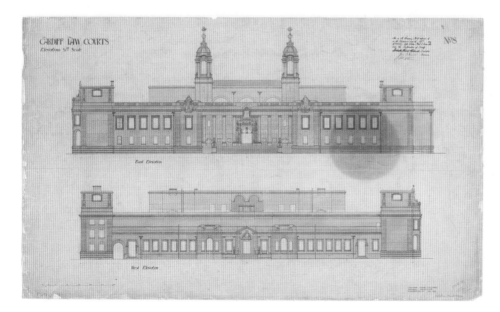

Grand Slam (it celebrated the centenary by winning its tenth in 2008).

The foundation of national institutions prompted a building programme that produced many of Wales's major public buildings. The National Library of Wales was prominently housed on a hillside in Aberystwyth – the home of Wales's first university college – in a striking custom-built edifice of Portland stone and Cornish granite. Building commenced in 1911 and occupation in 1916. The central block was completed in 1937 and the final portion of the ambitious original design by 1955. The library's Greek classical style, albeit with art deco details, placed Welsh culture firmly in the milieu of European civilisation. This was echoed in the design of the National Museum, another imposing structure of Portland stone and granite, begun in 1910. Though the simpler Doric order serves to emphasise the building's primary use for the display of art and artefacts, it is certainly a monumental structure in its own right, with a particularly arresting domed and marbled entrance hall.

The National Museum's location in Cardiff linked it closely with the city's emergence as capital, and the other buildings of the magnificent civic centre at Cathays Park, laid out from 1901 onwards, pointed towards Cardiff's growing sense of itself as the premier city of a nascent nation. It included the Law Courts, City Hall, County Hall and University Registry in a harmonious amalgam of Classical and Baroque styles, producing a civic centre of a grandeur to compete at a European level.

Gareth Edwards

077 Official Buildings: The PSA Collection

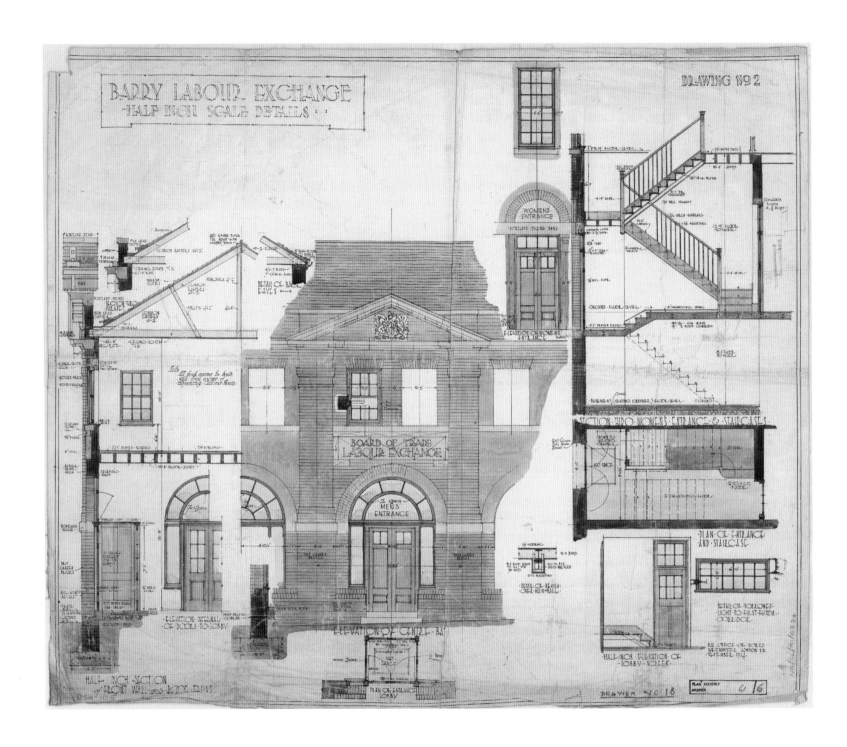

The drawing for the Board of Trade Labour Exchange, Dock View Road, Barry, 1914.

DI2008_0571 NPRN 406839

The early twentieth century witnessed an unprecedented level of investment in new government buildings outside London. They included law courts, post offices, tax offices and labour exchanges. Many of these are recorded through drawings deposited in the National Monuments Record of Wales by the Property Services Agency, set up in 1972, which inherited responsibility for the construction and maintenance of public, government and municipal buildings from H. M. Office of Works. Around 5,000 measured drawings were transferred to the Royal Commission from the Cardiff branch of the agency shortly before its privatisation in 1989. The earliest drawings were usually produced by or for the Engineering Division of H. M. Office of Works, based in London. There are some exceptional design and operational drawings for significant buildings.

Among earlier buildings represented by the collection is the Head Post Office in Westgate Street, Cardiff, the original designs for which were produced in 1893-4 by Sir Henry Tanner, the government's chief architect of works. Its elaborate classicism and use of sparkling Portland stone set the pattern for the government and civic buildings that were to distinguish Cardiff's rapid growth to prominence in the early twentieth century, especially those in the new civic centre, Cathays Park [076]. Before the focal point of government buildings in Cardiff was drawn to the more rarified civic centre, however, the Post Office was joined in Westgate Street, at the heart of Cardiff's business life, by the Inland Revenue and County Court Offices. This second building was completed to a similar design, again using Portland stone, in 1904. The spirited Edwardian offices revelled in balconies, crests, columns, pediments, sweeping roofs and a miniature cupola. The drawings for the building include not just plans and elevations in ink and wash but working construction details throughout the complex.

Not all new official buildings were in Cardiff. Along the coast in Barry docks, the new purpose-built Labour Exchange was completed for the Board of Trade in 1914. This dignified building featured three entrances to the front elevation: the main central entrance for men only, and two smaller flanking entrances, one for women and the other for boys. Another fine set of drawings exists for the Post Office in Barry docks, which includes interesting details of fixtures and fittings of a late nineteenth-century post office.

The fragility of some of these drawings has led to them receiving special archival attention. They have been catalogued down to individual item level and many have been digitised.

Susan Evans

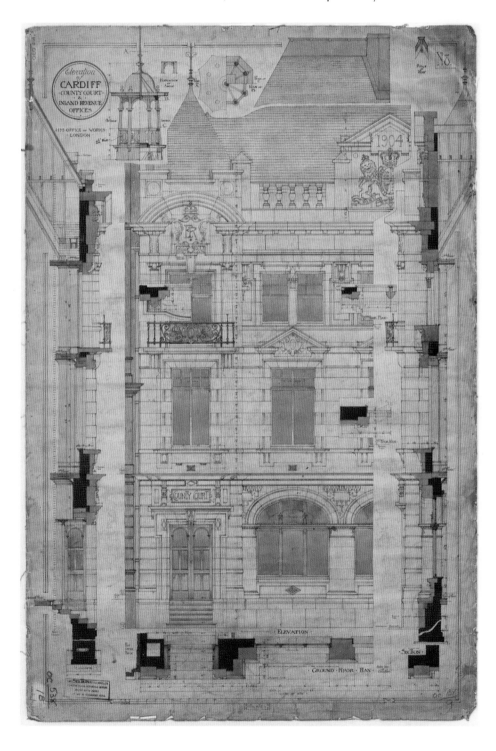

Drawings for Cardiff Inland Revenue and County Court Offices, built 1904.

DI2008_0149 NPRN 31750

078 Water for Birmingham: The Elan Valley Water Scheme

Construction of the Garreg Ddu dam, looking upstream from the road, September 1897.
GTJ63718 NPRN 752

The dams, reservoirs, tunnels and aqueduct of the Elan Valley Water Scheme were built to supply clean water to the city of Birmingham which, in the latter part of the nineteenth century, was experiencing increasing difficulty in providing adequate water supplies for its rapidly expanding population.

The Elan valley, set in rugged upland terrain to the west of Rhayader in mid-Wales, is over seventy miles from Birmingham. It was chosen for its high average rainfall of seventy inches a year and its altitude, which allowed the water to be carried to Birmingham entirely by gravity. The most prominent features of the scheme visible today are the reservoirs and their massive masonry dams. Largely hidden from view but no less remarkable is the 117-kilometre aqueduct carrying water from the take-off point at Foel tower in Garreg-ddu reservoir to Frankley reservoir in Birmingham.

This ambitious civil engineering project lasted thirteen years, from 1893 to 1906, under the direction of James Mansergh. It was substantially finished when the scheme was opened officially, with great pomp and ceremony, by King Edward VII and Queen Alexandra on 21 July 1904. A century later the scheme is still supplying Birmingham's water, and it was expanded in the mid-twentieth century by the construction of another dam on the Claerwen river, thereby doubling the capacity of the original scheme to 76,000,000 gallons of water a day.

A superb collection of contemporary photographs in the National Monuments Record of Wales documents the building of the dams, tunnel,

Above: Pen y Garreg dam; the inlet end of the culvert under construction, September 1897.

GTJ63732 NPRN 32534

Right: Blasting the cutting called 'Devil's Gulch' on the railway built to serve the construction of the dams, October 1897.

GTJ63750 NPRN 309635

Below: Aqueduct carrying the pipeline over the Nant Caethon under construction, February 1897.

GTJ63740 NPRN 309608

aqueduct and construction railway, and illustrates dramatically the massive scale of the engineering works. The images provide insights into the lives of the engineers and the workforce, including their accommodation and the techniques they used to cut through rock, move vast blocks of stone and raise the walls of the dams. The construction of the new Nantgwyllt church, replacing one drowned by the reservoirs, was also recorded.

A relative of one of the scheme's engineers donated to the Royal Commission a copy of *The Vale of Nantgwilt – a submerged valley* (1894), a book by R. E. Tickell, who worked on the scheme from its inception. His book is a romantic celebration of the area, its houses and its literary associations with the poet Shelley. His drawings provide a contemporary record of the buildings and landscapes submerged by the scheme.

Hilary Malaws

079 A North Wales Architect:
The Herbert L. North Collection

Design for the lodge at Newry, Llanfairfechan, Caernarfonshire, built for C. W. May-Massey in 1906.

DI2008_0151 NPRN 469. Copyright: Herbert North

*Proposed design by North
for a church at Caerhun,
Caernarfonshire, not built.*

DI2008_0152
Copyright: Herbert L. North

The well-known architect Herbert Luck North made a significant impact on the landscape of north Wales in the early twentieth century through his progressive and airy Arts and Crafts designs and his influence on other architects. The National Monuments Record of Wales holds a large collection of drawings and some photographs from his architectural practice, which was based at Llanfairfechan in north Wales during the first half of the twentieth century, known latterly as the North and Padmore Partnership.

North was born in Leicester in 1871 and moved to Llanfairfechan with his family in the early 1880s. In 1885 he was sent to Uppingham public school and in 1890 went up to Jesus College, Cambridge. Following graduation he became an articled pupil of Henry Wilson, a leading Arts and Crafts architect with a particular interest in church architecture. This was followed by a number of years in the employ of the great English architect Edwin Lutyens, until 1901 when North returned to Wales to set up his own practice. His interest in local buildings and sensitivity to the use of local materials and details led him to write several books, including *The Old Cottages of Snowdonia* (1908) and *The Old Churches of Snowdonia* (1924).

The Herbert L. North Collection includes some fine drawings of churches, schools and houses. Many of the distinctive buildings that North designed can still be seen, particularly in the vicinity of Llanfairfechan. Among the most charming are the lodge at Newry, Llanfairfechan, built for C. W. May-Massey in 1906, and Penrhyd Lodge, Eglwysbach, built for Reuben North in 1899. North demonstrated a considerable interest in social architecture, not only through his development of the garden village style of housing on his own land at the Close, Llanfairfechan, but in individual buildings such as St Winifred's School, Llanfairfechan, designed in 1922, which contained a hall, music room and two classrooms (demolished in the 1970s), and the earlier and more Gothic Gyffin National School at Conwy, built in 1904, with its high-pitched roof and diagonally patterned roof slates. There are also uncompleted designs, such as the ones proposed by North for wall tiling and an altar canopy at a new church at Caerhun, of which there is no record of construction.

The records in the collection number over 160 individual items. Many of the drawings have been digitised in order to make them available for study online by the wide audience that North's distinctive work deserves.

Susan Evans

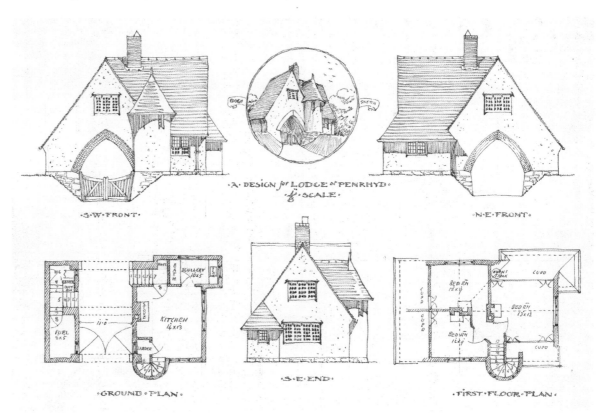

*Penrhyd Lodge, Eglwysbach,
Denbighshire, built for
Reuben North in 1899.*

CD2005_604_004 NPRN 96658
Copyright: Herbert L. North

080 The Garden Village Movement

Glebelands Housing Estate, Milford Haven: a concentric inter-war development with a central green.
DI2006_0564 NPRN 402790

Sundial at Y Groes.
DS2008_187_008 NPRN 403393

1913 date-stone at Y Groes.
DS2008_187_009 NPRN 403393

Socially, the ideas behind the Garden Village movement lay somewhere between the picturesque estate cottages of the eighteenth and nineteenth centuries and the mass public housing schemes that came afterwards. Garden villages and suburbs were both visionary and practical, providing uncostly but well-designed housing for worker-tenants who were sometimes shareholders. In Wales the movement was associated with a rigorous theoretical and practical interest in housing that found expression in a largely forgotten journal, *The Welsh Housing Yearbook*, which had a sociological concern for the facts and figures relating to housing, promoted the ideal of good design and reflected the growing strength of the Welsh architectural profession and the new Welsh School of Architecture. The movement was remarkable for its personalities, who included many eminent planners, economists, and social scientists.

The Garden Village movement became influential in Wales immediately before the First World War. The Welsh Town Planning and Housing Trust of 1913 was formed with the goal of providing garden villages for workers. Schemes were set afoot at Newtown, Llanidloes, Machynlleth, and Acton Park in Wrexham with the architect T. Alwyn Lloyd, who had worked for Raymond Unwin, the Garden Village and Garden City pioneer. Sidney Colwyn Foulkes was responsible for schemes in north Wales at Abergele, Llanrwst, and Beaumaris. There were large schemes in the coastal towns of Glamorgan (Cardiff, the embryonic Townhill in Swansea, and Barry), and in several south Wales valleys settlements, notably Oakdale. After the First World War concern to provide homes fit for heroes reinforced the movement, and the garden village at Tre Elidyr (Llanover in Monmouthshire), was built as a war memorial by the Llanover estate, whose heir had not returned from the conflict.

The most successful scheme, and the best preserved, was in north Cardiff at Rhiwbina. The Housing Reform Company Limited, founded by the economist H. Stanley Jevons, bought the Pentwyn estate. Raymond Unwin prepared a development plan for the 44.5 hectares with A. H. Mottram as architect. It started remarkably quickly, and in July 1913 a date-plaque and sundial were unveiled on the first houses. A first phase of thirty-four houses in a simplified Arts and Crafts style comprised three-bedroom houses in Y Groes in semi-detached pairs around a village green, and four-bedroom houses in Lon-y-dail. In the boom years of the 1920s the village was consolidated by private developments.

The residents were not always the worker-tenants originally envisaged. Some in the original garden village were intellectuals sympathetic to the utopian ideals of the founders, and Rhiwbina was sometimes known as Little Moscow. As Rhiwbina grew, it became known as the Debtors' Retreat, since some residents allegedly owed money to Cardiff tradesmen. Throughout the inter-war period and beyond the character of Rhiwbina was maintained by the control of the society, Rhiwbina Garden Village Ltd, which had its own maintenance team. Increasing costs eventually led to the winding-up of the society and the sale of the houses to the tenant-shareholders. It was declared a conservation area in 1977 and retains its distinctive character.

Richard Suggett

Y Groes and the green, Rhiwbina. Details of the sundial and date-stone on the first houses are shown above.

DS2008_187_009 NPRN 403393

081 The Experience of War: Penally Practice Trenches

One of the best-preserved First World War practice trench systems in the United Kingdom. The majority of others were simply backfilled and the land reverted to agriculture, but here at Penally, Pembrokeshire, they are cut into solid rock.

DI2006_00376 NPRN 268143

After a period of rapid military maneouvres, in four months the war on the Western Front slowed to a deadlock and the numerous small dugout rifle pits slowly developed into elaborate interconnecting fortified systems, adapted to make best use of the local terrain and conditions, which varied from muddy clay to chalk. Although trench warfare during the First World War was not an entirely new concept (trenches had been used extensively during the American Civil War and the Russo-Japanese conflict of 1904-5), this was on a massive scale, extending some 764 kilometres from the shores of the North Sea in Belgium to the Swiss border. By 1916 British and Commonwealth armies were concentrated in a 137-kilometre sector between Boesinghe and the River Somme.

All over Britain training camps were established and the soldiers had to learn the basic skills needed on the Western Front, including techniques of construction, daily routines, observation, communication and supply, as well as essential offensive and defensive tactics. These had to be used whatever the weather, day or night. Some of the remains of First World War practice trenches can be seen in Wales. The best examples are the fully developed standardised system at Penally in Pembrokeshire – well preserved because they were cut into rock – and in the grounds of Bodelwyddan Castle. Others are now only visible as cropmarks on aerial photographs, for example near Beaumaris on Anglesey and at an ANZAC (Australian and New Zealand Army Corps) camp at Rhuddlan, Flintshire. Evidence of many other training trenches was destroyed when the land reverted to agricultural use or camps were reused to train troops for the highly mechanised conflict of the Second World War.

The system developed and refined by British forces consisted of three parallel lines of earthworks: the firing, command, and reserve or support trenches. The firing trench was the actual front line, protected from the opposing enemy positions only by barbed wire. It was a continuous, stepped line with earth buttresses at regular intervals to give some shelter against shell bursts and raking fire along the line. Each trench bay was manned by a small unit commanded by a junior officer. Often a 'sap' trench jutted from the firing trench into no-man's land to serve as an observation position, a warning post or a staging point for raids into enemy trenches.

Behind the firing trench was the parallel command trench, linked to it at regular intervals by meandering communication trenches used for troop movements, supply of rations and ammunition and telephone cables to headquarters. The command trench could be used as a shelter to protect troops during heavy bombardment. The third line, the reserve or support trench, accommodating front-line support troops, was also often used as shelter during bombardment or for regrouping after an enemy attack.

In the field of conflict, rather than on the cliffs of Pembrokeshire, trenches remained almost unchanged for four years, when gains in territory that cost thousands of lives could be measured in just a few paces.

Medwyn Parry

A detailed view of the stepped pattern of the firing trench, with a sap trench meandering towards the enemy, top right. Communication trenches connect to the command trench, bottom left.

DI2006_0375 NPRN 268143

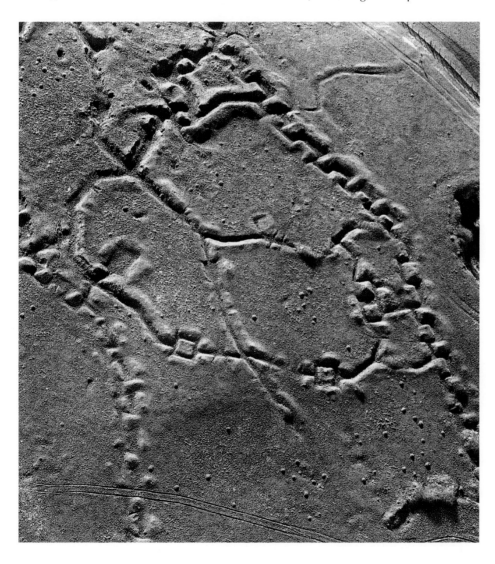

082 Remembering the Great War

The Welsh National War Memorial, Cardiff (1924-8, Ninian Comper).

DS2006_038_001 NPRN 32845

Aberystwyth: peace emerging from the thickets of war (Mario Rutelli, 1923).

DI2006_0300 NPRN 32643

The Chirk Memorial by Eric Gill (1920).

DS2008_146_001 NPRN 32717

The shock of loss during the First World War was shared by almost every community. Wales suffered some 35,000 dead in the conflict. Its commemorative monuments have been catalogued by the United Kingdom National Inventory of War Memorials, established by the Imperial War Museum with the Royal Commission on the Historical Monuments of England and the collaboration of the heritage organisations in Wales. The catalogue is available as an online database, www.ukniwm.org.uk.

There are over 40,000 memorials in the United Kingdom and 2,590 in Wales. They range from free-standing monuments and sculptural masterpieces to simple plaques in chapels, churches, schools, post offices and banks. Collectively, these are by far the largest body of public memorials in Wales, with examples in all communities. In addition, there are war memorial halls in villages and suburbs across Wales, recognisable by the Welsh words emblazoned prominently on their facades: 'Neuadd Goffa'.

The process of commemoration began immediately after the war and many committees – not without tensions of class, locality and language – were established in the 1920s to provide their communities with war memorials. Many took a sculptural form and listed the names of those who had fallen. The memorial cross – often Celtic in form – was frequently favoured, especially in smaller communities, but there are surprising numbers of expensive figurative sculptures. Many rural communities commissioned monuments with a cast or sculpted soldier in mourning leaning on his rifle butt: the 'Tommy' stood for all those who had served in the Great War and depictions of other servicemen (like the sailor at Holyhead) are rare. Goscombe John's soldiers at Lampeter, Carmarthen and Llandaff gaze into the distance, but Eric Gill's carved relief of a soldier at Chirk is very different; surely he represents the stoical 'Dai Greatcoat'. Allegorical representations of peace are rarer still. The obelisk at Aberystwyth (by Mario Rutelli, 1923) is outstanding, and the nude figure of peace emerging from the thickets of war has been admired by generations of schoolboys.

There was a hierarchy of war memorials, ranging from community to county to region and nation. Regional memorials were architectural rather than sculptural. The North Wales Heroes' Memorial at Bangor (by D. Wynne Thomas, 1923) took the form of a Tudor gatehouse with the names of 8,500 servicemen inscribed on wooden panels in the upper chamber. This rather diminished the status of the elegantly simple Welsh National Memorial at

Cardiff (1924-8, by Ninian Comper), a circular Classical colonnade evocatively open to the sky and enclosing bronzes representing the three services. A final memorial to the First World War, completed on the eve of the Second, was the Temple of Peace and Health (1937-8, by Sir Percy Thomas), also in Cathays Park: an institution founded by Lord Davies of Llandinam to promote peace and health with a hall and crypt below. The Second World War did not lead to many new memorials; but the names of fallen servicemen were added poignantly to the lists already inscribed on the monuments of the earlier conflict.

Richard Suggett

083 Coal's Heyday: Taff Merthyr Colliery

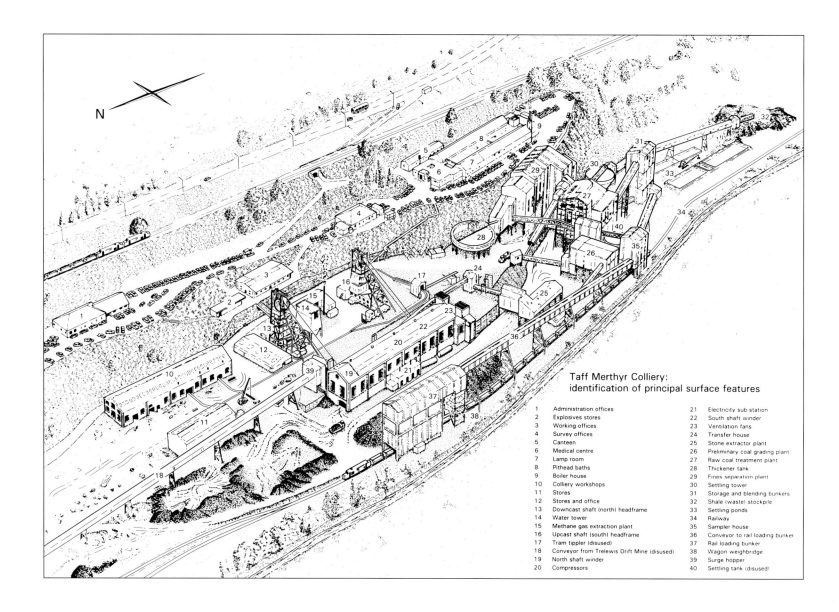

Taff Merthyr Colliery:
identification of principal surface features

1	Administration offices	21	Electricity sub-station
2	Explosives stores	22	South shaft winder
3	Working offices	23	Ventilation fans
4	Survey offices	24	Transfer house
5	Canteen	25	Stone extractor plant
6	Medical centre	26	Preliminary coal grading plant
7	Lamp room	27	Raw coal treatment plant
8	Pithead baths	28	Thickener tank
9	Boiler house	29	Fines separation plant
10	Colliery workshops	30	Settling tower
11	Stores	31	Storage and blending bunkers
12	Stores and office	32	Shale (waste) stockpile
13	Downcast shaft (north) headframe	33	Settling ponds
14	Water tower	34	Railway
15	Methane gas extraction plant	35	Sampler house
16	Upcast shaft (south) headframe	36	Conveyor to rail loading bunker
17	Tram tippler (disused)	37	Rail loading bunker
18	Conveyor from Trelewis Drift Mine (disused)	38	Wagon weighbridge
19	North shaft winder	39	Surge hopper
20	Compressors	40	Settling tank (disused)

A Royal Commission interpretative drawing of Taff Merthyr Colliery.
DI2005_1114 NPRN 80488

Above: The downcast shaft headframe at night.
DI2008_0708 NPRN 80488

Right: The headframes and part of the tram circuit.
DI2005_0678 NPRN 80488

Below: Pit bottom, upcast shaft, from the John Cornwell collection.
GTJ28914 NPRN 80488

The phenomenal growth of the south Wales coal industry during the nineteenth century brought both output and employment to a peak just before the First World War. Even with the gradual shift from coal to oil and increasing competition from coalfields around the world, new collieries continued to be developed after the war. Taff Merthyr colliery near Bedlinog, in the centre of the south Wales coalfield, was sunk between 1922 and 1926 by the Taff Merthyr Steam Coal Company (owned jointly by the two greatest Welsh coal combines, Powell Duffryn and Ocean). It was devised on the most advanced principles of the period and was fully electrified from the outset. The surface buildings were squeezed into a narrow, steep-sided valley and occupied an area only 400 metres by 180 metres.

In 1992, responding to the collapse of the traditional coal industry, the Royal Commission began a photographic survey of all the remaining collieries in Wales. It also acquired for the National Monuments Record the underground and surface photographic collection of John Cornwell and helped to rescue threatened archive material for transfer to the most appropriate repositories. Taff Merthyr was chosen to make a comprehensive record of one colliery's operation. The mine had two 640-metre deep shafts; latterly the north shaft carried coal in nine-tonne skips and the south was used for ventilation and transport of men and materials. One large engine hall housed most of the power applications at the colliery: two winding engines and their generator sets, three compressors and two electric motors driving the ventilation fans. Around this lay examples of all the structures typical of south Wales collieries at the industry's peak: two headframes, large workshops, a lamp room, a main office, a water tower, an explosives store and coal screens –

all dating from the original construction of the complex. Later in the 1920s the Miners Welfare Committee added the pithead baths, medical centre and canteen. During upgrading of the colliery by the National Coal Board in the 1970s, the coal preparation plant was reconstructed, incorporating earlier buildings, and other facilities were added.

Taff Merthyr colliery was selected for several reasons: although opened at the end of the great south Wales coal boom it carried on traditions and techniques common in earlier collieries; it was still fully operational; and it was largely of a single build, obviating the need to unravel a complex history of alterations. Due to the imminent closure, priority was given to a programme of intensive photography to record the architectural and engineering features of all the surface structures and a detailed investigation to record diagrammatically all the stages of coal processing. Recording the operation of the colliery at first hand, rather than gathering existing technical records, served to emphasise the importance of observing industrial processes while still operational. The National Monuments Record now holds an accurate and comprehensive record of coal processing at an early twentieth-century colliery, as carried out in the late twentieth century. This record is both typical and unique, in that coal was prepared in a similar way at many collieries while there was evidence of modification to fit the local conditions.

Brian Malaws

084 Modernisation in the Countryside:
Pont Llanio Milk Factory

Pont Llanio railway station, with the milk factory behind.
DI2008_0702 NPRN 91430

The growth of the railway network in the late nineteenth century allowed the London market to be provided with milk from the great dairy-farming region of west Wales, which encompassed north Pembrokeshire, Carmarthenshire and south Cardiganshire. However, in the closing years of the century, there was much inefficiency in some parts of the region despite the presence of agricultural cooperative societies. Poor use of transport facilities meant that mid-Cardiganshire produced butter and cream because it was unable to enter the more profitable market for fresh milk. A small dairy factory built in 1896 at the instigation of the county council at Pont Llanio railway station, between Tregaron and Lampeter, used the railway only for local traffic. In the 1920s Cardiganshire dairying cooperatives encouraged a revival and even tried marketing liquid milk. However, few farmers were able to afford milking machines and other equipment that would increase productivity; as late as 1939 only 8 per cent of dairy herds nationally

Right: An elaborately constructed milk-churn stand at Old Abbey farm, Pontrhydfendigaid, Cardiganshire.

DI2008_0711 NPRN 308020

Right: An unusual milk-churn stand cut into a rock outcrop adjacent to the main road at Pontarsais, Carmarthenshire.

DI2008_ 0707 NPRN 300209

Below: A postcard showing the milk factory at Pont Llanio under construction in 1937.

DI2008_0706 NPRN 91430

were machine-milked, but in Cardiganshire fewer than 15 per cent of farms even had electricity.

With the establishment of the Milk Marketing Board (the MMB) in 1933 milk collection, distribution and marketing began to be carried out in a more organised way and on a greater scale, allowing Cardiganshire to become increasingly involved in producing milk (it is still the county's principal agricultural product). Improvements by the MMB included the 'zoning' of farms and collection points to reduce transport costs, and the construction of a modern rail-connected factory to serve the 'northern zone' at Pont Llanio. This new factory, a steel-framed building with reinforced concrete walls and a flat roof – entirely functional with no architectural embellishment – opened on 1 October 1937 and was eventually equipped for liquid milk handling, milk separation, butter-making and powdered skimmed milk production. Milk was collected by lorries daily (or twice daily in summer) from farms in the Pont Llanio zone in standard 45-litre (10-gallon) churns. Farmers left the churns on small roadside stands, some of quite elaborate design and others extremely basic, but all of standard dimensions set by the MMB. Many of these churn stands are still to be seen.

The increase in milk output meant that by 1950 daily intake at the dairy was 136,200 litres (30,000 gallons), a very high figure. The factory at Pont Llanio employed over 120 staff and worked twenty-four hours a day in summer. It had a huge impact on the local economy. When it was threatened with closure a vigorous campaign for its retention was fought by the farmers' unions and Plaid Cymru, but a strike by lorry drivers in 1969 confirmed the official determination to close both the factory and its rail link, for what were stated to be 'economic reasons', in September 1970.

Brian Malaws

085 Defence from Invasion in the Second World War

A Luftwaffe aerial photograph of Holyhead taken on 24 November 1940 as part of an intelligence gathering sortie (Feindflug F1039),
probably from a Junkers 88. Several warships at anchor in the inner harbour are visible, protected by the massive breakwater.
The railway line gently curves out of the town over the Stanley Embankment. Although 'Operation Sealion' had been postponed,
the German High Command were still compiling information on all potential invasion areas.

DI2008_0122 NPRN 32990

As the Second World War began the government focused much of its attention on defending the south-east coast of England against invasion from France and the Low Countries. However, there was also considered to be a real danger of a Nazi invasion from the neutral Irish Republic. The Irish government was in the unenviable position of facing potential invasion from two adversaries: the Germans from the sea (an operation codenamed 'Unternehmen Grün' planned in early 1940), and the British overland from Northern Ireland to take the Irish ports and deny German access ('Plan W' proposed in early 1939). If the Nazis used the Irish Republic as a staging point they would require port facilities for unloading troops and heavy supplies in order to follow up a light, fast-moving first wave of attack. Their prime targets for invasion through Wales would be the deepwater harbours at Holyhead and Milford Haven, which were close to airfields and to beaches suitable for secondary troop landings.

The approaches to the harbour at Holyhead were protected by coastal gun batteries, anti-aircraft guns and minefields. A complex interlocking system of three concentric rings of machine-gun posts and pillboxes was improvised to surround the harbour. The inner ring concentrated on the harbour and nearby beaches, while a secondary line guarded nodal points on the outskirts of the town. The defences of the outer ring faced away from the harbour to counter any outflanking manoeuvre.

The majority of the Holyhead pillboxes were of a basic, cylindrical design. The core of the structures was built in reinforced concrete but a shortage of building supplies meant that the outer faces were finished with local rubble; some were even topped with mock crenelations, giving the appearance of a small folly. This use of traditional materials camouflaged the structures effectively into their surroundings.

Had enemy forces established a foothold in Holyhead, they would have needed to move quickly through Anglesey. On their way they would have found sporadic, concentrated resistance from Home Guard units, whose prime objective was 'To delay mechanized units of the Nazi invader trying to use our roads, and to make them waste their ammunition as well as their time'. This was crucial to buy time for the arrival of regular troops and heavy armour. To get from Anglesey to the mainland the invaders would have needed to cross the Menai Straits. During the early years of the war the Menai suspension bridge was undergoing a massive reconstruction scheme and an explosive device was discovered. This was probably planted by saboteurs linked to 'Plan Kathleen', the Irish Republican Army support for the German scheme, but it could equally have resulted in trapping invading forces on the island if the Britannia railway bridge had been blocked.

Had the Nazis crossed the Menai, the mountainous terrain of north Wales would have favoured the defenders. Systems of strongpoints were concentrated in the mountain passes, comprised of pillboxes, tank traps, spigot mortars, petroleum flame positions and roadblocks. Many of these survive today and are identified and protected for their national importance.

Medwyn Parry

Set into the perimeter wall of Soldiers' Point House, Holyhead, one of the 'folly towers' had unhindered views over the harbour. The ground floor was converted to a pillbox – firing loops are visible in the bricked-up window openings.
DSCN2613 NPRN 270424
Courtesy Medwyn Parry

A typical 'Type 24' pillbox, which had commanding arcs of fire to hinder any vehicle movements on the only road through the Horseshoe Pass near Llangollen.
DSCN2576 NPRN 270455
Courtesy Medwyn Parry

Post-war Wales

Richard Suggett[1]

The Second World War left Wales's two largest ports, Swansea and Cardiff, badly mauled as a result of air raids: important buildings were destroyed or damaged, and the configuration of Swansea was altered permanently. Along the coast and elsewhere, wartime structures that were no longer needed survived rather like beached whales. Despite the scattered physical evidence of the war, its political, economic and social legacies, together with those of the 1930s, were profound, affecting communities, their ways of life and their environment throughout Wales. The Royal Commission has recorded significant elements of this extraordinary transformation within its own lifetime as an organisation.

One radical change in the post-war period was the increasing awareness of conservation. People became more conscious of, and curious about, the meaning of their surroundings, and this extended to subjects not conventionally regarded as of historical importance. From the 1960s onwards an enthusiastic and knowledgeable community of industrial archaeologists recorded the remains of vanished and vanishing industries, from slate and coal to copper and lead. The Royal Commission was in the vanguard of this work, not least in recovering Swansea's early industrial landscape, hidden by layers of subsequent development, and in charting the development of Wales's canals. Historic parks and gardens were rediscovered and increasingly valued, their study being promoted by the Welsh Historic Gardens Trust and Cadw among others. All over Wales, civic societies, local history groups and special interest organisations increasingly took an interest in the past and argued for the conservation of historic buildings and sites. Concerns about the consequences of the decline of organised religion highlighted the need to record threatened or redundant churches and chapels and to fight for their protection. Retrospectively, the nineteenth-century religious buildings of Wales, and more particularly chapels, began to be perceived as a kind of national architecture.

It is important to emphasise the economic and social diversity of Wales, which produced variations in the pace and type of change – the experience of large conurbations of the south was not the same as that of country towns, and coastal areas fared

differently from the rural heartland. In north Wales the slate quarries had long been in decline, a process that continued after the war. Around the coasts the fishing industry and ports contracted with the results that docks were closed and fleets decreased to just a few boats. In rural areas depopulation and the decline of agriculture were often accompanied by the disappearance of small farms. In upland Wales the Forestry Commission expanded its programme of tree planting with an enormous impact on historic landscapes; with the felling of mature plantations, historic settlements and structures unseen for half a century have since reappeared and been recorded. From the 1990s onwards wind farms began to be increasingly common visual symbols of the changing energy economy, both on land and off shore.

The industrialised south, especially the coal and steel towns, dominated the rest of Wales in terms of population, and it saw the most massive changes of all. Many communities of nineteenth-century origin depended on traditional heavy industries that were vulnerable in the post-war economic climate. Industrial reorganisation through nationalisation restructured 'King Coal' in 1947 and the steel industry in the early 1950s, but these sectors were still vulnerable. Despite all efforts, Ebbw Vale's steelworks closed in 1975-6, to be followed by East Moors in Cardiff in 1978. There were successive phases of closure of coal mines

Opposite: Cwm Coking Works in production, near Llantrisant, Glamorgan.
DI2007_0155 NPRN 91585

The high tide of post-war coniferous plantations, Tywi Forest, Llanwrtyd Wells.
AP_2007_5078 NPRN 268323

[1] With contributions on modernism by John Newman.

*Above: Ffos-y-fran opencast
scheme, Dowlais,
Merthyr Tydfil.*
AP_2008_0849 NPRN 407892

*Above right: Criggion Radio
Station mast, Montgomeryshire,
shortly before demolition
in 2003.*
DI2007_0326 NPRN 309697

from 1947 onwards. When the giant Penallta colliery
was shut in 1992 only three pits out of hundreds
remained in south Wales – the last, Tower Colliery,
succumbed in 2007. The giant coal spoil tips had
remained prominent features of the landscape in many
a southern valley, but in 1966 the Aberfan disaster,
in which a school was overwhelmed with the loss of
144 lives, resulted in extensive clearance. The only
growth of coal mining was in opencast operations,
which began in Wales to support the war effort and
became commonplace around the rims of the
coalfields from the 1950s onwards, altering whole

landscapes and their human environment permanently.
In 2006 what is described as 'the largest coal mining
opencast operation in Europe' was given the go-ahead
at Ffos-y-fran, on the eastern edge of Merthyr Tydfil's
bowl of hills.

The economy of south Wales was restructured as
heavy industry gave way to manufacturing, but some
of the successor industries also declined. The most
notable example was the Dunlop Semtex factory at
Brynmawr [086], which closed down in 1982 and
became Britain's first post-war building to be listed. A
monument to social and architectural innovation, the
factory was demolished after continued failure to
find appropriate reuses. Technological change radically
altered many industries and made specialist processes
obsolete. At Gwasg Gee, the oldest press in Wales,
new technology rendered a range of specialised
buildings redundant [094]. In telecommunications the
exchanges that had enlarged as the numbers of
subscribers increased became obsolete: the banks of
redundant selectors recorded at Shotton before
decommissioning, looking quaintly archaic but only
thirty years old, are a striking example of the shrinking
effect of digital technology. The masts at Criggion
Radio Station were demolished in 2003 after over
fifty years of service from the end of the Second
World War through the Cold War and beyond.

Infrastructure and the public sector, broadly defined, mushroomed in the period after the war. The railways fell under the 'Beeching axe' from 1963 [089], but road communications were revolutionised, symbolised by dual carriageways in the north and south and the two successive Severn bridges. Improved roads have provided the fundamental networks for massive suburban development, new and expanded towns like Cwmbran and Newtown, and retail parks and 'enterprise zones' on the outskirts of towns and in rural areas. The gas pipeline constructed across south Wales in the first decade of the twenty-first century, for 317 kilometres from Milford Haven to Gloucestershire, was perhaps the most ambitious British development for the transport of fuel since the canals were built to carry coal in the Industrial Revolution. It attracted criticism from nearby communities but provided a remarkable opportunity to discover and record historic sites.

The collectivist social traditions of the industrial areas had long found expression in workingmen's clubs and institutes that combined education, leisure and politics in remarkable ways. A few such buildings were built after the war, but they were severely depleted as a result of the loss of the traditional industries and the all-pervading changes in personal life brought about by the motor car and the television. Friendly

societies formed an older and broader collectivist bedrock to industrial and rural communities, providing unemployment and sickness benefits and a decent burial, but they declined with the growth of the post-war welfare state. Generally, friendly societies met in public houses – one of the last meeting-rooms was recorded by the Royal Commission at The Fountain Inn in Troedrhiwgwair, Monmouthshire.

Increasing public provision, especially in health and education, created opportunities to enhance the social environment. As grammar schools gradually disappeared from the 1960s onwards, large new comprehensives, further education colleges and expanding universities transformed the world of

Above: The natural gas pipeline from Milford Haven, east of Sennybridge at Maes-car, Breconshire.
AP_2007_1129 NPRN 25853

Above left: Shotton Telephone Exchange (Connah's Quay ATE): redundant selectors before decommissioning.
DI2008_0485 NPRN 3088

Trawsfynydd Nuclear
Power Station.

DS2008_007_001 NPRN 301092

The 'Buff's Room' (for the
Buffaloes Benefit Society) at
The Fountain Inn,
Troedrhiwgwair,
Monmouthshire.

DI2008_0483 NPRN 36863

Llantrisant. Nuclear power stations were built at Wylfa and Trawsfynydd in the north.

Immediately after the war 'prefabs' were built to answer the housing shortage [087], and these were followed by extensive development of council housing estates and occasional high-rise blocks. Slum clearance driven by modernisation and concern for welfare could lead to the destruction of historic buildings: the demolition of slums in Abergavenny was accompanied by an early exercise in the emergency recording of Tudor and Stuart buildings (the results of which are preserved in the Thacker collection in the National Monuments Record). By the 1960s the rise in prosperity was accompanied by extensive new private housing estates and modernisation of Victorian terraces. Twentieth-century planners and architects often replaced decayed or redundant buildings in haste with structures that sometimes proved surprisingly transitory – 'modernism' in twentieth-century architecture involved a self-conscious break with the past, in function and materials as much as in image. It is not surprising that the most daringly unconventional buildings were also those most likely to have a short life-span, or to cost the most to maintain. Changes in fashion left some buildings, hailed as landmarks in their day, friendless and vulnerable when they lost favour with a new generation.

One of the most momentous changes of the post-war period was administrative: the sweeping away in 1974 of the Welsh shire system that had existed since the reign of Henry VIII. The new counties were themselves replaced by twenty-two unitary authorities in 1996. These changes in local government led to the redundancy of many municipal buildings. The effects of the reorganisation of the court service, especially the 1971 abolition of the quarter sessions and assizes, was perhaps not as profound in Wales as in England – and several crown courts still function in historic buildings, notably at Carmarthen – but some magistrates' courts became disused. On the other hand, local government reorganisation led to a crop of new civic buildings, though in most cases they lacked architectural distinction.

education. Many town and cottage hospitals, some in former workhouse buildings, were replaced by purpose-built hospitals and health centres. However, the emptying of the mental-health hospitals was among the most dramatic post-war changes in public health, leading to the closure of all the historic asylums [093]. Some major national bodies were brought to Wales through a United Kingdom-wide process of regional planning and government investment, among them the Driver and Vehicle Licensing Agency to Swansea and the Royal Mint to

Small cottages as well as substantial farmhouses were at risk in these decades of rapid and extensive change, particularly in north and west Wales, partly from dereliction and partly from unsympathetic development [088]. However, the main category of vernacular buildings most at risk was traditional farm buildings, as they were both the most numerous and the least protected. Eurwyn Wiliam's overview of *The Historical Farm Buildings of Wales* (1986)

showed that farm buildings could conform to highly localised types and their building chronologies were not well understood. These buildings have become redundant because of both farm amalgamation and their declining usefulness for modern practices; whole farmsteads (farmhouse as well as farm buildings) have become derelict through amalgamation, especially in the uplands. In the more prosperous lowland areas, particularly Monmouthshire, the Vale of Glamorgan and parts of north-east Wales, farmsteads have been the nodes for new residential development in the countryside.

At the other end of the spectrum, many mansions of landowners and industrialists continued their decline after the Second World War, vanishing behind a sea of rhododendrons, eventually becoming irretrievably ruined, as Thomas Lloyd documented in *The Lost Houses of Wales* (1986). The case of Cefn Mably, once one of the greatest south Wales houses, is remarkable. It managed to survive despite sale, adaptation as a hospital, and a disastrous fire. The gutted house was rescued and converted to exclusive apartments (with Michael Davies as architect) alongside a scheme of parkland development. Only a few miles away, Ruperra Castle remains an example of the challenges of bringing back a great house and its setting from decades of abandonment.

The plight of the large urban houses of the industrialists, entrepreneurs and prosperous professional middle class in the later twentieth century was also

serious. These houses were often built on the peripheries of towns in the late nineteenth or early twentieth centuries but were engulfed by later housing and became prime sites for redevelopment or conversion. They were often built from excellent materials with lavish and sometimes idiosyncratic decoration. Stelvio House in Newport, the home of a maritime entrepreneur, was partly demolished despite listed status. A successful prosecution was brought against the owners for unlawful demolition.

The processes affecting appreciation and use of modernist buildings are various, and ideas and fashions have changed. The architectural confection

Cefn Mably, Glamorgan: a photograph of the hall interior, later destroyed by fire (above) in 1994.
DI2008_0482 and DI2008_0476 NPRN 18286

Stelvio House, Newport: the illegal part-demolition of a listed late nineteenth-century urban mansion.
DI2008_0477 NPRN 3066

Bettws High School, Newport after its closure, in 2008.

DS2008_006_006 NPRN 407385

of Clough Williams-Ellis at Portmeirion is increasingly perceived as an idiosyncratic masterpiece [090]. Aversion to reinforced concrete, together with structural changes in the holiday business, led to the demise of Pwllheli holiday camp [098]. On the other hand, Sully Hospital near Barry, an exceptional expression of a modernist aesthetic dating from l932-6, was built more conventionally of rendered brick, so that after it went out of use as a hospital in the 1990s it found a new, domestic use. Such threats have alerted the Royal Commission to the need to record the most significant and adventurous buildings of the recent past before they are lost or disfigured. Sites range from the Dupont nylon factory near Pontypool to an unaltered group of 'brutalist' houses in Dinas Powys near Cardiff [091] and Bettws High School at Newport. This concrete and glass, modular-planned comprehensive school rose in three tiers from a lakeside setting. Designed by Evans & Shalev, it was built as recently as 1969-72. It was photographed in 2008 after demolition had been proposed.

In Cardiff the Empire Pool and Cardiff Arms Park were stylish public buildings characteristic of the optimistic post-war world. The Empire Pool opened in 1958 and marked Cardiff's new status since 1955 as the capital. It was a welcoming building and, for many, the conspicuous investment in sport and leisure represented an end to post-war austerity. It was the first modernist public building in the city. The design by the city architects' department caught the Festival of Britain mood and was influenced directly or indirectly by some early twentieth-century continental buildings, notably the 1908 AEG turbine factory in Berlin. Generous well-stairs at each end of the glazed

foyer took visitors to the first-floor changing rooms, and on the second floor there was a café with parquet floors and chromium embellishments. At ground-floor level there were rather mysterious Turkish and other baths. The 50-metre pool was flanked by tiered seats with a capacity for 1,772 spectators, exceeding that of most entertainment venues then available. The Arms Park stood north of the Empire Pool and was slightly later. Construction began in 1967 and was a resolutely Welsh affair. The stadium was designed by Cardiff architects Osborne V. Webb and Partners and was built by Welsh engineers and contractors using material largely from the reconstructed post-war industries of south Wales. The design was extraordinarily successful, with the 'predatory' concrete frame tantalisingly glimpsed from different points in the city and fully revealed from the River Taff. It is rare that a concrete-framed structure becomes a much-loved building, but this 'temple of sport' was hallowed by the golden era of Welsh rugby in the 1970s.

As sports historians have pointed out, success on the rugby field mirrored the success of the Welsh economy. Both the Empire Pool and Cardiff Arms Park were much-loved buildings, partly because they

Empire Pool, Cardiff, photographed after closure in 1998.

DI2008_0465 and DI2008_0471
NPRN 3065

An aerial view of old and new at Cardiff Bay provides an interesting comparison with the 1929 photograph (page 236).
AP_2005_0044 NPRN 403908

Stadium – which is admired but not yet loved.

A major aspect of urban policy from 1987 was the redevelopment of Cardiff's docklands through the Cardiff Bay Development Corporation. A new administrative capital on the waterfront began taking shape at the beginning of the new century where the permanently flooded bay forms the back-drop to the Senedd building of the National Assembly for Wales and the Wales Millennium Centre – both expressing aspects of Welsh heritage in design and materials. Hindsight will tell the extent to which these buildings capture the popular and professional imagination, but there is growing interest in Wales's architectural heritage generally and recognition of its richness and diversity. Increasingly, the vernacular building tradition of the countryside seems particularly inspirational. The early tradition in timber attracts those who are interested in developing sustainable buildings [095]. For others, the stone-building tradition, especially the massive masonry of Snowdonia, expresses ideas of cultural continuity and sympathy with the landscape [092]. As the inscription on the Millennium Centre says, 'In these stones horizons sing'.

were well designed, and partly because the public – especially those growing up in the 1960s and 1970s – felt that they had ownership of them and (by extension) of the city centre. Neither was listed, but both were photographed as part of the Royal Commission's emergency recording programme before demolition in 1998 [096] to make way for the Millennium

Wales Millennium Centre, Cardiff Bay.
DS_2006_037_009 NPRN 403908

086 Modernism: The Dunlop Semtex Factory

Concrete grandeur. Huge 'shell' domes supported by raking columns spanned the production area.
DI2008_0464 NPRN 41229

The Dunlop Semtex factory in Brynmawr was Britain's first post-war building to be listed. Its protection at grade II* in 1986 by the Welsh Office was a bold decision that took listing beyond the conventional cut-off date of 1939. The building was impressive for its modernist flair and superb engineering, and for the sheer scale of its site, which extended to about three hectares. The factory made the rubberised flooring used in quantity by post-war schools and hospitals. It was built as part of the post-war restructuring of the south Wales valleys and opened in 1953. The story of its innovative design and social purpose, and the vision of its promoter, Lord Forrester, is told in Victoria Perry's *Built for a Better Future* (1994). At the height of production the factory had 1,000 employees, many of them former miners.

The Architects' Co-Partnership and the engineers Ove Arup produced a design that was eclectic and exciting. The factory was designed around a vast manufacturing space spanned by nine concrete shell-domes or vaults, pierced by 'oculi' or circular roof-lights that on sunny days produced angled shafts of light down to the factory floor – creating an impression that has been compared to the dome of St Paul's Cathedral. At the time of construction they were the largest shell-domes in the world, yet they were only three inches (7.5cm) thick. The central workspace was bounded on two sides by storage and milling ranges with undulating barrel-vaulted roofs, and a 'brutalist' service range fronted the storage lake.

The architects were proud of the socially progressive features incorporated in their design, which eroded the distinctions between workers and managers: among them were a common entrance ramp and shared canteen. Decoration by students

Right: The detached boiler house with its high vaulted roof of ribbed concrete.
DI2005_1078 NPRN 41230

Below: Aerial view of the Dunlop Semtex site showing the nine concrete domes of the main production area flanked by the barrel vaults of the north 'drug room' (right) and the west 'mill room' (top), with the service range (left) and the boiler-house (bottom right).
DI2007_1403 NPRN 41229

from the Architectural Association included Picasso-inspired painted masks. Victoria Perry's book tells some amusing stories of the social awkwardnesses created by these daringly non-hierarchical spaces.

The factory had a working life of barely thirty years and closed in 1982. Additions made in the 1960s and dereliction in the 1980s and 1990s obscured the superb sculptural qualities of the design. A new use for the building failed to materialise and it became regarded as an eyesore. Consent was eventually granted for demolition despite representations from the amenity societies. Awareness of the grandeur and value of the building and local support for its retention increased over the years before demolition took place, but it was too late to change the decision.

The detached boiler house, which escaped destruction, hints at what has been lost. The brick and concrete ground-floor boiler room is utilitarian but the upper floor has a soaring, parabolic vaulted roof of ribbed, reinforced concrete. A curving elevated railway brought coal wagons to the hoppers. Upper and lower levels were linked by an innovative helical staircase, which had been removed by 1986.

The factory was photographed by the Royal Commission in 1999 as part of its emergency recording programme. By then, the interior had disconcerting voids in the floor and an exterior invaded by giant hogweed. On the eve of demolition on 21 June 2001 the factory was recorded from the air using stereo photography. Three-dimensional anaglyphs generated from these stereo pairs form a unique image of the shell-domes.

Richard Suggett

087 Post-war Housing: The Newport Prefabs

Prefabs awaiting demolition at Bishpool, Newport, in 2004.
DI2007_0408 NPRN 309133

Newport has a good range of distinctive nineteenth- and twentieth-century public and private estate housing. In the post-war period Newport and its new neighbour Cwmbran avoided high-rise public housing and stayed faithful to the residential close lined with small-scale houses and gardens. Newport Council maintained and kept in use a remarkably large number of 'prefabs', built in 1946-7 to provide emergency housing after the Second World War and with an intended lifespan of no more than fifteen years. Newport's prefabricated houses were of the Arcon type, originally designed in 1944, made of prefabricated panels bolted to a tubular steel frame. Some 750, mostly of the Arcon Mark V type, had been built in Newport by May 1948, primarily for the families of ex-servicemen. Fifty years later the Bishpool estate was one of the last, and largest, concentrations of prefabs remaining in Britain.

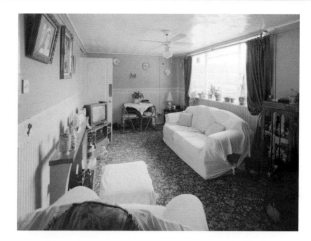

Right: Living-room interior of a Newport prefab in 2004.

DI2008_0473 NPRN 309133

Right: A quiet close at Bishpool.

DI2007_0406 NPRN 309133

At Bishpool there were rows of close-set prefabs standing with neat gardens in quiet closes, their distinctive corrugated roofs, curved at the apex, painted red and their asbestos-cement walls painted cream. The most complete examples retained their garden sheds, looking rather like diminutive Anderson air-raid shelters. Only a few privately-owned prefabs had broken out into other colour schemes, had added lean-tos and patios, or had seen their roofs recovered in tiles. Internally, the planning was uniform, convenient and easily modernised. A small entrance hall with bathroom and toilet off it separated the two bedrooms from the living-room and the kitchen. In the original design there was a free-standing solid-fuel stove in the living-room that fed hot air via ceiling ducts to the other rooms.

Newport Council decided in 1999 to replace the prefabs with bungalows. The Royal Commission photographed a selection of them as the programme by Newport Housing Trust was in progress. Upgrading was out of the question but residents and planners wanted as little disruption as possible. Bishpool was a stable community and many of the residents were retired and had lived in the area for most of their lives, so it was decided to replace the prefabs in a phased programme. This required a reduction in the size of gardens, but that was seen as a reasonable compromise since greater access was required for disability vehicles. To start the scheme some residents had to be moved to mobile homes. The work then progressed with the demolition of groups of prefabs, building new bungalows and moving groups of residents back in.

There is now prefab nostalgia. A celebration and photographic survey of the Newport prefabs and the way of life associated with them has been published by Gary Robins, *Prefabrications – Newport's Temporary Bungalows: The First Fifty years* (2001). One of Cardiff's prefabs has been re-erected at St Fagans, where this 'temporary' dwelling restored to its original condition has now found a permanent site.

John Newman, Richard Suggett and Iain Wright

Below: Prefabs and garden sheds.

DI2007_0240 NPRN 309133

088 The Decline of Cottage Life:
A Letter from Kate Roberts to Peter Smith

Cae'r Gors, Rhosgadfan, Caernarfonshire, before restoration.

DI2005_1137 NPRN 26171

Above: The kitchen chimney or simdde fawr.
DI2005_1136 NPRN 26171

Below: Peter Smith's plan and reconstruction and Kate Roberts's sketch-plan of Cae'r Gors (1972).
DI2008_0494 and DI2008_0495 NPRN 26171
Courtesy Plaid Cymru

Small-scale cottages are buildings often at risk, partly from dereliction and partly from unsympathetic development. In Carmarthenshire and Cardiganshire cottage architecture in the clay-walled tradition virtually disappeared in the second half of the twentieth century. Cottages in north-west Wales survive in some numbers because of their robust stone construction – examples can be rescued from dereliction even when roofless.

While academic interest in vernacular cottages was shown in some of the Royal Commission's earliest inventories, it dates primarily from Iorwerth Peate's *The Welsh House* (1940) and Peter Smith's *Houses of the Welsh Countryside* (1975). Smith illustrated Cae'r Gors, the home of the novelist Kate Roberts (1891–1985) in the slate-quarrying village of Rhosgadfan, near Caernarfon. This cottage dated from the heyday of slate quarrying and its dereliction mirrored the decline of the industry. It was the home of the quarryman-smallholder described in Roberts's novels. Smith wrote to her for information. He received this reply dated 11 November 1972 from the novelist, then in her eighties, with a plan of her childhood home drawn from memory.

Dear Mr Smith,
I thank you for your letter which took six days on its journey.

There was a wooden partition between the kitchen and the dairy and between the kitchen and the bedrooms. There was no window between the kitchen and the cowshed, the back of the chimney (y simdde fawr) was the partition there, with a big oven on one side and a cupboard on the other. There was only one dairy with the door near the simdde fawr, thus forming a small addition to the dairy. There was no back door.

I have no idea when the house was built. The owner and occupier died in 1891 and we moved in about 1896 when his widow built a new house on the other side of the road.

I guess that cottages of this kind in Rhosgadfan were built between 1840 and 1860. But I am sure there are some older ones than Cae'r Gors in the neighbourhood.

Now, the roof has been taken off, and also the partitions and the beautiful tiled kitchen floor. I understand the latter was given away by the builder to a friend who had made two surrounds for fireplaces with them.

If there is anything else you want to know please let me know. Many thanks for your kind words about my books.
Yours sincerely,
Kate Roberts

[Reproduced courtesy of Plaid Cymru]

The image of the ruined cottage is a poignant literary trope but the cottage itself is now a powerful symbol of community. Care for Cae'r Gors and celebration of the work of Kate Roberts are goals for the Friends of Cae'r-gors: Cyfeillion Cae'r Gors. The cottage has been reroofed and the late nineteenth-century interior recreated. A heritage centre (Canolfan Dreftadaeth Kate Roberts) has been built alongside.

This restored cottage looks back to the Welsh-speaking community that is celebrated in the novels of Kate Roberts. All over Wales similar cottages built from local materials now inspire debates about sustainability and local distinctiveness that are highly relevant to the twenty-first century. Another book continuing the study of vernacular cottages, by Eurwyn Wiliam, will soon be published by the Royal Commission.

Richard Suggett

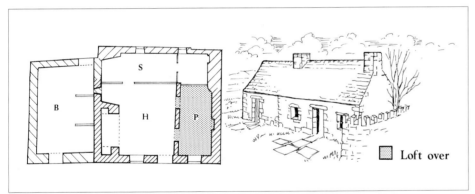

Loft over

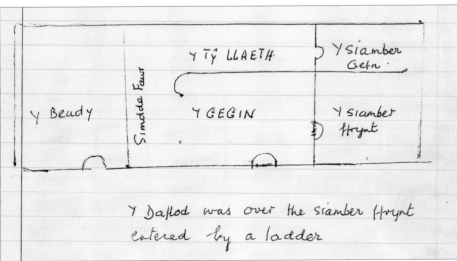

089 The Decline of the Railways: The Rokeby Collection

The two lost stations of Abergavenny: Brecon Road (above), photographed by Rev. Rokeby on 12 July 1957, and Abergavenny Junction, photographed on 28 December 1957 by D. W. Winkworth, many of whose images were collected by Rokeby.

DI2008_0606 NPRN 407764 and DI2008_0603 NPRN 407763
Courtesy National Churches Trust

An event momentous in its effect on the post-war landscape was the drastic pruning of the railway network. The elimination of duplicate or uneconomic services had begun earlier, but in the post-war years the nationalised rail system was losing money and cuts continued. After the Beeching report of 1963, *The Reshaping of British Railways*, they took on a breathtaking swiftness and severity. Enthusiasts for the railways set about making records of the infrastructure before it vanished. One of the largest collections was assembled by Rev. H. D. E. Rokeby of Norfolk. The National Monuments Record of Wales holds the Welsh section of this collection, comprising over 1,500 photographs of stations, halts and other installations. They were taken mainly in the late 1950s and early 1960s, though some dated back to the 1930s.

The loss of stations was particularly remarkable. For almost a hundred years the market town of Abergavenny had three: Oxford Road on the Hereford to Newport line, Brecon Road on the line to Merthyr Tydfil, and Junction, where the Merthyr and Newport lines met. Brecon Road was rendered redundant by the closure of the Merthyr line in 1958 and was demolished. It had opened in 1862 and boasted a large locomotive depot, a goods yard and a barracks for staff. Junction also closed in 1958. In Swansea the London, Midland & Scottish Railway had its own terminus, Swansea Victoria, by virtue of having absorbed the London and North Western Railway. Its meagre traffic could be accommodated by the Great Western station at High Street, so it was closed in October 1965.

The rivalries between railway companies during the nineteenth and early twentieth centuries had given rise to anomalies. The Manchester and Milford Railway was begun with the ambition to connect Milford Haven with the Lancashire cotton district, but the reality was a line that struck out for the Cambrian Mountains from Carmarthen, lost heart just north of Tregaron and headed for the coast at Aberystwyth. It was taken over by the Great Western in 1906, which hoped to capture some of the Cardigan Bay holiday traffic. Among the improvements by the new owners was the refurbishment of Llanilar station, far exceeding the requirements of this rural community. The branch succumbed to floods in 1964 and was closed officially the next year. Like many abandoned railways, it is now a cycle path.

David Percival

Top: The village station at Llanilar, Cardiganshire, closed in 1965.

DI2008_0607 NPRN 41354

Above: A map of the former Manchester and Milford Railway collected by Rev. Rokeby in about 1959. The services to Newcastle Emlyn and Aberaeron had already ended, but three passenger trains a day went from Carmarthen to Aberystwyth until 1964.

DI2008_0608 NPRN 91660

Right: The Swansea Victoria terminus, opened in 1867. The site was redeveloped in the 1970s for the Swansea leisure centre.

DI2008_0604 NPRN 34874

090 Clough Williams-Ellis and Post-1945 Portmeirion

A summer view of Portmeirion.

AP_2005_0582 NPRN 28697

Above: The site identified as the late twelfth-century castle of Aber lâ, once a stronghold of a prince of Gwynedd. A battlemented parapet was added by Clough in the 1960s.
DS2008_172_001 NPRN 302700

Right: The town hall with the statue of Atlas.
DS2007_449_020 NPRN 28697

Below: Aerial view of Portmeirion village.
GTJ25743 NPRN 28697

Clough Williams-Ellis wrote that he 'owns and is designer and builder of the new model resort of Portmeirion'. This constant in his life for over fifty years had two phases: the 1920s to 1930s and the 1950s to 1970s. Clough began Portmeirion in 1925, in the heyday of towns like Llandudno, with the group of cottages round the Campanile, a realisation of his beliefs about humane building, fitting structures to landscape, visual pleasure, and sense of history. Its spark came from the 1920s push from those who survived the First World War to make a better Britain, and his anger that this came to mean not architecture but ribbon development.

In the post-1945 stage the Arts and Crafts belief in craftsmanship and lettering, the introduction of gateway arches on the drives, an eye-catching dome, colours as never before and a sense of stylistic progress (Clough and his wife, the writer Amabel Strachey, joked about 'the Early Curly and the Late Straight'), all appeared as an unanticipated encore. Holidays for all had become the norm, and for the book-readers he wrote *Portmeirion: the Place and its Meaning* in 1963. This was handsomely introduced by the American critic Lewis Mumford, and Clough basked in far-away admiration, including that of Frank Lloyd Wright. Many other serious architects found the frivolity baffling.

There are differences between the village's two editions. The Second World War meant both closing his London architect's practice and adding the name of his son Christopher to the war memorial he had built in Llanfrothen in the 1920s. When building restrictions were lifted, his architectural and social conscience was reinvigorated, but there were younger Turks in the fight: he wrote the book for the Festival of Britain but was not invited to build at it. He became drawn to the new big ideas – founding the Snowdonia National Park, chairing the first New Towns commission

– and eventually he came to be living history himself and the oldest knight ever dubbed.

Chantry Row realised the monopitch terraces of council housing designed in 1941 for Workington but never built; miniatures of Classical mansions sprang insubstantially from Portmeirion's rocky declivities; teasing historic images like late eighteenth-century Gothick garden loggias were gathered round the central square; there were moments of homage like the introduction of Brodie's bronze sculpture of Atlas in 1959; and finally in 1973, when Clough was 93, to cope with the immense popular success of his creation, a new ticket lodge (of which John Cornforth remarked that it would be automatically listed as soon as finished).

The paradoxes of it all were clear. Clough was a convinced proponent of the Town and Country Planning Acts and of architectural preservation, but was surprised that regulation applied to his own work. What began as a seaside retreat for a London elite became an engine of Welsh life and tourism, but his friends thought he had spoiled it by so much infilling. Portmeirion was built to address twentieth-century architectural issues and freedoms, but it became identified with Cold War paranoia through the cult television series, *The Prisoner*. It is an important architectural essay, yet to be fully understood.

Richard Haslam

091 Award-winning Houses: 1-6 Little Orchard

The lounge at 6 Little Orchard, 1973, as furnished by Thomas Glyn Jones, photographed in 2006.
DS2006_015_017 NPRN 404533

The story of twentieth-century architecture in Wales does not always receive the attention it deserves. There is much to celebrate in the way in which modernity was espoused and assimilated, and not least in how a sense of identity was maintained in the face of new challenges. Perceptions of modern architecture are dominated by large-scale schemes – engineering projects, factories, housing estates – but there are also some exceptionally fine examples of small-scale development. Like historical architecture, these have the capacity to illuminate the culture and context of their time, reminding us that even the relatively recent is part of our history.

Little Orchard in Dinas Powys is one such development, comprising six houses by the Cardiff architects Thomas Glyn Jones and John R. Evans, who themselves lived in two of the houses. The scheme was implemented in two phases, plans for the first being approved in 1966. Four houses had been completed by 1968, the other two in 1973. The first phase won a Welsh Office Housing Medal in 1968 and a Concrete Society Award in 1969. In 1972 the scheme won the gold medal in architecture at the National Eisteddfod.

The development expresses progressive architectural thinking of its day. It represents a modern picturesque idiom, in which the six houses form a self-contained group, linked to each other in a rhythmic sequence which makes a harmonious composition in a carefully designed setting, working with the existing plot and retaining several of its trees. The houses boldly embrace tenets of modernity, notably in their use of materials and their handling of space. The use of concrete in various forms to articulate different elements of the plan is visually interesting and structurally honest.

Particularly striking is the use in the principal storey of ribbed concrete, cast *in -situ* and then hammered to create broken edges. This expressive assertion of the properties of the material took up a theme of modern architecture in both Europe (in the work of Le Corbusier) and the United States (Paul Rudolph had used this technique in the Art and Architecture Building at Yale University in 1966). The architects considered that the rough texture of the concrete made reference to the rugged Welsh landscape. Large areas of glazing enabled the interpenetration of interior and exterior spaces, reinforcing the relationship of the houses to their setting and providing interesting contrasts between solid and void, rough and smooth. There is a rigorous and elegant geometry at work in the sequences of planes and volumes, which contain, but do not seem to constrain, the living spaces.

Although some of the houses have seen a degree of change, the coherence of the original scheme has survived well and number 6, which was the home of Thomas Glyn Jones, has changed remarkably little since its completion in 1973. In 2006 a full photographic survey of this house was carried out by the Royal Commission, while it was still furnished as the architect intended, and the whole group of houses was listed as being of special architectural and historic interest. Copies of the original plans were placed in the National Monuments Record.

Judith Alfrey

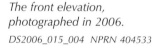

A detail of the ribbed and hammered concrete walls of the principal storey.

DS2006_015_010 NPRN 404533

The front elevation, photographed in 2006.

DS2006_015_004 NPRN 404533

092 Architecture for Wales: Plas Menai

Plas Menai in its landscape setting, viewed from the Anglesey side of the Menai Strait,
showing the roofs of Plas Menai in the middle ground between sea and mountains.

DS2008_413_004 NPRN 406861

Plas Menai, the National Watersports Centre, was built for the Sports Council for Wales as an outdoor pursuits centre in 1982. The site overlooks the Menai Strait midway between Caernarfon and Bangor, and is within easy reach of sea, rivers and mountains. The accommodation required by the brief included teaching rooms, a swimming pool, extensive stores for boats and equipment, workshops, a kitchen and dining room, hotel-quality bedrooms for sixty, and separate staff accommodation. The architects were the Bowen Dann Davies Partnership of Colwyn Bay and Bangor, led by Bill Davies with Jonathan Knox as job architect. This was their first large commission but it won the firm a Civic Trust award in 1984, an Eisteddfod Gold Medal and a Royal Institute of British Architects Regional Commendation.

Plas Menai: seaward (top) and landward (bottom) elevations.

DS2007_413_003 and
DS2007_413_002 NPRN 406861

The elements that make this centre one of the best new buildings in north Wales in the latter half of the twentieth century can be discussed on several related levels. First, the response to the site is masterly. The ground slopes gently to the Menai Strait, while in the opposite direction a backdrop is provided by the mountains of Snowdonia. The designers created a new landscape echoing this natural fall of the land. The large expanses of roof, all of Penrhyn purple slate, cascade down the slope in disjointed plates which slide and step past each other. Although the building reaches four storeys in height, nowhere does it feel tall.

The organisation of the large building is skilful, too. Where the accommodation needs the views, it is placed along the contours; where views are not important, the building turns at right angles to follow the slope (but with the roofs still sliding downhill). This results in a loose, E-shaped plan, with two relaxed, open courtyards between the wings. The lower yard relates to the boats and the water's edge, and was designed to have the character of a working quay. The upper yard, between the bedroom wings, is softer and greener. A third courtyard is provided in a separate block for the staff.

The palette of materials is simple and traditional: off-white roughcast, dark-stained timber windows and the purple slates. Occasionally, the walls are lined with slates or trimmed with granite. Eaves' overhangs are generous, giving a sense of shelter, and where semi-external space is covered there is more dark-stained carpentry, elegantly designed without being elaborate.

There is nothing inherently Welsh about the building's form or detail, yet there is a sense at Plas Menai and the firm's other buildings of an architectural 'vernacular' appropriate to the area. This is the same as the feeling from the buildings of Herbert Luck North [079], and it is not surprising to detect his influence as Frank Dann worked with North's partner and son-in-law, P. M. Padmore. In these days of globalisation, when buildings so often look the same no matter where they are put, Plas Menai reminds us that they can be, and should be, rooted in their context.

Adam Voelcker

093 Closing the Asylums

Aerial view of the North Wales Hospital, Denbigh, after closure, showing the final scale of an asylum complex that had grown progressively over a century and a half.

AP_2006_1006 NPRN 3010

Untearable (tick) dress and lockable shoes preserved in the hospital museum.

DI2008_0468 and DI2008_0467
NPRN 3010

The closure of asylums was one of the most dramatic aspects of public policy in the 1980s and 1990s. Several factors were involved: the establishment of outpatient clinics, the development of long-acting tranquilisers and the organisation of community-care programmes. There were several large and architecturally impressive asylums in Wales, including the cottage-like hospital at Pen-y-fal, Abergavenny, the Italianate St David's Hospital at Carmarthen with its huge water-towers, and the hill-top complex at Cefn Coed, Swansea. Most were less than a century old, but little of distinction had been added to them since the Second World War, with the exception of Carmarthen's noteworthy library. All of them have now changed in function or closed.

The largest former asylum is the North Wales Counties' Lunatic Asylum at Denbigh, built by public subscription, primarily out of concern for the welfare of Welsh-speaking patients who had previously been sent to asylums in England. The original core of the hospital was an impressive U-shaped range in Jacobean style with a central clock-tower, designed by Thomas Fulljames of Gloucester and opened in 1848. The principal benefactor, the local landowner Joseph Ablett, was commemorated by a bust in a niche in the entrance hall. The original building housed 200 patients, but there was progressive enlargement. By 1908 there was a self-sufficient 'village' of 1,000 patients and staff with a chapel, a farm, workshops, and private water and electricity supplies. Significant inter-war developments included schemes for dispersing patients and staff: six detached villas for patients were planned (though only two were built), a substantial nurses' home was added and a reception hospital for voluntary patients (the 'nerve hospital') was established in an adjoining villa.

Closure of the North Wales Hospital was envisaged by the 1980s and it was finally closed in September 1995. It was visited by Royal Commission staff shortly before closure to make a photographic record. Among the most affecting items were garments formerly worn by inmates, including 'tick' dresses and lockable boots. These were specially made for patients who kicked off their shoes or tore their clothes. Other moving artefacts included a painting by a patient which depicted the male airing court of the asylum devoid of patients. Astonishingly, many of the patients' records remained, some dating back to the foundation of the hospital, and this archive formed the basis of a research project on the history of mental illness in north Wales led by Dr Pam Michael of the University of Wales, Bangor.

These extraordinary complexes of buildings have posed problems of conservation and adaptation to new uses. Talgarth and Denbigh asylums have remained empty and semi-derelict for many years. The most frequent solution has been to demolish accretions and additions and retain the original buildings. Various health service functions are maintained in some cases, as at Whitchurch hospital in Cardiff. At Abergavenny conversion to apartments has been achieved successfully since the hospital closed in 1996, with the cost of refurbishing the original buildings offset by 'enabling development', building houses in the extensive grounds. This solution is hoped for at Denbigh.

Richard Suggett

The front elevation of the original 1847 asylum building at Denbigh.

DI2008_0486 NPRN 3010

094 Survivors: The Gee Printing Works

The linotype machine: the mainstay of the provincial printer.
DI2008-0481 NPRN 41216

Above: Gee Printing Works entrance (exterior).
DI2006_0271 NPRN 41216

Right, top: Gee Printing Works entrance (interior) with the proprietor's bay window.
Right, below: The bindery.
DI2008_0475 and DI2008_0480 NPRN 41216

Below: The print shop.
DI2008_0479 NPRN 41216

At the time of its closure in 2001 the original Gwasg Gee printing works in Denbigh was an astonishing survivor of a traditional printing shop. It was the oldest surviving example in Wales and had a strong tradition of Welsh-language printing and publishing. The press was founded in 1808 and acquired in 1813 by Thomas Gee, whose son of the same name (1815-98) took over its management in the 1830s and developed an ambitious programme of publication. The premises in Chapel Street were occupied continuously by the press from the 1830s and are substantially unchanged since the mid-nineteenth century. Increasing mechanisation led to expansion in the 1850s. The press buildings grew to enclose a courtyard, with an entrance large enough for carts, overlooked by Thomas Gee's first-floor office window. The Gee family remained closely associated with the press in the twentieth century, but shortly before World War II it was taken over by Morris T. Williams and his wife, Kate Roberts, a major literary figure whose novels and short stories portray the life of Welsh quarrymen and their families [088].

The press assumed its final form in the post-war years. Williams died in 1946 but Roberts continued to run the press and publish its Welsh-language national newspaper, *Baner ac Amserau Cymru* (or *Y Faner*), for another ten years. To the rear of the premises is a small furnace where the lead type was cast. The machinery is mainly twentieth century in date, much of it German. It includes a Polar-Mohl guillotine, a Brehmer Leipzig book-sewing machine, a Stahl folding machine and the Heidelberg presses in the printing room. The compositing room, for setting the type, contains six linotype machines. These machines, latterly used for printing funeral and

wedding services and the like, were the mainstay of a provincial printer. Gwasg Gee still retained old-fashioned racks of poster type and compositing stones.

The printing works was photographed in 1998, before its closure. Technological changes have simplified the number of processes involved in printing but the enormous investments require economies of scale, and large buildings on industrial estates are more suitable premises than constrained historic buildings in a town centre. However, Gwasg Gee remains an important component of the built heritage of Denbigh. A trust is investigating new uses for the building, which it is hoped will incorporate a museum of printing.

Richard Suggett

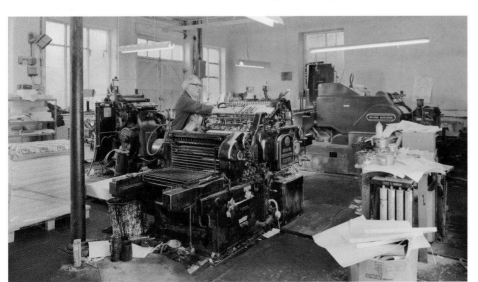

095 Eco-housing

Malator at Nolton, Pembrokeshire, nestling under a turf carpet with a glass wall looking out to sea.
DI2006_1034 NPRN 309561

Understanding of the history of Welsh architecture has led to a greater appreciation of the use of vernacular building materials, particularly timber, clay and turf. The modern interest in these materials dates to the early part of the century – exemplified by Clough Williams-Ellis's book of 1919, *Cottage Building in Cob, Pisé, Chalk and Clay*. It coincides today with a growing interest in sustainability and eco-friendly buildings.

Wales has a record of innovative work in sustainability, with the Centre for Alternative Technology at Machynlleth playing an important role in developing and demonstrating new approaches since it was established in 1973. Nearby, Dyfi Eco Park of 1997 is a green business park built with locally-sourced natural materials wherever possible, for example using sophisticated timber framing in place of the ubiquitous steel portal construction. Environmentally sustainable technology has also been demonstrated by the National Museum of Wales at St Fagans with the construction of Tŷ Gwyrdd (Green House).

Notable examples of 'eco-housing' in west Wales were photographed by the Royal Commission in preparation for the Pevsner *Buildings of Wales* guide to Pembrokeshire. There is a distinction to be drawn between houses in the 'home-made homes' tradition and those designed by architects. Home-made homes are in some cases unofficial and erected without planning permission. One of these, the Round House at Brithdir Mawr near Newport, Pembrokeshire, has become a planning *cause célèbre*. It is an 'eco-home' of timber, cob and recycled windows, with a turf roof. It has solar power and wind-turbines for electricity, a compost toilet, and reed beds to recycle grey water. It was built in the mid-1990s without planning permission but was spotted by a National Park survey plane. Demolition has been ordered but there have been demonstrations in favour of keeping it.

The Round House caught the public imagination but there are other notable 'eco-friendly' buildings

Right: Nant-y-cwm Steiner School: interior (below) and exterior of the turf-roofed kindergarten.

DI2008_0470 and DI2008_0472 NPRN 32113

Below: Malator in its landscape setting.

DI2006_1036 NPRN 309561

in Pembrokeshire. The Pevsner volume describes the emergence of a body of work on ecological principles, much of it of a pioneering nature. Nant-y-cwm Steiner School at Clynderwen is a modified Victorian Board School with a new-built kindergarten of 1982 by Christopher Day. According to the authors of the Pevsner architectural guide, 'Day achieved an iconic building of the then barely nascent ecological movement, a little building where the forms flow from the earth in battered roughcast walls, anchored by a turf roof'. Educational buildings, including visitor centres, have proved a fruitful focus for innovative architecture in a mainstream context. The Pembrokeshire Pevsner notes the visitor centre at Scolton Manor by Peter Holden Architects (1993), the tourist information centre at St Davids, and the visitor centre at the Castell Henllys hillfort (1993–4).

In these and other eco-buildings the turf roof has become expressive of late twentieth-century innovative architecture, symbolically replacing slate. One Pembrokeshire example has received particular attention: Malator, Nolton, by Future Systems (1998), which nestles under a turf carpet with a glass wall looking out to sea. It is an appealingly contemporary house matching futuristic design with the environmentally friendly.

Richard Suggett

Into the Future

Peter Wakelin

Today's landscape would be unrecognisable to Palaeolithic hunter-gathers who happened to arrive in twenty-first-century Wales. The sea has inundated their familiar lowland plains and the climate has become far milder. Even more incomprehensible to them would be the human alterations of the landscape – from Neolithic tombs to modern cities – which have accelerated along with mankind's appetites and capabilities. We cannot even guess how the landscape will change over the coming millennia, but recent experience does provide clues about the next few decades, as our lives today become the future's history.

In the near future the familiar landscape and building stock will persist. The vast majority of people will live in houses dating from the nineteenth or twentieth centuries and most of Wales will still be rural. Some current trends are likely to continue: housing and commercial development will probably go on expanding, high streets may still experience frequent renewal, old schools and hospitals may well be replaced with new, and churches and chapels may close if congregations continue to dwindle. In the countryside traditional farmsteads will become disused or be adapted and land uses based on leisure will probably increase.

Radical change is often unexpected. There may be twenty-first-century equivalents of shocking transformations such as the virtual eradication of traditional heavy industries; it is worth remembering that as recently as the 1980s the National Coal Board was predicting that coal reserves would last for two more generations. If pressure on food supplies increases and the climate warms, pasture might be turned to arable and marginal farmland might be brought back into use. The trend for out-of-town retail development could reverse with rising oil prices and the renaissance of town and city centres. It is even possible that deep mining will begin again to meet the demand for power generation.

The greatest impetus for change may come from the climate. Studies of the potential impacts of climate change warn of major consequences. Sea level is expected to rise 40 centimetres by 2080 and storm surges could affect land a metre above the present sea level. A 30 per cent rise in winter precipitation is predicted by 2100, which would increase flooding

along rivers and accelerate the erosion of fragile upland peat, especially if it is desiccated by the expected warmer, drier summers. As many towns and settlements cluster along riversides and nearly a fifth of all Wales's known archaeological sites are in peat soils, this is a major threat to the heritage. Actions to mitigate climate change may include the building of onshore and offshore windfarms and perhaps a Severn barrage, the alteration of buildings to improve their environmental performance, tree planting and drainage works to reduce peat erosion, and the construction of flood defences.

Such changes pose many challenges for the Royal Commission and its partners. Shifts in economic activity may put pressure on recording programmes, as occurred in the 1990s when steelworks and coal mines closed in rapid succession. Important strands of social history also deserve to be recorded, such as

Opposite: Contemporary projects will produce the heritage of the future, such as the great glasshouse at the National Botanic Garden, designed by Norman Foster and Partners, nearing completion in February 2000.
GTJ26987 NPRN 307111

Below: The speed with which traditional industries have vanished has been shocking, especially for valleys communities: Ebbw Vale steelworks in 2001 (top) and 2003.
DI2008_0415 and
CD2003_603_017 NPRN 34135

Above: The remains of the north Wales slate industry are on an enormous scale and much will be lost to processes of natural decay. The multiple working levels of Dinorwic quarry at Llanberis occupy a whole mountainside.

AP_2007_5203 NPRN 40538

the holiday camps that have disappeared in recent years [098]. Observing living processes rather than reconstructing them from fragmentary remains can be particularly productive [083], and it might prove far-sighted to record, for example, the myriad small shops threatened by the global shift to internet purchasing.

Even protected sites and buildings are not always safe. Crop-mark sites are liable to ploughing, Iron Age promontory forts are falling into the sea, and derelict country houses, churches and industrial

Right: Traditional buildings continue to be lost but careful recording can aid restoration or preserve information about them. Cottages of clom or cob are particularly vulnerable once abandoned.

DI2005_0852 NPRN 17223

buildings may fail to find saviours. The early steam engines at Glyn Pits, Pontypool, which have been recorded in detail by the Commission, are among the most remarkable industrial monuments in the country, yet years of effort have so far failed to safeguard them. Only a fraction of the thousands of relict slate-quarrying structures in north Wales can be preserved, but this was a distinctive industry of international importance which had great cultural significance: further investigation of it will enable the features most worthy of care to be identified and others to be recorded for posterity. There will be occasional, disastrous fires, like those that have destroyed, in recent years, a group of Georgian houses in Tenby, a listed chapel in Aberystwyth and the interiors of Hafodunos Hall. Where records have been made beforehand, they can be used to inform restoration or enable people in the future to understand what has been lost.

Some of the most frequently consulted items in the National Monuments Record show construction projects in progress, such as the album recording the building of the Elan valley reservoirs [078]. Major construction schemes of the future should also be

periods, including when and how the earliest humans arrived and left and the international transfer of technologies in the Industrial Revolution. An armoury of new techniques is offering exciting opportunities to answer important questions. Environmental archaeology is generating invaluable information from peat deposits about past climate and vegetation. The potential is now better understood for using bathymetry and underwater sampling to investigate the landscapes off the present coast that Palaeolithic people occupied. Tree-ring dating has begun to refine the chronology of vernacular architecture, allowing buildings to be understood in their contemporary context [097]. Examination of airborne laser imagery (Lidar) is certain to discover additional archaeological sites. The Royal Commission's systematic chapels programme is beginning to identify patterns in the 'national architecture' of Wales, and the mass of data produced by the Uplands Archaeology Initiative should generate conclusions about mining, agriculture, Neolithic ritual and past climates, among many other themes.

These are exciting and challenging times. As the First Minister, Rhodri Morgan, said in his centenary message to the Royal Commission in summer 2008, the core functions of the organisation to develop our knowledge and record of Wales remain as important as ever. He wrote, 'The arrival of a centenary is an important moment to look back on achievements and take pride in them. At the same time, there is much to look forward to in the coming years. I'm sure that the Commission will face the challenges of its second century with the same determination and readiness to embrace innovation that it has shown in the past.'

represented and the Commission has photographed, among important recent projects, the National Botanic Garden, the Senedd of the National Assembly for Wales and the Millennium Stadium [096].

As public interest and expectations have grown, the National Monuments Record has metamorphosed from an inventory and archive used largely by professionals into a widely-enjoyed resource. The World Wide Web has become a tool of daily life and historians and archaeologists are grasping the opportunities it affords to work in partnership and make their resources available to all [099]. New interpretative tools include computer animation and mobile audio tours and e-trails. However, the burgeoning of digital materials also imposes responsibilities on professional archivists to ensure that they will still be accessible in another hundred years.

There has been a revolution in what people judge to be their heritage. The definition extends far beyond the interests of a century ago. Sports venues are seen to be as significant in their way as monasteries or castles, and modernist buildings elicit almost as much passion and enthusiasm as Victorian ones. Historic battle sites have begun to generate considerable public interest, posing new challenges associated with less tangible heritage [100]. *Introducing a Research Framework for the Archaeology of Wales* (2008) has identified gaps in our understanding of all

096 Major Construction Projects:
The Millennium Stadium

The Millennium Stadium photographed during its early construction in August 1998.
At the far end is the part of the old stand kept to maintain the structural integrity of the attached Cardiff stand.

DI2008_0346 NPRN 309686

Above: 'The entry of the Gladiators': The players' tunnel in Cardiff Arms Park, the former national stadium, photographed in 1997.

GTJ22272 NPRN 3064

Right: The National Stadium, showing its distinctive U-shaped roof, and early stages in the demolition of the old West Stand.

D12007_1432, GTJ 22268 NPRN 3064

Below: The Millennium Stadium, showing its prime location and its immense retractable roofing structure. Adjacent is the Cardiff rugby ground.

CD 2003_606_023 NPRN 309686

The Royal Commission is unique in making permanent records of important contemporary developments in Wales – the heritage of the future even as it is being created – as well as of historic structures and sites under threat. The construction of the Millennium Stadium for the Rugby World Cup in 1999 represented an opportunity to observe the demolition of an icon of Welsh heritage and the genesis of a new one. The Commission's expertise in architectural photography and aerial archaeology provides unique perspectives of the old stadium and the development of its replacement.

The Millennium Stadium is a Welsh structure that is already recognised worldwide. Constructed between 1995 and 1999, it is built on the site of two previous international rugby venues – the original Cardiff Arms Park and the later National Stadium, with the axis of the pitch turned through ninety degrees. It was constructed at a cost of £126 million, partly financed by the Millennium Lottery Fund. It accommodates 74,500 spectators on three tiers, the lowest of which is below ground level to reduce the stadium's visual impact in the city centre. The many remarkable features of the stadium include a retractable roof with a moveable area of 8,960 square metres and a playing surface laid on 7,412 moveable pallets, which can be carried off-site in 188 articulated lorry loads. Perhaps its most distinctive feature is the excellent sight-lines that give every spectator a sensation of being close to the action of the game: the back seat of the upper tier is the same distance from the pitch side as the back row in the old stadium.

From the mid-nineteenth century the river meadow alongside the old Cardiff Arms Park Hotel

was used for military and sporting events. Cardiff Rugby Football Club held its first practice match here in 1878. In those early days the Marquis of Bute charged the Cardiff rugby and cricket clubs a peppercorn rent for the use of the site. The hotel was demolished in 1882 and the first major grandstand opened on Boxing Day 1885, built at a cost of £365. There followed a series of grandstands to accommodate the growing crowds, and the land was eventually sold by the marquis to a consortium of the Welsh Rugby Union and Cardiff Rugby Club in 1922. Further developments took place incrementally until the Cardiff Arms Park was completely replaced in the 1960s by the purpose-built National Stadium, with its distinctive U-shaped roof structure, at a cost of £9 million. This was to become the scene of an extraordinary period of sporting dominance by the Welsh national team, making it famous across the world. Despite its official title, the stadium still remained generally known as Cardiff Arms Park. The name of the new building – the Millennium Stadium – was a requirement of the Millennium Lottery Fund. So well loved was the old stadium that it led to questions in the New South Wales Legislative Council in Australia as to why the replacement had not been named the New Cardiff Arms Park.

Neil Harries

097 Dating the Work of the Master Carpenter: Old Impton

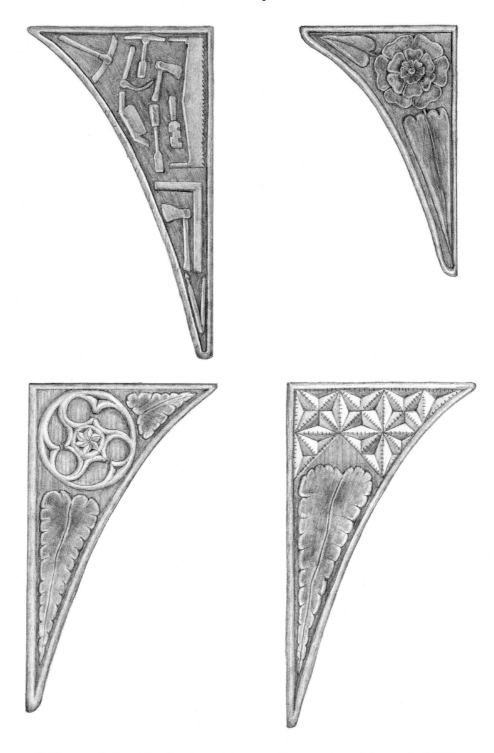

Old Impton, Radnorshire: Drawings of the carved jetty brackets of the porch (1542),
including (top left) the depiction of the carpenter's tools.

DI2005_0043 NPRN 81445

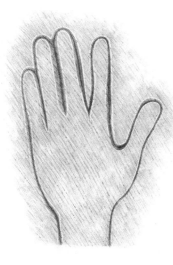

Top: Upper Dolley (Presteigne), Pembrokeshire, the carpenter's hand incised on a jetty bracket.

DI2005_0041 NPRN 81574

Right: The porch at Old Impton, a masterpiece of timber framing.

DI2007_0335 NPRN 81445

Below: Old Impton: A reconstruction sketch showing the relationship between the stone-built hall (1471) and the timber-framed additions (1542).

DI2008_0852 NPRN 81445

Some buildings more than others clarify aspects of building history and pose questions for future investigation. Old Impton in Radnorshire is such a building. The house exemplifies the transition in late-medieval Wales from stone building to building in timber, and it has timberwork of the highest quality completed by an unknown master. In later medieval Wales the craft of the carpenter in church and house was of great significance. The names of the master carpenters were not usually recorded and their personalities are elusive, but in their day they were as well known as the best poets and musicians, and in as much demand. The recovery of the exceptional, hidden history of Welsh timber building has been one of the achievements of the Royal Commission's survey work since *Houses of the Welsh Countryside* was published in 1975. Tree-ring dating is refining our understanding further.

Old Impton is a complicated house, best appreciated from a bird's-eye view. But we now know from tree-ring dating that its phases of development were simpler and earlier than formerly thought. There were only two phases: a stone-built hall-house of 1471 and sophisticated timber-framed additions of 1542. Documentary research sheds light on what was happening at these two dates. In 1471 the receiver of the lordship of Maelienydd built a stone-walled hall here. Two generations later his grandson, Thomas ap Watkin, married the daughter of a Shropshire knight, Sir John Bradshaw. It appears that the 1542 rebuilding of Old Impton was a consequence of his advantageous match.

The timber-framed additions to the house were all of the highest quality, but the best decoration was displayed in the new entrance. The porch built at

that time is two-storeyed and jettied out in best Tudor fashion. The ceiling joists are gently domed and expensively moulded. The door-head and the brackets that support the jetty are carved with foliage and interlacing squares and circles. These are virtuoso displays of the carver's craft. Even more strikingly, high on an upper jetty bracket and not readily visible from the ground, the carpenter has represented all the tools needed to build a house – from felling-axe to saw and auger – vividly expressing the pride of the carpenter in his craft.

Precise tree-ring dating has been crucial to developing an understanding of Old Impton, providing an illuminating instance of how the method is recovering and reinterpreting the timber-building tradition nationally. Precise dating is indispensable as it enables a building to be put in historical context. It can be accurate (if complete sapwood survives) to the year and even the season of felling. More than fifty buildings have been dated by the Royal Commission with the Oxford Dendrochronology Laboratory. This work is constructing a master chronology that will help tree-ring dating in all parts of Wales and beyond. In the next few years it has the potential to refine our understanding of Welsh building history and, of course, the mysterious figures who were the master carpenters of Wales.

Richard Suggett

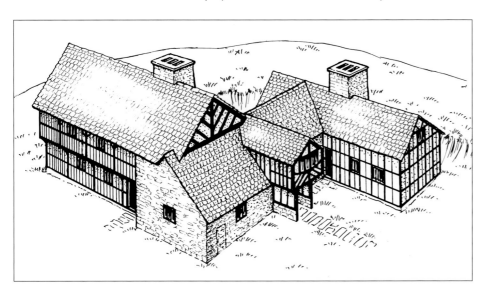

098 Buildings at Risk: Prestatyn Holiday Camp

Prestatyn holiday camp: A stair turret and the curved end of the Britannia lounge.
DI2005_1093 NPRN 300218

Above: The reception block and the observation tower.

DI2008_0853 NPRN 300218

Below: Sunfish Bay chalets and the ballroom in the background.

DI2008_0855 NPRN 300218

Buildings of historic interest are at risk perennially. The Royal Commission encourages nominations from local authorities, Cadw and members of the public of buildings vulnerable to decay or damage that may be priorities for recording. Most of these are legally protected from demolition but are at risk nevertheless. Some may be rescued; others may be lost. In either case, a survey is important, aiding restoration or preserving information for the future. Unprotected buildings, too, are often of historical interest. One of these was the art deco holiday camp at Prestatyn in Flintshire, which was due to be cleared for redevelopment without any record in 2001. The Royal Commission approached the owners to make an emergency photographic survey while demolition was in progress.

Prestatyn holiday camp was opened in 1939 by British Holiday Estates Limited, a joint venture between the London, Midland and Scottish Railway and Thomas Cook. It was designed by William H. Hamlyn, the railway company's architect. Originally there were 900 chalets with accommodation for 1,700 people around a central amenity area. The seaward side had tennis courts, a running track, an open-air swimming pool and other facilities for outdoor activities. A large entrance piazza was flanked by distinctive art deco complexes connected by covered walkways with characteristic rounded corners and curved windows. One block contained the reception, a gymnasium, a billiards room, a large communal lounge and an observation tower over 30 metres high with a glazed viewing platform. The other contained another lounge, a ballroom, service areas and a dining room over 55 metres long and almost 30 metres wide. The buildings were constructed with steel frames infilled with rendered brick.

The chalets were of three types: family units in blocks of four, twin-person units in back-to-back pairs, and single-person chalets in back-to-back terraced blocks. Concrete foundation rafts supported grooved concrete uprights into which prefabricated wall panels were slotted. The panels were made of wood-wool fibre reinforced with cement, and the end units incorporated steel-framed windows and a door. The roofs were flat, extending to form a storm-shelter at the front. Chalets were lit by electricity and had washbasins with cold water; toilets and showers were in communal blocks.

After the Second World War, during which the camp was requisitioned, the public's expectations changed. The need for family accommodation far outstripped that for singles and couples, and en suite facilities and hot water were expected as standard. Single units were combined into two-bedroom chalets with private bathrooms. The camp continued to be improved and expanded but it could not keep pace with changes in the holiday market.

Prestatyn was not the first holiday camp but it was an early attempt to combine mass travel, accommodation and entertainment in one package, an innovative exercise in prefabrication, and a remarkable architectural set piece. The photographs, despite the dereliction of the site, evoke the optimism and style of new leisure opportunities for ordinary people in the mid-twentieth century. The Royal Commission has surveyed thousands of buildings under threat, and the need to record others for posterity continues.

David Percival

099 Pointing to the Future:
Digital Technologies

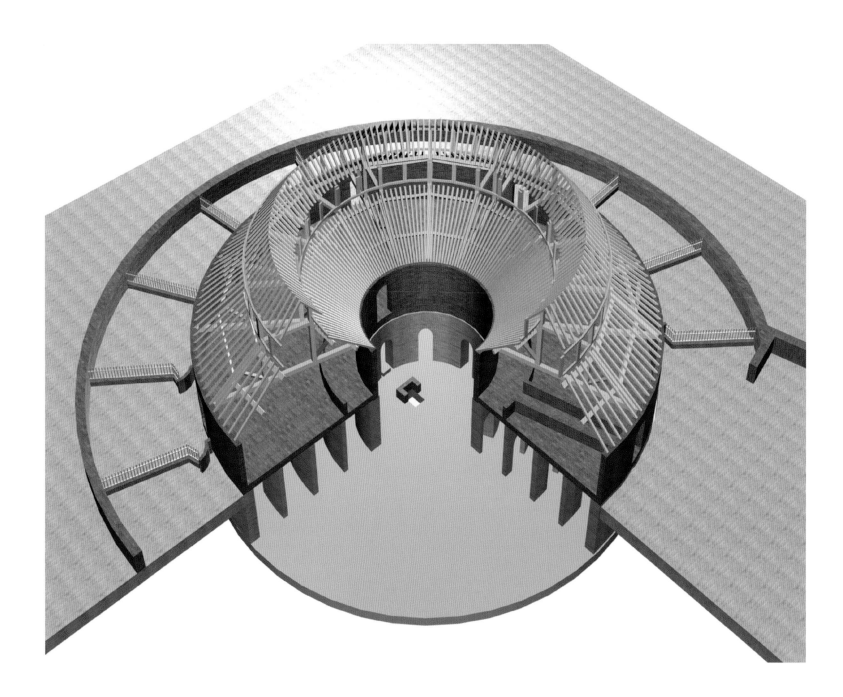

A digital interpretative cutaway drawing of the piggery at Leighton Park model farm near Welshpool, Montgomeryshire [072].
The slurry from the circular-roofed building flowed into the tank below, where it was mixed with water and pumped to the fields.
NPRN 80542

Above: The Royal Commission's booklet giving guidance on developing e-trails, published in 2008.

Below: The Historic Wales Portal in its first phase of development, 2006-8.

The explosion in the use of the internet has transformed the ways in which the Royal Commission can deliver its information and collections to larger and more diverse audiences than ever before. It has created a succession of digital resources since the 1980s and, with its partners, has been a pioneer of high-quality online services – these have already answered hundreds of thousands of queries. Its web technology partnership with the Royal Commission on the Ancient and Historical Monuments of Scotland, Shared Web Information Services for Heritage (SWISH), is widely admired.

In 2004 the free online database, Coflein, was launched, providing details of features of archaeological and historical interest across Wales. Coflein enables visitors to search for sites by name or type, or to explore through maps, as well as to view the archive catalogue and many digitised images. Expectations of its contents will continue to increase. Not least among the challenges for the future is how to enhance the records made by specialists in the past with no idea that they would be available to a wider public. Time and expertise are required to catalogue the records and prepare concise descriptions of each site.

In 2006 the Historic Wales Portal was launched to build on Coflein and to allow simultaneous viewing of the Royal Commission's material alongside 200,000 objects from the National Museum's archaeological collections, Cadw's data about statutorily protected sites, the historic environment records held by the four Welsh Archaeological Trusts, and other sources. This created a holistic portal to the historic environment of enormous potential. In 2008 the Commission took on a role in interpreting social history engagingly and innovatively as a development partner in the Welsh Assembly Government's People's Collection.

As use of the internet continues to mature and further advances are made in its technology and content, new challenges and opportunities arise. Regular relaunches of Coflein and the Historic Wales Portal ensure that these opportunities are grasped. Improvements in design, querying and data presentation inspired by leading international websites such as Google, Flickr and Google Earth are made possible by flexible engineering of the underlying databases. An important area for further development is the creation of more personalised versions of Coflein that allow users to add their own content, extending the information base in Wikipedia style, without prejudicing the authority and impartiality for which the National Monuments Record is valued.

The Commission has been a pioneer in the delivery of information to mobile devices. Its pilot projects were received enthusiastically in Ruthin and Blaenavon, bringing information about the historic environment to new audiences in new ways, and its experience was shared with other organisations. Digitisation and photography programmes constantly add material, and information captured in the field is made available far more quickly than was possible in the past. Developments of video and three-dimensional modelling, equally, allow sites to be represented and explained engagingly, both by conventional media and through the web.

The Royal Commission is dedicated to exploiting new technologies to improve its services and ensure that its work and collections remain relevant to the needs of a society both fascinated by its history and eager to gain the most from its rich heritage.

David Thomas

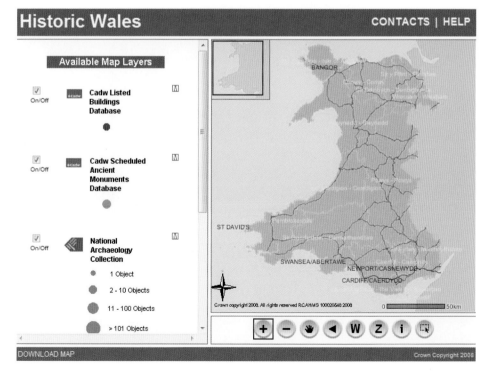

100 Uncertain Heritage: The Search for Battle Sites

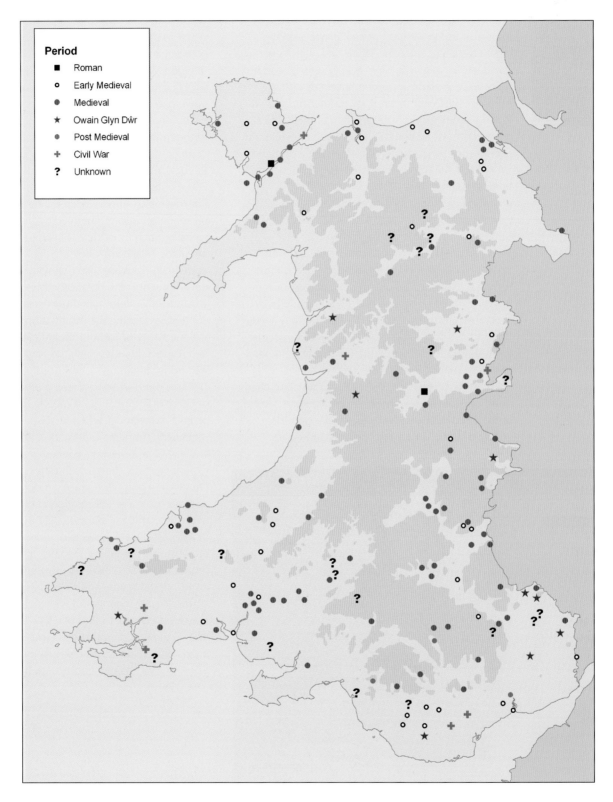

Bloodier times in Welsh history are recalled by a map of over 170 military conflict sites so far identified by the Royal Commission.
Crown copyright: All rights reserved. Ordnance Survey licence number 100017916.

At Pwll Melyn in Monmouthshire the attack by Owain Glyn Dŵr's son, Gruffydd, on Usk Castle was routed by English forces in 1405. The site is largely built over but it can be located by the pool that still bears the name Pwll Melyn (wooded, centre), in which skeletons were found in the nineteenth century.

AP_2006_1916 NPRN 402320

The Civil War battlefield at St Fagans, near Cardiff, where parliamentary forces defeated royalists in 1648 is cut through by a dual carriageway.

AP_2006_1802 NPRN 307776

Right: At Cymerau in Carmarthenshire in 1257 a Welsh force attacked an Anglo-Norman troop returning from Llandeilo to Carmarthen, killing two to three thousand, probably at the confluence of the rivers Tywi and Cothi.

GTJ26916 NPRN 404717

The sites of battles are a subject of great public interest. They can shed light on the turbulence of history and the course of pivotal events, and many people feel a need to honour the fallen of past conflicts by recognising where combatants fought and died. However, in most cases little or nothing is visible to identify the sites of battles, and documentary sources seldom provide information about their location. Investigating historic battles therefore poses special challenges.

The Royal Commission's early county inventories often contain notes of historic battles or field names that suggest a conflict. In 2005 the Commission began to identify battles systematically with several outcomes in mind – the depiction of the most important sites on maps, raised public awareness, priorities for further investigation, and provision of information for the Welsh Assembly Government to help it consider the possible protection of sites. The term 'battle' can cover events of many types and levels of significance; it was decided to consider all locations where a conflict occurred involving military forces. Work began with battles that involved massed troops and is gradually extending to other kinds of conflict that might be equally important historically, such as sieges, skirmishes, ambushes, maritime engagements and confrontations between the military and civilians such as the Merthyr Rising of 1831.

Some 170 sites so far have been given entries in the National Monuments Record (all accessible through Coflein), dating between the Roman conquest (which provides the first documentary evidence of battles) and the Second World War. Early medieval battles – such as at Rhuddlan in 795 – are particularly difficult to locate, as contemporary references are scant. Many have been identified from the Middle Ages: those associated with Owain Glyn Dŵr between 1400 and 1410, such as Pilleth (or Bryn Glas) in Radnorshire and Pwll Melyn in Monmouthshire, are a particularly important group. Post-medieval battles include Civil War engagements such as St Fagans near Cardiff and Colby Moor in Pembrokeshire. Undated sites have been deduced from archaeological finds or place names such as 'Bloody Field' at Beguildy in Radnorshire.

Before sites can be proposed for addition to maps or a battlefields register it is important to judge their significance and whether a location can be identified and delimited. The Commission has consulted historians, the Welsh Archaeological Trusts and special interest groups about the information it has gathered. Twenty-two battles are so far generally agreed to be of primary importance, of which twelve can be located with reasonable confidence. Recommendations have been passed to the Ordnance Survey for depiction of these on small-scale maps. However, some important battles in Welsh history are not easily located authoritatively – for example, although there is a monument to Glyn Dŵr's victory at Hyddgen in 1401, it was put up centuries after the event.

In partnership with Cadw, further research is being undertaken to investigate primary sources, interrogate historic maps to strip away later landscape features, compile aerial photography, assess site topography, and plan programmes of geophysics and archaeological evaluation. This work may bring greater certainty to these most hidden and significant components of Wales's heritage.

Brian Malaws and Peter Wakelin

St Llawddog's Church, Cenarth, Carmarthenshire: a twelfth- or thirteenth-century font carved with five heads, possibly representing Christ and the Evangelists, originally from Llandysiliogogo, Cardiganshire.

DI2006_0214 NPRN 309895

Royal Commissioners, 1908-2008

Chairmen

Sir John Rhys 1908-1915
Evan Vincent Evans 1916-1934
Ivor Miles, earl of Plymouth 1935-1943
Thomas Jones 1944-1948
Robert Richards 1948-1954
John Goronwy Edwards 1955-1967
William Francis Grimes 1967-1979
Hubert Newman Savory 1979-1983
Richard John Copland Atkinson 1984-1986
Glanmor Williams 1986-1990
Jenkyn Beverley Smith 1991-1998
Ralph Alan Griffiths 1999 –

Secretaries

Edward Owen 1908-1928
Wilfred Hemp 1928-1946
Courtenay Arthur Ralegh Radford 1946-1948
William Eric Griffiths 1948-1949
Alexander Hubert Arthur Hogg 1949-1973
Peter Smith 1973-1991
Peter Robert White 1991-2005
Alexander Peter Wakelin 2005 –

Commissioners

Edward Anwyl 1908-1914
Robert Carr Bosanquet 1908-1925
Robert Hughes 1908-1925
Griffith Hartwell Jones 1908-1944
William Edwin Llewellyn Morgan 1908-1925
Evan Vincent Evans 1908-1934
  (Chairman 1916-1934)
Henry Owen 1914-1919
Joseph Alfred Bradney 1916-1933
Sir John Morris-Jones 1920-1929
John Fisher 1925-1930
Cyril Fred Fox 1925-1960
John Edward Lloyd 1930-1947
Charles Frederic Roberts 1930-1942
Ivor Miles, earl of Plymouth 1934-1943
  (Chairman 1935-1943)
Courtenay Arthur Ralegh Radford 1935-1948
Henry Harold Hughes 1935-1940
William Garmon Jones 1935-1937
Robert Richards 1943
  (Chairman 1948-1954)
Ifor Williams 1943-1963
John Goronwy Edwards 1949
  (Chairman 1955-1967)
Thomas Alwyn Lloyd 1949-1960
William Francis Grimes 1949
  (Chairman 1967-1979)
Idris Llewelyn Foster 1949-1983
Victor Erle Nash-Williams 1955
Arthur Herbert Dodd 1956-1966
Arnold Joseph Taylor 1956-1983
Richard John Copland Atkinson 1963
  (Chairman 1984-1986)
Glanmor Williams 1963
  (Chairman 1986-1990)
Raymond Bernard Wood-Jones 1963-1982

Edward Martyn Jope 1963-1986
John Davies Knatchbull Lloyd 1967-1973
John Gwynn Williams 1967-1991
Dewi-Prys Thomas 1970-1985
Hubert Newman Savory 1970
  (Chairman 1979-1983)
David Morgan Rees 1974-1978
George Counsell Boon 1979-1990
David Gordon Tucker 1979-1984
Michael Ross Apted 1983-1992
Ronald William Brunskill 1983-1997
David Ellis Evans 1984-1996
John Geraint Jenkins 1984-1989
Jenkyn Beverley Smith 1984
  (Chairman 1991-1998)
Leslie Alcock 1986-1990
Richard Michael Haslam 1986-1998
Geoffrey John Wainwright 1987-2003
Stuart Brian Smith 1990-1996
Ralph Alan Griffiths 1991
  (Chairman 1999 –)
Daniel Gruffydd Jones 1991-2001
Geraint Dyfed Barri Jones 1991-1999
Eurwyn Wiliam 1992-2006
Alexandra Nicol 1993-2001
Patrick Sims-Williams 1998-2008
David Wyatt Crossley 2000-2007
John Arthur Newman 2000 –
Llinos Olwen Wyn Smith 2000 –
Anthony David Carr 2001 –
James Neil Osborne Harries 2001 –
John Wilson Lloyd 2001 –
Anne Sara Eastham 2004 –
Jonathan Matthews Hudson 2006 –
Henry Stuart Owen-John 2006 –

Further Reading

The following sections recommend some of the best introductory sources for the heritage of Wales. Wide-ranging surveys and general reference works are followed by suggestions for each period. More comprehensive bibliographies are in the Royal Commission's own publications and in many of the works noted below.

General

The Royal Commission's inventories and other publications have made fundamental contributions to knowledge, and they are listed separately on page 311. They provide authoritative information and interpretations for most periods of the past and for much of Wales. Information for more than 80,000 individual sites may be found on the Commission's free online public database, www.coflein.gov.uk. This can be searched by map or text, or by using the National Primary Record Number (NPRN) given for each photograph in this book.

Recent one-volume introductions to the history of Wales are: Morgan, P. (ed.), *The Tempus History of Wales: 25,000 BC–A D 2000* (Stroud, 2001), a collection of expert essays; Davies, J., *Hanes Cymru* (Harmondsworth, 1990), translated as *A History of Wales* (2nd edn. London, 2007); and Jenkins, G. H., *A Concise History of Wales* (Cambridge, 2007). Davies, J., *The Making of Wales* (Stroud, 1996) is a well-illustrated introduction to the history of the landscape. Rees, W., *An Historical Atlas of Wales* (new edn. London, 1972), is a classic, while more detailed twentieth-century maps are in Carter, H. and Griffiths, H. M. (eds.), *National Atlas of Wales* (Cardiff, 1980).

Cadw's *A Guide to Ancient and Historic Wales* (4 vols., London) is a succinct regional gazetteer of ancient and medieval sites: *Dyfed* (by Rees, S., 1992); *Glamorgan and Gwent* (by Whittle, E., 1992); *Clwyd and Powys* (by Burnham, H., 1995); and *Gwynedd* (by Lynch, F., 1995). Cadw's regularly updated guidebooks to individual monuments in state care provide an authoritative and well-illustrated source of information.

The Pevsner series, *The Buildings of Wales*, provides detailed descriptions of buildings, arranged by city, town and village: Haslam, R., *Powys* (London and Cardiff, 1979); Hubbard, E., *Clwyd* (London and Cardiff, 1986); Newman, J., *Gwent/Monmouthshire* (London and Cardiff, 2000); Lloyd, T., Orbach, J. and Scourfield, R., *Pembrokeshire* (New Haven and London, 2004); and Lloyd, T., Orbach, J. and Scourfield, R., *Carmarthenshire and Ceredigion* (New Haven and London, 2006).

Several counties have an authoritative *County History* complete or in progress: Lloyd, J. E. (ed.), *A History of Carmarthenshire*, 2 vols. (Cardiff, 1935, 1939); Williams, G. (ed.), *Glamorgan County History*: vol. I, *Natural History*, ed. Tattersall, W.M. (Cardiff, 1936); vol. II, *Early Glamorgan*, ed. Savory, H. N. (Cardiff, 1984); vol. III, *Medieval Glamorgan*, ed. Pugh, T. B (Cardiff, 1971); vol. IV, *Early Modern Glamorgan,* ed. Williams, G. (Cardiff, 1974); vol. V, *Industrial Glamorgan*, ed. John, A. H. and Williams, G. (Cardiff, 1980); vol. VI, *Glamorgan Society, 1780-1980*, ed. Morgan, P. (Cardiff, 1988);

Davies, E. and Howells, B. (eds.), *Pembrokeshire County History*: vol. II, *The Middle Ages*, ed. Walker, R. F. (Haverfordwest, 2002); vol. III, *Early Modern Pembrokeshire*, ed. Howells, B. (Haverfordwest, 1987); vol. IV, *Modern Pembrokeshire*, ed. Howell, D. W. (Haverfordwest, 1993); *History of Merioneth*: vol. 1, *From the Earliest Times to the Age of the Native Princes,* ed. Bowen, E. G.and Gresham, C. A. (Dolgellau, 1967); vol.2, *The Middle Ages*, ed. J. B. Smith (Dolgellau, 2002); Griffiths, R. A. (ed.), *Gwent County History*: vol.1, *Gwent in Prehistory and Early History*, ed. Aldhouse-Green, M. and Howell, R. (Cardiff, 2004); vol. 2, *The Age of the Marcher Lords, 1070-1536*, ed. Griffiths, R. A., Hopkins, T. and Howell, R. (Cardiff, 2008); *Cardiganshire County History*: vol. 1, *From the Earliest Times to the Coming of the Normans*, ed. Davies, J. L. and Kirby, D. P. (Cardiff, 1994); *Cardiganshire County History*: vol. 3, *Cardiganshire in Modern Times*, ed. Jenkins, G. H. and Jones, I. G. (Cardiff, 1998).

Volumes of *Archaeologia Cambrensis*, the archaeological journal of the Cambrian Archaeological Association, and *The Welsh History Review* and *Cof Cenedl* contain a wealth of papers on diverse subjects.

Prehistory

Good introductions to prehistory are: Lynch, F., Aldhouse-Green, S. and Davies, J. L., *Prehistoric Wales* (Stroud, 2000); Burrow, S., *The tomb builders in Wales 4000-3000BC* (Cardiff, 2006); and Bewley, R., *Prehistoric Settlements* (Stroud, 2003).

Particular themes are explored in: Green, S. and Walker, E., *Ice Age Hunters: Neanderthals and Early Modern Hunters in Wales* (Cardiff, 1991); Aldhouse-Green, S. (ed.), *Paviland Cave and the 'Red Lady'* (Bristol, 2000); Burrow, S., *Catalogue of the Mesolithic and Neolithic Collection in the National Museums and Galleries of Wales* (Cardiff, 2003); Britnell, W. J. and Savory, H. N., *Gwernvale and Penywyrlod: Two Neolithic Long Cairns in the Black Mountains of Brecknock* (Bangor, 1984); Cummings, V. and Whittle, A., *Places of Special Virtue: Megaliths in the Neolithic Landscapes of Wales* (Oxford, 2004); Oswald, A., Dyer, C. and Barber, M., *The Creation of Monuments, Neolithic Causewayed Enclosures in the British Isles* (English Heritage, Swindon, 2001); Bruck, J. (ed.), *Bronze Age Landscapes – Tradition and Transformation* (Oxford, 2001); Gibson, A., *Stonehenge and Timber Circles* (Stroud, 1998); Gibson, A., *The Walton Basin Project: Excavation and Survey in a Prehistoric Landscape 1993-7* (CBA Research Report 118, York, 1999); Lynch, F., *Excavations in the Brenig Valley. A Mesolithic and Bronze Age Landscape in North Wales* (Bangor, 1993).

Iron Age and Roman

Good up-to-date introductions are: Green, M. and Howell, R., *A Pocket Guide to Celtic Wales* (Cardiff, 2000); Ralston, I., *Celtic Fortifications* (Stroud, 2006); Arnold, C. J. and Davies, J. L., *Roman and Early Medieval Wales* (Stroud, 2000); and Manning, W., *Roman Wales* (Cardiff, 2001).

Particular Iron Age themes are explored in: Avery, M., *Hillfort Defences of Southern Britain* (3 vols. Oxford 1993); Bevan, B. (ed.), *Northern Exposure: interpretative devolution and the Iron Ages in Britain* (Leicester, 1999); Cunliffe, B., *Iron Age Communities in Britain* (London 2005); Gwilt, A. and Haselgrove, C. (eds.), *Reconstructing Iron Age Societies, New approaches to the British Iron Age.* (Oxford, 1997); Haselgrove, C. and Moore, T. (eds.), *The Later Iron Age in Britain and Beyond* (Oxford, 2007); Haselgrove, C. and Pope, R. (eds.), *The Earlier Iron Age in Britain and the Near Continent* (Oxford, 2007); Hogg, A. H. A, *Hill-forts of Britain* (London, 1975); Howell, R., *Searching for the Silures. An Iron Age Tribe in South-east Wales* (Stroud, 2006); Musson, C., *The Breiddin Hillfort: A later prehistoric settlement in the Welsh Marches* (York, 1991); Williams, G. H. and Mytum, H., *Llawhaden, Dyfed: Excavations on a group of small defended enclosures, 1980-4* (Oxford, 1998).

Various aspects of the Roman military presence are treated in: Nash-Williams, V. E., *The Roman Frontier in Wales* (2nd edn. Cardiff, 1969); Davies, J. L., Fragile Heritage: the archaeology of the early Roman campaigns in Wales and the borderland, *Archaeologia Cambrensis,* 155 (2006), 1-21; Brewer, R., *Caerleon and the Roman Army* (2nd edn. Cardiff, 2000); Zienkiewicz, J. D., *The Legionary Baths at Caerleon* (Cardiff, 1986); Brewer, R. (ed.), *The Second Augustan Legion and the Roman Military Machine* (Cardiff, 2000). The two *civitas* capitals are described in: Brewer, R., *Caerwent Roman Town* (3rd edn. Cardiff, 2006); James, H., *Roman Carmarthen: Excavations 1978-1993* (Exeter, 2003).

Some aspects of the Romano-British countryside can be studied in: Allen, J. R. L. and Fulford, M. G., Romano-British settlement and industry on the wetlands of the Severn estuary, *Antiquaries Journal* 67 (1987), 237-89; Blockley, K., *Prestatyn 1984-5: An Iron Age Farmstead and Romano-British Industrial Settlement in North Wales* (Oxford, 1989); Jarrett, M. G. and Wrathmell, S., *Whitton: An Iron Age and Roman Farmstead in South Glamorgan* (Cardiff, 1981). For other aspects of Roman Wales see: Burnham, B. and Burnham, H., *Dolaucothi-Pumsaint. Survey and excavations at a Roman gold-mining complex 1987-1999* (Oxford, 2004); Nayling, N. and McGrail, S., *The Barland's Farm Romano-Celtic Boat* (York, 2004).

Early Medieval Wales

The main themes of early medieval Wales are discussed in: Alcock, L., *Economy , Society and Warfare among the Britons and Saxons* (Cardiff, 1987); Davies, W., *Wales in the early Middle Ages* (Leicester, 1982); Davies, W., *Patterns of Power in Early Wales* (Oxford, 1990); Edwards, N. and Lane, A. (eds.), *Early Medieval Settlements in Wales, A.D. 400-1100* (Cardiff, 1988); Redknap, M., *The Christian Celts. Treasures of Late Celtic Wales* (Cardiff, 1991); Redknap, M., *Vikings in Wales: An Archaeological Quest* (Cardiff, 2000); Redknap, M. and Lewis, J. M., with Charles-Edwards, G., Horák, J., Knight, J. and Sims-Williams, P., *A Corpus of medieval inscribed stones and stone sculpture in Wales, vol. 1: South-east Wales and the English Border* (Cardiff, 2007); Edwards, N., with Jackson, H., McKee, H. and Sims-Williams, P., *A Corpus of medieval inscribed stones and stone sculpture in Wales, vol. 2: South-west Wales* (Cardiff, 2007); Bromwich, R., Jarman, A. O. H. and Roberts, B. F. (eds.), *The Arthur of the Welsh* (Cardiff, 1991); Davies, S., *Welsh Military Institutions, 633-1283* (Cardiff, 2004).

The Middle Ages

Dependable general accounts are: Walker, D., *Medieval Wales* (Cambridge, 1990), and Carr, A. D., *Medieval Wales* (London, 1995). Detailed and masterly surveys are: Davies, R. R., *The Age of Conquest: Wales,* 1063-1415 (revised edn. Oxford, 2000), and Williams, G., *Wales, c.1415-1642* (Oxford, 1987).

Particular themes may be explored in: Lord, P., *The Visual Culture of Wales: Medieval Vision* (Cardiff, 2003), from the fourth century to the sixteenth, lavishly illustrated; Edwards, N. (ed.), *Landscape and Settlement in Medieval Wales* (Oxford, 1997); Griffiths, R. A., *Conquerors and Conquered in Medieval Wales* (Stroud, 1994); Jones, N. A. and Pryce, H. (eds.), *Yr Arglwydd Rhys* (Cardiff, 1990); Carr, A. D., *Medieval Anglesey* (Llangefni, 1982); Reeves, A. C., *The Marcher Lords* (Llandybïe, 1983); Taylor, A. J. (ed.), *The Welsh Castles of Edward I* (London, 1986); Davies, R. R., *Lordship and Society in the March of Wales,* 1282-1400 (Oxford, 1978); Williams, D. H., *Welsh History through Seals* (Cardiff, 1984); Williams, G., *The Welsh Church from Conquest to Reformation* (2nd edn. Cardiff, 1976); Cowley, F. G., *The Monastic Order in South Wales, 1066-1349* (Cardiff, 1977); Nayling, N., *The Magor Pill Medieval Wreck* (York, 1998); Robinson, D. M., *The Cistercians in Wales: Architecture and Archaeology, 1130-1540* (London, 2006); Griffiths, R. A. (ed.), *Boroughs of Medieval Wales* (Cardiff, 1978); *Montgomeryshire Collections* 89 (2001) is a special volume describing the late medieval house of Tŷ-mawr, Castle Caereinion; Suggett, R. F., The interpretation of late medieval houses in Wales, in Davies, R. R. and Jenkins, G. H. (eds.), *From Medieval to Modern Wales: Essays Presented to Kenneth Morgan and Ralph Griffiths* (Cardiff, 2004), 81-103; Suggett, R. F., Dendrochronology: progress and prospects, in Briggs, C. S. (ed.), *Towards a Research Agenda for Welsh Archaeology* (Oxford, 2003), 153-69, lists all tree-ring dates up to 2003.

Early Modern Wales

Good general surveys are: Williams, G., *Recovery, Reorientation and Reformation, Wales, c.1415-1642* (Oxford, 1987); Jenkins, P., *History of Modern Wales, 1536-1990* (London, 1992); Jones, J. G., *Early Modern Wales, c.1525-1640* (London, 1994); Jenkins, G. H., *Hanes Cymru yn y Cyfnod Modern Cynnar, 1530-1760* (Cardiff, 1998); and Jenkins, G. H. *The Foundations of Modern Wales: Wales 1642-1780* (Oxford, 1993).

For particular themes, see: Williams, G., *Wales and the Reformation* (Cardiff, 1997); Jones, J. G., *The Welsh Gentry, 1536-1640* (Cardiff, 1998); Jenkins, G. H., *The Foundations of Modern Wales,* 1642-1780 (Oxford, 1993); Jenkins, G. H., *Protestant Dissenters in Wales, 1639-1689* (Cardiff, 1992); Dodd, A. H., *Studies in Stuart Wales* (2nd edn. Cardiff, 1971); Jenkins, P., *The making of a ruling class: The Glamorgan gentry, 1640-1790* (Cambridge, 1983);

Morgan, P., *The Eighteenth Century Renaissance* (Llandybïe, 1981); Suggett, R. F., Timber versus Stone in late-medieval and early modern Wales, in Coulson, M. R. (ed.), *Stone in Wales: Materials, Heritage and Conservation* (Cardiff, 2005), 70-6; Davies, C. (ed.), *Dr John Davies of Mallwyd: Welsh Renaissance Scholar* (Cardiff, 2004); Jenkins, G. H. (ed.), *A Rattleskull Genius: The Many Faces of Iolo Morganwg* (Cardiff, 2005).

The First Industrial Nation

Among the best introductions to the Industrial Revolution in Wales are Dodd, A. H., *The Industrial Revolution in North Wales* (2nd edn. Cardiff, 1951); Minchinton, W. E. (ed.), *Industrial South Wales 1750-1914: Essays in Welsh Economic History* (London, 1969); Rees, D. M., *Mines, Mills and Furnaces: Industrial Archaeology in Wales* (London, 1969); Rees, D. M., *Industrial Archaeology of Wales* (Newton Abbot, 1975); Rees, W., *Industry before the Industrial Revolution* (2 vols. Cardiff, 1968); Langton, J. and Morris, R. J., *The Atlas of Industrializing Britain, 1780-1914* (London, 1986) ; and Gwynn, D., *Gwynedd: Inheriting a Revolution* (Chichester, 2006).

Particular industries are explored by: Bick, D., *The Old Metal Mines of Mid-Wales* (Newent, 1991); Hadfield, C., *The Canals of South Wales and The Border* (2nd edn. Newton Abbot and Cardiff, 1967); Jones, N., Walters, M. and Frost, P. *Mountains and Orefields: Metal Mining Landscapes of Mid and North-east Wales* (York, 2004); Lowe, J., *Welsh Industrial Workers' Housing 1774-1875* (Cardiff, 1994); and Richards, A. J., *A Gazetteer of the Welsh Slate Industry* (Llanrwst,1991).

Urban topics are covered in: Boorman, D., *The Brighton of Wales: Swansea as a Fashionable Seaside Resort c.1780-c.1830* (Swansea, 1986); Miskell, L., *An Intelligent Town: An urban history of Swansea, 1780-1855* (Cardiff, 2006); Carter, H., *The Towns of Wales: A Study in Urban Geography* (2nd edn. Cardiff, 1966); Evans, C. 'The Labyrinth of Flames'. *Work and Social Conflict in Early Industrial Merthyr Tydfil* (Cardiff, 1993); Williams, G. A., *The Merthyr Rising* (Cardiff, 1978). Rural and landscape themes are discussed in: Inglis-Jones, E., *Peacocks in Paradise* (London, 1950); Macve, J., *The Hafod Landscape* (The Hafod Trust, 2004); Howell, D. W., *The Rural Poor in Eighteenth-century Wales* (Cardiff, 2000). Other social and cultural trends are studied in: Lord, P., *The Visual Culture of Wales: Industrial Society* (Cardiff, 1998).

Victorian Society

Useful general surveys are: Evans, D. G., *A History of Wales 1815-1906* (Cardiff, 1989), and Harrison, J. F. C., *Early Victorian Britain, 1832-51* (Glasgow, 1988).

The rich themes of this period may be explored in: Dixon, R. and Muthesius, S., *Victorian Architecture* (London, 1995); Orbach, J., *Blue Guide: Victorian Architecture in Britain* (London, 1987); Brooks, C. and Saint, A. (eds.), *The Victorian Church: Architecture and Society* (Manchester, 1995); Stevens Curl, J., *Book of Victorian Churches* (London, 1995); Jones, A., *Welsh Chapels* (Stroud, 1996); Girouard, M., *The Victorian Country House* (London, 1990); Howell, D. W.,

Land and People in Nineteenth-century Wales (London, 1977); Horn, P., *Labouring Life in the Victorian Countryside* (Guernsey, 1995); Pimlott, J. A. R., *The Englishman's Holiday: A Social History* (Hassocks, 1976); Jones, I. G., *Communities: Essays in the social history of Victorian Wales* (Cardiff, 1987); Adamson, S. H., *Seaside Piers* (London, 1977); Seaborne, M., *Schools in Wales, 1500-1900: A Social and Architectural History* (Denbigh, 1987); Morgan, K. O., *Wales in British Politics, 1868-1922* (3rd edn. Cardiff, 1980); Williams, J., *Was Wales Industrialized? Essays in Modern Welsh History* (Llandysul, 1995); Davies, J., *Cardiff and the Marquesses of Bute* (Cardiff., 1981); Jones, D. J. V., *Crime in Nineteenth-century Wales* (Cardiff, 1992); Darby, M., *John Pollard Seddon* (London, 1983); Lewis, W. J., *Born on a Perilous Rock* (Aberystwyth, 1980)

The Early Twentieth Century

General surveys include: Evans, D. G., *A History of Wales, 1906-2000* (Cardiff, 2000); and Morgan, K. O., *Rebirth of a Nation, 1880-1980* (2nd edn. Oxford, 1998).

Particular topics are covered in: Croll, A., *Civilizing the Urban: Popular culture and public space in Merthyr, c. 1870-1914* (Cardiff, 2000); Daunton, M. J., *Coal Metropolis: Cardiff, 1870-1914* (Leicester, 1977); Smith, D. B. and Williams, G. W., *Fields of Praise: Official History of the Welsh Rugby Union, 1881-1981* (Cardiff, 1980); Williams, C., *Capitalism, Community and Conflict: The South Wales Coalfield, 1898-1917* (Cardiff, 1998); Lieven, M., *Senghennydd: The Universal Pit Village, 1890-1930* (Llandysul, 1994); Gaffney, A., *Aftermath: Remembering the Great War in Wales* (Cardiff, 1998); Miskell, P.M., *A Social History of the Cinema in Wales, 1918-1951* (Cardiff, 2006); Judge, C., *The Elan Valley Railway* (Oakwood Press, 1987); Lowry, B. (ed.), *Twentieth Century Defences in Britain – An Introductory Guide. Handbook of The Defence of Britain Project* (York, 1995); Jenkins, A., *Drinka Pinta: The Story of Milk and the Industry that serves it* (Heinemann, 1970); and Culpin, E. G., *The Garden City Movement Up-to-date* (London, 1913); Johnes, M., *Soccer and Society: South Wales*, 1900-1939 (Cardiff, 2002).

Post-War Wales

General surveys are: Morgan, K. O., *Rebirth of a Nation, 1880-1980* (2nd edn. Oxford, 1998); Herbert, T. and Jones, G. E. (ed.), *Post-war Wales* (Cardiff, 1995); Smith, D. *Wales! Wales!* (London, 1989) and Jones, R. M., *Cymru 2000: Hanes Cymru yn yr Ugeinfed Ganrif* (Cardiff, 2000).

Particular subjects are discussed in: Francis, H. and Smith, D., *The Fed: A History of the South Wales Miners in the Twentieth Century* (Cardiff, 1998); Suggett, R. F., Recent Emergency Recording in Wales, *Transactions of the Ancient Monuments Society* 45 (2001), 81-108; Herbert, T. and Jones, G.E., *Post-War Wales* (Cardiff, 1985); Gildart, K., *North Wales Miners: A Fragile Unity, 1945-1996* (Cardiff, 2001); Pryce, D. W. T., *History of the Church in Wales in the Twentieth Century* (Penarth, 1990).

The magazine of the Royal Society of Architects in Wales, *Context*, is a useful periodical for current architecture.

Principal Publications by the Royal Commission, 1911-2008

The following list includes the principal official publications by the Royal Commission. Its leaflets, newsletters and annual reviews are excluded. The volumes were published by HMSO on behalf of the Royal Commission unless otherwise stated. In more recent years the principal authors have been identified by name (given in brackets).

1911: *An Inventory of the Ancient Monuments in Wales and Monmouthshire. I. – County of Montgomery.*

1912: *An Inventory of the Ancient Monuments in Wales and Monmouthshire. II. – County of Flint.*

1913: *An Inventory of the Ancient Monuments in Wales and Monmouthshire. III. – County of Radnor.*

1914: *An Inventory of the Ancient Monuments in Wales and Monmouthshire. IV. – County of Denbigh.*

1917: *An Inventory of the Ancient Monuments in Wales and Monmouthshire. V. – County of Carmarthen.*

1921: *An Inventory of the Ancient Monuments in Wales and Monmouthshire. VI. – County of Merioneth.*

1925: *An Inventory of the Ancient Monuments in Wales and Monmouthshire. VII. – County of Pembroke*

1937: *An Inventory of the Ancient Monuments in Anglesey*

1956: *An Inventory of the Ancient Monuments in Caernarvonshire Volume I: East – The Cantref of Arllechwedd and the Commote of Creddyn*

1960: *An Inventory of the Ancient Monuments in Caernarvonshire Volume II: Central – The Cantref of Arfon and the Commote of Eifionydd*

1964: *An Inventory of the Ancient Monuments in Caernarvonshire Volume III: West – The Cantref of Lleyn. Together with the General Survey of the County*

1970: *National Monuments Record for Wales Report 1970*

1970: *Hand-lists of the Field Monuments of Wales (1) Cardiganshire*

1972: *National Monuments Record for Wales Report 1971*

1973: *Hand-lists of the Field Monuments of Wales (2) Monmouthshire (Gwent) (a) Early Monuments*

1975: *Houses of the Welsh Countryside – A study in historical geography* (Peter Smith)

1976: *An Inventory of the Ancient Monuments in Glamorgan Volume I: Pre-Norman Part I The Stone and Bronze Ages*

1976: *An Inventory of the Ancient Monuments in Glamorgan Volume I: Pre-Norman Part II The Iron Age and The Roman Occupation*

1976: *An Inventory of the Ancient Monuments in Glamorgan Volume I: Pre-Norman Part III The Early Christian Period*

1981: *An Inventory of the Ancient Monuments in Glamorgan Volume IV: Domestic Architecture from the Reformation to the Industrial Revolution Part I: The Greater Houses*

1982: *An Inventory of the Ancient Monuments in Glamorgan Volume III: Medieval Secular Monuments Part II: Non-defensive*

1986: *An Inventory of the Ancient Monuments in Brecknock (Brycheiniog) The Prehistoric and Roman Monuments Part ii: Hill-forts and Roman Remains*

1988: *An Inventory of the Ancient Monuments in Glamorgan Volume IV: Domestic Architecture from the Reformation to the Industrial Revolution Part II: Farmhouses and Cottages*

1988: *Houses of the Welsh Countryside – A study in historical geography* (Peter Smith; second enlarged edition)

1988: *The Archaeology of the Montgomeryshire Canal – A Guide and study in Waterways Archaeology*, Aberystwyth: RCAHMW (Stephen Hughes)

1989: *Llantwit Major and Cowbridge – The archeology of an Early Railway System*, Aberystwyth: RCAHMW (Stephen Hughes)

1990: *The Archaeology of an Early Railway System: The Brecon Forest Tramroads*, Aberystwyth: RCAHMW (Stephen Hughes)

1991: *An Inventory of the Ancient Monuments in Glamorgan Volume III – Part Ia Medieval Secular Monuments The Early Castles From the Norman Conquest to 1217*

1992: *A Guide to the Industrial Archaeology of the Swansea Region*, Aberystwyth: RCAHMW (Stephen Hughes & Paul Reynolds)

1992: *An Architectural Study, Newport Castle (Pembrokeshire)*, Aberystwyth: RCAHMW (David M. Browne and David Percival with A.J. Parkinson)

1994: *Lighthouses of Wales – Their Architecture and Archaeology*, Aberystwyth: RCAHMW (Douglas Hague, ed. Stephen Hughes)

1994: *An Architectural Study: The Cathedral Church of St. John the Evangelist, Brecon*, Brecon: Friends of Brecon Cathedral/RCAHMW (A. J. Parkinson)

1994: *Collieries of Wales – Engineering and Architecture*, Aberystwyth: RCAHMW (Stephen Hughes, Brian Malaws, Medwyn Parry & Peter Wakelin)

1994: *Wales from the Air – Patterns of Past and Present*, Aberystwyth: RCAHMW (Chris Musson)

1994: *Cardiganshire County History Volume 1 From the Earliest Times to the Coming of the Normans*, Cardiff: University of Wales Press for the Cardiganshire Antiquarian Society in association with RCAHMW (ed. J. L. Davies & D. P. Kirby)

1995: *John Nash – Architect in Wales/Pensaer yng Nghymru*, Aberystwyth: RCAHMW and The National Library of Wales (Richard Suggett)

1996: *Snowdonia from the Air – Patterns in the Landscape*, Penrhyndeudraeth: Snowdonia National Park Authority/RCAHMW (Peter Crew & Chris Musson); Welsh edition: *Eryri o'r Awyr – Patrymau yn y Tirlun*

1997: *An Inventory of the Ancient Monuments in Brecknock (Brycheiniog) The Prehistoric and Roman Monuments Part i: Later Prehistoric Monuments and Unenclosed Settlements to 1000 AD*, Aberystwyth: RCAHMW

1997: *Mynydd Du and Fforest Fawr – The Evolution of an Upland Landscape in South Wales*, Aberystwyth: RCAHMW (David K. Leighton)

1998: *Cardiganshire County History Volume 3, Cardiganshire in Modern Times*, Cardiff: University of Wales Press for Cardiganshire Antiquarian Society in association with RCAHMW (ed. Geraint H. Jenkins & Ieuan Gwynedd Jones)

2000: *An Inventory of the Ancient Monuments in Glamorgan Volume III – Part Ib Medieval Secular Monuments The Later Castles From 1217 to the Present*, Aberystwyth: RCAHMW

2000: *Copperopolis – Landscapes of the Early Industrial Period in Swansea*, Aberystwyth: RCAHMW (Stephen Hughes)

2001: *Bryngaer Pen Dinas Hill-Fort – A Prehistoric Fortress at Aberystwyth*, Aberystwyth: RCAHMW (David Browne & Toby Driver)

2001: *Guns Across the Severn – The Victorian Fortifications of Glamorgan*, Aberystwyth: RCAHMW (A. Saunders, C. J. Spurgeon, H. J. Thomas & D. J. Roberts)

2003: *The Archaeology of the Welsh Uplands*, Aberystwyth: RCAHMW (ed. David Browne & Stephen Hughes)

2005: *Houses and History in the March of Wales – Radnorshire 1400-1800*, Aberystwyth: RCAHMW (Richard Suggett)

2006: *Thomas Thomas, 1817-88: the first national architect of Wales*, reprinted from *Archaeologia Cambrensis* 152 (2003) (Stephen Hughes)

2006: *Cefnllys Castle, Radnorshire*, Aberystwyth: RCAHMW (David Browne and A. Pearson) http://www.rcahmw.gov.uk/HI/ENG/Publications/Electronic+Publication/Cefnllys+Castle

2006: *Roman Camps in Wales and the Marches*, Cardiff: University of Wales Press, in association with RCAHMW (Jeffrey L. Davies & Rebecca H. Jones)

2007: *Pembrokeshire – Historic Landscapes from the Air*, Aberystwyth: RCAHMW (Toby Driver)

2008: Hanes Wrth Law: *Defnyddio Dyfeisiau Symudol I Ddehongli Trefhadaeth/History in Your Hands: Using Mobile Devices in Heritage Interpretation*, Aberystwyth: RCAHMW (Tom Pert)

2008: *Denbigh Town Hall*, Aberystwyth: RCAHMW (Susan Fielding) http://www.rcahmw.gov.uk/HI/ENG/Publications/Electronic+Publications/Denbigh+ Town+Hall

2008: *Pontcysyllte Aqueduct & Canal Nomination as a World Heritage Site – Nomination Document*, Wrexham/Aberystwyth: Wrexham County Borough Council/RCAHMW

List of Contributors

Judith Alfrey BA, MA, FSA is an inspector of historic buildings and landscapes with Cadw. She is the co-author of two books on industrial heritage and has written on Welsh rural vernacular architecture as well as twentieth-century buildings in Wales.

Louise Barker BA has been an archaeological investigator at the Royal Commission since 2004. Prior to this she worked in the archaeological survey section of English Heritage. She has a particular interest in landscape archaeology.

Richard J. Brewer BA, FSA is keeper of archaeology at Amgueddfa Cymru–National Museum Wales, chair of the Ancient Monuments Advisory Board for Wales and a research fellow in the School of History and Archaeology, Cardiff University. His main area of research is Romano-British archaeology.

C. Stephen Briggs BA, PhD, FSA, FGS, MIFA was a senior investigator with the Royal Commission from 1973 until 2006 and is an independent heritage consultant and researcher. He has published widely on antiquarianism, prehistory, industrial and garden archaeology and is a director of the Institute of Field Archaeologists.

Harry Brooksby OBE, FSA was a member of staff at the Royal Commission from 1963 to 1994 as a photographer, an investigator dealing with domestic architecture, acting secretary and deputy secretary.

David Browne BA, MA, FRAI, FRGS is head of publications and outreach at the Royal Commission, which he joined in 1975. He has published on general archaeology and prehistoric, Roman and medieval subjects and is an authority on the prehistoric Nasca culture of Peru.

Steve Burrow BA, PhD, AMA, MIFA, FSA has been curator of Neolithic archaeology at Amgueddfa Cymru–National Museum Wales since 1997. His books include *The Neolithic culture of the Isle of Man* and *The tomb builders in Wales 4000-3000 BC*, which won the British Archaeology Popular Publication Award, 2006.

Antony Carr MA, PhD, DAA, FSA, FRHistS is emeritus professor of medieval Welsh history at Bangor University, where he was on the staff from 1964 until 2002. A former archivist, he was also responsible for the archive training course from 1979. He has published extensively on medieval Wales and has been a Royal Commissioner since 2001.

Timothy Darvill BA, PhD, DSc, FSA, FSA(Scot), MIFA, RPA is professor of archaeology at Bournemouth University. He has written more than a dozen books, including *Ancient Monuments in the Countryside, Prehistoric Britain, The Concise Oxford Dictionary of Archaeology* and *Stonehenge: the biography of a landscape*.

Toby Driver BA, PhD, FSA is the aerial investigator for the Royal Commission and author of *Pembrokeshire: Historic Landscapes from the Air*. His doctorate was on the Iron Age in Ceredigion. He is a former chairman of the Aerial Archaeology Research Group and an honorary research fellow at the University of Wales Lampeter.

Gareth Edwards BA, DAA is the archivist and records manager for the National Monuments Record of Wales.

Susan Evans joined the Royal Commission in 1978. She is a member of the team employed to look after the records held in the National Monuments Record of Wales.

Susan Fielding BA, MA has been an architectural investigator at the Royal Commission since 2005. She worked previously as a buildings archaeologist for commercial companies. Her specialisms include castles and three-dimensional visualisation.

Alex Gibson BA, PhD, FSA, FSA(Scot), MIFA is reader in British prehistory at the University of Bradford. Prior to this he was with English Heritage's Centre for Archaeology. From 1989 to 1998 he worked for the Clwyd-Powys Archaeological Trust and in 2002 received the G. T. Clark Award for contributions to Welsh prehistory.

Ralph A. Griffiths OBE, BA, PhD, DLitt, FRHistS is emeritus professor of medieval history at Swansea University. He has been a Royal Commissioner since 1991 and chairman since 1999. Among his recent books are the later medieval volume of *The Short Oxford History of the British Isles* and *The Household Book (1510-51) of Sir Edward Don*.

Deanna Groom BSc, MLitt, MIFA, FSA(Scot) joined the Royal Commission as its maritime officer in 2007. Previously, she was a project manager with Wessex Archaeology and worked on the establishment of maritime recording for the National Monuments Record of Scotland and for several historic environment records.

David Gwyn MA, PhD, MIFA, FSA is an archaeological and heritage consultant and editor of *Industrial Archaeology Review*. His recent publications include *Understanding the Workplace* and *Gwynedd: Inheriting a Revolution*.

Jenny Hall BSc formed the Trysor partnership with Paul Sambrook in 2004 and undertakes uplands field projects for the Royal Commission. Previously, she worked as sites and monuments record officer at the Dyfed Archaeological Trust. She has a particular interest in helping people gain greater access to their heritage.

Neil Harries BA, MEd, FCMI was director of education, leisure and library services at Caerphilly County Borough Council. He has since been head of education policy at the Welsh Local Government Association and first director of the National Grid for Learning Cymru. He chairs the Royal Commission's publications and outreach committee.

Richard Haslam MA, FSA is a writer and consultant on buildings. He served as a Royal Commissioner from 1986 to 1998. He has published extensively on historic houses and churches, gardens and landscape and has contributed to the Buildings of Wales series.

Stephen Hughes BA, MPhil, FSA, FRHistS is head of survey and investigation at the Royal Commission. His books include *The Archaeology of the Welsh Uplands, Copperopolis, Collieries of Wales* and *The Archaeology of the Montgomeryshire Canal*. He has coordinated international studies for the World Heritage Secretariat.

Penny Icke BA has worked at the Royal Commission since 1996 in recording and reader services. She is a trustee of the Welsh Religious Buildings Trust and was secretary of Capel: The Chapels Heritage Society, from 1997 to 2002.

Olwen Jenkins BA, DipBdgCons, MLib was an inspector of ancient monuments and historic buildings from 1969 to 1987 and then became an investigator with the Royal Commission. She co-wrote *The Cathedral Church of St John the Evangelist, Brecon* and worked on projects on chapels, housing in Blaenavon and Leighton model farm.

Rebecca Jones BA, PhD, FSA, FSA(Scot), MIFA is survey and recording operational manager at the Royal Commission on the Ancient and Historical Monuments of Scotland. Her special interest is the Roman army and Roman frontiers. She co-wrote *Roman Camps in Wales and the Marches* with Dr Jeffrey L. Davies.

David Leighton BSc, MIFA, FSA is a field monuments investigator with the Royal Commission and currently manages the Uplands Archaeology Initiative. He has written on the uplands of the Brecon Beacons, prehistoric ritual and funerary monuments and aspects of medieval history and archaeology in Gower.

Thomas Lloyd OBE, MA, FSA is an architectural and art historian. In 1986 he wrote *The Lost Houses of Wales*. He is a former chair of the Historic Buildings Council for Wales and the Buildings at Risk Trust. He was co-author of the Buildings of Wales volumes covering Pembrokeshire, Carmarthenshire and Ceredigion.

Frances Lynch MA, FSA lectured in prehistory at Bangor University and has directed excavations in Wales and Ireland. She has been secretary of the Council for British Archaeology Wales and a member of the Ancient Monuments Board, and she is chairman of the Clwyd-Powys Archaeological Trust.

Hilary Malaws BLib, MIFA is head of the information management branch at the Royal Commission.

Brian Malaws is head of archaeological mapping at the Royal Commission.

David McLees MA, FSA(Scot) was the inspector of historic buildings at Cadw with professional responsibility for the resurvey of historic buildings throughout Wales. He has a particular interest in nineteenth-century architecture and wrote Cadw's guide to Castell Coch and its booklet on industrial workers' housing.

Christopher Musson MBE, BArch, MIFA, FSA joined the Royal Commission in 1986 as its first investigator in aerial photography after working with the Rescue Archaeology Group and the Clwyd-Powys Archaeological Trust. He promotes aerial archaeology throughout Europe with the Aerial Archaeology Research Group.

John Newman MA, FSA was reader in architectural history at the Courtauld Institute of Art, University of London. He has written the volumes of the Buildings of Wales series for Glamorgan and Gwent/Monmouthshire and was awarded the G. T. Clark Prize for the latter. He has been a Royal Commissioner since 2000.

Chris Nicholas BA, MA is the data officer at the Royal Commission and is responsible for enhancing its online databases and supporting its information technology infrastructure. He was trained as a medieval historian.

Julian Orbach BA is an architectural historian and co-author of the volumes for Pembrokeshire, Carmarthenshire and Ceredigion, and Gwynedd in the Buildings of Wales series.

Henry Owen John BA, MIFA, FSA is English Heritage's regional director for north-west England. Previously, he directed excavations on prehistoric and Roman sites for the Glamorgan-Gwent Archaeological Trust and was an inspector of ancient monuments for English Heritage. He has been a Royal Commissioner since 2006.

Anthony J. Parkinson MA, FSA was an investigator for the Royal Commission from 1970 to 1995, and is now a Methodist minister. He has published articles on architectural history and industrial archaeology and is an honorary research fellow at the National Museum of Wales.

Medwyn Parry works in the Royal Commission's library and enquiries service. He was the regional coordinator for Wales for the Defence of Britain project and lectures, broadcasts and writes on the impact of twentieth-century conflicts on the landscape.

David Percival was manager for detailed recording of sites and buildings at the Royal Commission until 2008. He joined the Commission in 1984 from the Ordnance Survey. His special interests are nonconformist chapels, industrial landscapes and transport.

Tom Pert BA, PGDip has been mapping officer for the Royal Commission since 2002. He specialises in the development of mobile mapping and information systems and wrote *Hanes wrth Law/History in Your Hands* in 2008.

Mark Redknap BA, PhD, FSA, MIFA is curator of medieval and later archaeology at Amgueddfa Cymru–National Museum Wales. In 2002 he received the Archaeological Book Award for his book *The Vikings in Wales* and the G. T. Clark Prize for his work on early medieval Wales.

Sian Rees BA, PhD, FSA is an inspector of ancient monuments for Cadw with responsibility for north-east Wales and marine archaeology. She edited the *Ancient and Historic Wales* guides and has written Cadw guidebooks to Dinefwr Castle, Dyfi Furnace and Haverfordwest Priory.

Paul Sambrook BA, PGCE formed the Trysor partnership in 2004 with Jenny Hall, which undertakes uplands field projects for the Royal Commission. Previously, he worked at the Dyfed Archaeological Trust as a project manager. He has a particular interest in community archaeology.

Malcolm V. J. Seaborne MA, PhD, HonLitt, FRHistS, FRSA died in 2008. He was emeritus professor of the University of Chester and was principal of Chester College from 1971 until 1987. He published on the architecture of schools, Celtic crosses, churches, chapels and stained-glass.

Patrick Sims-Williams MA, PhD, FBA is professor of Celtic Studies in Aberystwyth University and was a Royal Commissioner from 1998 to 2008. Previously, he was reader in the department of Anglo-Saxon, Norse and Celtic at Cambridge. He received the G. T. Clark Award for his book *The Celtic Inscriptions of Britain*.

Anna Z. Skarżyńska BA, MSc(Econ), PhD is an archivist at Ceredigion Archives and an enquiries assistant at the Royal Commission. She read Celtic Studies at Aberystwyth and her doctorate was an edition of an early modern Irish trickster tale.

J. Beverley Smith MA, FRHistS is emeritus professor of Welsh history at Aberystwyth University. He was a Royal Commissioner from 1984 to 1998, and chairman from 1990. He has written widely on medieval Wales and especially on the age of the thirteenth-century princes.

Llinos Beverley Smith BA, PhD, FRHistS has been a Royal Commissioner since 1990 and is vice-chairman. Formerly a senior lecturer in Welsh history at Aberystwyth, she has published widely on the social and economic history of late medieval Wales.

Richard Suggett BA, BLitt, FSA, FRHistS has worked in buildings recording at the Royal Commission since 1984. His publications include a study of John Nash, *Houses and History in the March of Wales*, for which he was awarded the G. T. Clark prize, and *A History of Witchcraft and Magic in Wales*. He is an honorary fellow of the University of Wales Centre for Advanced Welsh and Celtic Studies.

Robert J. Sylvester BA, FSA, MIFA is deputy director of the Clwyd-Powys Archaeological Trust. He is the archaeologist for the diocese of St Asaph and is a member of the Welsh Cathedral and Churches Commission. His current studies are in medieval and post-medieval rural settlement and landscape history.

David Thomas BA is data manager at the Royal Commission and is responsible for developing its digital content and online applications. Previously he worked as a project officer for the Clwyd-Powys Archaeological Trust.

Adam Voelcker MA, DipArch, RIBA is an architect and specialises in the repair of old buildings, particularly churches in Gwynedd. He is a member of the Bangor Diocesan Advisory Committee and is co-author of the Gwynedd volume in the Buildings of Wales series.

Geoffrey Wainwright MBE, FSA, PhD, HonMIFA is president of the Society of Antiquaries and was formerly chief archaeologist at English Heritage. He has served on the Royal Commission as a member and vice-chairman. In 2007 he received the Graham Clark medal of the British Academy for services to archaeology.

Peter Wakelin BA, MSocSc, PhD, FSA has been secretary of the Royal Commission since 2005. He was previously an inspector with Cadw. He has published on industrial archaeology and the history of Welsh art, and wrote the guidebook to the Blaenavon World Heritage Site. He is an honorary fellow of Aberystwyth and Swansea universities.

Geoff Ward Cert.Arch.Hist. has been with the Royal Commission for over thirty years, initially as an illustrator and then an investigator. He specialises in vernacular architecture, timber-framing and farm buildings. His recent work includes a survey of Denbigh's historic houses.

Peter White OBE, BA, FSA was secretary of the Royal Commission from 1991 to 2005, having previously been head of historic buildings listing at English Heritage. He chairs the Hafod Advisory Panel and Cytal/Association of Preservation Trusts Wales. He is an honorary research fellow of the University of Wales Lampeter.

Eurwyn Wiliam MA, PhD, FSA is director of collections and research and deputy director general of Amgueddfa Cymru–National Museum Wales. He is the author of numerous works on Welsh vernacular architecture. He served as a Royal Commissioner from 1992 to 2006 and vice-chairman from 2002 to 2006.

Angharad Williams BSc, PGCE has been education officer for the Royal Commission since 2003. Previously, she was a primary school head-teacher and an advisory teacher for Ceredigion Local Education Authority. She writes about the historic environment for educational publications.

Iain Wright FBIPP is the Royal Commission's photographer. He has provided illustrations for the past four volumes in the Buildings of Wales series and the corpus of early medieval inscribed stones currently in production. In 1989 he was awarded a fellowship by the British Institute of Professional Photography for his work at the Commission.

Aerial ropeways, or 'Blondins', at Pen-yr-orsedd quarry, Caernarfonshire, are among the remains of the slate industry vulnerable to decay.
DI2006_0029 NPRN 40565

Acknowledgements

The editors wish to acknowledge the assistance of all the named contributors listed on pages 313-15 and of Karen Andrews, Stephen Bailey-John, Susan Billingsley, Glenda Carr, Jane Durbin, Richard Edwards, Frances Foster, Sal Garfi, Charles Green, Cheryl Griffiths, Lilwen Jones, Dewi Vaughan Owen, Joanna Pettitt, Nicola Roberts, Andrew Wakelin, and Cadw, Welsh Assembly Government, BBC Cymru Wales, and Element Productions.

All of the images in this book are in the collections of the National Monuments Record of Wales with the exception of those belonging to the following individuals and organisations to whom we are grateful:

  Amgueddfa Cymru – National Museum Wales: pages 47, 49, 53, 59, 93, 99, 105, 111, 115, 147
  Cadw, Welsh Assembly Government: page 119
  Clwyd-Powys Archaeological Trust: page 65
  Fiona Grant: page 49
  Mrs Migallon: page 21
  Trysor: page 201
  Professor Geoffrey Wainwright/SPACES Project: pages 51, 57

Most of the images have been created by the Royal Commission on the Ancient and Historical Monuments of Wales and are Crown copyright. We have made best efforts to contact the copyright holders of other images. If we have failed to trace or acknowledge any copyright holder we would be glad to receive information to assist us. We are grateful to the following individuals and organisations who have allowed images held in the National Monuments Record of Wales to be reproduced:

  Environment Agency, Lidar data: page 295
  Geoperspectives, Digital Terrain/Surface Model: pages 60, 74, 200
  Thomas Lloyd Collection: page 232
  Howarth-Loomes Collection: pages 135, 209
  Heather James (photograph by Terry James): page 239
  Landmark Information Group Ltd: pages 74, 200
  National Churches Trust (for the photograph taken by D. W. Winkworth in the Rokeby Collection): page 278
  National Trust: page 172
  Medwyn Parry: page 263
  Mrs P. J. Phillips (for the Herbert L. North Collection): pages 250, 251
  Plaid Cymru: page 277
  Dylan Roberts: page 76
  Unit for Landscape Modelling/Cambridge University Collection of Air Photographs: page 54

Maps on the following pages are based upon Ordnance Survey material with the permission of Ordnance Survey on behalf of the Controller of Her Majesty's Stationery Office © Crown copyright. Unauthorised reproduction infringes Crown copyright and may lead to prosecution or civil proceedings. Licence number: 100017916: pages 29, 34, 55, 60, 69, 87, 88, 179, 202, 304.

Map of Historic Counties

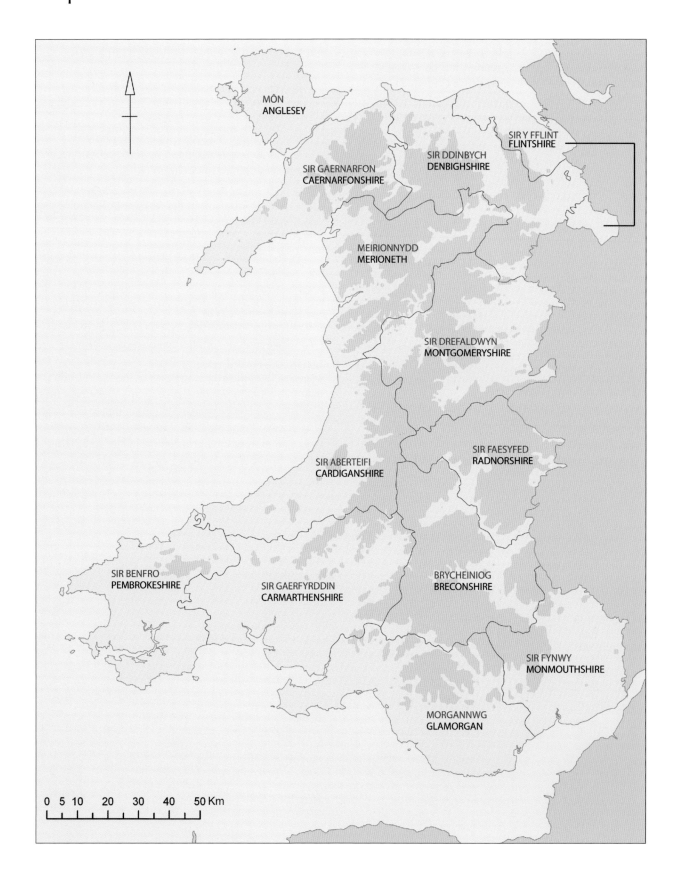

Index

Italic page numbers indicate illustrations and material in illustration captions.